MEN, WOMEN & MANNERS IN

Colonial Times

Volumes I & II

SYDNEY FISHER

INTRODUCTION BY
WAYNE LAPIERRE

Skyhorse Publishing

First published 1897 by J. B. Lippincott Company

Introduction copyright © 2012 by Palladium Press for the Library of American Freedoms

First Skyhorse Publishing edition 2015

All inquiries should be addressed to Skyhorse Publishing, 307 West 36th Street, 11th Floor, New York, NY 10018.

Skyhorse Publishing books may be purchased in bulk at special discounts for sales promotion, corporate gifts, fund-raising, or educational purposes. Special editions can also be created to specifications. For details, contact the Special Sales Department, Skyhorse Publishing, 307 West 36th Street, 11th Floor, New York, NY 10018 or info@skyhorsepublishing.com.

Skyhorse® and Skyhorse Publishing® are registered trademarks of Skyhorse Publishing, Inc.®, a Delaware corporation.

Visit our website at www.skyhorsepublishing.com.

10 9 8 7 6 5 4 3 2 1

Library of Congress Cataloging-in-Publication Data

Fisher, Sydney George, 1856–1927.
  Men, women & manners in colonial times / by Sydney Geo. Fisher ; illustrated with photogravures and with decorations by Edward Stratton Holloway. — First Skyhorse Publishing edition.
     pages cm
  "First published 1897 by J. B. Lippincott Company"—Title page verso.
  ISBN 978-1-62914-502-0 (paperback : alkaline paper) 1. United States—Social life and customs—To 1775. 2. United States—Description and travel. 3. United States—History—Colonial period, ca. 1600–1775. I. Title. II. Title: Men, women and manners in colonial times.
  E162.F53 2015
  973.2—dc23

                         2014042625

Print ISBN: 978-1-62914-502-0
Ebook ISBN: 978-1-63220-045-7

Printed in the United States of America

INTRODUCTION

by Wayne LaPierre

In analyzing periods of history, historians tend to focus on significant events and the accomplishments of famous people of the time. In the case of the development of colonial America and the foundation of the American republic, this conventional approach emphasizes events such as the Boston Tea Party, the First Continental Congress, the Battle of Bunker Hill, the drafting of the Declaration of Independence, Washington's crossing of the Delaware, the British surrender at Yorktown, and the Philadelphia Convention of 1787; along with the lives of men such as George Washington, Thomas Jefferson, James Madison, John Adams, and Benjamin Franklin.

But what about the common man? What about the everyday lives of the colonists? After all, it was their votes that elevated the Founding Fathers to power, and their voices that were reflected in the choices these great men made in rejecting British rule and establishing a new republic. What were the important influences — social, moral, racial, and political — that created the base of public opinion?

In *Men, Women & Manners in Colonial Times*, author Sydney George Fisher examines the lives of the first settlers: why they immigrated to America and how their European past affected their dispositions, customs, and laws. Volume I discusses the colonies of Virginia, Massachusetts, Connecticut, Rhode Island, New Hampshire, Vermont, Pennsylvania, and New Jersey. Volume II looks at New York, Maryland, North Carolina, South Carolina, and Georgia.

In his preface, Fisher remarks on the variety seen in the colonies:

> In travelling from Massachusetts to the Carolinas one passed through communities of such distinct individuality that they were almost like different nations. Each had been founded for a reason and purpose of its own. Each had a set of opinions and laws peculiar to itself, and it was not uncommon to find the laws and opinions of one a contradiction of those of another.

The American author and lawyer Sydney George Fisher (1856–1927) wrote a number of significant books on American history.

They include *The Evolution of the Constitution of the United States, The Struggle for American Independence, The Making of Pennsylvania, The True Benjamin Franklin, The Quaker Colonies,* and *The True History of the American Revolution.*

This Library of American Freedoms edition is an exact facsimile of the Lippincott edition of 1898.

Wayne LaPierre

FAIRFAX, VIRGINIA
OCTOBER 9, 2012

Liberty Hall, Elizabethtown, N.J

SHIRLEY

James River, Va.

Built 1760

MEN, WOMEN & MANNERS IN COLONIAL TIMES · · · ·

BY

SYDNEY GEO. FISHER

ILLUSTRATED WITH PHOTOGRAVURES
AND WITH DECORATIONS BY
EDWARD STRATTON HOLLOWAY

VOL. I

PHILADELPHIA & LONDON
J. B. LIPPINCOTT COMPANY
1898

At Hartford, Conn.

PREFACE

THE charm of a journey through the colonies was its variety. In travelling from Massachusetts to the Carolinas one passed through communities of such distinct individuality that they were almost like different nations. Each had been founded for a reason and purpose of its own. Each had a set of opinions and laws peculiar to itself, and it was not uncommon to find the laws and opinions of one a contradiction to those of another.

They were a strange and picturesque collection of settlements on the extreme eastern verge of a vast continent; a mere fringe along the seacoast from Georgia to New Hampshire. Most of the people lived close to the shore, and all were within two hundred miles of it. Behind them stretched the great unknown continent, which for a thousand miles was nothing but trees,—a vast forest that seemed to them inter-

5

minable, for they did not know that beyond it were the open prairies with their long grass and herds of buffalo stretching to the Mississippi, and beyond that the plains, the desert, and the Rocky Mountains.

The wild fowl that every autumn came to them in countless millions from Alaska could have told them all; and now we know what the canvas-back and the mallard have always known. But we must be careful not to think ourselves on that account the superiors of the colonists. We have at our command more facts and more material wealth, but it is a question whether we are any wiser or better than the fathers; and it is extremely doubtful whether we enjoy ourselves as much as they did, when, in their scarlet cloaks, yellow waistcoats, and abundant leisure and room, they ornamented the Atlantic seaboard, with the continent behind them.

Those were brave days when the judges on the bench wore scarlet robes faced with black; when the tailor-shops, instead of the dull-colored woollens which they now contain, advertised, as in the *New York Gazetteer* of May 13, 1773, "scarlet, buff, blue, green, crimson, white, skye blue, and other colored superfine cloths;" when John Hancock, of penmanship fame, is described in his home in Boston with a red velvet skull-cap lined with linen which was turned over the edge of the velvet about three inches deep, a blue damask dressing-gown lined with silk, a white stock, with satin embroidered waistcoat, black satin breeches, white silk stockings to his knees, and red morocco slippers.

It has been said that the minuet and other stately dances of colonial times were the natural result of the wonderful clothes the upper classes of the people wore. It would have been extremely difficult for a lady to waltz with her hair done up in a great pyramid of paste, with perhaps a turban or a large feather on it. She scarcely dared move her head, except very slowly.

The man with his variety of wigs—tie-wig, bob-wig, bag-wig, nightcap-wig, and riding-wig —usually selected one for a ball on which he dared not put his hat, which, with its gold-lace trimming, was carried under his arm ; and the sword, which was the essential of full dress, would have been very much in the way in a modern waltz in a crowded ball-room.

But all that we have and all that we are those colonists gave us, and this we are now beginning to realize. We are re-discovering the debt we owe to the colonies. We are turning to investigate every detail of colonial life with a loving devotion which it is hoped may be a sign of stronger national feeling, or at least of an attempt to have a true national feeling, and to give up the so-called cosmopolitanism and vulgar worship of everything foreign which so long has been our bane.

Fifty years ago, or even twenty years ago, there was little or no interest in colonial history. It was regarded as a time of slavery. It seemed as if we had then been a different people, unworthy of our present selves, and the bitter feelings of the Revolution were continued by the remembrance of the war of 1812. Whatever was written about the colonial period was so dull or so full of vague generalities that no one cared to read it.

It was taken for granted that everything had begun suddenly at the time of the Revolution, and behind that there was nothing of importance. The slow growth of almost two hundred years which had led up to that event was ignored. Many writers assumed that our national Constitution was made off-hand on the spur of the moment, or that we copied it from European models.

One of the most remarkable proofs of the vital interest which the colonial times possess for us is the beautiful revival in our domestic architecture which has followed from the return to the types of those days which we once supposed were only days of slavery. The Revolution killed architecture. Any one familiar with old buildings knows the steady deterioration from the year 1780, until by the time of the civil war we were in a reign of horrors, with the scroll-saw of the carpenter triumphant.

The Philadelphia Centennial Exhibition of 1876 aroused an unfortunate interest in European forms of building. Our people, having suddenly awakened to the thought that they had no architecture beyond the proportions of a dry-goods box, ran riot, and, under the name of Romanesque, disfigured the country with all manner of grotesqueness and individual conceit, in which Gothic, Classic, Queen Anne, and every other style were mingled. Then it was discovered that in our own land and in the line of our own development we had a pure and perfect type for inspiration and suggestion, a type which belonged to the nation and had been wrought out by more than a hundred years of natural effort and experience without hysterical imitation of alien sources. It has accomplished great things for us already, and there is more in store.

The present volumes complete a purpose I have long had in mind, to present the various aspects and influences of colonial life in a way that would interest ordinary readers. A large part of these volumes was written some time ago ; but their progress was delayed when I found in the course of my investigations that

Preface

Pennsylvania alone had a most curious and complicated history, almost totally neglected and unwritten, which deserved separate treatment.

"The Making of Pennsylvania," which describes the elements of the very miscellaneous population of that province, was accordingly published first, and was followed by "Pennsylvania: Colony and Commonwealth," as a supplement, giving the narrative history. I have also written "The Evolution of the Constitution," which shows how the plan and principles of our national government were developed by a natural process of growth on our own soil during the two hundred years of the colonial period, instead of being imitated from European institutions, as the cosmopolites have vainly imagined. These volumes, with the present ones, disclose the important influences, social, moral, racial, political, and constitutional, which created the American Republic.

I am indebted to Mr. Henry T. Coates, of Philadelphia, for the picture of Shirley, and for the use of photographs from which the head- and tail-pieces of the first chapter were drawn. The Doughoregan manor-house and the decorations for the chapter on New Jersey have been newly drawn from illustrations in *The Magazine of American History*, by permission of Messrs. A. S. Barnes and Company, of New York.

TABLE OF CONTENTS

VOL. I

LIST OF PHOTOGRAVURES

VOL. I

13

The Gate at Westover

CHAPTER I

CAVALIERS AND TOBACCO

THE Commonwealth which could produce Washington, Jefferson, Henry, Madison, Marshall, Monroe, the Lees, the Randolphs, the Carters, the Harrisons, and a host of other eminent men, which was called the Mother of Presidents, and which exercised such a controlling influence in the Revolution and the formation of the Constitution, must have been a remarkable community; for such distinguished men are the result of the conditions in which they live, and cannot spring up by accident or of their own will.

We are still dominated by the ideas of these Virginians; we follow their thoughts, obey the fundamental laws and principles they framed, without even a desire to change them. What was the secret of their life and their success?

When we wander through the land they lived

in we find the remains of handsome old brick churches which were evidently intended for a larger population than now lives upon the soil, and large mansion-houses with ornamentation and gardens implying a luxury and exuberance of life which their successors do not enjoy. From these houses we gather the remains of silverware and furniture which give us glimpses not only of their wealth, but of their taste and accomplishment in the arts of life, which we are glad to imitate.

Fascinated with further research, we pore over records and manuscripts and histories only to find that they were a gay, happy people; a race of sportsmen, cock-fighters and fox-hunters; bright, humorous, and sociable; in the saddle by day and feasting and dancing by night; and we go away with the impression that the hounds were always baying in Virginia, that the sun shone all day long, and all night the fiddles scraped and the darkies sang.

But these men were among the strongest intellects of their century. With no pretensions or show of book-learning, they seem to have possessed themselves of all the essential information of their time. They had a soundness of judgment, a breadth of grasp, a lofty ambition, and a high-strung sense of honor which made them master-minds.

Cavaliers and Tobacco

When in September, 1774, Washington, Henry, Randolph, Harrison, Bland, and Pendleton rode up, sunburnt, on their thoroughbreds to attend the first meeting of the Continental Congress at Philadelphia, they carried everything before them. "Fine fellows," "very high," "not a milksop among them," are the descriptions we read in the diaries or letters of people who were in the town at that time; and other delegates who succeeded them, such as the Lees and Carter Braxton, were equally efficient.

Some subtle combination of climate, life, and thought produced this result, which, like all such things, becomes difficult in the last analysis; and unfortunately the Virginians, while they were great makers of history, were not writers of it. Scraps, relics, and ruins are all that remain of their curious and interesting civilization, and for many phases of their life we have only the one-sided comments and criticisms on its excesses.

The beginnings of Virginia by a handful of reckless, improvident men, who in 1607 settled on a little, swampy, malarious peninsula on the James River, were as humble, weak, and unpromising as anything of the kind could be. But they were starting the great British colonial empire, the vastness of which, stretching round the world through Africa, Asia, America, and Australia, is to-day the wonder among nations, and but for a mistake in policy might be larger by seventy millions of people and the whole territory of the United States.

Up to that time England had done nothing in colonizing, although more than a hundred years had passed since Columbus had discovered South America, and meanwhile Spain had built up for herself a strong colonial power. In all that time England had been entitled to North America by the discovery of the Cabots in 1497; but the nation which in the end was to be the greatest colonizer was unable to move, and her first attempt must have seemed very ludicrous to those who knew what Spain had accomplished.

The company of one hundred and five persons that began the colony at Jamestown in 1607 was not of the kind to conquer the wilderness or found a commonwealth, and no one would have ever suspected them of being the forerunners of a stupendous colonial power. More than half of them were poor gentlemen who were unaccustomed to manual labor and despised it; many were small tradesmen or servants; some are described as " Jewellers, gold refiners, and a perfumer ;" and they were nearly all odd sticks who had not been very successful at anything in England.

Cavaliers and Tobacco

There was only one real man among them, a short, stout, vigorous little fellow with red hair and beard and a face flaming with energy, Captain John Smith by name. He was about twenty-seven years old, and, if his own account can be believed, had recently returned from most extraordinary adventures among the Turks, where he had slain champions in single combat and broken the hearts of the most illustrious Turkish ladies.

Idle and shiftless, Smith's companions often had to be driven by force to work, and sometimes would not work even to save their lives, and they dissipated their energy in continual disputes and quarrels. On the voyage over they had suspected the redoubtable little captain of aspiring to be " King of Virginia." They put him under arrest, and, as he says, had a gallows ready to execute him.

They intended to go to Roanoke Island, a desolate sand-bank on the coast of North Carolina, where some years before a colony sent out by Sir Walter Raleigh had perished. But a storm drove them northward into Chesapeake Bay, and they turned into Hampton Roads, where vessels have ever since sought refuge. They called the cape at the mouth of the river Point Comfort, in memory of the relief they felt when they reached it, and it still bears the name.

Sailing about fifty miles up the river, which

they called the James in honor of the king, they selected a low, swampy peninsula on the north bank of it for their settlement, which they called Jamestown. It was a most unhealthy spot, and between their arrival in May, 1607, and the following October half of them died of malarial fevers. But being a peninsula surrounded on three sides by the river, it was easy to fortify and defend, and they depended on the wild fowl and fish of the river for their food. If they had chosen a more wholesome spot in the interior among the pines, they might have starved to death or have been all killed by the Indians, and left no trace of their fate.

The James River is surpassingly lovely in the month of May, and the soft climate, the flowers, the whispering pines, and the myriads of birds convinced them that they had surely reached the land of the idle man's delight. They were a strange contrast to the stern Puritans who afterwards founded Massachusetts. They were royalist in politics and Episcopal in religion. They were not flying from persecution. They had no grievance. They had nothing against either the English government or the English Church, and they brought both with them. So slight was their zeal that their object in coming to America has been disputed. Their motives were probably restlessness, the hope of finding gold, and a conviction that they could not be much worse off in America than they were in England.

Their governing body consisted of a president and council. Wingfield, their first president, was utterly incapable, and so was his successor, Ratcliffe, who was finally sent back to England for fear, as Smith said, that the colonists would kill him. When the hot months of summer came all were stricken with fever and lay groaning in their huts with scarcely enough energy left to bury the dead. Some were determined to return to England, and Wingfield, the president, was concerned in two attempts to seize the pinnace for this purpose. In the second attempt, Kendall, one of the ringleaders, was tried, convicted, and shot. Another attempt made by Ratcliffe was frustrated by Smith.

For some time after landing Smith was still under arrest for his supposed design to be king. But he now demanded a trial, and on his acquittal, being the only man possessed of brains or vigor, he became the leader of the colonists and saved them from destruction. He fought off the Indians, obtained supplies of corn and venison from them, and during a few weeks' captivity was saved, as he relates, by Pocahontas. When the cool weather of autumn drove away the fever he had only about forty men left. With this handful he not only maintained the existence of Jamestown, but made explorations in the surrounding country.

It is extremely doubtful, however, if he could have carried his forty colonists through another summer of fever in the swamps of Jamestown. But in spring more ships and people arrived, and during the summer Smith made his famous exploration of Chesapeake Bay.

He hoped, no doubt, to find the long-sought passage through the land to the South Sea, which was supposed to lead to the kingdom of the Grand Khan and other places of fabulous wealth. The colonists had been specially instructed to search carefully for this passage. Smith was disappointed in this search, but he made a most thorough examination of the Chesapeake in its entire length, and drew a map of it which remained the authority for the geography of that part of the continent for more than a hundred years. When Lord Baltimore obtained his charter for Maryland, in 1632, and when William Penn obtained his charter for Pennsylvania, in 1681, they both relied on this map for the boundaries of their provinces.

Smith's account of his exploration can still be read with interest and the places he describes recognized. He speaks of the red-winged blackbirds, which he calls blackbirds with a red shoulder. With his boat and men clad in armor he entered the mouth of the Susquehanna, and ended his exploration at the point where the bridge of the railroad between Philadelphia and Baltimore now spans the stream. He speaks of the high bluffs farther up the river which we now see from the bridge; and it was here that he met the tribe of Indians called the Susquehannocks, remarkable, he says, for their lofty stature.

Smith continued to be the ruler of the colony for two years, maintaining command among his turbulent people by courage and address and his known willingness to strike and kill when occasion required. Arrivals from England increased his people to about five hundred, composed for the most part of rakes, broken tradesmen, and impoverished gentlemen. The bankrupt element began now to appear, as afterwards in Carolina, but it never became so numerous.

The beginnings of Virginia were, however, more disorderly and hopeless than those of South Carolina, and for many years the people had to be held down with a strong hand. There were continual fighting and treaty making and treaty breaking with the Indians; and the colonists were kept together by the Indian hostility like the early South Carolinians, and hardly dared at first to cultivate the land.

Their property was all held in common for the general good, and there were scarcely any women among them. They built fifty or sixty wooden houses and a church on the swampy peninsula where they had established Jamestown, and in the narrow neck which connected it with the mainland they had a fort. They lived on the game and fish they killed or procured from the Indians, with a few little patches of corn which they cultivated.

Smith attempted to establish branch settlements farther up the river, but the Indians were so hostile that for a long time very little could be done. The peninsula with water on three sides and a fort at the neck was the safest place, and there they huddled together for several years, the only white men on all the vast continent of forests and mountains which in time their race was to people from sea to sea.

Smith, to whom belongs the honor of keeping alive this first company of Englishmen that had ever lived in North America, was a curious character. By some writers he has been described as a "wonder of nature" and "a mirror of our time," and his own description of himself is never uncomplimentary. By others he is called a lying braggart, an adventurer, a Gascon, and a beggar.

Cavaliers and Tobacco

In this country his own estimate was usually accepted and even enlarged upon until Mr. Charles Dudley Warner's careful biography of him sifted the evidence. That he had a most valuable faculty of commanding rough men, leading exploring expeditions, and preparing maps of wild countries which were as accurate as any of that time is unquestioned; and he seems to have been free from the vagabond vices of drinking and gambling which were so rife among his followers. But his own estimate of himself and the descriptions of his wonderful adventures can hardly be accepted without a great deal of allowance.

He was a boaster in the fullest sense of the word, and every page of his books and pamphlets is full of it. Everything he wrote, especially his adventures in Turkey, is in the inflated romantic style of lords, ladies, Tartars, Turks, swords, blood, and death. We can scarcely think of him without seeing the pistols in his belt and his sword slashing infidel heads. If he had not been such a thorough believer in civilization and progress he would have made an admirable pirate.

He rouses suggestions of the gorgeousness of the East, the rich garments, the camels, and the blazing sun. He tries to give outlandish names to places. Cape Ann he wanted to call Cape

25

Cavaliers and Tobacco

Tragabigzanda, which was the name of a Turkish lady whose smiles he declared he had won and who had befriended him when he was a slave. She would, he assures us, feign herself sick and stay home from the bath and avoid all amusements in order to hear him relate the history of his achievements.

Through all he says there runs a conscious effort to defend his reputation and a craving for notice and sympathy : his merits have been overlooked ; his sacrifices have been in vain ; people, he thinks, do not sufficiently appreciate his glorious life of adventure.

It is now generally held by the best authorities that the story of his deliverance from death by Pocahontas was one of the efforts of his chivalric imagination. There undoubtedly was a playful little Indian maiden named Pocahontas, who, at the time of Smith's stay in Virginia, used to come to the fort at Jamestown and turn somersets with the white boys, and at times her friendship was of assistance to the colonists ; for she appears to have liked the English better than her own people.

She finally married an Englishman and was exhibited in London society as a curiosity, very much as we have known in our own time African chieftains or other oddities exhibited there. In his early writings about the colony, Smith never mentions his obligation to her; but when she had become famous by her marriage and exhibition in England, he laid claim to the interesting episode. He always professed to have found favor with the fair and to have been assisted by them, and the romantic career of Pocahontas was a great opportunity and temptation.

It seems probable that his ideals of life were founded on the extravagant stories of chivalry and knight-errantry which Don Quixote (which appeared about the time Smith came to Virginia) was written to satirize. His style of writing is ludicrously like the style of those romances, and, as Mr. Warner has pointed out, some of his adventures are most suspiciously like certain stock tales of the time.

But Smith was not a Don Quixote in Virginia; for when it came to practical affairs his common sense was always in the ascendant, and romance was forgotten until he sat down to write again. He had no faith in the gold mines so many expected to find, and when Captain Newport loaded a ship with a quantity of yellow earth he had found, Smith bluntly informed the people that he was " not enamored of their dirty skill to fraught such a drunken ship with so much gilded dirt;" and he always declared that wealth could be obtained from America only by labor.

Cavaliers and Tobacco

But the council of the colony in England failed to appreciate him. He found no gold, he was harsh, they said, to the Indians, he failed to find the passage to the South Sea, he sent back no ships freighted with products, he was rude and rough, and they were not growing rich by his administration. He was deposed and returned to England just after he had almost been assassinated when lying wounded and helpless from an accidental explosion of some gunpowder.

In 1614 he made a voyage to the northern coast of America, explored New England, giving it its name, and made one of his excellent maps, which was the guide of navigators and geographers until far within the next century. He died in London in 1631, after writing full descriptions of his explorations and adventures.

That he had been a useful leader in Virginia seems to be proved by the depletion which began there as soon as he had gone. Crops, work, and fortifications were neglected and disease and famine set in. These first Americans seem to have been utterly incapable of self-government, and some of them left the colony to become pirates in the West Indies. Six months after Smith's departure only sixty of the five hundred inhabitants were alive. After three years of effort, all that could be said of the Virginia colony was that it consisted of about sixty persons and five hundred graves.

The miserable remnant are said to have finally resorted to cannibalism to maintain themselves; but as this charge rests on an assertion afterwards made by Smith, and seems to be denied by other sources of information, its truth is doubtful. It is certain, however, that they were reduced to great straits; and when two ships arrived with food for only fourteen days, the wretched colonists refused to remain any longer in the country. They were taken aboard the vessels, which set sail for England, and Jamestown was abandoned. But they had scarcely reached the ocean when they were met by a new governor, with ships, food, and men, and Virginia was restored to life.

Lord Delaware, the new governor, remained with the new colony only from June, 1610, until the following March, when a severe attack of ague sent him to England never to return. He was a courtly nobleman, and even there in the wilderness affected the state of a little monarch with his privy council, his lieutenant-general, and his admiral. He maintained his authority well, and during his short reign there was peace as well as plenty in Virginia.

His successor, Sir Thomas Dale, was a rough soldier, who professed to be very religious and to possess a great knowledge of divinity. He punished a conspiracy against himself by keeping one man chained to a tree with a bodkin thrust through his tongue until he died, and the others he disposed of by hanging, shooting, and breaking on the wheel. He asked Powhatan, the Indian chief, to give him his daughter in marriage; but the monarch of the woods declined.

Dale's successor was Yeardley, a mild man, who was governor of Virginia several times. Of the other governors, Argall was a buccaneer who robbed and abused the colony, and when deposed, loaded a vessel with his plunder and sailed away. Sir John Harvey appropriated the fines and revenues to his own use and granted away the land of individuals until the council thrust him out. Such was Virginia's fortune, sometimes ruled by a mild and reasonable man, sometimes by a tyrant or a robber, until the year 1642, when Sir William Berkeley appeared and was twice governor for many years.

Virginia lacked at first the two essentials of a colony: there were no women and there was no private ownership of land. The early settlers came without wives, and their form of government was communism. Everything they raised from the soil or obtained from the Indians or took in hunting went into the common store and was equally divided. The colony seemed to be constituted expressly for failure, for the climate made men lazy and there was no incentive to work. A man could not gain a future home for himself by clearing and cultivating land; he had no family to inspire his exertions; he lived only for himself and for the present, and therefore he lived from hand to mouth and from day to day. The colony was nothing but a military camp, and could be maintained only by pouring fresh men into it from England, at great cost and with terrible loss of life.

But in Dale's administration communism was abolished and the land given to individuals; and in 1619 Sir Edwin Sandys, seeing the absolute necessity of women, shipped ninety maidens to Virginia, who were free to marry whomsoever they chose; but the husband each one selected must pay for her outfit and voyage to the province. Arrangements were made for the support of those who should not happen to select or be selected. But no difficulty was experienced on that point. Within a short time after their arrival they were all married and paid for. So well pleased were they with the result that they wrote letters to England which induced a shipment of sixty more.

After the colonist got his wife and his land there was no longer any doubt about the success of Virginia. Immigration rapidly increased and the colony grew by its own vigor. In 1622 there were over four thousand inhabitants, in 1650 about fifteen thousand, and in 1670 about forty thousand.

These later immigrants were mostly of the royalist party in England, cavaliers as they were called, a fine body of men, far superior to the disorderly crew whom Smith kept from famine. They completely changed the character of the colony and blotted out the disorderly, indolent past. They spread along both sides of the James, a broad, beautiful river, navigable for almost a hundred miles from its mouth. Then they occupied the York, which is the next river to the north, and afterwards the Rappahannock and the Potomac. At the time of the Revolution they had planted themselves on all these streams from their outlets in Chesapeake Bay to their sources in the Blue Ridge, where the hunter and the Indian fighter guarded the advance of civilization.

But their success was entirely due to one product, tobacco, which with the assistance of negro slavery built up a most curious and interesting civilization, as rice afterwards did in Carolina. The cultivation of tobacco began early, the demand for it rapidly increased, and great profits were made. The crop was one which required close attention and labor for only a short period of the year, and Virginia held the monopoly of its production. It was a business which made a man rich and at the same time gave him a great deal of leisure. It created a tobacco aristocracy, and aristocracy, as time proved, was better suited to Virginia than democracy. Tobacco pervaded everything. It was for a long time the money of the colony. Salaries and wages were paid in it, taxes were levied in it, and criminals were fined so many pounds of tobacco.

The Virginians were never seafaring, like the South Carolinians or the people of the Northern colonies. They neither built nor owned any ships except a few small coasting vessels, and they never engaged in manufacturing. They imported everything they used—implements, clothes, tables, chairs, and even brooms—and exported nothing but tobacco and a little wheat. They even had not mills to grind their own grain.

They were less varied in their occupations than even the South Carolinians, and they had no towns. The South Carolinians, as we shall see, were driven by circumstances to concentrate their life in Charleston, and were stimulated by the close association ; but the Virginians seem to have been stimulated by a life of individual isolation which in the end produced

better results than the close contact of the Carolinians.

But during the first seventy years of Virginia's existence, or from 1607 to Bacon's Rebellion in 1676, her progress was comparatively
slow, and at the end of that time her population
was only about thirty-eight thousand whites
and two thousand slaves. The cause of this
slowness seems to have been the continued
Indian hostility, which repressed the people
as it repressed the South Carolinians and prevented their spreading out; and there was one
frightful massacre in 1622, the memory of which
intimidated the people for many a year.

In that time the planters lived in small wooden
houses carefully palisaded, and though they are
described by travellers as contented and having
abundance of game and products from their
land, their life, like that of the early Carolinians,
was one of continual guard duty. The large
mansion houses of which we now see the remains were not built in those days. The great
period of Virginia, as of Massachusetts, did not
begin until after 1700.

They had, however, many advantages over
the Carolinians. The climate was cooler and
more healthy, the white man could hunt and
work in both summer and winter, and although
he had the fear of the Indian constantly before

his eyes, he had comparatively little fear of an insurrection among his slaves.

In " A Perfect Picture of Virginia," published in London in 1669, we meet with some of that enthusiasm of description which was so often applied to the Southern colonies. Virginia is an earthly paradise, the writer says, fertile and rich, full of trees and bees, rare colored parroketoes, " and one bird we call the mock-bird, for he will imitate all other birds' notes, even the owls' and nightingales' ;" a great contrast to New England, where, " Except a herring be put into the hole you set the corn or maize in, it will not come up."

After the year 1700, the Indians being subdued, the Virginians were able to spread out and occupy the broad rivers which flow into the west side of the Chesapeake. All the tobacco plantations were on these rivers, and the largest vessels could come up those deep streams and load at the private wharves of the plantations.

Each plantation was a kingdom in itself, with its own mechanics, carpenters, coopers, and workmen of all sorts, even to a greater degree than the South Carolina plantations, which usually sent their rice and other products to the merchants at Charleston. But in Virginia each planter was his own merchant and shipper, and imported and exported at his own landing-place as though he were an independent state. Both provinces were essentially river provinces; but the Carolina rivers all led to Charleston and created a merchant class, while the Virginia rivers led direct to England and dispensed with the provincial merchants and towns.

In 1676, seventy years after Virginia had been founded, Jamestown, its capital, consisted of a state-house, a church, and only eighteen houses. It was even smaller than it had been in Captain Smith's time. One hundred years afterwards, in 1776, Williamsburg, to which the seat of government had been removed, was a mere straggling village. Attempts were continually made to bring towns into existence by legislation. Statutes were passed establishing them at convenient cross-roads; but they met with the fate which usually befalls attempts to change the essential nature of a community. The greatest size to which any of them attained was one or two small stores, and they became known as paper towns.

Slavery was introduced into Virginia in 1619, when a Dutch ship landed twenty negroes. But the people were not particularly anxious for them. There were no rice swamps to be cultivated, as in Carolina. The climate was cooler, and white men could labor in the tobacco fields all the year round. In fact, the people were at first rather opposed to slavery; so that in 1670, fifty years after their introduction, there were only two thousand slaves in the colony. But gradually they were found to be valuable both for work and for sale in other parts of the country. In 1756 there were one hundred and twenty thousand of them, and after the Revolution Virginia became a breeding-place for slaves to supply the rest of the Southern States.

But the slaves never outnumbered the whites, and although there were one or two servile insurrections, there was less dread of them than in South Carolina. The black population was usually about forty per cent. of the whole.

The laws against them on the statute book were severe and very much like those in Carolina. A slave was punished for being found off his plantation without a certificate from his master; he was not allowed to carry a club, gun, or other weapon; and if he resisted when corrected it was not a felony to kill him. If he gave false testimony he was to have one ear nailed to the pillory, stand for an hour, and then have the ear cut off. After that the other ear was to be served in like manner, and, in addition, he was to receive thirty-nine lashes well laid on. Meetings and assemblies of negroes were forbidden, and incorrigible runaways could be killed at sight.

Cavaliers and Tobacco

But these laws were seldom enforced, and the treatment of slaves in Virginia is generally admitted to have been mild and kindly, more so than anywhere else in the Southern colonies, and with the usual result that the slaves bred more rapidly and were more profitable to their masters.

Indented servants, often called redemptioners, bound to labor for a term of years were numerous, and were sold like the slaves from master to master. Some had bound themselves in this way to pay for their transportation, some were criminals or had been kidnapped in the streets of London, and some had been rebels, like the followers of the Duke of Monmouth.

White and black slavery and the plantation system built up a landed aristocracy which was an aristocracy in the true sense of the word because it controlled the political power. It was supported also by a system of primogeniture and entail more thorough than that of England. The eldest son inherited the land, and it could be entailed on him and his descendants so as to be beyond the reach of creditors. Not only could the land be entailed, but the slaves necessary to work it could be entailed so as to follow the land. In England, as early as 1473, entails could be broken by bringing an action in court; but by an act of the House of Burgesses the barring and breaking of entails in Virginia were expressly forbidden, and this remained the law until, at the time of the Revolution, all entails were abolished by Jefferson and his democratic followers.

The Virginia lord of his entailed land, with slaves to work it, independent of towns and merchants, making an easy living by the sale of tobacco, a royalist in politics and a member of the Church of England, was a most striking and curious character. Although his system was essentially an aristocracy, he enjoyed at the same time all the benefits of liberty and free government; for the stockholders of the company in England which owned Virginia under the charter from the Crown had been a very miscellaneous and democratic body, composed of grocers, candle-makers, and artisans in company with knights, gentlemen, noblemen, and members of both houses of Parliament. Unsuccessful in money-making in Virginia, the meetings of these stockholders became the scenes of political debate. It was a miniature parliament and, as the royalists thought, a very seditious one.

Its debates seem to have attracted considerable attention, and its importance and influence are shown by the contempt with which the royalist writers speak of it, and its discussion of the great questions of popular rights. The popular or democratic party in it seems to have been in the majority, and voted to give Virginia a representative government elected by every freeman in the colony. In 1619, twelve years after the founding of the province, Governor Yeardley issued writs for the first American legislature.

Virginian prosperity dates from that year. It is a curious fact that women, free government, universal suffrage, and negro slavery were all introduced into Virginia at about the same time. The right to vote was after a time restricted to freeholders and housekeepers; but neither the right to vote nor representative government, though sometimes injured and weakened, was ever seriously impaired. The Virginians steadily developed them and were developed by them.

So Virginia elected her own legislature, which was called the House of Burgesses, and the governor and his council were appointed by the king. The burgesses were chosen, two from each county, and at first sat in the church at Jamestown with their hats on like the British House of Commons. Their laws were sent to the king for approval, but until he disapproved they remained in force.

The governor's council was also the general court for the hearing of causes civil and ecclesiastical. Membership in the council was a great honor, raised a man's social position, and was much coveted by Virginia families. Every member of the council was commissioned colonel, and hence in all probability arose the custom in Virginia and the South of applying colonel as a complimentary title to prominent men. The commander of the militia of each county was also a colonel, and in the eyes of his neighbors occupied very much the same position as the lord lieutenant of a county in England.

Within five years after the burgesses were established the king dissolved the company and annulled all the charters, and for the rest of the colonial period Virginia, like some of the other colonies, was under the direct government of the Crown.

The excuse given for destroying the company was that it had mismanaged its affairs; but there seems to have been very little evidence to support this charge. The company was at that time composed of about a thousand stockholders, and they had spent over one hundred and fifty thousand pounds and sent out nine thousand colonists. The real reason was, probably, that their debates on free government were disliked by the royalists and it was determined to put a stop to them. But the representative government which they had given the province was allowed to stand unharmed, and within the next few years its position was greatly strengthened.

In 1631 the burgesses enacted that the governor should neither raise money nor levy war except by their consent. At the same time they were exempted, when in the performance of their duty, from arrest and judicial process. In 1635 the usurpations and tyranny of Governor Harvey became so unbearable that the House of Burgesses thrust him out of his government, as the ancient record has it, and appointed Captain John West to act as governor until the king's pleasure should be known. Short of actual rebellion, there could not have been a more high-handed measure. To depose the king's duly appointed governor was the next thing to deposing the king himself.

Charles I. was now on the throne, and he directed that Governor Harvey should be restored; but the burgesses never suffered for their daring. They existed only by sufferance; they had never been recognized or established by the king; and it must have been a tempting opportunity for annihilating them. But Charles I. was always extremely liberal with the colonies, and in 1642 he formally recognized the burgesses.

The cause of the people prospered in England. Cromwell and the Roundheads came and

Cavaliers and Tobacco

Charles I. was beheaded. When Cromwell had secured England, he sent a fleet across the sea to secure Virginia, where he knew the people were royalists and opposed to him. The men-of-war appeared before Jamestown, preparations for defence were made, and everything looked like battle. Then negotiations were entered into and resulted in a treaty of peace which is a most remarkable document. It is skilfully drawn, and its tone is more like an agreement between independent nations than the surrender of a colony.

Full indemnity is given for words and acts done or spoken against the Parliament of England. The surrender is acknowledged to be a voluntary act, not forced or constrained by a conquest. Free speech and free trade to all parts of the world are guaranteed to the colony. No customs or taxes are to be levied, and no forts or garrisons are to be maintained in Virginia without the consent of her House of Burgesses. Thus more than a hundred years before the Revolution the principle of no taxation without representation was declared by Virginia and assented to by Great Britain.

While Cromwell ruled England, Virginia, like all the other American colonies, was let alone, and she elected her own governors. A dispute between one of these governors and the burgesses shows the increasing power of the popular assembly. The governor and his council were accustomed to have seats in the House of Burgesses, and when a law was passed excluding them, Matthews, who was then governor, declared the assembly dissolved. They remained in session, however, and passed a resolution to the effect that they were the representatives of the people and not dissolvable by any power in Virginia but their own. To show their strength, they deposed Governor Matthews and then re-elected him. He accepted the situation, received his office from their hands, and took the oath anew.

The event, however, that best shows the temper of the Virginians is Bacon's rebellion. Nathaniel Bacon was born in England, and came to Virginia about four years before he took part in the rebellion. He was of good family and education, and had studied law at the inns of court. He was possessed of a moderate fortune, and lived with his wife on a plantation on the upper waters of the James River; and it is interesting to note that his rebellion took place in 1676, exactly a hundred years before the Revolution.

Bacon had little or nothing to do with creating the rebellion. It arose from causes beyond his control; but when the time for an outbreak arrived he became its leader. The colonists had for some time considered themselves oppressed and injured by the British government. Their first complaint was the navigation acts, which prohibited the colony from trading with any country but England and in any vessels but English vessels. Every hogshead of tobacco and every other export must go to England for sale and pay heavy duty. The Virginians, when they surrendered to Cromwell, had stipulated that they should be free to trade with all the world, and they claimed that this clause had relieved them from the obnoxious provisions of the navigation acts.

During the Commonwealth times they had little to complain of, for Cromwell let them govern themselves. But when Charles II. was restored to the throne he re-enacted the navigation acts and they were enforced. The Virginians tried to avoid them by smuggling, but the king's officers were vigilant, and prosecutions and penalties increased the discontent.

The Virginians tried to increase the price of tobacco by diminishing the crop. They passed laws regulating the quantity of tobacco that should be planted, and secret parties were organized to go about and destroy the young plants. But these methods were of little avail. The price went lower and lower ; but no matter how low it went, the tobacco must go to England

and the duty be taken from the price. Virginia incomes were diminished, and this was undoubtedly one of the principal causes of the rebellion.

Another grievance was the conduct of Charles II. in giving away the land. At one time he had given to some of his favorites the whole country between the Rappahannock and the Potomac. In 1673 he gave to Lord Arlington and Lord Culpeper the right for thirty-one years to all the quit-rents and lands escheated to the Crown. They were to receive the revenues of the colony, appoint the public officers, lay off new counties, and present to parishes. In effect they were to be the proprietors of Virginia.

An excessive tax of one hundred pounds of tobacco on each inhabitant had to be levied to send commissioners to England to have this grant modified or to buy it back from the rapacious noblemen who held it. The colonists were naturally indignant at such treatment, and they had a further cause of complaint in the erection of expensive forts, which were no protection, because the Indians, by aid of the dense forests, easily passed round them. They also complained of the recent restriction of the right of suffrage to householders. The restriction of the suffrage, however, was an act of their own legislature.

Cavaliers and Tobacco

The truth was that the Virginians were ready to complain of anything. They had conquered the wilderness, were growing rich, and began to feel their independence. It was this consciousness of wealth and success that was the most potent cause of the rebellion. They were in a state of feeling that easily took fire from oppression. They did not care to be governed at all, still less to be misgoverned.

Sir William Berkeley was governor at this time. He was a polished, agreeable man, of the cavalier class, with all the arts of a courtier and a diplomat. He kept open house, lived profusely, spent a large part of his private fortune in improving the colony, and had the confidence and to a great extent the affection of the people. But he was a haughty, arrogant old royalist, thoroughly convinced of his own importance, and a most bigoted conservative. He was a king's man, and blind, unquestioning devotion to royalty was part of his nature.

Indian hostilities gave an occasion for the rebellion. A force was sent against them under the command of Sir Henry Chicheley, but just as Chicheley was about to march Governor Berkeley revoked his commission. It has been said that Berkeley feared that the expedition would interfere with his monopoly of the Indian trade in beaver skins, but this is very unlikely.

Berkeley was not a sordid man ; he had the welfare of the colony at heart, and, so far as his own interests were concerned, they would be apt to suffer severely if the depredations of the Indians were left unchecked.

There was something in his mind more important than beaver skins. He knew that the colony was in a seditious state and ripe for a revolt, and he feared that when Chicheley's men had been successful against the Indians they would be turned into a sort of parliamentary army and overthrow the power of the governor.

His apprehension was justified by the event. There was an outburst of indignation among the people against the ruler who would not protect them from the savages. This was Bacon's opportunity. The Indian attacks continued until their victims numbered hundreds. The people petitioned to be led against them under any commander whom the governor would appoint, and as he would appoint no one, they elected Bacon for their leader, but the governor refused to give him a commission. Then Bacon took the responsibility on himself, and, calling his volunteers together, promised them that when the Indians were disposed of he would attend to the questions of civil rights and taxes.

He was successful against the Indians and won a victory over them at the battle of Bloody Run, not far from the present site of Richmond. But he had no sooner gone on this expedition than Berkeley declared him a rebel and started in pursuit. The pursuit was not far, however, for Jamestown and the lower counties joined the rebellion and Berkeley had to come back to quiet them.

He quieted them by yielding. They demanded a new assembly of the burgesses and he gave it to them. The present one had remained unchanged for fifteen years; had been, in fact, another Long Parliament, was strongly cavalier in sentiment, and had passed the act restricting the suffrage. Berkeley issued writs for a new assembly. Bacon became a member of it, and so little was the limitation on suffrage regarded that men who were not householders voted, and in some instances were elected members. The new burgesses repealed the limitation on the suffrage and made some provisions against fraudulent tax levies and fraudulent election returns by sheriffs; but they were not a very revolutionary body, and their reforms were neither violent nor far-reaching.

Bacon had been arrested the moment he appeared to take his seat with the burgesses. Berkeley asked him if he was still a gentleman, and, on being assured that he was, paroled him. He was then persuaded to repent and read a confession of his guilt. Whereupon Berkeley pardoned him, restored him to his seat in the council,—a very politic act to keep him out of the burgesses,—and, in addition, promised him a commission as general to go against the Indians.

The commission was, of course, not granted, and Bacon stole out of Jamestown, collected about five hundred armed men, and, having stirred them with one of his eloquent harangues, marched them to the State-House. The aged governor came down, bared his breast before the multitude, and said he would rather be shot than grant a commission to such a rebel. He offered to settle the question by fighting Bacon in single combat, but Bacon declined. He wanted not, he said, the governor's blood, but only permission to fight the heathen horde who were murdering his countrymen every day. Again Berkeley yielded. He not only gave the commission, but, together with the burgesses and council, signed a paper to be sent to the king, extolling Bacon and commending his loyalty and patriotism, so that Bacon's triumph was complete.

He again started in pursuit of the Indians, and his success was greater than before. By a thorough campaign he hunted them out of every thicket and swamp, and the colony was relieved from danger. Meanwhile Berkeley resorted to his old tactics, proclaimed him a rebel, and then summoned a convention of the people in Gloucester County. But although he addressed the meeting in person, they declared before his face in favor of Bacon, and used the very natural argument that they could not call a man a rebel who was at that moment defending them from the Indians. Berkeley could not raise a sufficient force to oppose Bacon, so he fled across Chesapeake Bay to the Eastern Shore, then called the Kingdom of Accomac.

When Bacon heard that the governor had fled, he marched his men to a place called Middle Plantation, which afterwards became Williamsburg, the capital of the colony. While there he was advised by his friends to depose Berkeley and appoint Sir Henry Chicheley in his place. But Bacon had a plan of his own.

He issued what he called a Remonstrance, setting forth the grievances of the people and calling for a mass-meeting. The men of Virginia assembled and Bacon completely controlled them. He actually persuaded them to bind themselves by an oath that until the king could be communicated with they would not only rise in arms against Berkeley, but also against any force which should be sent from England to his aid. These daring Virginians, like the South Carolinians in their revolution of 1719, intended to fight the king's forces until they could get a message to the king showing him the real state of affairs. This whole movement was indeed very much like the South Carolina revolution which occurred nearly fifty years afterwards.

Bacon issued writs for the election of a new House of Burgesses, and assumed full powers in himself on the theory that Berkeley, by his flight, had abdicated the government, and he argued to his followers that they were the loyal party and Berkeley the rebel and traitor.

He made another successful expedition against the Indians and was beginning to settle himself in power when Berkeley returned from Accomac with a thousand men and seventeen vessels and entered Jamestown. Bacon immediately besieged the little town, and, throwing intrenchments across the narrow neck which connected it with the mainland, imprisoned Berkeley within it. To protect his men while they were at work on the trenches, Bacon collected from the neighboring plantations some of the wives of prominent followers of Berkeley and placed them between himself and the enemy.

An assault was made by Berkeley on the trenches, but it was an unequal contest. His followers from Accomac were a rabble of fishermen and loose characters whose only motive was plunder. The rebels were householders and men of substance who were fighting for a principle. They repulsed Berkeley, drove him back into the town and from the town to his ships, and then they burnt the town so that the Berkeleyites could harbor there no more. Berkeley retreated down the river, and Bacon was again successful.

And now word was brought to him that he was threatened from the north. Colonel Brent was marching on him with a thousand men from the Potomac. Again he called together his soldiers and addressed them. They had become like the soldiers of Cromwell: success had given them a strong taste for fighting. They were eager for battle, but battle was denied them. Before they had come within striking distance of Brent his force melted away and most of his men went over to Bacon.

A few hundred men in Gloucester County still considered themselves royalists. Bacon assembled them in convention and explained the situation. They seemed, he said, to desire to be saved, and yet would do nothing to secure their salvation. He would have all or nothing; they must be either wholly for him or wholly against him; they must either take his oath or fight him. His armed veterans stood by as a grim background to this argument, and the oath was taken.

Berkeley had again retreated to Accomac.

Bacon was determined to destroy the last vestige of opposition to the popular cause, and planned an expedition against him. But in the midst of his preparations he died. He had contracted a fever in the trenches before Jamestown, and some time in October, 1676, this soldier and orator and leader of the people passed away and was buried in secret by his friends. He began the rebellion in May and had finished it in October. From comparative obscurity this youth steps into history, makes himself famous and successful for five months, and then dies.

So soon as Bacon was gone the revolution collapsed. There was no one who could fill his place even for a moment. Berkeley returned from Accomac and almost without a struggle took possession of the colony. Then his vengeance began. He executed twenty-three of the prominent rebels. He had them shot or hung in chains and left their bodies swinging from the gibbets as a warning. He reviled and taunted them before their death, and on one occasion basely insulted a woman who offered to die in place of her husband.

The old man had a craze for blood, and disgusted even his own party and the king whom he thought he was serving. He would have slaughtered half the country if the burgesses and a commission that had been sent out from England to investigate the rebellion had not stopped him. All his agreeable qualities seemed to have turned to bitterness, and the love the Virginians once bore him had certainly turned to hate.

When they heard of his recall a few months after the rebellion, they celebrated the event with an illumination. On reaching England he sought the king,—the king to whom he had devoted his life, and in whose divine power he believed. But Charles II., when asked if he would see him, said, " That old fool has hanged more men in that naked country than I have done for the murder of my father." He never granted Berkeley an audience, and the old man died of a broken heart.

Bacon's rebellion destroyed many fine lives and apparently accomplished nothing. It was certainly a strange event, and implies an immense amount of independence and hardihood in these Virginians, who, without the aid of any other colony or nation, rushed recklessly against the whole British empire and committed acts which they knew were treason and would be punished as such. The whole population numbered at that time only about forty thousand; and with this in mind we can the more easily understand the outbreak in the Revolution, when the population of Virginia was more than three hundred thousand.

Cavaliers and Tobacco

The story of Bacon's rebellion was for a long time lost to the world. The uprising had been completely crushed and for many years was a forbidden subject of conversation. By the time the eye-witnesses of it were dead, only a vague tradition survived, and that tradition was colored and distorted by the influence of royalists. It was generally believed that the rebellion had been a petty affair without adequate cause and without the least success, and the name of Bacon was held in infamy.

It was not until more than a hundred years had passed that the subject was placed in its true light by a manuscript discovered in England by the American minister and made public by Thomas Jefferson. This document showed that the revolt was by no means unimportant and by no means without cause, and further investigations have made this view more certain. The occurrence of such a powerful rebellion shows that seventy years of tobacco raising and plantation life had developed a remarkable community of people. No other American colony made such an open and desperate revolt before the time of the Revolution, and it was the only revolt accompanied by bloodshed.

For some years after the rebellion Virginia suffered from very evil governors. Culpeper swindled the people by raising and lowering the value of the coin, Lord Howard swindled by a new seal, and Sir Francis Nicholson and others contrived petty tyrannies or means of enriching themselves. There was none of the contentment and easy relations with the British government which prevailed in South Carolina. The commercial restraints and most of the troubles which had caused the rebellion continued. Instead of receiving bounties on its products, like South Carolina, Virginia's great staple, tobacco, was taxed, and in 1750 the annual revenue to Great Britain from this tax was one hundred and fifty thousand pounds.

Virginia was managed by the mother country as a mere source of revenue, without regard to her welfare or discontent. We find one governor recommending that an act of Parliament should be passed forbidding the Virginians to make their own clothes. If the British merchants complained of one of the colony's laws, it was promptly suspended. The disputes between the royal governors and the colonists in the next hundred years were petty but frequent. Discontent and complaint became the habit of the Virginian mind; and there might, perhaps, have been another rebellion if there had been another Bacon to lead it.

On the accession of William and Mary to the throne, the burgesses, by their agents in England, asked many favors of their majesties, and among other things announced their familiar doctrine that no tax or imposition should be laid upon the colony, except by its consent. But they gained little or nothing from William and Mary's reign.

When Anne came to the throne their political affairs were quieter; the governors from that time were somewhat better; and two of them —Alexander Spotswood and William Gooch— had long and prosperous administrations. It was in this hundred years that followed Bacon's rebellion that the real Virginia was developed. The population in that time increased from thirty-eight thousand whites and two thousand blacks to three hundred thousand whites and two hundred and fifty thousand negroes; it often doubled itself every twenty-seven years; and this increase was largely a natural one of native births, and was very little assisted by immigration, except of negroes.

This large population of over half a million was scattered on plantations, and, as in the early days of the province, there were no towns of any size, except Norfolk, near Cape Henry, which contained some years before the Revolution about seven thousand people. Jamestown had dwindled to almost nothing, and the paper towns which the burgesses tried so hard to establish had not succeeded.

Cavaliers and Tobacco

Williamsburg, which had become the capital, contained the College of William and Mary, about two hundred houses, and a dozen families of the gentry, who made it their home. There were few doctors deserving the name, and no lawyers, except a few pettifoggers and sharpers, for the litigation of the province was unimportant. Towards the time of the Revolution, however, the great increase of population and products and the growth of wealth made business affairs more complicated, and at that time Mason, Wythe, Patrick Henry, and Jefferson became lawyers, and there were others of good repute.

The only profession of importance was the clergy. The Church of England was established by law, was part of the governing machinery of the province, adherence to it was the pathway to social and political eminence, and it became more of a power than in Maryland and South Carolina, where it was also established.

Dissenters were persecuted and driven out of the colony. In 1642, when Boston sent down a supply of Puritan ministers to take care of such dissenters as were already in Virginia, the burgesses passed an act banishing them, and it was rigidly enforced. But after Bacon's rebellion the Presbyterians, Baptists, and Quakers seem to have quietly increased in numbers in spite of efforts to keep them out, until at the time of the Revolution they included, according to Jefferson's estimate, two-thirds of the population.

If this estimate is correct it shows an immense change, and in fact almost a complete reversal of the religious feeling of Virginia. One hundred years before, or even seventy five years before, if we can believe the accounts of travellers, the dissenting sects were a mere handful and the influence of Episcopacy was overwhelming. The change was no doubt largely due to the great revival which was aroused in all the colonies by the preaching of the Wesleys and Whitefield about the middle of the eighteenth century.

The dissenters in Virginia had always bitterly hated the established church, and after the Revolution they had their day of vengeance. They not only disestablished it, but tore it out root and branch. Its property, glebe lands, church buildings, and sacred vessels were taken away from it and put to profane uses; a baptismal font was in one instance, it is said, used as a horse-trough. When, in the beginning of the present century, Chief-Justice Marshall was asked to subscribe money towards the revival of the church, he gave the money, but said it was useless; the church was dead.

Jefferson, Madison, and many of the best men in Virginia took part in this disestablishment. They meant, however, to accomplish only disestablishment, and not robbery; and their reason for disestablishment was the valid one that a state church was inconsistent with republican institutions. But the church had been so intolerant, some of its clergy had led such loose lives, and so many of them had been tories in the Revolution, that the vengeance of the majority of the people could not be restrained.

In colonial times the most inefficient clergymen were the ones who could be most easily induced to leave England and accept the hardships of the wilderness. In some instances men who had been discarded by the church in England obtained livings in the colony. These men, as a class, not only lacked zeal and spiritual life, but many of them were addicted to open vice.

Horse-racing, gambling, and drunken revels were among their sins. One of them was for many years president of a jockey club. They encouraged among the people the custom of celebrating the sacrament of baptism with festivities and dancing, in which the officiating clergyman often took a part, a custom which, by the way, shows some signs of returning in England. One of them is said to have called out to his church-warden during the communion, "Here, George, this bread is not fit for a dog." Another fought a duel in the grave-yard; and still another thrashed his vestry,—as no doubt they deserved, for it is said that the vestries in Virginia exercised too much power,—and the next day preached from the text, "And I contended with them, and cursed them, and smote certain of them, and plucked off their hair."

This liveliness of disposition was not so much of a scandal then as it would be now, because everybody was rather gay; and, moreover, they were not all of this sort. Those who were natives of the colony and had been educated at the College of William and Mary are admitted to have been good men. The faults of those who were reckless and dissolute have been so much dwelt upon that many people have an impression that every parish in Virginia was presided over by a drunkard or a gambler; but it is certain that there were earnest and useful men among them. Many of them were tutors for the children on the neighboring plantations, and not a few of the most prominent colonial Virginians, like Madison, Jefferson, and Marshall, received a fairly good education at their hands.

Each one of them usually had a plantation or glebe, which he cultivated and lived upon, and it was entirely possible for some of them to indulge in fox-hunting and many of the sports of their neighbors and be more moral and useful men for it. Indeed, it is doubtful if they were, on the whole, any worse than the clergy of that time in England, where a large part of the corruption which had caused the Reformation was still retained; and it has never yet been satisfactorily shown that the old-fashioned sporting parson was in any way inferior to his modern ritualistic successor.

Religion was not as powerful an element in the formation of the community as it was in Massachusetts. The churchmanship of the Virginians would now be called very low. They often omitted the use of the prayer-book altogether, and it is said that the surplice was unknown in the colony for the first hundred years.

Governor Spotswood describes the Virginians of his time as living "in a gentlemanly conformity with the Church of England," a phrase which is more expressive than volumes of writing. Gentleman was always a powerful word in Virginia. But the church, nevertheless, had a decided influence on them, and that quietude, good taste, refinement, and freedom from cant which marked Washington, Madison, Jefferson, Marshall, and the other prominent men of the colony were its results.

There has always been much discussion among writers on Virginia as to the comparative influence on the province of the Puritan and the Episcopalian, the roundhead and the cavalier.

Cavaliers and Tobacco

Some give all the influence to the cavalier and the Churchman. Others give all to the Puritan and the roundhead. That there was some Puritan influence, especially during the time of the commonwealth, when the governors of Virginia were Puritans, is undeniable. But on the whole the cavaliers were in the ascendant, and they poured into the colony by thousands even at the very time when it had Puritan governors. Grigsby, however, in a passage which has often been quoted, resents with indignation this stain on the honor of Virginia :

"The cavalier was essentially a slave, a compound slave, a slave to the king and a slave to the church. I look with contempt on the miserable figment which seeks to trace the distinguishing points of the Virginia character to the influence of those butterflies of the British aristocracy."

But nearly all the great Virginians were descended from cavaliers. Washington was the great-grandson of one of them, and Madison, Monroe, the Randolphs, Richard Henry Lee, Pendleton, and Mason were also descendants of royalists. These men were not butterflies; and the followers of Bacon who fell into the hands of that arch-royalist Governor Berkeley would hardly have described him as a beautiful and harmless insect.

Equally futile is the charge sometimes made

against the Virginia people that they were the descendants of adventurers, bankrupts, and felons, and instead of being, as they claimed, accomplished gentlemen, were only accomplished jail-birds.

The early settlers were no doubt a shiftless set, and in after-years some convicted felons were sent over by the British government in spite of the earnest protests of the colonists. But the felon importation was stopped. They numbered altogether only about two thousand, and, like some of the early adventurers, being shiftless and improvident, seldom had families, and in time left few if any descendants. One of the other colonies, Maryland, received twenty thousand of these low characters and was greatly injured by them, but Virginia, like Massachusetts, succeeded in keeping them out.

A considerable number of indented servants, or redemptioners as they were called, came to Virginia, but they were not an inferior class of men. They were numerous in all parts of the colonies except New England, where there were scarcely any of them. They were mostly people who sold their services for a term of years to pay for their passage to America. They were bound by law to serve the stipulated time, and seem now as if they had occupied the position of white slaves.

Cavaliers and Tobacco

But they were not so regarded, and there is not the slightest trace of any stigma being cast upon them. They were, as a rule, merely men without means, who had adopted a recognized method of the time to pay for a service rendered them. Many of them were founders of respectable families whose descendants are still in the country; and there were instances of gentlemen's sons who had got themselves in a scrape or lost property resorting to this method for a fresh start in life.

When they had once bound themselves they could be sold from one person to another until their term expired, and in this respect they were like slaves. There were also some of them who resembled slaves in having been kidnapped in the streets of London by ruffians, who sold them to the captains of vessels bound for the colonies, a nefarious traffic which the public opinion of the time could not suppress. Others were political prisoners, rebels who had assisted some of the pretenders to the English throne, and, instead of being executed or imprisoned, the government sold them as redemptioners to the captains or other speculators who traded with the colonies. Poverty or misfortune was generally the only crime of a redemptioner, and very often he was a useful man.

There is no doubt that the vast majority of

the Virginians were of the very best blood of England. The cavaliers were among the best of their class, and the dissenters, although not so severe and capable as the Puritans of New England, made good colonists. There was a large Scotch-Irish immigration which went out on the frontier, where their descendants can still be found; and there were also some Huguenots, from which such families as Maury, Dupuy, Cocke, Chastaine, Trabue, Fontaine, and Marye are descended.

Although men who had been royalists in England were the preponderating influence in Virginia, and the structure of society was that of a landed aristocracy, yet the spirit of the people was always strongly on the side of liberty. The large royalist migration a few years previous to the breaking out of Bacon's rebellion appears to have had little or no influence in checking that event. In fact, there is reason to believe that many of these royalists, after a short residence in the colony, became arrant rebels.

Self-interest soon changes a man's political belief. The Virginians admired the king and the nobility, but they liked their own rights better. They looked back towards old England with fondness; they loved its ancient customs, the pride and pomp of its aristocracy, the dignity and solemnity of the ritual of its church, and they strove as far as possible to reproduce these things in the wilderness. But beyond that they would not go. When it came to the question of losing money or property or a freeman's right, the king might count on them as enemies. Their devotion to royalty was merely a matter of taste.

The conditions of life in Virginia were those which the political and social economists assure us can never lead to prosperity or make a people great. There were no manufacturing industries, no merchants or tradesmen, few mechanics, except of the rudest sort, no money except tobacco, and all the methods of exchange and business were cumbersome and slow. The country was capable of producing iron, indigo, lumber, and beef, but these sources were never developed, and the artificial attempts to stimulate them and the cultivation of wine, silk, linen, and cotton came to naught. There were scarcely any schools, and the people all lived on large isolated tobacco plantations where they could have none of that association and conflict of mind which is said to be essential to intelligence.

The logical result of these circumstances should have been a race of stupid, ignorant boors. But, instead of that, the Virginians became the most high-spirited, intelligent, and capable men on the continent, the leaders of the

Cavaliers and Tobacco

Revolution, the framers of the Constitution, and the creators of a large part of the political thought of the country. The Americans of to-day live largely in towns, and believe no other life possible for progress; but they live by the principles of government of men whom they worship as demigods, and who not only did not live in towns, but had scarcely seen a town until they went to Philadelphia to pass the Declaration of Independence.

What was the cause of the tobacco planter's success and how did he live? Is it that the ability to live in the country without stupidity is one of the lost arts? Have the vigor and ingenuity of mind and the independence of character which enabled a man to create an intellectual world of his own on a plantation passed away from the race? Have we become so institutionalized and specialized and interdependent that each individual of us pines and perishes when separated from the swarm?

What means the enormous list of subjects in language, science, history, and philosophy through which the pale school-children are dragged only to meet in college another complicated curriculum which would have made the fathers of the republic gasp and stare? Which is the superior, the Virginia boy drilled in the simple rudiments of Latin, English, and mathematics by the fox-hunting clergyman of the parish, or the modern graduate of stupendous knowledge, kept in life only by the utmost skill of specialists for his eyes, teeth, and nerves, and happy if he can but understand thoroughly the system of government and civilization which the Virginia boy created?

The tobacco planter, like the rice planter of Carolina, had undoubtedly a great advantage in slavery, for it saved him from absorbing labor and gave him leisure. It also stimulated his pride, gave him the habit of command and the desire for ascendancy, and these qualities were further stimulated by the aristocracy of which he was a part.

In none of the other colonies were class distinctions so clearly marked and so thoroughly believed in. After the negroes came the indented servants and poor whites, with a distinct position from which few of them arose ; then the middle class of small planters, who were distinct but constantly rising into the class of the great landlords who were the rulers of the province, the creators of opinion, and always the most typical and representative men of Virginia. There was a constant effort to maintain position or to acquire it, which was a safeguard against mental stagnation.

As in South Carolina, politics and the theories and principles of government were the subject of endless conversation. The people were proud of whatever freedom they enjoyed, and in their political campaigns and contests met each other freely, and there was ample opportunity to exchange ideas.

In fact, their lives were isolated only in appearance. The plantations, like those in South Carolina, were little kingdoms in themselves, full of varied interests and requiring versatility in their management. The climate and life quickly gave the people of all classes great social facility and an ease of manner and intercourse which still often astonishes travellers from the North; and it is not uncommon to find a Virginian who has been born with a natural politeness and social instinct which the best people in other parts of America spend half a lifetime in acquiring.

The Virginians loved amusements of all kinds, and there was continual visiting between plantations. Fox-hunting, cock-fighting, horse-racing, wrestling-matches, and dancing parties, mingled with gambling and hard drinking, were their delight.

In the early days before 1700 the cattle and horses had been allowed to wander in the woods, and many of them became wild. Hunting them became a popular sport, and dogs were trained to assist in it. The pursuit of the wild horses, which were hunted down and caught or shot, was very exciting, and it was a daring and skilful rider and a strong horse that could follow them at full speed among the trunks and branches of the forest.

Up to the year 1686 the Virginia horses were very small, the result of their wild, roaming life and the scant pasturage in the woods. But in that year a law was passed for improving the breed, and before long those excellent saddle-horses were produced which are still famous. Men and women passed a large part of their time on horseback, riding over their large plantations or visiting their neighbors.

The devotion of all the people to sports and amusements is now hard to realize, and never since has there been anything quite like it in America. It was merry England transported across the Atlantic, and more merry, light, and joyous than England had ever thought of being.

" To eat and drink delicately and freely," says Campbell; " to feast and dance and riot; to pamper cocks and horses; to observe the anxious, important, interesting event which of two horses can run fastest or which of two cocks can flutter and spur most dexterously ; these are the grand affairs that almost engross the attention of some of our great men, and little, low-lived sinners imitate them to the utmost of their power."

Cavaliers and Tobacco

In the town of Norfolk fairs were constantly held in the market-place, which are described as most uproarious, the people abandoning themselves to laughter, shouting, and fun beyond anything known in subsequent puritanic times. A gilt-laced hat was placed on top of a pole, well greased and soaped, and, as man after man climbed it only to slip down with a rush before he reached the prize, the crowd screamed with delight until some enduring one succeeded.

Young men ran races with young women; pigs were turned loose and the whole crowd chased them among each other's legs to catch them by their greased tails. Some were sewn up in sacks and ran races, tumbling and rolling over each other. Others raced through sugar hogsheads placed end to end with the ends out, and as the great barrels got rolling to and fro the affair ended, it is said, in nothing but " noise and confusion."

Then a man would appear with a pot of hot mush, and eaters with distorted faces and tearful eyes gobbled at it to see which was the fastest. At the close the women and children were hurried away and a bull-bait began.

The *Virginia Gazette* of October, 1737, gives the sports in Hanover County for that month :

" We have advice from Hanover County, that on St. Andrew's Day there are to be Horse Races and several other Diversions, for the entertainment of the Gentlemen and Ladies, at the Old Field, near Captain John Bickerton's in that county (if permitted by the Hon. Wm. Byrd, Esquire, Proprietor of said land), the substance of which is as follows, viz : ' It is proposed that 20 Horses or Mares do run round a three miles' course for a prize of five pounds.

" ' That a hat of the value of 20 s. be cudgelled for, and that after the first challenge made the Drums are to beat every Quarter of an hour for three challenges round the Ring, and none to play with their Left hand.

" ' That a Violin be played for by 20 Fiddlers; no person to have the liberty of playing unless he bring a fiddle with him. After the prize is won they are all to play together, and each a different tune, and to be treated by the Company.

" ' That 12 Boys of 12 years of age do run 112 yards for a Hat of the cost of 12 shillings.

" ' That a Flag be flying on said Day 30 feet high.

" ' That a handsome entertainment be provided for the subscribers and their wives; and such of them as are not so happy as to have wives may treat any other lady.

" ' That Drums, Trumpets, Hautboys, &c., be provided to play at said entertainment.

" ' That after dinner the Royal Health, His Honor the Governor's, &c., are to be drunk.

" ' That a Quire of ballads be sung for by a number of Songsters, all of them to have liquor sufficient to clear their Wind Pipes.

" ' That a pair of Silver Buckles be wrestled for by a number of brisk young men.

" ' That a pair of handsome Shoes be danced for.

" ' That a pair of handsome silk Stockings of one Pistole value be given to the handsomest young country maid that appears in the Field. With many other Whimsical and Comical Diversions too numerous to mention.

" ' And as this mirth is designed to be purely innocent and void of offence, all persons resorting there are desired to behave themselves with decency and sobriety; the subscribers being resolved to discountenance all immorality with the utmost rigor.' "

These sports were the hearty and rude ones which prevailed in England at that time among the cavaliers and the members of the established church, and were the horror of the strict Puritans.

The passion for card-playing and gambling which we read of in English books as so excessive among the upper classes in the mother country was reproduced among the Virginians. It prevailed in all the colonies wherever there were large towns, and Chastellux describes the upper classes of Boston at the time of the Revolution as very fond of high play. But it is a mistake to infer, as some writers have done, that all this enjoyment was excessive or that it shows the Virginians to have been a rude and uneducated people given over to mere animal pleasures.

After the Revolution the American people passed into a puritanic state of mind in which the pleasures which had been the life of all of the colonies outside of New England were put under the ban and disappeared. In the rapid development of the continent which has continued throughout nearly the whole of the nineteenth century entire devotion to business has been the test of manhood. The sports and amusements which were once followed by all ages and classes have been uniformly considered as degrading or immoral, and not allowable even to people of wealth and leisure who respected the opinion of the community. We are only just emerging from this state of feeling, which has inspired many of the books which have been written about the Virginians, and their reputation has in consequence suffered.

But much of what is written and has come down to us describes merely their excesses. They had vast leisure; for the heavy work of tobacco culture was carried on by slaves, and close attention on the part of the master was required only during a few months of the year, and the master was not driven by the nervous intensity of modern life. When everybody had so many opportunities and was so much devoted to pleasure, there was necessarily excess, as there was excess at the same period in England, and the lower classes in Virginia were no doubt very rough in their sports.

But there is every reason to believe that by far the greater part of these sports and amusements had a very wholesome influence, especially among the middle and upper classes. In our own time the sullen and depressed state into which a large part of our farming population has fallen is largely due to the lack of amusements and the ban under which amusements have been placed. In some parts of the country where fox-hunting and other sports of colonial times have been retained a superior brightness, intelligence, and happiness can be observed, and where a farming population lives near the water and follows the sports of the water it always has a distinct advantage.

In our crusade during the past century against all sports except billiards and drinking, we have forgotten that they have an educational value, that they develop some of the most practical and effective of the faculties, and that they are a safeguard against narrowness and weakness of character and against a great deal of positive immorality.

The Duke of Wellington was not the only Englishman who learned to win a Waterloo on the cricket-fields of Eton. Washington was always a persistent fox-hunter; his youth was devoted to these Virginia sports, and the results of his life do not seem to show that he was at all inferior to the men who have thought such pleasures degrading.

Patrick Henry's youth is described as passed

in a rather excessive indulgence in the woods and fields and trout streams; and he is said to have spent too many evenings at lively plantation houses, where he played the fiddle and danced in apparent utter disregard of the momentous questions of the Revolution which he would soon be called upon to face.

But how many men have there been who have faced those questions better than he, and how many could equal him in arousing the enlightened sentiment of a continent? When the time came Henry was found to have all the knowledge that was necessary, more wit and intellectual keenness than most, and he became one of the able lawyers of the country, as well as an important public man. The joyous evenings of the fiddle and the vigor of the pine forests and the mountains appear to have interfered as little with the development of a great career as the schooling received by Jefferson, Marshall, and Madison at the hands of those much-belied parish clergymen.

The colonial Virginians are generally charged with being inveterate gamblers, but the Marquis de Chastellux describes two days which he spent at Offly, General Nelson's plantation, during which, although there were fifteen or twenty people in the house, kept in-doors by bad weather, cards and play were not even mentioned. He comments on the circumstance because, as he says, in France, under the same conditions, there would have been no end of trictrac, whist, and lotto.

Music, drawing, and public reading, he adds, were not sufficiently cultivated by the Virginia women, but on this occasion a Miss Taliaferro (Tolliver he spells it, which was the way it was pronounced) sang some songs. " A charming voice, and the artless simplicity of her singing were a substitute for taste if not taste itself."

The Virginia women might, he thought, become musicians if the fox-hounds would only stop baying for a little while each day. There were also, he says, sources of amusement in the house " in some good French and English authors," and in subsequent journeys he met with several Virginia ladies who sang and played on the harpsichord.

Chastellux was very fond of music, and proud of the efficiency in it which his old regiment in France had possessed. He was a general in the French army who came over with our allies at the time of the Revolution, and being a distinguished and polished man of the world, familiar with the best society in France, the pleasure he found among the upper classes in Virginia is sure proof that they were not as rude as some have supposed.

Cavaliers and Tobacco

There were many foreigners who wrote their impressions of the colonies,—Abbé Robin, Brissot, Burnaby, Crèvecœur, Smyth, Kalm, Rochefoucauld, Blanchard, and Dankers; but none of them were quite equal to Chastellux in ability and keenness of observation.

He describes one of the Nelsons who had been secretary of the province before the Revolution as an " old magistrate whose white locks, noble figure, and stature, which was above the common size, commanded respect and veneration ;" and, like all true Virginians, he was badly afflicted with the gout. On the plantation where he lived he could within less than six hours assemble thirty of his children and grandchildren, besides nephews and nieces in the neighborhood, amounting in all to seventy. These enormous families which were to be found in colonial times in Virginia and New England, where the people were very homogeneous and united, always astonished the Frenchmen.

It may be added that Chastellux found the word " honey," now so common in the South and indeed in all the United States, used in Virginia as a term of endearment; and he explains that it is equivalent to the French *mon petit cœur*.

Washington may be taken as a fair type of

the usual result of Virginia life among the upper classes when it did not run to excesses. He was very fond of card-playing. We find the entry in his journal, " At home all day over cards;" and his account-books show innumerable purchases of cards, usually a dozen packs at a time.

He played for money and small stakes, especially when he was young, and his winnings and losings are recorded in the books he kept without the slightest consciousness that there was anything that might be criticised; and there was not, for he was merely following the universal custom of the time in which he lived. With his usual moderation of character, he did not play for large sums. Three pounds is the largest gain and nine pounds the largest loss we find recorded by him. In the same way he played billiards, betting on the games, and in the midst of these records we also find that he was reading Addison's *Spectator*.

His greatest passion, as we all know, was for horses. He bred them carefully at Mount Vernon, ran them in races, and won and lost bets on them. As for fox-hunting, he followed it persistently and devotedly in his youth and returned to it again with as great relish as ever when he retired from public life and was settled at Mount Vernon. In fact, he kept it up until a fall from his horse wrenched his back and he could hunt no more. The descriptions in his diary of the details of hunting are those of an enthusiast. His hounds were carefully trained, sometimes running so well together that the pack could be " covered by a blanket," and he had pet names for them like Mopsey, Trueman, Music, Bell Tongue, and Sweetlips.

The stupid, wooden, sanctimonious character into which he has been manufactured to suit modern hypocrisy is not in accordance either with his own account of himself or with statements of his contemporaries. Instead of being reserved and frigid, he was an extremely sociable man, and he could not have lived in Virginia and been otherwise. He belonged to the clubs which in his day met at all the taverns and cross-roads. He spent days and nights, like Patrick Henry, as a visitor at plantations. When he came into possession of Mount Vernon, although he was a bachelor, he describes himself as " having much company," which meant that within two months he had had people to dinner or to spend the night on twenty-nine days and had gone away to dine or visit on seven.

His passion for dancing was almost as strong as his passion for horses. He complained when in the woods or on the frontier that there were no balls or assemblies to while away the time;

and he would often ride ten miles from Mount Vernon to a dance.

During the Revolution, although he was the commander-in-chief, he never thought it beneath his dignity to dance at every opportunity, and he encouraged balls and dancing assemblies among the officers. On one of these occasions we find it recorded that " His Excellency and Mrs. Greene danced upwards of three hours without once sitting down." When we add to this his superb physical strength, which instantly impressed every one who saw him, and that he habitually drank from half a pint to a pint of Madeira, besides punch and beer, we have a picture of the sort of man the Virginia colonial life produced when at its best.

Such being the broadening effect of his pleasures, what were the serious occupations of a great planter ? Each one of them ruled over a little world of his own, consisting of from one hundred to four or five hundred people. At Mount Vernon there were about three hundred, constituting a self-supporting community, and Washington gave orders to " buy nothing you can make within yourselves."

There were a blacksmith-shop, wood-burners to keep the house supplied with charcoal, brick-makers, masons, carpenters, a mill which ground flour for sale as well as for the family's use, coopers to make barrels for it, and a schooner to carry all produce to market. Besides these there were a shoemaker, and weavers who in the year 1768 produced eight hundred and fifteen yards of linen, three hundred and sixty-five yards of woollen, one hundred and forty yards of linsey, and forty yards of cotton goods. There was an important fishery on the shore, and large herds of cattle, horses, and sheep, not to mention the great waving fields of grain, for Washington planted little or no tobacco.

It was a large enterprise, somewhat resembling in the ability required our modern manufacturing industries, but more varied. In fact, in colonial times the Southern plantations were the great business undertakings of the country, and more broadening in their effect on character than the petty trades and small farming that were followed in the North.

The man who successfully ruled this property and its retainers and at the same time led the life of a sportsman and a gentleman, mingled with military service on the frontiers in the French and Indian wars, was receiving an education which cannot be given in modern times by any university, city, or community in the United States. No amount of book-learning, no college curriculum imitated from plodding, mystical Germans, no cramming or examinations, and no system of gymnastic exercises can be even a substitute for that Virginia life which inspired with vigor, freshness, and creative power the great men who formed the Union and the Constitution.

There is no mystery about it. There is no need that we should wonder that such men should come from a place we know is now incapable of producing them. As soon as we unravel the details of colonial life it is all plain enough. It was that same mingling of sport, scholarship, social intercourse, and knowledge of the world in country life which has made England the leader among nations; and the Virginians had the advantage of a new country, easily acquired wealth, the freshness of the wilderness, and a climate which sharpened the intellect.

The test of genius and force of character is the effortlessness with which it performs its tasks. Washington went to the front by a natural ascendency, a subtle magnetism of character. Those who knew him could not pass him by or disregard him even when they tried. There is no evidence of the schemes and plans, the self-advertising, the intrigues and bitter heart-burnings by which the second-rate crawl to power. The brow of the greatest American was, it is said, often thoughtful, but never disquieted.

Cavaliers and Tobacco

The critics analyze him. He was not this, they say; he had not read that; it would have been done better in this way; and conclude by informing us that it was impossible he could have been what he was. But he did it. He was always there. Nothing could stop him, and he would not go away.

As we read the life of Jefferson we meet with a similar difficulty. His recorded words and what is said of him seem inadequate to account for the stupendous influence he exercised, the political party he created, the ideas he established, and the worship which follows him to this day. But it was the personality, the native force which he exercised unconsciously, which while he lived subdued the minds of men, and, now that it is dead with him, there is nothing to explain the result.

Marshall, one of the most noble and charming of all the Virginians, trained in the typical Virginia manner by a parish clergyman and out-door athletic sports in which his long limbs were very proficient, has, however, left behind him a great deal to explain the power of his life. The thirty volumes of the Reports of the Supreme Court of the United States, which contain his decisions as Chief-Justice, are the foundations of American constitutional law. He handled the most difficult and momentous judicial questions with giant ease, and no one has ever attempted to deny his wonderful intellectual power or its vast influence on the destinies of the American Union.

Like Washington and Jefferson, he was a thoroughly natural and native product of Virginia life; and when we reflect on what that life was we are led irresistibly to the conclusion that the highest forms of intellect are beyond the power of mere books and colleges to produce. They originate in physical vigor and are developed by association.

As long as the old colonial life lingered, Virginia continued to produce such men; not all so great as Marshall and Washington and Jefferson, but all with some measure of that instantly recognized leadership which carried them up without an effort. They wandered off into Kentucky and other States, and were as irrepressible there as in the Old Dominion. They filled Congress and all the offices of government, and far down into the present century it was the continual complaint that it was impossible to keep out the Virginians.

A great deal that has been written about Virginia is by Northern writers inspired by the anti-slavery movement, which compelled them to see even in the colonial Virginian an ignorant, licentious, cruel brute. But Governor Spotswood, after ruling the colony for twelve years, was so pleased with it that he lived there the rest of his life ; and he tells us that there was " less swearing, less profanity, less drunkenness and debauchery, less uncharitable feuds and animosities, and less knavery and villany than in any other part of the world."

The more we study the life in colonial days on the James and the Potomac the brighter and better it appears. Travellers from England and France like Smyth or Rochefoucauld were invariably delighted with it. "A taste for reading," says Rochefoucauld, " is more prevalent among gentlemen of the first class than in any other part of America ;" * and Smyth's testimony is to the same effect :

" The gentlemen are more respectable and numerous than in any other province in America. These in general have had a liberal education, possess enlightened understanding and thorough knowledge of the world that furnishes them with an ease and freedom of manners and conversation highly to their advantage . . . they being actually, according to my ideas, the most agreeable and best companions, friends, and neighbors that need be desired." (Smyth's " Travels in America," vol. i. p. 65.)

Although there were no towns, the Virginia rivers during the tobacco season were full of

* Vol. ii. p. 117.

ships coming and going to each plantation and leaving the luxuries of English manufacture which the wealth of the planters enabled them to buy. The investigations into the contents of old Virginia houses show that they were crammed from cellar to garret with all the articles of pleasure and convenience that were produced in England: Russia leather chairs, Turkey worked chairs, enormous quantities of damask napkins and table linen, silver- and pewter-ware, candlesticks of brass, silver, and pewter, flagons, dram cups, beakers, tankards, chafing dishes, Spanish tables, Dutch tables, valuable clocks, screens, and escritoires.

Chastellux describes the Nelson house at Yorktown as very handsome, " from which neither European taste nor luxury were excluded; a chimney-piece and some bas-reliefs of very fine marble exquisitely sculptured were particularly admired."

He also tells us that " the chief magnificence of the Virginians consists in furniture, linen, and plate." This we shall find to be characteristic of all the colonies, especially with regard to linen and silver-ware, of which the people had what often seem to be unnecessarily large quantities. The reason for the quantities of silver-ware may have been that, in the absence of savings banks and investment securities, the people used their savings to buy silver, which they believed would always have a permanent value; so that in the Northern colonies it was not uncommon to find ordinary farmers' families with what seems a large supply of it.

The people dressed extravagantly in the bright colors that were fashionable in Europe, and their garments are sometimes described as a little ludicrous in contrast with the wilderness around them and the slovenliness of the slaves. Silk stockings, beaver hats, red slippers, green scarfs, gold lace, and scarlet cloaks among the men and silk and flowered gowns, crimson taffetas, and pearl necklaces among the women became such a common indulgence that the legislature tried to suppress them.

These extravagant costumes were usually given full display at church on Sunday, which was a weekly meeting for the people of all the neighboring plantations. Those old brick churches must have looked very glorious within when the people were all seated according to social rank in their high-backed pews and their wonderful clothes; and when the congregation poured out after service, the yellow and scarlet, the silk and satin, must have been a curious contrast against the dark green of the pine forest and the rough surroundings.

Although leading a country life, the women

Cavaliers and Tobacco

seem to have been able to go about a great deal to dancing parties and amusements. They rode on horseback, and long distances never deterred them. We read of no whining complaints of the impossibility of enjoying life in the country which are now so common. Without professing to be advanced or strong-minded, the colonial women of Virginia seem to have been able to create pleasure out of almost any sort of surroundings, and in their homes young girls were full of gayety and mischief. We may smile at their simplicity; but it was the simplicity of health and vigor.

" We took it into our heads to want to eat. Well, we had a large dish of bacon and beef, after that a bowl of sago cream, and after that an apple pye in bed. After this we took it into our heads to eat oysters. We got up, put on our rappers, and went down in the seller to get them. Do you think Mr. Washington did not follow us and scare us just to death! We went up tho' and ate our oysters." (Goodwin's " Dolly Madison," p.8.)

Burnaby says that the women were seldom accomplished and could not be relied upon for very interesting conversation. Burnaby was a learned doctor of divinity and set a rather high standard, to which comparatively few even now could conform in any part of the country. They were immoderately fond of dancing, but not graceful in it. When tired out with ordinary dances, they resorted to jigs which they had learned, he says, from the negroes. A man and a woman danced about the room, one retiring, the other pursuing in a fantastical manner until another woman got up, when the first must sit down, being cut out, as they called it; and the men cut out one another in the same way.

The fondness for extravagant dress among the women, of which we find so many instances in colonial times, was as prevalent in the woods of Virginia as elsewhere. Chastellux describes two young ladies arriving at a house " in huge gauze bonnets, covered with ribbands, and dressed in such a manner as formed a perfect contrast to the simplicity of the house in which they were;" and his translator, an Englishman, George Grieve, who had also travelled in Virginia, gives his own experiences in a foot-note:

" The rage for dress amongst the women in America, in the very height of the miseries of the war, was beyond all bounds; nor was it confined to the great towns, it prevailed equally on the sea coasts, and in the woods and solitudes of the vast extent of country from Florida to New Hampshire. In travelling into the interior parts of Virginia I spent a delicious day at an inn, at the ferry of Shenandoah, or the Catacton Mountains, with the most engaging, accomplished and voluptuous girls, the daughters of the landlord, a native of Boston transplanted thither; who with all the gifts of nature possessed the arts of dress not unworthy of Parisian milliners, and went regularly three times a week to the distance of seven miles, to attend the lessons of one De Grace, a French dancing master, who was making a fortune in the country." (Chastellux, Travels, vol. ii. p. 115.)

British men-of-war were constantly in the rivers. The easy access from the sea and the hospitality of the planters doubtless made the province seem a very convenient anchorage. The recollections of a lady who lived near Norfolk show some of the phases of this part of their life :

" My father was very hospitable and used to entertain all the strangers of any note that came among us, and especially the captains and officers of the British Navy that used to visit our waters before the war. Among these I remember particularly Capt. Gill, a fine old man, afterwards Admiral Gill. He commanded at this time a fifty gun ship called the Lanneston . . . He had thirty-two midshipmen on board, mostly boys and lads of good families and several of them sprigs of nobility. These used to come to my father's house at all hours and frequently dined with us. Sometimes, too, they would go into the kitchen to get a little something to stay their appetites, when old Quashabee would assert her authority, and threaten to pin a dish—something to their young lord-ships if they did not get out of the way. I remember particularly a young stripling by the name of Lord George Gordon, afterwards so famous as the leader of the riots in London, whom I have seen begging old Quashabee for a piece of the skin which she had just taken off the ham which she was about to send into the house for dinner, and eating it with great relish. Of course I had many beaux who flattered me and danced with me, and one or two who loved me, and would have married me if I would have said yes. Among these was a young Mr. Smith, a lieutenant in the British Navy with a fine florid face and auburn hair, who came here in a merchant vessel on his way to join his ship in the West Indies, who would have given his eyes for me if I would have taken them." ("Lower Norfolk County Antiquary," No. 2, part i. p. 26.)

Family life and family ties were strongly developed in Virginia. Every one wanted to found a family or extend and perpetuate the influence of the one he already had, and relationship was claimed to a degree which has made the term Virginia cousin a recognized method of expressing remote kinship.

There was, of course, the same profusion and hospitality which was to be found on the Carolina plantations: plenty of good horses, plenty of servants and slaves, and plenty to eat and drink, combined with a considerable disregard of appearances. The negroes were not neat and could not be made so. Elkanah Watson, a New Englander who travelled in Virginia at the time of the Revolution, was very much shocked at the nudity of the young negroes. Naked negro children sometimes waited at table, a custom which is said to have also prevailed in the West Indies. Attempts to have them well dressed almost invariably failed, and those who wore livery were apt to make themselves ludicrous in it.

The French travellers Brissot and Rochefoucauld complain that amidst the troops of slaves and beautiful horses and the masses of silver plate on the sideboards there was a touch of the barbaric. Silk stockings were worn with boots, window-panes were broken, and the coach-horses were not carefully matched. But the stables were kept in good condition.

On the frontiers the smallness of the cabins, which were usually only one room, where the whole family lived, ate, and slept, led to curious habits, of which we shall have more to say in describing bundling in Massachusetts and Connecticut.

" Being fatigued he presently desired them to show him where he was to sleep; accordingly they pointed to a bed in a corner of the room where they were sitting. The gentleman was a little embarrassed; but being excessively weary he retired, half undressed himself, and got into bed. After some time the old gentlewoman came to bed to him, after her the old gentleman and last of all the young lady. This, in a country excluded from all civilized society, could only proceed from simplicity and innocence : and indeed it is a general and true observation that forms and observances become necessary and are attended to in proportion as manners become corrupt, and it is found expedient to guard against vice." (Burnaby, Travels, 111.)

Cavaliers and Tobacco

Rude plenty combined at times with great toleration for heavy drinking was the life the people loved, and Thackeray has given a fair description of it in " The Virginians." A planter was never so happy as when his house was full of his neighbors and his stable full of their horses. An invitation to a neighboring family to come to dinner usually meant to come and spend the day. Men and women arrived in the morning on horseback, lounged about, strolled or slept at noon on the couches in the hall-way, carrying on with each other continual raillery and fun mingled with the ever-present politics, and feasting far into the night.

Kennedy's " Swallow Barn," a book which had considerable reputation some years before the civil war, gives a picture of Virginia life about fifty years after the Revolution, when some of the colonial ways still survived. Although impaired by many faults of style, it is worth reading for the conditions which it describes.

One of Kennedy's best characters is the lawyer who was also fox-hunter and farmer, whose hounds often insisted on following him on the circuit of the county courts, and who never could be restrained from joining a hunt which came in his way.

Less violent and aggressive than the South

Cavaliers and Tobacco

Carolinians, the Virginians were nevertheless, like the Carolinians, ready to stand alone before the world, and always thought of themselves as an independent nation. The cloudless skies and genial air had changed the heavy, sombre Englishmen into the spirited, keen, vivacious beings who produced the Jeffersons, Madisons, Randolphs, and Lees.

They were united and homogeneous, and, like the people of Massachusetts, firm believers in themselves, and this was one of the causes of their greatness. They admired everything of their own and exaggerated the merits of their prominent men. The man who had become the wonder of his county or parish they took for granted must be known to the whole continent.

The lower classes and poor whites were very rough and disorderly in colonial times, and spent a large part of their time drinking, gambling, and fighting at taverns and at elections. They were unfortunately very numerous compared with the aristocratic planter class, and when that class lost its power and control in the Revolution, these lower orders became the ruin of all that was great and distinguished in Virginia.

It was these lower-class people who indulged in the practice of "gouging." If they could get their adversary down, they seized a side-lock of his hair, and pressing their thumb against the eyeball, forced it from the socket unless he called out " king's cruse !" They were always anxious to swap horses or watches with a stranger, and if he declined might threaten " to try the strength of his eyestrings."

Elkanah Watson had on several occasions in his travels sharp experience with some of this class :

" In passing Hanover Court House, Virginia, we found the whole county assembled at election. The moment I alighted, a wretched pug-nosed fellow assailed me to swap watches. I had hardly shaken him off, when I was attacked by a wild Irishman, who insisted on my swapping horses with him, and in a twinkling ran up the pedigree of his horse to the grand dam. Treating his importunity with little respect, I became near being involved in a boxing match, the Irishman swearing that I did not 'trate him like a jintleman.' I had hardly escaped this dilemma when my attention was attracted by a fight between two very unwieldy fat men, foaming and puffing like to furies, until one, succeeding in twisting a forefinger in a side-lock of the other's hair, and in the act of thrusting by this purchase his thumb into the latter's eye, he bawled out ' king's cruse !' equivalent in technical language to ' enough.' " (Watson's " Men and Times of the Revolution," p. 60.)

The translator of Chastellux's Travels also had an experience :

Cavaliers and Tobacco

" The indolence and dissipation of the middling and lower classes of white inhabitants of Virginia are such as to give pain to every reflecting mind. Horse racing, cock fighting and boxing matches are standing amusements, for which they neglect all business, and in the latter of which they conduct themselves with a barbarity worthy of their savage neighbors. The ferocious practice of stage boxing in England is urbanity compared with the Virginian mode of fighting : In their combats, unless specially precluded, they are admitted (to use their own term) ' to bite, ——, and gouge,' which operations, when the first onset with fists is over, consists in fastening on the nose or ears of their adversaries with their teeth, . . . and dexterously scooping out an eye; on which account it is no uncommon circumstance to meet men in the prime of youth deprived of one of those organs.

" This is no traveller's exaggeration; I speak from knowledge and observation. In the summer months it is very common to make a party on horseback to a limestone spring, near which there is usually some little hut with spirituous liquors, if the party are not themselves provided, where their debauch frequently terminates in a boxing match, a horse race, or perhaps both. During a day's residence at Leesburg I was myself accidentally drawn into one of these parties, where I soon experienced the strength of the liquor, which was concealed by the refreshing coolness of the water. While we were seated round the spring, at the edge of a delightful wood, four or five countrymen arrived, headed by a veteran cyclops, the terror of the neighborhood, ready on every occasion to risk his remaining eye. We soon found ourselves under the necessity of relinquishing our posts and making our escape from these fellows, who evidently sought to provoke a quarrel.

Cavaliers and Tobacco

" On our return home, whilst I was rejoicing at our good fortune and admiring the moderation of my company, we arrived at a plain spot of ground by a wood side, on which my horse no sooner set foot than, taking the bit between his teeth, off he went at full speed, attended by the hoops and hallooings of my companions. An Englishman is not easily thrown off his guard on horseback; but at the end of half a mile my horse stopped short, as if he had been shot, and threw me with considerable violence over his head; my buckle, for I was without boots, entangled me in the stirrup, but fortunately broke into twenty pieces. The company rode up, delighted with the adventure; and it was then, for the first time, I discovered that I had been purposely induced, by one of my own *friends*, to change horses with him for the afternoon; that his horse had been accustomed to similar exploits on the same *race ground*; that the whole of the business was neither more nor less than a Virginian piece of pleasantry." (Chastellux, Travels, vol. ii. p. 192.)

As against this description of the translator we have Chastellux's account of a cock-fight he saw at one of the inns. The planters had collected from a distance of thirty or forty miles, bringing their cocks, money for betting, and also their own provisions, because the inn, or ordinary, as it was usually called at that time in Virginia, was small. So many arrived that they were obliged to sleep in blankets on the floor. But he mentions no roughness or excesses, except that the bets were very high. The sport did not interest him; there was too much of the Anglo-Saxon in it to suit a Frenchman; and he was amused at a boy who kept leaping for joy and crying, "Oh, it is a charming diversion!"

With that part of Virginia near Williamsburg, along the James River, where the oldest civilization of the colony was to be found, Chastellux was delighted. "We travelled," he says, "six and twenty miles without halting, in very hot weather, but by a very agreeable road, with magnificent houses in view at every instant; for the banks of James River form the garden of Virginia." He stayed at Westover, where Mrs. Byrd, the widow of the famous colonel, received him with great hospitality, and he amused himself exploring the neighboring country-seats, observing the humming-birds, and also the sturgeon, which at that time were so numerous in the river that on a summer's evening hundreds of them could be seen at a time leaping out of the water.

The indolence of the masses of the people did not escape the observation of Chastellux, and he comments on it in many passages. He also noticed that in Virginia there were many poor and even poverty-stricken people living in misery and rags in wretched huts, which was a class he had not seen in the Northern colonies, where in colonial times there was scarcely any poverty at all in the sense in which it is now known or as he had known it in Europe. These Virginia poor were of course what afterwards became known as the poor white trash, the result of indolence and the degradation of slave labor.

His visit at Westover and wanderings in the neighborhood led him into many reflections, one of which is well worth noticing. It seemed to him that the cause of Virginia's success up to that time—the prominent position she had taken in the Revolution, and the remarkable men she had already produced—was that she had been ruled exclusively by the great planters, whom he, like all other travellers, found to be a very enlightened and unusual class of men.

For the rest of the people he seems to have had a great contempt, and he certainly had no confidence in them. Their indolence and ignorance, he said, had been an advantage in the Revolution, because it obliged them to rely on the high-spirited and intelligent planters, who led them much farther than they would have gone without such guides and relying on their own dispositions.

He prophesied that under the new order of things since the Revolution, by which the masses of the people were being given more and more influence and control, Virginia would gradually sink into insignificance, and that the change had already begun. His keen observation showed him that although the masses of the people were of an excellent race and stock, the natural conditions of climate, soil, and the presence of the negro (whose depressing influence, even if given his freedom, he clearly foresaw) would keep them in an indolent and unprogressive state. The conditions of tobacco planting combined with slavery and intellectual influence from England which had built up the great planter class were merely temporary, and when they were gone that class would sink into the masses and the whole become mediocrity.

Some of the Virginians of the upper classes went to England to complete their education; but it is noteworthy that none of the distinguished men the colony produced were educated abroad. The great men of Virginia were all natural products of their native soil. Most of them were graduates of William and Mary College, which was founded in 1693, and is next after Harvard the oldest college in the country. It is significant of the position which Virginia and Massachusetts occupied that they were the first colonies to establish colleges.

At the outbreak of the Revolution nearly all the students of William and Mary joined the Continental army. Among the graduates who distinguished themselves were Benjamin Harrison, Carter Braxton, Thomas Nelson, and George Wythe, all of whom signed the Declaration of Independence. Besides these, the college has produced among her alumni two attorney-generals, seventeen members of Congress, fifteen senators, seventeen governors, thirty-seven judges, a lieutenant-general, two commodores, seven cabinet officers, a chief-justice, and three Presidents of the United States.

Peyton Randolph, President of the First American Congress, was an alumnus; so was Edmund Randolph, Washington's attorney-general, and afterwards Secretary of State. So was Thomas Jefferson, a stupendous influence, and to this day a living, active force. We have his own word that it was the instruction of Dr. Small at William and Mary which fixed the destinies of his life. James Madison was another alumnus; so also were James Monroe and John Tyler; and last and greatest, John Marshall, the Chief-Justice. Marshall alone would have been enough to make a college famous, for our constitution, nationality, and indissoluble union are largely the work of his hands.

When we examine more closely into details, we find that the roll of honor is even longer than at first sight appears. Not only has the college produced conspicuously great men, whose names have become household words, but she has graduated a very large number of alumni who have been distinguished in a minor way. Not to mention General Winfield Scott, we find William C. Rives, at one time a very prominent man; also Bushrod Washington, James Breckenridge, James P. Preston, George M. Bibb, William H. Fitzhugh, H. St. George Tucker, and so on. In a list of graduates of this sort it is possible to count thirty names of men who, though by no means equal to Jefferson or Marshall, were nevertheless in their day prominent and powerful leaders in the service of either the nation or the State.

To this must be added a large number of influential Virginia families, many of whom were educated at the college. The catalogues of colonial times bristle on almost every page with Carters, Pages, and Randolphs. Nor are the Harrisons, the Blands, the Nicholases, the Burwells, the Lewises, and the Carringtons without a goodly representation. It is very interesting sometimes to see the names of a whole family side by side, followed by their country-seat or county, and a statement telling whose sons they are. This is one branch of the Carter family:

Cavaliers and Tobacco

Names.	Residences.	Remarks.
John Carter,	Corotoman,	Son of Robert Carter, known as King Carter.
Robert Carter,	Sabine Hall,	Son of Robert Carter, known as King Carter.
George Carter,	Nomini,	Son of Robert Carter, known as King Carter.
Landon Carter,	Cleve,	Son of Robert Carter, known as King Carter.
Edward Carter,	Blenheim,	Son of Robert Carter, known as King Carter.

It has sometimes been said that the instruction at William and Mary was probably very inferior, and hardly equal to that of an ordinary academy. This may be true if we compare it with modern institutions of learning which are obliged to furnish the excessively varied list of modern studies; but, compared with colleges of its own time, William and Mary was as good as any. Chastellux, who certainly was competent to judge, examined it very carefully in the year 1782, and, although he may have been biassed by the degree of Doctor of Laws which it gave him, his extremely favorable opinion is worthy of respect.

The college was situated in Williamsburg, the capital of the colony, and there the planters and their families often congregated in winter time, coming on horseback or driving in their great lumbering coaches, to attend the courts and the sessions of the burgesses, talk politics, see their sons, nephews, and cousins at the college, and take part in the balls. It was to them a miniature Court of St. James, and, with that ludicrous pride which often infects provincial people, they sometimes asserted that its receptions and festivals were more brilliant than anything in England.

The college chapel and the old church-yard, where many eminent men of the province were buried, was a sort of Westminster Abbey. The college contained curious and rare books and manuscripts, the gifts of kings, archbishops, and governors. The governor's palace, as his large plain house was pretentiously called, was the scene of much festivity, for which every anniversary or important event in England or the colony served as an excuse. The "Apollo Room" of the Raleigh tavern was a famous place for assemblies, and it was there that Jefferson danced with his sweethearts and the first acts of the Revolution were planned.

The charge which has been so persistently repeated, that the colonial Virginians were ignorant and illiterate as compared with the New Englanders and other people in the Northern colonies, is not borne out by the facts. The clever phrases of Governor Berkeley in his report on the condition of the colony, which have been so often quoted, largely account for the prevailing impression :

"I thank God," he said, "there are no free schools nor printing; and I hope we shall not have, these hundred years; for learning has brought disobedience and heresy and sects into the world, and printing has divulged them, and libels against the best government. God keep us from both."

But this testy statement of the old royalist governor was made in the early days of the colony, before Bacon's rebellion, and before William and Mary was founded; and even if true at the time, did not necessarily imply that the people were ignorant, for Berkeley himself explained in his report that each man educated his family in his own way by the parish clergyman or by the instruction of himself or tutors. They never had free schools, and there was never much printing done in the colony because they relied on England for their books, as for their tables and chairs and everything they used ; and private tutors, the parish clergyman, a very few schools, and a great deal of social intercourse were their means of education.

The lower class of poor whites was undoubtedly uneducated, and in this respect inferior to the similar class in New England ; but the middle and upper classes were as well educated and accomplished as any other people in the country, and in natural brightness and mother-wit there were very few that could equal them. The occasional glimpses we get of plantation life not infrequently disclose an interest in culture and in other subjects besides politics.

The works of Addison, Steele, Pope, Congreve, and Prior were common in the great plantation houses. Isham Randolph, a planter on the James with a hundred slaves, was interested in botany and corresponded on the subject with learned men. There were several other gentlemen in the province interested in the same science.

That genial character Colonel William Byrd devoted his leisure to literature and the sciences, and his private library, said to have been the best in the colonies, contained three thousand six hundred and twenty-five volumes. John Randolph's library was almost as large, and some said larger. Madison, Jefferson, Mason, and other noted men had also good collections of books; and in a note to the introduction to the volume of the Spotswood Letters there is an account of thirty families which seem to have had fairly good libraries, from which books often containing armorial book-plates have come down to our time.

If the upper-class Virginians had not been educated men it would certainly have been most extraordinary, for the ineffaceable mark they have left on history is one of intellect and not of brute force. Judge the tree by its fruit. If Washington, Jefferson, Madison, Marshall, Mason, Henry, Pendleton, and Lee were the result of an ignorant and illiterate community, then let us have as much ignorance and as little education as possible.

Tobacco-planting, like the rice-planting of Carolina, was a very speculative occupation, and added a dash of recklessness to the Virginian's character, tempting him to great risks and bold undertakings. The price varied so much at different periods that sometimes there was an enormous profit and sometimes a heavy loss. This, combined with the inveterate propensity of both the men and women to gamble, made fortunes uncertain, and many, like Colonel Byrd's, were lost in this way, and many families had to begin life anew.

It was a strange civilization, this tobacco aristocracy of about two hundred years, dependent for its success on a single product, not altogether a useful one, and supported by negro slavery, which the moral sense of the world has always considered a crime. But the system produced wealth, leisure, and the results of independence and intelligence; and the long-leaved narcotic plant accomplished as much in creating the American Union as the rice of Carolina and the schooners and codfish of New England.

Cavaliers and Tobacco

It of course had within it the seeds of its final overthrow. There was a rift in the lute, a rottenness at the core, and in this respect Virginia was inferior to Massachusetts, whose foundations were more stable. Slavery could not continue forever in face of the protests of the world, and tobacco-raising exhausted the soil.

The usual method of culture was to plant tobacco in the same ground for five years in succession. At the end of that time, fertility being exhausted, the land was allowed to grow up in pines, and the primeval forest was cleared from some other tract for another five years' cropping. So long as there was any virgin soil in Virginia this system was very profitable. Grain was cultivated in an equally wasteful manner. Corn and wheat were allowed to succeed each other on the same ground without the intervention of clover or any crop that would restore fertility, and there was no manuring.

Virginia lived by moving from one virgin tract to another, and she never restored any of the wealth she took from the earth. The slaves who passed the summer in harvesting the crops were employed all winter in cutting away the forests to supply fresh material for this spendthrift system of agriculture.

Virginia was always living on her capital, and she came to the end of it at last. When there was no more new soil for tobacco, and other countries had begun to compete in its culture, the great wealth of the Virginians was gone. After the Revolution the exhaustion of the soil and the competition in tobacco brought on a steady shrinkage of values, and the flame of Virginia's genius burnt lower and lower. One by one the distinguished families were reduced to poverty and oblivion, and among them none suffered more than Jefferson and Madison. The story of Jefferson's last years, when with failing fortunes he struggled to keep up on his plantation the old life and hospitality, is most pathetic; and Mrs. Madison, after her husband's death, was assisted by charity.

Virginia hospitality, which was so easy and generous, was intended for near neighbors, relatives, or the occasional traveller in a wild country. But in later times, when Jefferson and Madison had world-wide reputations, and all the means of travel had improved, they were beset by tourists and curiosity hunters who had heard of the Virginia hospitality and thought they would like to try it at a great man's house and save a tavern bill.

Not realizing that times and conditions had changed, Jefferson felt bound in honor to himself, his family, and his State to receive all these people with the open heart and hand of old times.

Cavaliers and Tobacco

His overseer, Captain Bacon, describes his hope-less efforts to prevent these so-called friends and admirers from eating his master out of house and home :

"They were there all times of the year; but about the middle of June the travel would commence from the lower part of the State to the Springs, and then there was a perfect throng of visitors. They travelled in their own carriages and came in gangs, the whole family with carriage and riding horses and servants, sometimes three or four such gangs at a time. We had thirty-six stalls for horses, and only used ten of them for the stock we kept there. Very often all of the rest were full and I had to send horses off to another place. I have often sent a wagonload of hay up to the stable, and the next morning there would not be enough left to make a bird's nest. I have killed a fine beef and it would be all eaten in a day or two."

John Randolph of Roanoke, as he was called, shows the Virginia intellect in the beginning of its decay. He was born in 1773, and his formative period was passed after the Revolution, when the old life was changing and, as Chastellux would say, the ignorant and lax lower classes were beginning to overwhelm the high-strung spirit of the aristocracy. He was an odd character, dressed in the old-fashioned manner, and used to come into Congress with top-boots on, followed by two pointer dogs, which were constantly running in and out to the annoyance of the members. He, however, always rode a fine horse, and was accompanied by a negro body-servant mounted on an equally good one. He was very particular never to ride his servant's or allow the servant to ride his.

He had undoubted ability, and dominated Congress with a force and vehemence which were difficult to resist. Henry Clay was elected a member principally for the purpose of checking him. But Randolph's leadership and power were of the bullying kind; he did not win and convince forever, like the old Virginians. His triumphs were temporary and aroused vindictiveness and hatred. He was eccentric, vacillating, and inconsistent,—marks of weakness which are looked for in vain in the school of Washington and Marshall. He was also undignified,—a point in which his predecessors never failed; and he was inclined to fierce invective and personal violence,—caning and duelling,—which sprang up among the Virginians and other Southerners after the Revolution.

This sudden appearance of a fondness for personal violence, which afterwards developed to ridiculous excesses, is a strange phenomenon and difficult to account for, unless that after the Revolution the spirit of the gouging, fighting, and ignorant lower classes got possession of the whole community in consequence of the change to democratic government.

Cavaliers and Tobacco

In Randolph's time, however, the fighting disposition had developed no farther than the duel. Revolvers, bowie knives, blackguarding, and street assassination were not yet known; and Randolph had the honor of taking part in one of the last of the high-toned duels, as they were afterwards called.

He had grossly insulted Henry Clay, implying that he was a blackleg and a forger. Clay's first shot cut the skirt of Randolph's coat. He fired again; but Randolph, raising his pistol in the air, said, " I do not fire at you, Mr. Clay," stepped forward, and offered him his hand. This was his way of saying that he regretted the insult, but after being challenged could not apologize for it.

It required nearly half a century of gradual shrinkage to bring the inevitable end in Virginia, and when it came, the people, incapable of manufacturing or commerce, turned their attention to ordinary unprofitable farming on exhausted land and the breeding of negroes until the civil war stripped them of even this last resort. The important life in Virginia is now centred in towns, as in other parts of the Union, and the old plantation and country life has completely disappeared.

Whether the State will ever again be heard from and rise to superiority or ascendency as in the past is an interesting but an extremely difficult question. The same race, the pure Anglo Saxon blood which was once capable of such eminence, is still there; but it may remain sunk in the indolence of the climate and the terrible incubus of the free negro, with whom social equality is impossible and whose influence is degrading; for, as Chastellux said, the colonial Virginians seem to have been inspired and raised from the enervating conditions by which they were surrounded only by the pride and stimulus of the old tobacco aristocracy which has passed away. In a community where the mass of the people is composed of negroes and indolent whites the degenerating influences can scarcely be held in check by any form of government short of an oligarchy.

Old House Yorktown.

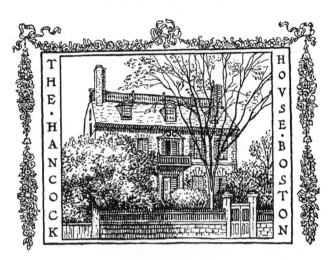

THE·HANCOCK HOVSE·BOSTON

CHAPTER II

FROM PURITANS AND WITCHES TO LITERATURE AND PHILOSOPHY

WHEN we leave Virginia and begin to consider Massachusetts and New England we are at once struck by the contrast. Instead of the soft climate, fertile soil, low sandy shores, and wide rivers of Chesapeake Bay, we have the rock-bound coast, the barren land, the fir-trees, and the harsh climate of picturesque but stern New England. Instead of men " in gentlemanly conformity to the Church of England," pleasure loving and easy and indolent in manners, we must deal with stiff, solemn individuals, devoted to schools, colleges, and learning, to whom amusement was a crime, whose lives were completely absorbed in religion, and who were among the most unrelenting fanatics the world has ever seen.

Instead of a people who lived for and loved the outer world and its pleasures, we have men and women whose thoughts were turned inward on themselves, and who developed their faculties of introspection and self-analysis to the utmost extreme. Instead of the Virginia form of government, strangely compounded of aristocratic pride and Saxon liberty, we have a civil polity modelled on the Kingdom of Israel, with the words of the Old Testament for a code, and believed by its upholders to be the voice of God on earth. Instead of an agricultural population, without commerce or manufactures, widely dispersed on large estates, without towns or villages, and leading the lives of planters and sportsmen, we have a people living exclusively in small towns and devoted to fishing, ship-building, and trade.

The early voyagers and settlers were always pleased with Virginia and the South. The mild air and the richness of the vegetation gave promise of comfort and wealth. But no one, except some enthusiast like Captain John Smith, could ever take much delight in his first experience of New England.* It might please

---

* This description of New England would not have been relished by the Puritan Fathers, and it would not have

the lover of nature, but it hardly satisfied the pioneer in search of prosperity and peace. It was comparatively easy to tempt colonists to go to fertile Virginia, but it required religious zeal of the most uncompromising kind to plant a colony in New England.

Massachusetts was settled by two colonies. First by the Plymouth colony, in 1620, and ten years afterwards by the colony of Massachusetts Bay. The first, or Plymouth colony, usually known as the Pilgrim Fathers, was composed of people who in religion were called Brownists, or Independents, and they established themselves on the coast at a place they named New Plymouth, opposite Cape Cod, about thirty miles south of Boston. The Massachusetts Bay people were Puritans, and settled on the shores of what is now Boston Harbor.

The two colonies were quite distinct in character and opinions. The Independents of the Plymouth colony were dissenters who had entirely separated themselves from the Church of England, and had been in consequence severely persecuted. Their opinions were very much the same as are now held by the Congre-

---

been safe to have uttered it among them. They once haled a man before the General Court because he had said that New England was nothing but " rocks, sand, and salt marshes." (Winthrop, p. 173.)

gationalists. They believed that each congregation should govern itself, and that there should be no general and united church organization controlling all the parishes and congregations.

They denied the necessity of regularly ordained clergymen deriving their authority from bishops who professed to be the legitimate successors of the apostles. Their worship was very simple, consisting of sermons and extemporaneous prayers without ceremony or ritual, and they of course repudiated all the doctrines which the Church of Rome had developed during the Middle Ages.

The small company of them, numbering about a hundred, which landed at Plymouth Rock, were mostly natives of Lincolnshire, England, where they had been hunted down and persecuted until they fled to Holland, where they lived first at Amsterdam, afterwards at Leyden for twelve years. They worked at various small trades, and helped one another like the Christians of the primitive Church. But they were wretchedly poor, and seeing no prospect of any improvement in their condition, they obtained, through the assistance of some merchants, the means of reaching America.

Crowded on board that immortal ship, the Mayflower, and guided by Captain John Smith's map, they reached the coast of Massachusetts in November, 1620. They intended to proceed southward to the Hudson River, where they had obtained a grant of land from the Virginia Company; but becoming involved in the shoals near Cape Cod, they landed on the extreme end of that cape, at what is now Provincetown, where vessels still seek shelter from the gales of the Atlantic, and after some weeks of exploration they established themselves at their final settlement on the mainland.

They were far superior in respectability and education to the people who had founded the colony of Virginia thirteen years before, but they resembled them in knowing nothing of camp life and the difficulties of a wilderness. The Virginians had had the advantage of arriving in the month of May, in a mild climate, with abundance of game, an advantage which was soon offset by the malarial fevers which destroyed so many of them. But the Plymouth colonists arriving in November were obliged at once to face the cold and barrenness of the New England coast, which proved to be almost as destructive as the fevers of Virginia, for nearly half of them perished within six months.

They were industrious and thrifty, and while they lacked skill as woodsmen and hunters, they made excellent soldiers. Miles Standish drilled and disciplined them, and their village was an armed camp rather than a colony. Isaac De

Puritans and Philosophy

Rasiers, a Dutchman from New York, who visited them in 1627, describes their life:

" Upon the hill they have a large square house, with a flat roof made of thick sawn planks, stayed with oak beams, upon the top of which they have six cannons, which shoot iron balls of four or five pounds, and command the surrounding country. The lower part they use for their church, where they preach on Sundays and the usual holidays. They assemble by beat of drum, each with his musket or fire-lock, in front of the captain's door; they have their cloaks on, and place themselves in order, three abreast, and are led by a sergeant without beat of drum. Behind comes the governor, in a long robe; beside him on the right hand comes the preacher with his cloak on, and on the left hand the captain with his side arms and cloak on, and a small cane in his hand; and so they march in good order, and each sets his arms down near him." (Bradford's " Plymouth," p. 126.)

This careful system of defence was forced on them by their small numbers and the danger from Indians. When their sentinel paced his rounds at night he had no waking companions on the vast continent of black forest save the Dutch guard two hundred miles away at Fort Amsterdam, on the Hudson, and the careless Virginian probably sleeping at his post at Jamestown, on the Chesapeake. They were unable to spread out and occupy the country. They had to remain huddled together in their village, with its fort on the hill, and live by fishing and

Puritans and Philosophy

trade with the Dutch or the English vessels that visited the coast. Their garden patches were kept close to the village, and it was with great caution and very gradually that they began to occupy outlying districts.

At the end of ten years, with the assistance of new arrivals from England, they numbered only about two hundred and fifty. At the end of seventy years, in 1691, when they were absorbed by the Puritans of Massachusetts Bay, they numbered only about nine thousand. They were not a success as a colony, and they were not, as the orators would have us believe, the creators of New England and the United States.

The dramatic incident of their first landing on Plymouth Rock has been used to exaggerate their merits and to credit them with all the good things that afterwards happened on the continent, and they are supposed to have established liberty, republican government, and all that is valuable in American institutions.

But, as a matter of fact, they were scarcely able to establish themselves, and they had none of that fierce energy for development which characterized the Puritans. They were excellent people in many ways, and less intolerant and illiberal than the Puritans; but they were completely overwhelmed by the Puritans, who were the real creators of New England, and who numbered thirty thousand in 1691 when the Plymouth people were only nine thousand.

Our historical literature is full of attempts to fix on some one point or set of men as the source of American liberty. Virginia has claimed the honor, so also Connecticut, Rhode Island, Massachusetts, the Dutch of New York, and the Pennsylvania Germans. But all the claims are unfounded, for there was no one set of people in England who in that time had a monopoly of the principles of free government.

The Englishmen who settled the American colonies, whether Cavaliers, Quakers, or Roundheads, were all familiar with the doctrines of liberty. The English revolution was beginning at that time, and such principles were the subject of intense discussion and were known to every one. Democratic ideas crept into America by Chesapeake Bay, by the Delaware, by the Hudson, by the Connecticut, by Narragansett Bay, and even the intolerant Puritans had democratic instincts which showed themselves as soon as the old shell of Puritanism was worn away.

The Puritans who formed the second colony at Massachusetts Bay were a party within the Church of England. They had not separated and become dissenters, like the Independents, but were working to change and, as they thought, purify the English church. They would not, they said, overset the house; but they wanted to sweep it.

It was not enough for them that the English church had thrown off the authority of the Pope, abolished the sale of indulgences and other corruptions, and rejected the great mass of dogmas that had been developed in the Middle Ages. Other things must go,—the prayers read from a book, the surplice, the sign of the cross in baptism, the ring in marriage, the rite of confirmation, bowing at the name of Jesus, and everything appealing to the imagination, which they described as "marks of the beast and dregs of antichrist." They wanted to reduce Christianity to its most primitive form of four bare walls and the literal words of the Bible.

They were also very much opposed to the authority of the bishops, and they had adopted the Calvinistic belief in predestination and election, which they wished to force on the English church as one of its doctrines. In church government they were somewhat divided. Some of them inclined to the independent plan; but most of them were unwilling to go so far. They had no desire to disorganize the English establishment and, as one of them put it, make every man's hat his church; and in the end they established in Massachusetts a system which was midway between the free democracy of the Independents and the more complicated republican form of synods and representative assemblies adopted by the Presbyterians. Their system has been called Massachusetts congregationalism because it was somewhat different from pure congregationalism or independency.

Unlike the Plymouth people, the Puritans were a great power in England, strong in numbers, unafflicted by poverty, and not compelled to hide or flee to Holland. In the early years of the reign of Charles I., before their party rose to power under Cromwell, many of them had become hopeless of reducing the Church of England to what they believed to be the true faith, and several expeditions went to the coast of Massachusetts in the neighborhood of Cape Ann to establish a settlement.

They were unsuccessful at first; but the increasing despotism under King Charles aroused a greater anxiety to leave England, and the Dorchester company was founded in 1628 and supported by the most influential and wealthy of the Puritans. The next year this company was enlarged, and under the new name of the Governor and Company of Massachusetts Bay, was incorporated by a royal charter and given a grant of the land lying between the Merrimac and Charles Rivers and extending westward to the Pacific Ocean, an extremely narrow strip

which did not include the Plymouth colony
which lay south of it.

The charter was most liberal in its provisions. The members of the company were
allowed to elect their governor and all other
officers without any control from the king; nor
were they obliged to submit their laws to the
crown for approval. In fact, it gave them virtual
independence; and the most probable explanation of this extreme liberality is that no definite
colonial policy had been formulated at that time,
except that it was important to encourage colonists to go to America in the hope that they
would check the expansion of the Dutch settlements at New York and gain the continent for
Great Britain. The Puritans were becoming very
troublesome in politics as well as in religion, and
it would be a relief to get rid of some of them.

A few months after they obtained their charter
they made a most judicious move, which they
had prepared for at the outset of their enterprise. The charter said nothing about the loca-
tion of the governing body. The Virginia
charter made England the head-quarters of the
company. But the Massachusetts charter was
silent on the subject. The company, therefore,
passed a resolution removing the charter and the
whole government of the colony to Massachusetts. If the governing body had remained

in England, the distance would have prevented the colonists from becoming active members of it ; but if transferred to Massachusetts, the colonists would become its officers : the colony and the corporation would be one. Thus these pious souls snapped the last thread of home influence and, taking in their hands their government as well as their goods, slipped off into the wilderness to become independent.

On the eve of their departure they announced that they were still members of the Church of England, and in their farewell address declared that they were not to be thought of as loathing the milk wherewith they had been nourished, that they esteemed it an honor to call the church their dear mother, that any hope of salvation they possessed had been received in her bosom and sucked from her breasts, and they concluded by asking for her prayers.

The address was all in the rather unctuous tone common among the Puritans, and has been somewhat unfairly described as a mere hypocritical cloak to cover their real intentions and check interference. They certainly had no sooner landed in Massachusetts than they gave up every vestige of the Church of England, banished two of their number who insisted on using the Book of Common Prayer, and organized their churches without either clergy or bishops, who, in the language of the time, they regarded as " biting beasts and whelps of the Roman litter."

When charged with separatism, they always denied it; but when closely pressed replied that they were separating from corruptions and not from the church. They believed themselves to be the true Church of England, just as every political party believes itself to be the true government, and they clung to that idea for many years after they had developed the Massachusetts system far beyond anything that was recognized by the mother-church in England.

They were the most sturdy, virile, and accomplished men that had thus far attempted to establish a colony, and in these respects they have perhaps never been equalled by any body of English colonists. Large numbers of them were men of more or less means who came amply provided, and a very large proportion were men of excellent education, bred in the English universities, and thoroughly convinced that religion was a question which demanded the deepest learning and research and the keenest logic.

They were on fire with the most determined enthusiasm to establish their own religion by this means and convince the whole world of its truth. Those who were so vicious or ignorant as not to accept it as the truth were to be banished, or if wicked enough actively to resist it, should be put to death.

They settled down in the wilderness as students and strong, determined men who intended to enforce the result of their studies with the musket and the hangman's rope. Their ministers and leading men had their books, and connected with their houses many of them had their little library or study, to which they were devotedly attached. In some of their diaries we read that their greatest dread of death was that they would never again enter the room of their books, which had given them such delight.

For ten years, from 1630 to 1640, they left England in increasing numbers, and at the close of that period fifteen thousand of them had settled in Massachusetts, far outnumbering the little Plymouth colony; and indeed a large part of the small increase in numbers at Plymouth seems to have been due to the overflow from the Puritans in the neighborhood of Boston.

After 1640 there was no more emigration to Massachusetts or the rest of New England, because the Puritans in England, under the leadership of Cromwell, were rising into power and saw their opportunity to accomplish all they desired in religion and politics. If Cromwell's party had not been successful, it is highly probable that nearly all the Puritans would have come to New England. In fact, their leaders seem to have had this in view, and they might have been able to establish such a powerful commonwealth that they could have declared and maintained complete independence.

From 1640, New England received no immigrants until after 1820, when the modern immigration of Irish and French Canadians began. In that period, from 1640 to 1820, her population, being of the same race and religion, became very homogeneous and united, and increased by the natural method of births at a more rapid rate than it has increased in modern times with the aid of all the foreigners that have been poured upon the country. In that period previous to 1820 the New Englanders not only filled up their own limits and became the leading section of the Union, but also overflowed into New York and the West.

The Puritans had no sooner established themselves at Boston and Cambridge, and spread along the shores of Massachusetts Bay, than they set about creating a religious oligarchy and making themselves as independent of England as possible. No one could become a freeman and have the privilege of voting unless he was a member of some church; and under the Puritan system membership in a church meant that one had shown visible evidence of conversion and change of heart, and had been accepted by some congregation. The examination into the religious experience of a candidate was very severe, and only a small part of the inhabitants could pass it; so that the fundamental principle of the Puritan government disfranchised a large majority of the population.

In 1634, when the colony numbered about four thousand, there were only three hundred and fifty freemen; and in 1670, when the population numbered about twenty-five thousand, there were only about eleven hundred freemen. As a general rule, out of every four or five adult males only one was a freeman; and this disfranchised majority, which included from three-fourths to four-fifths of the able-bodied men of the colony, had no more part or lot in the government than the women and children.

This aristocracy of saints which had so little regard for the liberty of those who had not taken strongly to religion was, however, very careful of the liberties of the colony, and had determined, as far as possible, to make it independent of England. They soon ceased to issue writs in the king's name. They dropped the English oath of allegiance and adopted a new oath, in which public officers and all the inhabitants swore allegiance, not to England, but to Massachusetts.

Any one who refused to take this oath was banished or disqualified from holding office. They also took upon themselves the sovereign attribute of coining their own money, and issued the famous pine-tree shillings. No appeals were allowed to the king or to the English courts; it was treason even to speak of them. By their definition of treason, the king himself would have been guilty of it if he had attempted to interfere with Massachusetts.

They hardly dared to adopt an ensign of their own; but some of them, instigated as is supposed by Roger Williams, cut out of the English flag the cross of St. George, which they said was idolatrous. Soon after, when some captains threatened to report in England that no flag was displayed on the fort at Castle Island, the assistants, as the governor's council was called, debated the question at great length, discussing after the Puritan fashion the nature of emblems in general and all the principles involved, and finally told the captains that they had no English flag.

A captain promptly offered to lend them one; and when at last they had to put the idolatrous thing on the fort, they excused themselves by saying that as the fort belonged to the king he had a right to have his flag there; but the rest of the colony they seemed to think was their own.

As early as 1646 the assistants actually debated the question whether they owed allegiance to England. Their conclusion was that they could govern themselves as they pleased, and that their allegiance consisted only in paying to England one-fifth of all the gold and silver they mined and praying for her welfare.

Besides the power of the assistants and of the freemen, there soon grew up a new power unknown to the charter, composed of the ministers of the different congregations; and on the whole the ministers were the more powerful, for although the assistants and governor carried on the practical work of governing, yet they invariably took the advice of the ministers, and difficult questions were referred to them.

Each minister was elected by his flock, and his authority came solely from the vote of his congregation. To all other churches except the one which elected him he was a layman. He could administer the communion only to his own congregation, and he became completely a layman when he ceased to be a minister in any particular church.

There was a great deal of work connected with a Puritan church, and at first each one had a pastor whose duty it was to exhort, and a teacher who explained doctrine; but gradually the distinction wore away and there were two pastors, who were often called the elders; and besides these there were ruling elders and teaching elders who had charge of the discipline, and deacons who managed the business affairs.

A minister maintained his position by his talents and his ability to please the people, and those people were not easy to please. Religion was the most absorbing subject of their lives, and they expected strong doctrine and strong reason. They came to church provided with note-books, they followed the whole argument of the sermon, and during the week held meetings to discuss it. They had the right to interrupt the preacher and ask him questions. The preacher had to uphold his authority among keen-minded men and women who were eager to cross-examine him, and whose training in religious controversy was in many cases equal to his own.

If a minister was suspected of unsoundness, written questions were presented to him and answers demanded. He dared not refuse. His answers were apt to draw forth replies; explanations and counter-statements followed; the discussion would grow intense; would sometimes spread to other churches and sometimes involve the whole community. Such a system produced able men, for a weak one could not exist in it; and so by a very natural process the ministers became the most powerful part of the Puritan government.

Each church governed itself to a great extent; but no church could be formed without the consent of the assistants and the ministers; and the assistants and the legislature as well as the churches could punish both individuals and churches for heresy and make laws for their government. The civil punishments for heresy were fines, banishment, imprisonment, whipping, and sometimes death, and the churches could excommunicate, which was in effect to disfranchise the victim and make him an outcast. Church and state were one, and that one was the church.

Every one's conduct was closely watched by the elders, and discipline administered for the most trifling offences. Robert Keane, a shopkeeper in Boston, was brought before the court of assistants because he charged too high for his goods. They fined him a hundred pounds and were greatly horrified at his conduct.

A minority of the court suggested that there was no law regulating profits, that it was common practice the world over to sell for as high a price as people would give, and that hundreds of others were as guilty as Keane. But it was of no avail. When the court had finished with him he was turned over to the church. He knew that there was only one safe course for him, and before both the court and the church he confessed his sin and with many tears bewailed his covetous and corrupt heart.

At every opportunity they raised some question of religion and discussed it threadbare, and the more fine-spun and subtle it was the more it delighted them. Governor Winthrop's journal is full of such questions as whether there could be an indwelling of the Holy Ghost in a believer without a personal union; whether it was lawful even to associate or have dealings with idolaters like the French; whether women should wear veils. On the question of veils, Roger Williams was in favor of them; but John Cotton one morning argued so powerfully on the other side that in the afternoon the women all came to church without them.

On one occasion Governor Winthrop paid a visit of state to Bradford, the governor at Plymouth. The journey from Boston to Plymouth can now be performed within two hours; but Winthrop spent two days on it, and was carried across the streams on the shoulders of Indians. Arrived at Plymouth, all repaired to church in the evening, and a religious question was started in honor of the distinguished guests.

Puritans and Philosophy

Many of the congregation spoke to it, and then the visitors were asked to speak.

The governors were usually preachers, and the judges preached and prayed with the criminals. And such sermons! When a Puritan preached he threw his whole soul and mind and body into his subject. It was no uncommon thing for a man to preach for several hours in the morning and have his congregation return in the afternoon to hear the sermon finished. Sometimes the sermons were serial. The minister would take up a subject and preach on it Sunday after Sunday until it was exhausted; and an able and learned Puritan could exhaust anything except the patience of his audience.

Besides the sermons, there were at first four lectures a week; but it was found that people neglected their affairs to attend the lectures, and they were reduced to two a week. Afterwards Thursday was lecture day for a great many years, and regarded almost as a second Sunday. Church meetings were so often prolonged far into the night that the assistants tried to have them break up early, so that people who lived at a distance could get home by daylight. In crossing the ocean to America the Puritans would set the watch with a psalm and a prayer; and it is said that on board the Griffin there were three sermons a day.

Puritans and Philosophy

Every form of amusement was of course forbidden, and even to have in one's possession a pack of cards or a set of dice was a criminal offence. They had no objection to wine; and in later colonial times hard drinking was very common, even among the ministers; but they were very much opposed to health drinking, which was too jovial and pleasant to suit their gloomy principles.

Through nearly all their journals and writings there runs a bitter, disappointed tone, mingled with a melancholy self-righteousness. One can almost hear their nasal drawl which in England was so disgusting to the Royalists and Cavaliers, who gave them the name malignants, which was in many respects an exact description.

In the Puritan commonwealth there was, of course, no freedom of speech. Hugh Bewett was banished for maintaining that he was free from original sin, and that a true Christian could, after a time, live without committing sin. Philip Ratcliffe was whipped, fined forty pounds, banished, and lost his ears for uttering what were called scandalous speeches against the government.

A woman, named Oliver, maintained that the magistrates and ministers together had the power to ordain ministers; that all who dwell in the same town and confess the same faith should be received at the communion. She also defined excommunication in her own way. For these harmless beliefs she was imprisoned. She afterwards reproached the assistants and was whipped. Winthrop remarks that she stood without tying and bore her punishment with a masculine spirit. She also spoke evil of the ministers, and for that had a cleft stick put on her tongue for half an hour.

Any one arriving in the colony and suspected of false doctrine was examined, and, if found unsound, was banished; and to prevent the secret presence of heretics there was a law forbidding any one to entertain strangers without permission from the assistants. Winthrop's Journal and the court records are full of accounts of fines, imprisonments, and whippings for all sorts of trifling differences of opinion. And yet, in spite of all this precaution and severity, heresy increased. In 1637, only seven years after the arrival of the Puritans, a convention held at Newtown found that there were in the colony eighty-two damnable errors.

Their minds, from constantly working on their consciences and exaggerating every subtle thought, were filled with gloomy terror. They believed in devils, signs, and portents. An upturned boat, a chance expression in a sermon, a dream, or any trifling incident might drive them into morbidness and depression. Winthrop tells of a man who cried out in the night, "Art thou come, Lord Jesus?" sprang from the window and ran through the snow, falling on his knees and praying at intervals until he died.

Other diaries relate the terrible inward struggles of imaginary guilt, or fear of damnation, which many were fond of describing at length for their own and others' edification. We often read in their diaries such passages as "Great dulness and deadness was in my heart. I am in despair of my salvation." A man seized with one of these feelings would often shut himself alone in his room and remain for days battling with the demon of his imagination, and perhaps come out with the resolve that he would be a minister of the church.

Sewall describes a large congregation who were so moved by the preaching of their minister that they all cried out, unable to contain themselves; and his description of the troubles of his daughter Betty reveals how this terrible religion often worked on the minds of the young:

"A little while after dinner she burst out into an amazing cry, which caused all the family to cry too. Her mother asked the reason; she gave none. At last said she was afraid she should goe to Hell; her sins were not pardoned. She was first wounded by my reading a sermon of Mr. Norton's, Text, ye shall seek me and shall not find me. And those words in the sermon, ye shall seek me and die in your sins ran in her mind and terrified her greatly . . . told me she was afraid she should go to Hell, was like Spira not elected."

Nathaniel Mather, when a mere boy, wrote in his diary,—

" Of the manifold sins which then I was guilty of none so sticks upon me as that being very young I was whitling on the Sabbath day ; and for fear of being seen I did it behind the door. A great reproach of God."

This morbid youth, who in Virginia would have been hunting wild horses and foxes, is said to have prayed in his sleep, made long lists of sins and things forbidden, " chewed much on excellent sermons," read the Bible, and " obliged himself to fetch a note and prayer out of each verse ;" but he lived in the deepest despair, full of " blasphemous imaginations and horrible conceptions of God," and died at the age of nineteen.

Living under such terrible repression, their human instincts sought pleasure in public confessions of guilt and a morbid prying into one another's consciences, which supplied the place of amusements. Adulterers described in church before the congregation all the details of their offence in a way which no doubt brought a large audience ; and confessions of error in doctrine, made with tears and groanings of spirit, were also of great interest and satisfaction.

A criminal condemned to execution was a choice opportunity that was never neglected. The poor wretch was visited in his cell in turn by the ministers, who probed his fears and conscience with their tireless skill, and on Sunday he was placed in the front seat of the church and preached at for hours. His crime was enlarged upon and explained and the dreadful torments that awaited him in hell foretold.

At the scaffold, to which he was drawn limp and trembling in a cart, a great crowd of men and women was collected, there were more prayers and preaching, and the prisoner was expected to break down and confess in terror, while the women shrieked and fainted.

We can easily sympathize with the women who in defiance of public sentiment sometimes leaped upon the cart to ride with the prisoner to his awful doom ; and it is gratifying to know that when the seven pirates were executed in Boston, one of them was proof against all the efforts of the ministers,—refused to go to church, jumped into the cart with a bouquet in his button-hole, and was drawn to the gallows bowing and smiling at the crowd.

The Puritans' extraordinary system of government was not established without protest. Many of the disfranchised majority were dissatisfied with their position, and complaints of all sorts were sent to England. Robert Child and some others ventured to present a petition to the assembly asking to have the laws of England administered, which was their guarded way of complaining that none but church members could vote, hold office, and sit on juries. They also complained that they were heavily taxed without being allowed a voice in the government, and could not establish churches of their own.

Child and several of the petitioners were arrested and fined; and when Child was about to leave for England, his papers were searched and one found which declared that the Puritans had forfeited their charter and were guilty of treason. For this he was again arrested to prevent his return to England. A young man named Joy, who asked one of the marshals if his warrant was in the king's name, was put in irons. But he understood the saintly character, humbled himself, confessed sin, blessed God for the irons on his legs, and was discharged.

The reason for this severity against Child and the other petitioners was that they were capable of arousing the disfranchised majority, which could have wrecked the Puritan commonwealth or have brought down on it the vengeance of the British crown, and this was also one of the principal reasons for the banishment in 1636 of Roger Williams, who founded Rhode Island.

Williams was an out-and-out separatist, who made no pretence of being still within the Church of England. He belonged to the class of people who at that time were called seekers. They believed that all church organization and government had been utterly corrupted during the Middle Ages, and they were seeking or waiting for a new and true dispensation.

In the case of most people whose minds were set free by the Reformation we find that their ideas very soon crystallized again, and settled down into some hard-and-fast form. This was notably true of the New England Puritans. But Roger Williams was altogether different; his ideas always remained in solution; he seemed to be attempting to carry out every thought that came to him. He was one of a small body of rationalists who had succeeded in getting almost entirely free from dogmatism.

He had had a university education, and was a man of some little knowledge in theology, an ardent lover of controversy, and a hard hitter, with a good vocabulary of invective. He rarely spoke without using some rough words. He feared neither the wilderness nor the Indians. He made most praiseworthy attempts to learn what he called the barbarous, rocky speech of the savages and convert them; and he tells us of the wearisome days and nights he passed in their filthy, smoky wigwams. On one occasion he went alone and unarmed among the Narragansett warriors when they were on the warpath, and persuaded them not to join the Pequods against the Puritans who had banished him.

His individuality was strong, and he could endure no rule or control but his own. Some of his opinions, especially those on religious liberty, were far in advance of his times, and the rest were mere eccentricities and hair-splittings. He was opposed to the oath of allegiance, because an oath, he said, was part of God's worship and establishment, and ought not to be administered to any mortal, whether good or bad. He held also that a man ought not to pray with the unregenerate, even if they were his wife and children.

The argument that was used to confute him on this point is a good illustration of the close way in which the Puritans reasoned about the smallest matters:

" If it be unlawful to call an unregenerate person to pray, since it is an action of God's worship, then it is unlawful for your unregenerate child to pray for a blessing on his own meat. If it be unlawful for him to pray for a blessing upon his meat, it is unlawful for him to eat it, for it is sanctified by prayer, and without prayer, unsanctified. (1 Tim. iv. 4, 5.) If it be unlawful for him to eat it, it

Puritans and Philosophy

is unlawful for you to call upon him to eat it, for it is unlawful for you to call upon him to sin. Hereupon Mr. Williams chose to hold his peace rather than make any answer: Such the giddiness, the confusion, the autocracy of that sectarian spirit." (Magnalia, Book 7.)

He complained of the charter because it described King James as the first Christian prince who had discovered New England, and because it took the land from the Indians without paying them for it. The Puritans, he said, should all go back to England and begin over again, or else make a public acknowledgment of their repentance, and he tried to have a letter signed and sent to the king admitting the wickedness of the charter.

The Puritans, he said, should also make a public repentance of having been in communion with the Church of England. Their combined government of church and state was all wrong, and confused politics with religion. Compelling people to attend public worship was a law to enforce hypocrisy. It was ridiculous to select public officers solely from church members. Would you, he said, select your doctor or your pilot according to his theology? The captain of a ship demands no compulsory prayers from his crew, and yet he maintains order and follows his course through the seas. And, finally, he declared that it was wrong to punish for religious error.

Puritans and Philosophy

This was too much for the Puritans, and it is rather remarkable that they endured Williams long enough to argue with him, for his principles struck at the foundation of their whole system. He was ordered out of the colony; and remaining on one excuse or another, they were about to seize him and send him back to England; but he fled away to Rhode Island through the winter snow.

There has been much controversy as to the exact reasons for banishing him, and some writers have denied that it was for his belief in religious liberty. The colony was at that time, they say, in danger of an Indian war, required unity among its people, and Williams was a disturber of the peace. No doubt his arguments tended to arouse the disfranchised majority, and the ministers, fearing this, were the more anxious to banish him. It is not likely that he was banished for any one opinion, but for all of them, and his advocacy of religious liberty would have been in itself enough.

There is no question that the Puritans were opposed to liberty of conscience. Their denial of it was the foundation of their system. It was preached against in Massachusetts as the cause of all immorality, and nearly every eminent man has left his written protest against it. It was called an evil egg, Satan's plea, hypocrisy.

Puritans and Philosophy

Nathaniel Ward called it hell above ground; it was, he said, one of the things his heart detested; and the Puritan oligarchy believed that its enforcement would ruin them.

The Puritans had by no means accepted all the ideas of the Reformation. They retained a large share of mediævalism, and among other things the dogma of exclusive salvation. Like Luther and Calvin, they still clung to the belief of the Roman Church, that there must necessarily be some one set of doctrines which would save all who accepted them and damn all who rejected them. After Roger Williams went to Rhode Island, John Cotton had a long controversy with him on this question of toleration, and the arguments show how the men of that age were struggling with the subject.

Williams cited the parable of the tares which were allowed to grow up with the wheat until the harvest, also the instance where Christ rebuked his disciples for suggesting that he should call down fire from heaven to destroy the Samaritans who would not receive him, and several other passages from Scripture which apparently imply a command not to persecute. He quoted the words of a number of famous princes and rulers who had announced themselves on the side of religious liberty, notably Stephen of Poland, who said, "I am king of men, not of consciences ; a commander of bodies, not of souls."

He also quoted passages from the fathers of the church,—from Hilary, Tertullian, Jerome, Augustine, and several others,—to the effect that Christianity should spread itself by the spirit and the word and not by the sword. The heathen, the Turks, and the Persians, said Williams, seldom persecute. He gave instances from ancient history and from the Old Testament where men have tolerated opposing religions ; and he reminded Cotton that although the Indians worshipped devils, the Puritans never persecuted them, but reserved their intolerance for their own brethren and fellow-countrymen.

Cotton astutely replied that what kings had said was no rule for the church of God, for kings often for the sake of policy tolerated heresies, and for every king Williams could name as in favor of religious liberty he could name a score who had put to death every heretic in their kingdoms. The commands of Christ to be gentle and tolerant were addressed only to the disciples, and the opinions of the fathers of the church referred to dealings with the heathen who had never enjoyed the light ; but such precepts could have no application to Christians who, knowing the truth, deliberately went astray.

Puritans and Philosophy

The rulers of Massachusetts, Cotton said, never punished the Indians, who had been born in darkness and ignorance, for not accepting Christianity. They punished only those who, having been enlightened, sinned against what they knew to be true; and they always warned them of their error before the punishment was inflicted. If, after fair warning, they still persisted, their punishment could not be called persecution for conscience' sake, but for sinning against conscience.

These arguments of Cotton seem now absurd enough; but at that time they were accepted not merely by the fanatical and cruel, but by tender women, magnanimous men, the sentimental and the timid as well as the strong. To the people of that age, living under the dominion of the doctrine of exclusive salvation, a man who would dare deny the truth of a system which alone could save the soul, a man who would dare to lead others from that system and thus insure their everlasting torment in hell, could not be honest and sincere; he was a pest, a danger which must be hunted down and stamped out as if he were a wolf or a snake.

The belief in religious liberty advanced during the Reformation in exact proportion as the belief in the doctrine of exclusive salvation was weakened, because men who really and thoroughly believe in exclusive salvation must necessarily persecute those who do not, and it is their evident duty to persecute them.

We can scarcely realize now what the old belief in exclusive salvation really was; but in the Middle Ages men accepted it not only as a belief but as a fact, just as to-day we know that the sun will rise to-morrow and are willing to risk our lives or fortunes on that event. Williams, having lost faith in every form of religion of his age, and believing the ordinances of every church to be invalid, had necessarily no confidence in the doctrine of exclusive salvation, and hence his belief in religious liberty.

He had hardly been in banishment a year before the colony began to be troubled by the prominence of Mrs. Anne Hutchinson. She was the sort of woman who would now be very welcome and popular in Massachusetts; but, unfortunately, she appeared about two hundred years before that good State was ready to receive her. She was a person of energy, force of character, and must have been possessed of considerable accomplishment and charm; but it is not probable that she was handsome, or it would have been mentioned in some of the writings of the time as one of the marks of Satan.

Like Roger Williams and many others who annoyed the Puritans, she led a life of righteousness and good deeds, and this her worst enemies have never denied or questioned. She exerted herself chiefly in caring for her own sex in sickness and in childbirth ; and it is probable that she made use of these occasions for inculcating her religious opinions. She took advantage of the weekly meetings for discussion held by the men, and persuaded the women of Boston to hold similar meetings of their own, a practice which they have not entirely forgotten.

Mrs. Hutchinson's heresy consisted in a perversion of the doctrine of justification by faith. She held that the fact of justification was known by an inward feeling and not by works. She was called an Antinomian,—a very terrible word in those days, like infidel in later times. It described those who trusted to their own mind and intention and were more or less independent of regularly organized churches and works, as they were called, which among the Puritans included sanctimonious speech, sour looks, groans and reproaches, and an austere routine of life.

Good works, Mrs. Hutchinson said, were often the result of justification ; but the inward feeling of comfort and assurance was the essential and only true proof, while forms and observances were not only unimportant but likely to mislead. In other words, she was drifting towards the doctrine of the inward light afterwards adopted by the Quakers, and her reliance on individual feeling and intuition was very much like the foundation principle of the transcendental school of Emerson which two hundred years afterwards appeared in Boston.

But the rulers of Massachusetts in the year 1637 did not want any light of this sort, for a person who relied on this inward feeling might come to believe anything. His conscience might some day tell him that it was wrong for the civil magistrate to punish for heresy, and that the Puritan combination of church and state was unsound.

But in spite of Puritan opinion this woman's doctrine, which has in all ages fascinated and comforted millions, began to run riot in the colony. It started with the women, but soon spread to the men. She was a far more dangerous heretic than Roger Williams. He had formed no party, and had had scarcely ten followers. But the American Jezebel, as she was called, won to her side nearly every member of the church of Boston, young Henry Vane, who was then governor of the colony, and many of the leading ministers.

Massachusetts was divided into two parties, the party of the covenant of works and the party of the covenant of grace. The grace party were most numerous in Boston, where

Puritans and Philosophy

Mrs. Hutchinson lived, but the smaller towns and the country at large held to the old belief.

The controversy grew bitter and divided families; the children in the streets took sides and quarrelled with one another; people went about from church to church to listen to the ministers and report their leaning, and after the sermon was finished these inspectors would often rise up and ask questions. The men of Boston who had acquired the new light were so much in earnest that they refused to march against the Pequods because the chaplain of the expedition was tainted with a covenant of works.

Wheelwright, the most prominent of the ministers on Mrs. Hutchinson's side, was tried and banished. Cotton was suspected and was more than half guilty. Mrs. Hutchinson always expressed great admiration for him, and declared that she had followed him to the colony to be under his preaching. He managed, however, to twist himself out of the difficulty. He complained that he had been grossly slandered, and that his enemies had drawn from his words inferences which he never intended. It is hard to tell exactly what he believed; but he probably held that the inward feeling and the good works were both necessary, and this shade of difference saved him.

Puritans and Philosophy

But it is useless to follow all the disputes and refinements of the excitement, for the ministers got Mrs. Hutchinson before them and began to badger and probe. She was singularly astute in evading them, and when they asked her if she was not a very seditious and unruly woman, promptly replied that if they had any charges to make against her they must prove them. Winthrop was finally driven to exclaim that they knew perfectly well what her opinions were, although they could not catch her in them, and one of the court expressed a fear that they would starve to death before they could finish with the lady.

But at last, to their unspeakable delight, the victim admitted in an unguarded moment that she had revelations and believed in them. Even this was rendered a little obscure by Cotton, who suggested that some revelations could be orthodox and according to the word. But the majority of the court understood her to mean that she had inspirations and an individual light independent of the churches; and this was enough. Individual revelations were a terrible heresy; for, said the Puritans, they might lead a person anywhere.

When the court had finished with her she was placed in charge of Welde for the winter. At his house she remained for three or four months, resorted to by many of the people and carefully cross-examined by the ministers, who took notes of her answers. Finally, when spring was near at hand, the ministers announced that they had entangled her in twenty-nine errors, and these errors were made the basis of her trial by the church.

She held her own so well in this trial that she was taken to Cotton's house, where she remained a week, again beset and pried into. This time they were successful, and she appeared at her second church trial completely broken down, admitted her errors, and made one of the regulation confessions of sin.

For a long time she had supplied the lack of theatre, ball-room, and horse-race, and the ministers had taken as great a satisfaction in her trial as the Virginians in a bull-baiting or a cock-fight. She was excommunicated and banished, and her followers banished or disfranchised, disarmed, and fined.

This severity was necessary, for the Antinomians were so numerous that at one election they had almost got possession of the government. But they were most thoroughly stamped out, some of the women among them accused of having given birth to monsters, and their reputations vilified.

Mrs. Hutchinson went to Rhode Island and

afterwards moved near New York, where she and nearly her whole family were massacred by the Indians, the just vengeance of God, as Winthrop said, for her heresies. But one of her descendants lived to be the royal governor of Massachusetts at the time of the Revolution.

Twenty years after the Antinomians had been disposed of the Puritans were compelled to face a still greater evil. The Quakers became a distinct sect about the year 1650, and soon after began to appear in Massachusetts. If there was anything that the aggressive, fighting, learned, intolerant Puritan detested it was a Quaker with his ways of peace, his devotion to religious liberty, and his indifference to learning as an essential of religion; and yet the men of war who had withstood the Antinomians and Roger Williams and driven them from the province found themselves powerless against this new form of meekness.

The first Quakers who arrived in Massachusetts were two women, who were imprisoned, starved, stripped naked and searched for witchmarks, and finally banished to the Barbadoes.

Other arrivals were treated with similar severity, and a fine of a hundred pounds was inflicted for bringing a Quaker within the jurisdiction. If a Quaker returned to the colony after having been banished, he should for the first offence lose one of his ears, and for the second offence his other ear; a woman was to be whipped for both offences; and for a third offence the culprit, whether man or woman, was to have the tongue bored through with a red-hot iron. Under this law no one had his tongue bored, but three Quakers lost their ears; and another law was soon passed which inflicted the penalty of death if a Quaker returned from banishment.

Under this law four of the sect were hung. One of them was a woman, Mary Dyer, who some years before had been a follower of Mrs. Hutchinson, and having settled in Rhode Island, had, like many of the Antinomians, become a Quaker.

Returning to Boston as a preacher of her new faith, she was banished, and when she appeared again was led out with due formality to the gallows and the halter put round her neck; but at the last moment she was pardoned at the intercession of her son. She went back to Rhode Island, but was dissatisfied. She felt that she had acted a weak part; and, without the knowledge of her husband, William Dyer, a very prominent man in the Rhode Island colony, she came again to Boston, and this time the saints succeeded in strangling her.

These persecutions of the Quakers were inflicted by a minority of the colony. Even in the House of Deputies, where the feelings of the dominant party were very strong, the law punishing the Quakers with death was passed by a majority of only one vote. If Massachusetts had had universal suffrage, like Virginia, we should never have heard of the Quaker massacre. But the General Court, headed by Governor Endicott and the ministers under the lead of John Norton, held the power and did what they pleased.

When the Quakers were executed, great precautions had to be taken to prevent an uprising of the community and a rescue. After the execution of Mary Dyer there was great indignation, with many threats of violence. The victims were always marched to the gallows surrounded by soldiers, and when they attempted to speak their voices were drowned by the beat of drums. Armed men were stationed in different parts of the town to guard against a surprise; the church members were kept up to the killing mark by fiery sermons on the passages from the Old Testament that justified killing unbelievers, and the argument was freely used that as it would be lawful to slay a man who brought into the town a pestilence which destroyed the body, how much more for a pestilence that destroyed the soul!

Puritans and Philosophy

The hanging business was soon found to have been overdone, for the indignation against it became very great, and in place of it a law was passed by which Quakers were to be stripped to the waist and whipped at the cart's tail through every town until they reached the border. Thirty men and women were whipped under this law by sentence of the General Court, and a much larger number by sentence of the county courts. An Indian, to whose wigwam a banished Quaker fled, exclaimed, " What a God have the English !"

The Antinomian difficulty had been disposed of within a year, but this contest with the Quakers was war to the death, and extended over a period of ten years. The Quakers became very numerous, and a large part of them were converted Puritans. Whittier, the poet, was a descendant of one of these Puritans converted to the way of peace.

They were so fearless and persistent that they wore out the endurance of the ministers, and finally were let alone. They lived at peace side by side with their enemies, and that was the last of religious persecution in New England. The meek Quaker had triumphantly enforced his lesson of religious liberty, and the fundamental principle of the Puritan commonwealth was destroyed.

Puritans and Philosophy

Another blow soon followed.   Massachusetts, as we have seen, was in effect almost independent of Great Britain, and up to the time of the Quaker massacre the condition of things in England was favorable to the colonists.   From the founding of the second colony in 1630 until the restoration of Charles II. in 1660, England was struggling with her great revolution.   The momentous events which occupied the attention of Charles I. and of Cromwell gave them no time to consider the affairs of a little colony three thousand miles away, and Cromwell, being himself a Puritan, was favorably inclined towards Massachusetts.   But her independent attitude was well known, and repeated demands were made for the surrender of her liberal charter that it might be cancelled.   At last the restoration came, and when Charles II. mounted the throne the Puritans, foreseeing their doom, held days of fasting and prayer.

Charles demanded that the Book of Common Prayer should be permitted to those who desired it, that the religious test for the right to vote should be abolished, and that writs should run in the king's name.   As the last requirement was a mere formality, the Puritans adopted it and disregarded all the others.   Proceedings were begun to forfeit the charter, and, although they were delayed for many years, the end came

Puritans and Philosophy

in 1684, when the charter was cancelled, and Massachusetts became a royal province under the direct rule of the king.

Sir Edmund Andros, who came out as the royal governor, ruled the colony as he pleased, seized the Old South Church for Church of England services, compelled land-owners to take out new patents and pay new fees, and with the aid of his council levied taxes as he thought proper. After four years of this rule, when William of Orange landed in England to drive James II. from the throne, the Puritans seized the opportunity to rebel. They rose almost as one man, seized Andros and his officers, sent them back to England, and took possession of the colonial government for themselves.

They sent agents to England to obtain a favorable charter from William; but the charter he finally granted abolished the religious restraint on the suffrage, and gave the right to vote to every inhabitant who had property above a certain value. This alone was enough to destroy the Puritan oligarchy.

But the charter went further, and abolished every principle that was dear to the Puritan heart. Liberty of conscience was given to all but Papists, appeals to England were allowed, and the oath of allegiance to Massachusetts was done away with and the English oath put in its place.

Puritans and Philosophy

By this charter the Plymouth colony was absorbed into Massachusetts, and she was also given Maine and Nova Scotia as part of her territory. Each one of these districts was to be represented in the upper house of her legislature very much as the States of the Union are now represented in the Senate.* The governor was appointed by the king; he could assemble the assistants at his pleasure, and could at his pleasure dissolve the General Court; he had the right of veto on every law, and the king also had the right of veto at any time within three years after the passage of a law. From this time until the Revolution Massachusetts was held down with an iron hand.

The attempt to establish extreme Puritanism in a colony ruling itself without interference from England had been moderately successful for about fifty years, which forms the first period of Massachusetts history. In the next period, from about 1680 until the Revolution of 1776, we find the power of the ministers gradually declining, and Puritanism becoming less and less peculiar and intolerant. But in the beginning of this period occurred a last outburst of some of the most peculiar characteristics of Puritanism, and a frantic at-

---

* Evolution of the Constitution, pp. 63, 125.

tempt of the ministers to regain their waning power, which is known as the Salem Witchcraft.

The Puritans were extremely superstitious, and still held to the old mediæval belief in devils and evil spirits. As their religion taught them to see in human nature only depravity and corruption, so in the outward nature by which they were surrounded they saw forewarnings and signs of doom and dread. Where the modern mind now refreshes itself in New England with the beauties of the sea-shore, the forest, and the sunset, the Puritan saw only threatenings of terror. The Greek gave every stream and mountain its graceful god or nymph who took a kindly interest in mankind, but the Puritan's imagination peopled every aspect of nature with his deadly enemy the devil.

Such people were in a state of mind to receive any strange delusion, and one of the worst delusions of those days was a belief in witchcraft, which at that time had begun to be doubted; but there was still enough of it in the air to infect the Puritans.

In former times no sect of religion and no class of life had been free from it, more than four thousand books had been written about it, it had assailed the highest intellects as well as the lowest, and Sprenger estimates that in the fifteenth century one hundred thousand persons were executed for it in Germany alone, and that during the Christian epoch nine million men and women had been put to death for this supposed crime. Those who doubted were reminded of the witch of Endor in the Old Testament and of the laws of Moses against witchcraft. In the books of the Middle Ages it is asserted over and over again that to doubt the existence of witchcraft is to deny the Holy Scriptures and to refuse confidence in the general belief of all mankind.

The belief in witchcraft might have lain dormant in Massachusetts, and not resulted in the killing of witches, but for Cotton Mather and the ministers, who saw an opportunity to regain their importance by arousing it.

Cotton Mather was the son of Increase Mather, and on his mother's side was descended from John Cotton,* who had been the leading minister of the colony, long and minute in

---

* When Cotton Mather was graduated at Harvard, President Oakes, in his Latin oration, said, " Mather is named Cotton Mather. What a name! But, my hearers, I confess I am wrong; I should have said, What names! I shall say nothing of his reverend father, since I dare not praise him to his face; but should he resemble and represent his venerable grandfathers, John Cotton and Richard Mather, in piety, learning, elegance of mind, solid judgment, prudence, and wisdom, he will bear away the palm." (Sparks, vi. p. 172.)

Puritans and Philosophy

preaching, and humble in confessing his errors when the cross-examination of an opponent or a congregation drove him to the wall. It was he who, when asked why he indulged in nocturnal studies, replied that before he went to sleep he liked to sweeten his mouth with a piece of Calvin,—a rather hot morsel, as Dr. Holmes has said. One of his best-known books was called " Spiritual Milk for Babes, Drawn out of the Breasts of both Testaments, for their Souls' Comfort and of Great Use for Children."

Cotton Mather, the final result of these two generations of Puritanism, was himself even more than an epitome of Puritanism, for he was Puritanism gone mad. Ingenious and learned, with boundless industry, able to labor sixteen hours of the twenty-four ; the author of three hundred and eighty-two books, written with all the fulsomeness, unction, and cant of his faith ; superstitious, vain, and arrogant, he was the most conspicuous figure of his time in New England. He fasted for days at a time ; he would lie flat on his face for hours on the floor of his study, praying and waiting for intimations and voices from heaven.

In order to stimulate the belief in witchcraft he related instances of it which he professed to consider well authenticated. A woman with her husband going over the river in a canoe, they saw the head of a man, and about three feet off the tail of a cat, swimming before the canoe, but no body to join them. A long staff danced up and down in the chimney, and afterwards was hung by a line and swung to and fro. A chair flew about the room until it lit upon the table where the meat stood. A man was taken out of his bed and thrown under it, and all the knives in the house, one after another, stuck into his back, which the spectators pulled out; but one of them seemed to the spectators to come out of his mouth.

In this way Mather and the ministers excited minds already terrorized by a belief in the constant presence of the devil and his angels, which had been dinned into their ears in every imaginable form from childhood. They were soon ready to see anything and believe anything: the yellow bird that lit on men's hats, the black man that whispered in their ears, the riding on sticks through the air, the written contracts with the devil, the signing of his book, and the feasts of the devil with the witches, where the sacraments of the church were blasphemously imitated.

The ministers soon had the opportunity they wanted. In the year 1688 two girls about thirteen years old began to mew like cats, bark like dogs, pretend to lose their hearing and sight, scream when rebuked by their parents, and went through other performances of strange postures for which they should have been whipped. After a day of fasting and prayer they were pronounced bewitched, and a poor washerwoman with whom they had quarrelled was hung.

Cotton Mather took one of the girls to his home to study her at leisure, and she made a complete fool of him,—stopped her ears when he prayed, refused to read the Bible or any Puritan book, but took great delight in a jest book, Popish books, and in the Church of England Prayer-Book. She also cleverly told him that Satan dreaded him, and that when he prayed the devils made her kick and sing and yell.

Mather and the other ministers now began to write and circulate pamphlets on the subject, and in about four years the minds of all the people were so wrought upon that the slaughter began.

Informers swarmed. No one was safe; the slightest peculiarity in manner, or an obscure chance remark that could be given a double meaning, was enough to secure a conviction. Many who had lost some household article or cattle, or who had suffered a misfortune or sickness, were allowed to relate their trouble before the court as evidence that one of their neighbors had bewitched them. The evidence against a minister named Burroughs was that he could lift up a barrel of molasses by the bung-hole, and hold a heavy gun at arm's length with his fingers in the muzzle.

Even in this awful delusion the Puritan mind still worked by its close reasoning processes. The few who were opposed to punishing for witchcraft argued that it might be possible for a devil to get into a person and make a witch of him against his will. In punishing witchcraft there was therefore great danger of punishing the innocent. If an ordinary man, they said, does anything supernatural, it must be by aid of the devil. Those that are possessed are therefore bad witnesses, both against themselves and against others, because it is making a witness of the devil, who is well known to be a liar. If they testify as witches, all that they know must come from the devil, and if the root of their knowledge be the devil, what must their testimony be?

But these arguments were of little avail. When a person was accused, his only hope of escape was in confession, and this process manufactured witches very fast. Children clung to their mother and begged her to confess and return to them; wives besought their husbands to confess and not desolate their home. Many escaped by confessing, and years afterwards the courts and the churches began to receive written retractions of these confessions which can be read to-day. Sad reading they are; but along with them are papers which are sadder still; these are the confessions of witnesses who by their lies and spite had caused the death of their neighbors.

Giles Corey was at that time eighty years of age. When accused of witchcraft, he would neither confess nor plead to the indictment. He knew himself to be innocent, and he despised a false confession. By the old English law a prisoner who refused to plead was pressed to death with weights. The Puritans were not much given to following the law of England; but this law they thought exactly suited Giles Corey's case, and accordingly the old man had rocks piled upon his stomach until he died. He begged his tormenters to increase the weight rapidly and end his misery, for there was, he assured them, no chance of changing his mind. When the weight forced his tongue from his mouth an attendant pushed it back with a cane.

The killing time lasted about four months, from the first of June to the end of September, 1692, and then a reaction came because the informers began to strike at important persons, and named the wife of the governor. Twenty persons had been put to death, fifty had confessed and escaped, one hundred and fifty were in prison waiting trial, and about two hundred more stood accused; and if the delusion had lasted much longer, under the rules of evidence that were adopted, everybody in the colony except the magistrates and ministers would have been either hung or would have stood charged with witchcraft.

In a short time all the people recovered from their madness, admitted their error, and laws were passed to prevent the recurrence of such a craze and to make some amends to the families of the victims. In 1697 the General Court ordered a day of fasting and prayer for what had been done amiss in " the late tragedy raised among us by Satan." Satan was the scapegoat, and nothing was said about the designs and motives of the ministers.

Among the few who would not admit that they had been wrong were Cotton Mather, Parris, one of the ministers, and Stoughton, the chief-justice. Stoughton was so disgusted when he found that no more witches could be hung that he resigned from the court. Mather attempted to arouse the delusion again, and made public a story of a woman who could suspend herself in mid-air so that a strong man could not pull her down. But the time had passed, his reputation suffered, and he never again regained the respect of the people. Parris, for a similar attempt, was dismissed by his congregation, and could never after obtain employment as a minister.

After the witchcraft delusion had subsided, Puritanism steadily declined for the next hundred years; and Sewall, one of the judges who had taken part in many of the witchcraft trials, has left us a most voluminous diary which gives valuable glimpses of Puritan life about the year 1700.

Sewall was very fond of going to funerals, to which people were invited in both England and some of the colonies by having a mourning scarf, a pair of gloves, or a ring sent to them. He was very proud of the rings and gloves he received in this way, and kept lists of them. When a funeral took place and no gloves or ring were received, he was much mortified; but, on the whole, he seems to have been in demand for these truly Puritan entertainments, which in time were carried to such excess, and were accompanied by so much drinking, that a law had to be passed to check the extravagance.

These funeral excesses seem to have prevailed only in the colonies north of Maryland, and the Virginians and other Southerners, having abundance of other amusements, were exempt from the excess. In Massachusetts we read of one funeral costing six hundred pounds, which was one-fifth of the man's estate. Families often had in their possession tankards and mugs full of rings which they had " made," as they expressed it, at funerals. One minister received in thirty-two years two thousand nine hundred and forty pairs of gloves, which he thriftily sold for six hundred pounds; and Sewall in thirty-eight years had " made" fifty-seven rings.

He had a great dislike for wigs, and was continually lecturing people for wearing them, using the most careful, close, and learned arguments. But the most curious part of his diary is the account of his courtships. He had three wives. The first he lived with more than forty years, the second he married within two years after the death of the first, and he began to court a third within five months after the death of the second. This was characteristic of the Puritans. They married early and frequently. Families of twelve or thirteen children were not uncommon; and women unmarried at twenty-six or twenty-seven were considered irredeemable old maids.

It was a natural state of society, in which marriage was the rule and children desired. Bachelors were carefully watched and treated almost as if they were incompetents or idiots. They were not allowed to live alone. Each one was assigned to a family, with whom he

Puritans and Philosophy

lived and who were responsible for his keeping proper hours.

When Sewall was courting for his third wife, he was sixty-eight years old. He and his son prayed together for success. This old beau gave his sweethearts books on theology, glazed almonds, meers cakes, and sometimes a quire of paper; and he frequently mentions the exact price of these presents. A lady who refused him gave as one of her reasons that she could not give up a course of lectures she was attending.

He describes some of the details of his gallantry. "Asked her to acquit me of rudeness if I drew off her glove. Enquiring the reason, I told her 'twas great odds between handling a dead goat and a living lady. Got it off." In another passage he says, "Told her the reason why I came every other night was lest I should drink too deep draughts of Pleasure." When his suit became hopeless, he enters in his diary, "I did not bid her draw off her glove as sometime I had done. Her dress was not so clean as sometime it had been, Jehovah Jireh!"

The Puritans would not allow instrumental music in their churches, and sung the Psalms in a drawling tone to three or four old tunes, which on one occasion gave Sewall some difficulty.

Puritans and Philosophy

"Spake to me to set the tune : I intended Windsor and fell into High Dutch, and then essaying to set another tune went into a key much too high. So I prayed Mr. White to set it, which he did well, Litchf. Tune. The Lord humble me, that I should be occasion of any Interruption in the worship of God." (Sewall Papers, ii. p. 151.)

The Psalms when sung were usually " lined," as it was called. The minister or clerk read a line, which was sung, and then the next line was read and sung. In this jerking way the drawling song proceeded through strange, distorted verses into which they had translated the beautiful language of David:

"Within their mouths doe thou their teeth
    break out o God most strong,
  doe thou Jehovah, the great teeth
    break, of the lions young."

We have already described the religious melancholy so characteristic of the Puritans which seized Sewall's daughter Betty. It seems to have been brought about, however, without any pressure from her father. But on another of his children, a son, he worked and pried, appealing to the boy's natural fear of death until the poor child shrieked in terror. Strong people they must have been who even in youth could endure such strains upon their nerves.

Sewall was, nevertheless, in many ways a kindly, good-hearted man in spite of his Puritanism. But he was an extreme conservative, struggled hard to uphold ecclesiasticism, and looked back with longing to the old days of intolerance. The presence of Quakers and Baptists in the colony annoyed him, and he regretted that the innovation of modern ideas prevented their being dealt with. One Sunday morning he appeared in the Old South Church, handed a paper to the minister, and stood while it was read. The paper described the remorse he felt for the part he had taken in the Salem witchcraft, and his conviction that all the proceedings had been a dreadful mistake.

Massachusetts life was altogether in towns, and the same system pervaded all the rest of New England. It grew out of the natural conditions and the necessity of protection from the Indians.* The farms were small, and the farmers could easily live in a village and go out from it to till their fields. One of the old laws forbade any one to live more than a mile from the meetinghouse, and the reason for this law was probably partly religious and partly military.

For the same reason, large tracts of wild land were at first seldom sold to individuals. A company would buy a tract, establish a village and

---

* For the origin of the New England town system see "Evolution of the Constitution," p. 336.

township, and portion out the land. Every man had his town lot and his farm lot with certain rights in the common. Massachusetts developed and spread herself into the wilderness by means of these village communities,—the very opposite of the large plantation life of Virginia. The township and not the county was the unit of government.

Each town was an instance of pure democracy, and the system increased the activity of mind and the united feeling of the people. The inhabitants of the town met together in a body, usually in their church building, elected their treasurer and selectmen, arranged the assessment of taxes, voted appropriations, and the legislature of the province was composed of representatives from these towns.

John Dunton, in his "Letters from New England," gives us some of the punishments in Massachusetts in the year 1686. For cursing and swearing the tongue was bored through with a hot iron. Scolds were gagged and sat at their own doors for all comers and goers to gaze at. For kissing a woman in the street, though but in way of civil salute, whipping or a fine. A white woman who indulged herself in an Indian lover had the figure of an Indian cut out in red cloth sewed upon her right arm and was compelled to wear it a year.

Puritans and Philosophy

In regard to kissing on the street, which was considered a great indecency, Burnaby, in his " Travels in America in 1759," relates that the captain of a British man-of-war, which was employed to cruise off the Massachusetts coast, left his wife in Boston. On one of his visits to the town she came down to the wharf to meet him, and was saluted by her husband as a true and loving sailor's wife deserved. But he was immediately brought before the magistrates, who ordered him to be whipped, and he was obliged to submit to the punishment. Whipping was not then the disgrace it is now ; the people seem to have thought as lightly of it as if they were English school-boys; and the captain soon became quite popular in the town, attending banquets and pleasure-parties, and entertained even by the very magistrates who had ordered him to be whipped.

When the time of his departure arrived he gave a farewell entertainment on board his ship. Just as she was on the point of sailing, and after every one had shaken hands with him and was going over the side, the magistrates were seized by the crew and stripped to the waist. Each one was led to the gangway, where the boatswain gave him forty save one on his bare back, and then hustled him over into the boat amid the cheers of the whole ship's company.

Puritans and Philosophy

When we read the writings of the leading Puritans we are led to infer that they were very strict moralists, and intended to allow of no irregularities among married or single people. Apparently their strictness was necessary ; but of course it is extremely difficult, especially in the absence of statistics, to know what was the real state of affairs.

In nearly all the colonies there appear to have been violent efforts made by the religious bodies to put down incontinence among the unmarried. The records of the Quaker meetings in Pennsylvania in colonial times are filled with instances of discipline administered to young people for this offence, and we find the same in Massachusetts among the Puritans. Dunton tells us that there hardly passed a court day but some were convicted, and although the punishment was fine and whipping, the crime was very frequent.

For the same offence by a married person the punishment was death ; and it may be said that, as a general rule, in all the colonies married life was very safely guarded. Married women usually became prudes and retired from all amusements and pleasures, while a great deal of liberty was allowed to the unmarried girls.

There was a method of courtship which prevailed in Massachusetts among the lower orders of the people, which was called tarrying or

bundling, and it was certainly either very innocent or very criminal. It was common in other
parts of New England, in the valley of the
Hudson, in New Jersey, and among the Germans of Pennsylvania, and is described with some
detail in the Rev. Dr. Burnaby's " Travels in
America." We shall have more to say of it
when we come to Connecticut.

Dunton has some further observations on
Massachusetts manners in 1686, and expresses
himself rather violently :

" For lying and cheating they outveye Judas, and all
the false other cheats in Hell. Nay they make sport of
it : Looking upon cheating as a commendable piece of
ingenuity, commending him that has the most skill to
commit a piece of Roguery; which in their dialect (like
those of our Yea-and-Nay-Friends in England) they call by
the genteel name of Out-Witting a Man, and won't own
it to be cheating." (" Letters from New England,"
Prince Society edition, 73.)

This statement must, of course, have been a
gross exaggeration. The Puritans were no doubt
very sharp at a bargain, and bargaining was one
of the amusements they allowed themselves. No
doubt some of them had amused themselves in
this way with Dunton. He was a phrase-maker
and fond of strong sensational assertions. He
afterwards qualified his statement by saying,
" For amongst all this Dross there runs here

and there a vein of pure gold. And though the Generality are what I have described 'em, yet is there as sincere a pious and truly a Religious People among them, as is any where in the Whole World to be found."

But although his first assertion is too strong, there seems to have been some ground for it. The mass of the Puritans were undoubtedly over-sharp, and John Adams himself complained of it. At the time of the Revolution, when on his way to the Continental Congress in Philadelphia, he met General Alexander McDougall in New York, and says of him in his diary, "He is a very sensible man and an open one. He has none of the mean cunning which disgraces so many of my countrymen." *

There are many touches of Puritan life in Dunton's letters. He was a bookseller, and seems to have done well in the business, for books and printing prospered in Boston from the beginning. He went about among the ministers, talking literature and encouraging them to buy.

He went to drill with the militia, and as soon as they had come into the field he tells us " the captain called us all into close order, in order to go to prayer, and then prayed himself." He

---

* Adams's Works, vol. ii. p. 345.

listened also to the terrible sermons which were preached to criminals, and took notes of them; but a great deal of what he says reveals the brighter side of life.

He professed to have had in Boston three very good friends among the women,—a maid, whose name he does not give, but calls her the Damsel; a wife, Mrs. Green; and a widow, Mrs. Brick. There was also, he says, a Mrs. Toy, "*parte per pale,* as the lawyers say, that is, half wife, half widow, her husband, a captain, having been long at sea;" and she was the most charming of all. "She has the bashfulness and modesty of the Damsel; the love and fidelity of Mrs. Green the wife; and the piety and sweetness of the Widow Brick."

He goes on describing these friends in the gallant, half-mocking way which was fashionable among smart English writers, enlarging much on the virgin state in speaking of the Damsel, of whom he finally says, "but once going to kiss her I thought she had blushed to death."

He and his friend Mr. King were one day a whole hour persuading the Damsel to take a ramble with them and accept of a small treat; "but on no other terms could we prevail but this, that she might have the company of Madam Brick and Mrs. Green and Mrs. Toy (of whom more anon) to go along with her."

Puritans and Philosophy

So we discover that the Puritans were human after all, and, in the midst of heresy, witchcraft, and slaughter of Quakers, went on little picnics. The Damsel, being a Puritan, must needs be thorough in everything, and insisted on three chaperons; and if we may judge of Dunton by his manner of writing, she was wise in her decision.

It is probable that the disfranchised majority were very human, and indulged in rambles and many other moderate amusements, but they have left no records from which we can know their life. Their tyrants and oppressors were the writers of the colony.

We find Dunton describing another of these rambles. He saw Morgan, the murderer, hung after he had stood an hour on the gallows to be preached at, and had given a most edifying confession to the surrounding crowd. From this scene, he says, "I rambled to the House of Feasting; for Mr. York, Mr. King, with Madam Brick, Mrs. Green, Mrs. Toy, the Damsel, and myself, took a Ramble to a place called Governour's Island about a mile from Boston, to see a whole Hog roasted, as did several other Bostonians. We went all in a Boat; and having treated the Fair Sex, returned in the Evening."

Before the year 1700 the Puritans attempted to be severe in their dress, and laws were passed to suppress "wicked apparel." But the things forbidden—the lace, the gold and silver thread, slashed sleeves and embroideries—imply an indulgence in brightness and color which is not attempted under the liberty of modern times.

There were orders of the General Court forbidding "short sleeves whereby the nakedness of the arms may be discovered." Women's sleeves were not to be more than half an ell wide. There were to be no "immoderate great sleeves, immoderate great breeches, knots of ryban, broad shoulder bands and rayles, silk ruses, double ruffles and cuffs." Long hair was prohibited as being not only "uncivil and unmanly," but too much like ruffians, Indians, and women. The women were complained of because of their "wearing borders of hair and their cutting, curling, and immodest laying out of their hair."

Later it appears that "wicked apparel" meant the attempt of persons of mean condition to ape "the garb of gentlemen by wearing of gold and silver lace or buttons or poynts at their knees, to walk in great bootes." Any tailor who should make clothes for children or servants more gorgeous than their parents or masters directed was to be fined. The poor must not appear with "naked breasts and arms; or as it were pinioned with the addition of superstitious ribbons both on hair and apparel;" and the select-men were to tax those who exceeded their rank and ability, especially in ribbons and great boots.

Even those who appear to have thought that they restricted themselves were dressed in a rather lavish manner. When we read the very ascetic and repressive writings of some of the ministers, we are surprised, on looking at their portraits, to find men with high boots like a cavalryman's, broad collars, and a general air of having paid much attention to their varied attire.

But after 1700 there was little or no effort at repression, and the bright colors, the silk, the velvet, the ruffles, the diamond shoe-buckles, and the powdered hair flourished in Massachusetts as in Europe. The women of Boston, who in the early days had debated whether it was wicked to come to church without a veil, had before the time of the Revolution expanded most extrava-gantly in silks and brocades, with ostrich feathers and high head-dresses.

The growth of wealth from the commerce and the thrifty habits of the people had its inevitable effect. The officials connected with the royal government and the Church of England people encouraged gayety and set the example of fashion. These people had no traditions of ascet-icism or severity, and the religion of the English church allowed amusements and pleasures.

Puritans and Philosophy

Their head-quarters was King's Chapel, where the services of the English church were held, at first in a wooden building, afterwards in the simple but beautiful stone structure which we see to-day. A wickedness and abomination it was to all true Puritan eyes, dispensing, as they thought, the doctrine of devils and tyranny; and the frequent entries in its records for repairs to the windows have been supposed by some to point to practical exhibitions of hatred by the lower classes.

The people who held the money, offices, and power of the government, who subscribed so liberally to King's Chapel, and represented in the colony the court of St. James, were an influence which could not be resisted. Their families, dependants, and followers took precedence in society and laid down rules of courtly conduct. The self-confidence and accomplishments of a courtier are in their way as strong as the zeal of a fanatic; for all men yield their homage to him who obviously plays well a difficult part.

Among the Wendells, Olivers, Amorys, Apthorps, Bollans, Chardons, and Shirleys who formed this circle was one whose presence was an act of poetical justice. Thomas Hutchinson, who, after filling many important offices, became the royal governor in 1771, was the grandson of Mrs. Anne Hutchinson, who had been cruelly

banished from the colony for her liberal opinions.
It was a most fitting revenge that he should rule
them; and in many ways he was an excellent
official, returning good for evil, until the Revolution came, when for his tory principles his
house was sacked and he himself was banished
in accordance with what seemed to be the inevitable fate of his family.

As the Quakers had taught the Puritans the
lesson of religious liberty, so the Church of
England people showed them the moral value of
enjoyment, good taste, and a happy, easy life;
and many a stern Puritan family surrendered.
The majority, of course, held back and stood by
the ancient traditions; but even these were
softened and enlightened; and as we read the
change of habits towards the time of the Revolution, it is strange to see this golden gleam pene-
trating the gloom which all the previous history
of Massachusetts has given us.

The Abbé Robin, who visited Boston during
the Revolution, tells us something of the scenes
in the principal churches:

" Deprived of all shows and public diversions whatever,
the church is the grand theatre where they attend, to display their extravagance and finery. There they come
dressed off in the finest silks, and over-shadowed with a
profusion of the most superb plumes. The hair of the
head is raised and supported upon cushions to an extrava-

gant height, somewhat resembling the manner in which the French ladies wore their hair some years ago.''

In the early days, especially in the country districts, there had not been so much display. The minister often had his musket by him in the pulpit, the congregation had their weapons in the pews, and armed sentinels watched outside. The church-going habits of the people, which placed nearly the whole population of a country side in one building, was a tempting opportunity to the Indians, and one or two tragedies compelled the most watchful precautions.

In the country the people came to church from long distances with their dinner; husbands riding on horseback, with their wives on pillions, and the younger people walking. Hundreds of horses were often seen fastened round the meeting-house; and when the first service was over, dinner was eaten, and gossip and discussion followed until it was time for the afternoon sermon.

Under the new influence of the royal governors and the general manner of dress of the age, Boston about the year 1765 was in some respects a gayer, brighter place in outward appearance than it is now. The governor drove in his great coach with six horses well groomed, and resplendent with harness and liveried servants. The wealthy citizens often had coaches with four horses, and they walked the streets in their cocked hats, and yellow, red, blue, or green coats and waistcoats according to their taste.

Their houses were large, and full of handsome silverware, furniture, glass, china, and tapestry imported from England. They began to indulge in riding, hunting, fishing, and skating as amusements. They took sleigh-rides in winter, with a supper and dance when they returned, and in summer they had picnics down the harbor and excursions into the country to drink tea. Some of them began to have country-seats. But they drew the line at theatres, and actors were not tolerated until after the Revolution.

Chastellux, on his visit to Boston at the close of the Revolution, when the French fleet was there and there was a great deal of entertaining, speaks of " a *ton* of ease and freedom which is pretty general at Boston, and cannot fail of being pleasing to the French." But the Bostonians did not dance well. In fact, he says they were very awkward, especially in the minuet; and the ladies, though well dressed, had " less elegance and refinement than at Philadelphia." He, however, mentions three ladies who were good dancers,—Mrs. Jarvis, Miss Betsy Broom, and Mrs. Whitmore.

KING HOOPER HOUSE
Danvers, Mass.
Built 1754

Puritans and Philosophy

Many of the people were taking advantage of the presence of the fleet to learn French. As the Revolution was just over, every one was expressing a great dislike for everything English, and Chastellux says they were much mortified to think that they spoke the English language. Instead of saying, " Do you speak English?" they would say, " Do you speak American?" And then he tells of a characteristic Boston suggestion :

> " Nay, they have carried it even so far, as seriously to propose introducing a new language ; and some persons were desirous, for the convenience of the public, that the Hebrew should be substituted for the English. The proposal was, that it should be taught in the schools, and made use of in all public acts. We may imagine that this project went no farther." (Vol. ii. p. 264.)

There were clubs then like those known in our own time, which met in turn at the houses of the members to dine and discuss questions of interest, and at some of these meetings songs were sung. Card playing Chastellux found very prevalent among the upper classes. Before the war it had been accompanied by a great deal of gambling for high stakes ; but by common consent almost every one had agreed not to play for money until independence was secured. " It is fortunate, perhaps," he says, " that the war happened when it did, to moderate this passion, which began to be attended with dangerous consequences;" and the translator explains in a note that there were frequent suicides.

From diaries and other sources we have glimpses of an amount of festivity and gayety at this time which would not now he found in any town of only sixteen thousand inhabitants, which Boston then contained. Indeed, at the outbreak of the Revolution the people of all the colonies were in a most flourishing and happy state, leading a glorious life of enjoyment, which the conflict with England and the ideas of the French Revolution which were introduced cruelly broke up. We gained independence and democracy, but we lost a great deal which we have only recently begun to restore; and the tories, who saw this loss and left the country in disgust, deserve a certain amount of sympathy.

One of the most pleasing pictures of the pomp and circumstance of colonial life in Boston a few years before the Revolution is John Adams's description of the scene at the argument of the great question of writs of assistance in the council chamber of the old State-House:

" The council chamber was as respectable an apartment as the House of Commons or the House of Lords in Great Britain, in proportion; or that in the State House in Philadelphia in which the Declaration of Independence was signed in 1776. In this chamber round a great fire were seated five judges with Lieutenant-Governor Hutchinson at their head as chief justice, all arrayed in their new, fresh, rich robes of scarlet English broadcloth; in their large cambric bands and immense judicial wigs. In this chamber were seated at a long table all the barristers-at-law of Boston and of the neighboring county of Middlesex, in gowns, bands, and tie wigs. They were not seated on ivory chairs, but their dress was more solemn and more pompous than that of the Roman senate when the Gauls broke in upon them. Two portraits at more than full length, of King Charles the Second and of King James the Second in splendid golden frames, were hung up on the most conspicuous sides of the apartment. If my young eyes or old memory have not deceived me, these were as fine pictures as I ever saw; the colors of the royal ermines and long flowing robes were the most glowing, the figures the most noble and graceful, the features the most distinct and characteristic, far superior to those of the king and queen of France in the senate chamber of Congress.''

Among these new people and manners which the royal governor and his courtly followers introduced, we have the interesting episode of Sir Harry Frankland, whose love-affair Dr. Holmes has celebrated in his poem " Agnes," and less skilful hands have at times made of it a novel or short story. His family was a very ancient one, and from time immemorial their seat had been Great Thirkleby Hall, at Thirsk, in Yorkshire. Through a female branch Sir Harry was descended from Cromwell; but he had none of the Puritan ideas of this ancestor, and, from entries in his diary, seems to have had no little contempt for the Great Protector.

He was educated in the liberal manner of a young English nobleman of his time, and was intended, as many of them still are, for employment under the government. In 1741, at the age of twenty-five, he was made collector of the port of Boston, and immediately took his place as a handsome and accomplished man among the royalists of the government circle who kept up the manners of the English aristocracy. His fortune from his English estates was a good one, with prospects of increase, and his salary and perquisites as collector gave him quite a large income.

His character was a rather curious mixture. He had the love of sport and out-door life and the loose habits of drinking and carousing which were common among his class; yet his face in his portrait is of a delicate cast, with an expression which seems to show great sweetness of temper. From his diary and other sources we gather that he was imaginative, nervous, somewhat inclined to ill health, and in the important public positions he occupied found that he must make considerable effort to keep himself cool and collected. He had with him a natural son whom he called Henry Cromwell. He was fond of literature and art, and botany and landscape gardening were among the strong passions of his life.

A year after his arrival he had occasion to visit Marblehead, or Marvil, as it was sometimes called, on public business, and at the tavern where he stopped he saw a beautiful girl of about sixteen scrubbing the floor. She was barefooted and meanly dressed, but with jet-black hair and sparkling eyes. Calling her to him, no doubt with that gallant but patronizing air the men of fashion were wont to assume towards women in her condition of life, he found that she answered his questions with remarkable brightness and intelligence, and he gave her a crown to buy a pair of shoes.

Afterwards, when he was again at Marblehead, he saw Agnes Surriage still scrubbing the floors and without shoes.

" Why have you not bought them ?" he said.

" I have, indeed, sir, with the crown you gave me ; but I keep them to wear to meeting."

Frankland was now completely captivated, and he obtained permission from her parents to take her to Boston, where she was given the best education the town could afford, and became the school-mate of the daughters of the most prominent people. She grew to be an accomplished young woman, and it is said was carefully instructed in religion under the Rev. Dr. Edward Holyoke, president of Harvard College.

Meantime Frankland amused himself with fox-hunting and the other sports which the wilderness of Massachusetts afforded, pursued smugglers with diligence, and assisted the governor and his followers to introduce more courtly manners among the Puritans. From the widowed mother of Agnes he bought a vast tract of wild land in Maine, between the Kennebec and St. Croix Rivers, for fifty pounds, evidently only for the purpose of assisting her, for the land was of little value, and afterwards became involved in confused litigation, which had to be settled by an act of the legislature in 1811. He was also a prominent member of the congregation of King's Chapel, to which he gave liberally.

Agnes had become a woman of twenty-three or four and of irresistible attraction; but Frankland's pride of family would not bend to the indignity of marrying the person who had been a scrubbing girl, and in this he was merely following the accepted rule of his class. But, like others of that class, he was self-willed and impulsive. He won Agnes's heart and took her to his house to live with him without a marriage ceremony and in spite of her religious instructor, the president of Harvard College.

Puritans and Philosophy

" But who would dream our sober sires
    Had learned the Old World's ways,
And warmed their hearths with lawless fires
    In Shirley's homespun days!"

Then there was an outbreak in the high life of Boston. For half a century the governor and his royalist retainers had been slowly teaching the Puritans the code of pleasure of the Cavaliers; but this last precept was a little too much. Agnes's schoolmates were indignant and their families were all indignant, and there was such an excitement in the town that Agnes and her lover could no longer live there in peace. Boston had always been severe to those who, from Roger Williams to the Quakers, had undertaken to teach her more than she cared to learn.

So Frankland bought a tract of nearly five hundred acres in the town of Hopkinton, about twenty-five miles southwest of Boston, and there, on the slope of a great hill where John Eliot had had an Indian mission, he built a mansion-house and began that Virginia life which Englishmen of his sort so dearly loved.

He had a few negro slaves; he built a great barn and granary; laid out orchards of apples, pears, plums, cherries, and peaches; set out elm-trees; planted shrubbery, lilacs, and hawthorns; and had a garden surrounded with box.

Puritans and Philosophy

Some years ago many of the trees he had planted were still standing, the box had grown ten feet high, and the trunks of the lilac bushes were eight inches in diameter.

> " The box is glistening huge and green ;
>   Like trees the lilacs grow ;
>   Three elms high arching still are seen,
>   And one lies stretched below."

The house was large, with a flower-garden in front; the hall with fluted columns, hung with tapestry; the chimney-pieces of Italian marble; and here Frankland and the erring Agnes lived an ideal life. They directed the slaves, read their favorite authors, cultivated the flowers, and Agnes was very fond of music. People from Boston who had concluded not to be as indignant as some of the others came to stay with them, and there appear to have been families in the neighborhood with whom they were familiar.

There was many a wassail bout, at which Frankland is said to have used a wine-cup of double thickness, so that he could drink his companions under the table and still keep his head, which in wine was not a strong one. He hunted the deer, which were numerous in the woods, and fished for the trout which filled the cool brooks. He had no doubt become familiar with Hopkinton in his shooting expeditions, and chose it for a home because it was a natural game preserve.

After about three years of this life Frankland and Agnes visited England; but here there was a terrible break in their happiness. The family of her lover not only would not receive her, but treated her with the brutal scorn and contempt which the English know so well how to administer. In Massachusetts she had had some friends,—a party, a following; but in England, in a strange land, she had none. The care and devotion of her lover—and it is probable that few men could excel him in tenderness to women —were no alleviation of her misery and melancholy. There was nothing that could be done but go away,—be banished again as in Boston.

After a year's travel on the Continent, they settled themselves at Lisbon, in Portugal, partly for pleasure and partly, probably, to look after some affairs of the British government with which Frankland had been intrusted. Lisbon was at that time one of the most lively, wealthy, and corrupt cities of Europe. It had a strong commercial connection with England, was full of English merchants, and Englishmen of all sorts came there for business, health, or amusement. It had been visited by George Whitefield, the preacher, and the novelist, Henry Fielding, who died there,

Puritans and Philosophy

Agnes and Frankland took a furnished house and adopted a very courtly style of living, which was warranted by the increased wealth which had recently come to them from a favorable decision in the English courts. They became prominent in the gay and dissolute life which must have made the sports and entertainments of the country place at Hopkinton seem very tame and commonplace. But they had been there hardly a year when, on All Saints' Day, at ten o'clock in the morning, the churches crowded with people, and the gorgeous ritual just begun, the earth began to heave and roll like the waves of the ocean, and the next instant churches, palaces, and humble houses came crashing down in massive piles, burying thirty thousand of the shrieking multitudes.

For twenty minutes the earth rocked, the sun was darkened, the water of the Tagus River rolled back to the sea, leaving the vessels on the mud, and then came roaring in again in a great wave. The prisons were open and the criminals were loose on the town, which was soon on fire.

Frankland was driving with a lady when the shock came, and was buried beneath the house he was passing. The horses were instantly killed, and the lady in her agony bit through the sleeve of his coat and tore a piece out of his arm. Still alive, but crushed beneath the mass of the building, he reviewed his life, and, among many errors to be atoned for, made a solemn vow to God that if he was delivered he would make Agnes his lawful wife.

The next instant she appeared. She had been rushing through the distracted town to find him, and, recognizing his voice beneath the ruins, offered large rewards for men who would dig him out. After an hour's labor he was dragged forth, wounded and bleeding. As soon as he recovered he was married to her by a Roman priest, for the ceremony was not allowed to be performed in Portugal by the minister of any other religion. They sailed for England, and, once on the ship and clear of Portuguese jurisdiction, he had the ceremony performed again by a clergyman of the Church of England.

Agnes was now well received in England, and the beautiful scrubbing girl of Marblehead became a familiar figure among the aristocracy of London. After another short visit to Lisbon, they returned to Boston, and, all reasons for exile being removed, they resolved to have a city as well as a country residence. They bought the Clarke mansion on Garden Street, a large house with twenty-six rooms, which they adorned with pictured panels, Italian marble and porcelain fireplaces in the most elaborate luxury.

Puritans and Philosophy

The floor of one of the rooms, it is said, was laid in a tessellated pattern of more than three hundred different kinds of wood.

In one of the rooms of the house at Hopkinton Frankland hung the coat he had worn on the day of the earthquake, with the hole in the arm where the lady had bitten through it, and also his rapier, bent by the falling stones. Every autumn, on All Saints' Day, he went alone to the room to view these relics and ponder solemnly on the event and his vows.

Agnes Surriage, of Marblehead, was now Lady Frankland; she had seen the best and the gayest as well as the worst life of her time, her reputation and character were saved, and she no doubt was an authority on court manners among the people of the royal government who were laying the foundations of fashionable life at Boston. But she was not proud, they say, and received cordially at her house her relations from the little village where Frankland had first seen her at the tavern.

He was appointed in 1757 consul-general at Lisbon, and again left Boston. He seems to have returned in 1763, and lived for a time at Hopkinton, to which he was sincerely attached, and would no doubt have spent the rest of his days there in the enjoyment of ease and the pleasures of books, trees, and sport, of which he never wearied; but his health was declining. He went to England and lived at Bath, where he died in 1768, in his fifty-second year.

After his death Lady Frankland almost immediately sailed for America, and went to live at Hopkinton with Harry Cromwell, her husband's natural son, of whom she seems to have been fond. She also took into her household her sister, with her children and some other relations, and the old life of her honeymoon was in part renewed. She managed the farm, planted and ornamented the grounds with shrubbery and flowers, rode on horseback, and indulged in her life-long love of music. She had many visitors, and seems to have made a point of entertaining the clergy of the English church.

She is described as slender, with a dark, lustrous eye, rather majestic carriage, and a melodious voice. An interesting woman she must have been, and her lover an attractive man; but the details of her life are few, and her strange career had been almost forgotten until revived in the present century by the researches of Mr. Nason, who became the owner of her country-seat at Hopkinton.

When the Revolution came in 1775 she found herself a tory, and there was nothing for her to do but suffer exile again. She started for Boston to get through the lines of the armed Puritan farmers, who were beginning to form the Continental army, and was soon stopped and put under arrest. Finally she was allowed to pass and take with her, as the order read, "6 trunks, 1 chest, 3 beds and bedding, 6 wethers, 2 pigs, 1 small keg of pickled tongues, some hay, 3 bags of corn," which seems a strange detail in such a romantic career.

The British officers in Boston received her with much kindness, especially Burgoyne, whom she had known in Portugal, and from the windows of her house in Garden Street she saw the battle of Bunker Hill. She sailed for England, and lived with the Franklands. Seven years after, at the age of fifty-six, she broke the spell of her romance and married John Drew, a rich banker; but she received the fate she deserved for such an act, and died within a year.

The changes in Puritan manners which such men as Frankland and the royal governors introduced were not accepted without protest. In 1740 the dancing assembly was making its way with difficulty, and the ladies who resorted to it were described by some as with but little regard for their reputation. In 1773, under the influence of the British officers in the town, a drum or rout given by the admiral on Saturday night lasted until two or three o'clock on Sunday morning, causing a great scandal; but after the officers had disappeared such performances were impossible.

The people were still Puritans. The new life was merely an outward varnish. They were stiff, formal, and reserved; and even among those who were accounted worldly and gay there was a simplicity of thought and con-duct which still lingers in Boston, and will in all probability be a characteristic for many years to come.

The old inquisitorial habits clung to them, and they pried into people's history and business in a way that was very offensive to strangers and travellers,—a habit which has since been known as Yankee inquisitiveness. A Virginian who had been much in New England in colonial times used to relate that as soon as he arrived at an inn he always summoned the master and mistress, the servants and all the strangers who were about, made a brief statement of his life and occupation, and having assured everybody that they could know no more, asked for his supper; and Franklin, when travelling in New England, was obliged to adopt the same plan.

As a class the Puritans of Massachusetts were a humorous, witty people. Their early writ-ings, even when very religious, often show a disposition to pun, and in some of their books describing the lives of pious ministers and godly churches statements are occasionally made in epigrammatic little verses. They had such a keen sense of the ridiculous that it is rather strange that they were not sooner delivered from their religious excesses. Their ordinary intercourse with one another seems to have been always characterized by sarcastic chaffing and a dry, sharp sort of humor, which, with shelling nuts round the fire and telling stories, was one of the few pleasures they allowed themselves in the early days.

This same humor and love of puns and epigrams have survived in a refined, elevated, and keener form in the poems of Lowell and Holmes, and there is often a touch of it in Hawthorne and Emerson, as well as in other Massachusetts writers. The " Biglow Papers" are largely a reproduction of this humor as it existed among the common people in Lowell's time. Indeed, there is no part of America where all the early traits of the people come down in such direct lines to the present. The grim humor in which the original Puritan thought it no sin to indulge has proved to be a most copious source of the literature of Massachusetts.

In the smaller towns outside of Boston the royal governors and their ideas had, of course, less influence. The people were suspicious of pleasures; and the handsome velvet suits and silverware which we are surprised to find so many of them had were often stored away and descended in the family as heirlooms which were never used. They resented any tendency in their preachers to expound comforting or pleasant doctrine in place of the old damnation and terrors. They did not want religion made easy; and there is a curious complaint against a certain minister because he had set forth "too many dainties."

Although the community was full of energy, power, and ability, it was all hard, economical, and repressed, and there was none of the generous and expansive hospitality of the Virginia planter. There was a certain accurate kindness and politeness; for prosperity was universal, beggars and paupers were almost unknown, and everybody felt that his respectability imposed duties which must be performed.

Chastellux is reported to have said that in several instances where he brought letters of introduction to people by whom he was pleasantly entertained, he was handed a bill for the trouble and expense, as if he had been at a tavern. An examination of his book does not reveal any such statement. The inns in New England were often overcrowded, and when that happened travellers were sent to respectable families near by who were willing to take them, and in such cases they always expected to be paid for their trouble.

In some respects there may be said to have been a decided aristocracy in Massachusetts. It was not a landed aristocracy like that of Virginia, although there were some large estates. Its members had not such absolute control of political power as the Southern planters, and yet they had control. It consisted more of a recognition of social distinctions, a deference paid to families of wealth, long-established position, and ability in public service ; and it was a settled rule that men of such families were to be elected to public office.

In all the churches the pews were assigned in accordance with social rank, or, as it was sometimes expressed, in accordance with " authority, age, wealth, and house lots," a custom which caused endless bickerings and heart-burnings, and gave the deacons in charge of the matter a very thankless task. At Harvard College the freshmen were arranged every year in a list according to the social rank of their parents, and each student was compelled to retain throughout his course the rank that was thus assigned him.

The English distinctions of the time among gentlemen, yeomen, merchants, and mechanics were sharply drawn ; and the ministers, of course, were ranked at the top, and often had the handsomest houses in the community. Indeed, the congregations usually took great pride in the houses they gave their ministers.

Many of the prominent people near Boston and the important towns like Salem and Marblehead had houses which might almost be described as magnificent. The Lee house at Marblehead is said to have cost ten thousand pounds, a sum which was the equivalent of nearly two hundred thousand dollars in modern times. Similar houses were scattered about, often built of stone, wainscoted in hard woods and mahogany, with carved mantel-pieces, pictures set in panels, and walls hung with tapestry.

The remnant of the old life which proved to be most enduring was the observance of the Sabbath, a name which has come into ill repute with many religious people because it was the favorite Puritan name for Sunday. But they often used the more touching expression, the Lord's Day.

The Sabbath began with the Puritans at six o'clock on Saturday evening and lasted until sunset on Sunday. No one could work, or amuse himself, or even be shaved by a barber. No travelling was allowed, and the inns were all closed. The story is told of Robert Pike that, having to go upon a journey, he waited patiently until the sun sank into the western clouds on Sunday evening and then mounted his horse. But he had gone only a short distance when the last rays gleamed through a break in the clouds, and the next day he was brought before the court and fined.

This strictness was observed until the Revolution and a long time afterwards, and many are still living who can remember the remains of this Sunday severity. Respectable people were not supposed to be seen on the street unless going to or returning from church. They could not stroll to the water's edge, and a group who stopped to talk would soon be dispersed by the constable. A young French officer, at the time of the Revolution, who tried to dispel the tedium of the dismal day by playing on his flute soon found an angry mob collected in front of the house, and was obliged by his landlord to desist.

Domestic affections and enjoyments were not supposed to be indulged in on Sunday. Some of the ministers, as Charles Francis Adams tells us in his excellent paper on Puritan church discipline, refused to baptize children born on Sunday, because there was a belief that such children must have been conceived on Sunday. But one of the ministers who was most severe in this rule was finally broken from it when his own wife on the Sabbath gave birth to twins.*

The people had a great dislike of foreigners and all outside influence. They were very original and ingenious, but it was always with their own material. They did their own thinking and their own work, and that other people or other nations had adopted an idea or a method was never in their eyes a recommendation. It was a most wholesome feeling and a strong incentive to nationality and greatness. They were extremely proud of their pure English blood, and this condition continued until fifty years after the Revolution, when the influx of foreigners and alien ideas began to break up their homogeneousness and destroyed that self-centred spirit which had given them their characteristic greatness and power.

When Massachusetts began to debate whether she should adopt the German system of education at Harvard, and when she yielded to the policy of the nation in encouraging alien immigrants of every race and nation, the end of those peculiar qualities which had given her such an ascendency in the intellectual and literary world was near at hand.

---

* Proceedings of the Massachusetts Historical Society, vol. vi. p. 494.

Puritans and Philosophy

The indented servants who were so numerous in many of the colonies were very rare in Massachusetts and the rest of New England, and there were none of the convicts and bankrupts whom Great Britain forced on some of the other provinces. Both Virginia and New England resisted the convict and pauper system which ruined Maryland and other commonwealths so far as concerned that high excellence and distinction of ability and character which form the greatest glory of a community.

It is a noteworthy fact in our history that during the Revolution and for sixty years afterwards the best and greatest men of the country were produced in two commonwealths, Virginia and Massachusetts; and these were the two which were more homogeneous than any of the others in race, religion, and general ideas, and had kept themselves clean of convicts, paupers, and inferior nationalities. They were also the most prosperous in material affairs, and increased their population very rapidly. Their overflow spread out westward, building up and increasing the peoples of communities of less unity and vigor. Their increase by the natural process of births was more rapid than it has since been with the assistance of enormous immigration.

The opinion which has prevailed of recent years that the people of beaten and inferior nationalities, the failures and incompetents of Europe, are good enough material with which to build up an American civilization which will carry on the high standard of intelligence, liberty, and republican government which Massachusetts and Virginia did so much to create, is unfortunately not supported by the facts of history. The Cavaliers and the Puritans were picked men, and they were wise enough to value their purity and save it from contamination. They represented the two great opposing parties of England, and they were the best of those parties, which, though conflicting, were yet in essentials very much alike. It was fortunate that the two commonwealths which they founded preserved their purity long enough for us to secure some of its results.

After the year 1700 the real development of Massachusetts began. Before that time the rule of the ecclesiastical oligarchy disfranchising the majority of the people, murdering Quakers and witches, and banishing the most high-spirited and enlightened men and women had not been representative of the people of the province. In fact, we can hardly consider it as even a fair exhibition of Puritanism, for it represented merely a few extremists who were in control of the government. But after 1700, with the power of the ministers reduced, with excesses in doctrine and superstition steadily declining, and with the opinions and feelings of the majority allowed fair expression, the colonists became as united, orderly, thrifty, and intelligent a body of men as could be found in the world.

They reasoned as keenly as ever on questions of religion, listened to their endless sermons and lectures with the same devoted attention, practised austerities and abstained from pleasures. They had lost their independence, but they never for a moment gave up their right to it. Nothing but the impossibility of resistance kept them quiet. They regarded the country as their own and not the king's. They believed that they had a perfect right to independence, and that they were kept from it only by superior force, and everything done by the British government tended to intensify this feeling.

Manufacturing in the colonies was discouraged by the British government, and Massachusetts at that time did very little of it. Her chief business was the building and navigation of ships and the trade in fish. She had some trade in furs and timber and a slight trade in grain and cattle; but the products of the ground were few and the soil was comparatively barren.

The sea, however, was for the Puritans a fertile field, and out of it they made their fortunes.

Puritans and Philosophy

There have seldom been better ship-builders, and their descendants are still among the best sailors in the world. It was on the shores of Massachusetts that the form of vessel known as the schooner was invented, and from the same source are many of the modern improvements in the rigging and shape of hulls.

They began to build ships and catch fish as soon as they arrived. Governor Winthrop, within a year after the colony was founded, built a vessel of thirty tons and called her the Blessing of the Bay. According to a report of the Board of Trade, made in 1721, Massachusetts built every year about one hundred and fifty vessels. Most of them were sold abroad, and about one hundred and ninety sail were owned in the colony. These employed eleven hundred sailors, and were engaged in the general carrying trade all over the world. Besides these the colony possessed about one hundred and fifty small vessels, which employed about six hundred men and were engaged in catching the fish which filled the waters from Cape Cod to the banks of Newfoundland.

Chastellux in travelling through Massachusetts noticed that the sailors were also farmers. The Puritan sailors, instead of being the desperate, reckless class of European countries, closely allied to criminals and knowing no other art but that of the sea, were usually respectable men who when ashore followed some handicraft or occupation. Very many of them owned farms which they cultivated part of the year, always ready to follow some captain, their neighbor, to the fisheries. The captain himself was frequently a mechanic or a farmer, and it was not uncommon to find a crew of excellent sailors with a most enlightened knowledge of their duties, not one of whom could be called a seaman by profession. A farmer often owned a sloop or a schooner which he had perhaps assisted in building, and which lay anchored in sight of his barn.

It is impossible to read the literature of Massachusetts, or to look through the materials of her history, without being impressed with the maritime instincts of her people. Everything savors of the salt sea. There are parts of Winthrop's journal which read like a log-book. Mingled with his accounts of wonderful conversions and miracles, and of the arrival in the colony of cows and mares, as well as of learned ministers, we find descriptions of voyages, and the latitude and longitude to which vessels were driven by storms; notes on the wind and tide, and on the price of salt and fish and other articles of commerce. Even Judge Sewall, though a landsman, uses technical language to describe the move-

Puritans and Philosophy

ments of vessels, and mentions several instances when he was invited, as a mark of honor, to drive a treenail into a new ship.

Coming down into the present century, when the great literary activity of Massachusetts began, we find books of ocean adventure and poems of the ocean, and we find that nearly all the families of wealth and refinement in Eastern Massachusetts are connected in some way with the shipping interest, and have recollections and memorials of India and China. We find members of these families going as captains of vessels. Small villages on the coast sometimes contain the homes of ten or fifteen captains of foreign-going ships. A careful observer cannot now spend a summer holiday on any part of the New England coast without constantly finding memories and suggestions of a great maritime life which has for the most part passed away.

Within six years after they landed the Puritans founded Harvard College. No fact of their history, no trait of their character, is more prominent than their zeal for learning. It has often been said that where the land was too stony to raise corn they planted school-houses to raise men.

Education was encouraged in every possible way. Every township of fifty families was directed by law to have a teacher, and when it numbered one hundred families it was to have a grammar-school to prepare boys for Harvard. For a long time this law was irregularly enforced, and it is not true, as has been sometimes said, that illiteracy was unknown in Massachusetts. There was a good deal of it, especially in early times. General Putnam, who was born at Salem, had scarcely any schooling, and was an illiterate man all his life; and there are numerous other instances of boys who seem to have been out of range of the school-house.

But the Puritan mind was trained in many ways besides schools and colleges. The habit of taking notes of sermons, the week-day meetings to discuss sermons, the lectures, and the frequent religious controversies were stimulating to mental growth. The Puritan was trained by these things as the Virginian by sports, social intercourse, and political discussions. Puritan life, like Virginia life, was in itself an education.

Nowhere was the printing-press more successful. In 1719 Boston had five printing establishments and only about ten thousand inhabitants. In 1750 it had five newspapers, the oldest of which had begun its career in 1704. The famous Eliot Indian Bible was printed in Boston, and those who examine any of the few remaining copies of it are always surprised to find it such a beautiful specimen of the book-maker's art.

Booksellers often made fortunes. Every man who had a new idea rushed into print with it. There was a fierce pamphlet war over the question of inoculation for the small-pox, another, of course, over the witchcraft proceedings, and every new opinion in theology had its pamphlet literature. Sewall mentions a little pamphlet describing a case of witchcraft, and relates that a thousand copies of it were sold and a new edition demanded.

This constant attrition of opinions had its natural result. The people not only acquired knowledge, but, what was more important, their power of reasoning and expressing themselves was highly developed. The excellence of New England schools and colleges has never been doubted, and the secret of their success lies not in the information they impart, but in the old Puritan love of logic and their habit of severe mental discipline.

The gradual decline of Puritanism until, after the Revolution, it drifted into liberalism and Unitarianism is difficult to trace, because it was so slow and imperceptible that no definite date or turning-point can be fixed for it. The year 1800 is in a general way near enough, and it is significant that it was not until about that time that actors dared show themselves in Boston.

The laws punishing heresy with death remained on the statute book for a long time. Even in very late times there were severe laws for the regulation of the Sabbath and against smoking in the streets, and men are still living who can remember when it was not considered respectable to be out of the house on Sunday afternoon. But these obsolete laws and few surviving customs were merely pieces of the old shell; the spirit and essential part of Puritanism had disappeared long before.

So long as that terrible incubus of Puritanism lay upon her it was impossible for Massachusetts to rise to the higher flights of which she was capable. In the Revolution she took a leading and most earnest part, which every school-boy knows. Independence was the ruling passion of her life, for she had enjoyed it once herself and knew its sweets by having been deprived of them. But at that period she did not produce as many great men as Virginia, and she never has produced military geniuses. Her great literary activity and eminence, as well as her great wealth and influence, were developed some years after 1800, when Virginia was declining.

The outburst of literature in Massachusetts, lasting only for about a generation, is one of the

Puritans and Philosophy

strangest phenomena in history. It was contemporary with the growth of Unitarianism and closely connected with it. The seeds of Unitarianism and transcendentalism were always in existence in Puritanism, and often showed a tendency to sprout and grow. Mrs. Hutchinson, when she announced that the inward feeling of each individual was the proof and test of his justification, touched the thought that was so powerfully developed on broader lines by Channing, Emerson, Parker, and Lowell.

Franklin, when a mere youth in Boston, a few years after 1700, belonged to a little coterie of deists who were in flagrant opposition to the prevailing opinion of the community, but too few and weak to accomplish anything. He could never have existed in the Boston atmosphere of that time, for his leaning towards liberalism and science was abhorrent to the people, and even his boyish attacks on the theology of the province got both himself and his brother into trouble. He fled to Philadelphia, where, although thought was not so intense and keen, yet every opinion was freely tolerated.

Both Franklin and Mrs. Hutchinson have had their revenge; for after the year 1800 the ideas of Massachusetts became the very reverse of what they had been a hundred years before.

Puritans and Philosophy

The most intolerant colony became the most liberal State; the home of bigotry became the home of free thought. From Cotton Mather to Ralph Waldo Emerson was a long journey, but it was the path that Massachusetts travelled. What a change! If John Cotton, or Increase Mather, or Cotton Mather could have known the gentle, all-tolerant Emerson, they would surely have called him a brand from hell.

Various reasons have been assigned for the rise of Unitarianism out of Puritanism; but the only probable explanation seems to be that as time passed and the severity of the Puritan discipline relaxed, and superstition and the terrors of holding heretical doctrine died out, the principle of individual judgment in religious matters which a century before had animated Mrs. Hutchinson and her followers began to spread again.

Mrs. Hutchinson's party had been very numerous; indeed, had almost controlled an election; and although they were formally suppressed, many of them, no doubt, continued to believe the heresy without obtruding it on the rest of the people in a way that would get them into difficulties. We know as a matter of fact that in Franklin's time, and afterwards, there were a few more or less avowed Unitarians in the province.

All that was needed was to have certain re-

Puritans and Philosophy

straints removed; for the minds of the Puritans tended naturally towards the heresy they had stamped upon. They were reasoners and philosophers; they loved logic and loved to search for causes. They had built up Puritanism as a hard-headed logical system based on a belief in devils and evil spirits and the doctrines of predestination and election.

In time, however, it became too narrow a field for them. They could walk all round it in a day; they had thrashed it over and over until they were tired of it, and the superstitious parts of it were crumbling away. But Mrs. Hutchinson's philosophy of intuition—the philosophy which ignored all testimony to spiritual truth except that of individual consciousness; the philosophy which allows full scope to reason and piles up ideas and subtleties in infinite variety; the philosophy which inspired Plato, Descartes, and Berkeley, as well as Coleridge, Carlyle, and Emerson, and which is capable of giving more comfort, satisfaction, and happiness than any other philosophy the world has ever known—was for the Puritans of Massachusetts a magnificent, new, and unexplored domain.

Step by step, cautiously, with fear and trembling, they entered this paradise where everything seemed so free and pleasant that they thought it surely must be sin. But they moved in so slowly that most of them were unaware of the process, until by 1780 the churches in the neighborhood of Boston were often preaching the new doctrine without accusing one another of heresy.

Before many years, however, the break came. The conservatives realized what was being done, and called a halt. The usual bitter controversies followed, dividing friend from friend; the usual disputes for the possession of church property; then the new separated from the old, and the thing was done.

But there was no oligarchy in possession of the government which could banish the new to New Hampshire or Rhode Island. They were very numerous, and they stayed and leavened the whole community, so that the conservatives from whom they had separated often differed from them only in matters of form. In fact, the new had set them all free; and when they found that no terrible signs and portents followed, that the sun still shone, the birds chirped, and the waves still beat the rocky shores, they broke out into an exuberance of joy and an intellectual debauch which can best be described by saying that it was the renaissance of Massachusetts.

The skilful and sarcastic pens of Emerson and Lowell have given us some of the details of this outburst when the Puritan mind first discovered that it could use the stored-up keenness and subtlety of centuries on any subject it pleased. From the streets and alleys of Boston, from the hill-side towns, and from the villages of Cape Cod came forth a host of sects, reformers, and extraordinary creatures, maintaining every imaginable doctrine and absurdity.

All the ills of life would be abolished if every one would take to farming; the use of money is the cardinal evil, and no one should buy or sell; we must eat pure wheat instead of bread; the whole difficulty lies in stimulating manures for crops instead of relying on the natural soil. Besides these there were the non-resistance societies, the societies of "come-outers," and the man who established a society for the protection of worms, slugs, and mosquitoes, and to prevent the use of horses; and all this was followed in later years by a frantic interest in spiritualism, Buddhism, mesmerism, and phrenology.

When we read of these things, and especially of the man who would abolish buying and selling, we are reminded of Sewall's crusade against wigs, of the long arguments against drinking healths, and of the sermon John Cotton preached to prove that it was wicked for a tradesman to buy cheap and sell dear. Was the attempt of the Puritans to establish an errorless church and state very much different from the attempt of the Brook Farm people to establish a community in which every man and woman should be a farm laborer for three hours of the day and a poet or philosopher for the rest? One was of the seventeenth century, the other of the nineteenth.

That same intense activity of mind, that same habit of sifting everything to the bottom, that same earnestness of purpose, traits which in small minds run to trifles or absurdities and in large minds produce the abolitionists, a Parker, a Channing, an Emerson, or a Lowell, were still characteristics of Massachusetts, just as they had been two hundred years before.

One of the most strange results of the renaissance was Thoreau, who carried almost to insanity his love of the woods and fields, in which the Puritan imagination had seen only signs of terror, and which they had peopled with devils and witches. He reacted so far that he got drunk with nature, and he is a curious connecting link between the really great poetical minds like Longfellow, Lowell, Holmes, and Hawthorne, who were always thoroughly sound and sane, and the unbalanced freaks and oddities which the renaissance produced.

He was midway between them, and the beautiful and immortal passages in his books are mingled with the crudest absurdities of a mind that had just cast off its shackles. His followers in the same peculiar school of the worship of nature, Burroughs, Bolles, and others, have restored the methods of the school to sanity; but there is still, in spite of his crudities, a great deal of attraction in Thoreau himself, and his fame is increasing.

At the time of this renaissance, which may be said to have begun about the year 1830, the people of Massachusetts had been a compact, intensely centralized, and united community for two hundred years. They had received no immigration since 1640, and being of the same race and religion, they had become more homogeneous in thought and feeling than any other body of people on the continent. They had become a numerous people, filling their own province and overflowing into the West, and by 1830 there was a large class which had wealth, leisure, and refinement.

Generation after generation had been trained in the enthusiasm for knowledge and education and in the keen, subtle methods of thought which made the literary art easily learned. They had always been able to express themselves well. Their sermons showed it; and in the numerous writings of Cotton Mather were to be found a power of statement which at times was almost literary genius. Franklin took him for the model of his own matchless style. Anne Bradstreet had attempted some ambitious poems, and not a few of the Puritan writers indulged themselves at times in verse. Although none of these productions rose to the level of poetry, they were usually well constructed and clever; while in the other colonies similar efforts were, with a few exceptions, unmitigated trash.

Under these conditions, as soon as their minds were free, they broke out on all sides and began to write the literature of Europe as well as of their own country. Prescott wrote immortal works on the history of the Spanish people and their conquests in Mexico and Peru; Motley, the history of the Netherlands; and these books became classics for the whole world. Bancroft took the United States for his theme, and Parkman the contest between England and France for the possession of the North American continent. The range of thought and power in the works of these four men alone is very significant and impressive.

In Longfellow we see the same breadth and force. A large number of his best poems deal with the history and episodes of New England and America, but many reach out across the

Puritans and Philosophy

Atlantic to Germany, England, and Italy, and he made one of the best translations of Dante. Lowell and Hawthorne also show the same characteristics. Massachusetts literature, like her ships of that time, was never content until it had sailed the seven seas.

Her newly awakened power found another theme ready to its hand which was perhaps even more congenial than literature. The great question of slavery, and whether it should be extended or restricted, was looming up in its most dangerous aspects and threatening to wreck the Union. The South was for extending it into the Western territories and making it a national institution ; the North was for confining it to the South. But even the North did not wish to go beyond the question of restriction or extension. The total abolition of slavery was a forbidden subject, and the mobs in every city were ready to kill the man who advocated it, and burn the building in which he spoke.

But the thorough-going Puritan who had believed in extirpating root and branch the most innocent heresies could not rest satisfied with such a weak compromise, especially of a question which involved moral right and wrong. The abolitionists—the Garrisons, the Phillipses, and the Whittiers—were merely the Cottons, the Mathers, the Endicotts, and the Winthrops transformed by the changes of a hundred and fifty years; and they never had had before such an opportunity to use their ancient power.

As we read the history of their onset, we are reminded of a trained pugilist wading into a crowd of ordinary men and striking right and left his terrible blows. Every stroke crushes a victim to the earth, and the rest melt away with fear. The men of Massachusetts who could torture a heretic into confession by weeks and months of questioning now turned to look the whole American people in the face and stretch their conscience on the rack. There never have been such piercing inquisitors; for the inquisitors of the Church of Rome inflicted their torture on the outward body and often left the mind triumphant in its error; but the intellect of the abolitionist reached within and gripped the soul with a power that converted the heretic into a fighting proselyte for the new faith.

One of the most remarkable features of the Massachusetts literature was its completeness. Although it lasted only for a generation, it was complete in all the departments of poetry, romance, oratory, philosophy, history, and theology, like the national literature of France, England or any country which is in the fullest sense of the word a nation, and by a long-continued homogeneousness of population has settled into a distinct type of people who think and act together as a unit.

Another striking characteristic besides its originality and force was the early age at which its writers matured and produced their best works. Even the historians, whose tasks, depending on research, usually require a longer time, were very forward in their fame. Prescott finished "Ferdinand and Isabella" in his forty-first year, and Motley "The Dutch Republic" in his forty-second. The fame of Longfellow and Bryant was made before they were forty. Their greatest poems were written before that age. Bryant's "Thanatopsis" was written when he was eighteen. Everett was drawing large audiences at nineteen. Lowell wrote the "Biglow Papers" at twenty-eight, and Holmes his poem on "Old Ironsides" at twenty-one. The forces that inspired them were evidently strong, rapid, and complete.

Why was it that a literature of so much power and genius, so complete in all its forms, could not last like the literature of England, in which we find a steady and continuous production of literary men of a high order for several hundred years, every decade producing several of them with remarkable regularity?

The literary men of Massachusetts were all

born between the years 1780 and 1823,* and they are now all dead, without leaving a single successor worthy to represent them. In the long perspective of Massachusetts history they are a mere isolated patch, and the period of their activity and influence is completely covered by fifty years.

Was it that this outburst was caused merely by the artificial stimulant of the sudden change from total repression to absolute freedom which attended the rise of Unitarianism acting on a people long accustomed to a love of knowledge and to the exercise of their minds in subtle expressions and delicate distinctions similar to the methods of the highest literature? This is the explanation which naturally first occurs to one, but it is not altogether satisfactory.

Unitarianism still exists and apparently all the other conditions. The people have grown richer, and developed their industries and enterprises; culture is more generally diffused; and all this one should suppose would be an assistance to literature. England has grown richer

---

* Channing, 1780; Everett, 1794; Bryant, 1794; Prescott, 1796; Bancroft, 1800; Emerson, 1803; Hawthorne, 1804; Longfellow, 1807; Whittier, 1807; Holmes, 1809; Parker, 1810; Sumner, 1811; Phillips, 1811; Motley, 1814; Lowell, 1819; Parkman, 1823.

and developed her industries, and has been doing so for several hundred years, and all the time her literature has been going on.

Indeed, it is generally supposed that the development of wealth and ease is beneficial to the fine arts. Education is as thorough to-day in Massachusetts as it was before 1825. In fact, it is believed to be more thorough, more generally diffused, and more liberal and enlightened. There are no signs of stupidity around Boston Harbor. The people read and appreciate good books as much as ever, and have plenty of money to buy them. All the conditions seem favorable to literature of a high order, and it is difficult to believe that the mere change, the sudden access of freedom, was the sole cause, and that a literature so powerful and complete in all its departments passed away because the novelty of the change wore off.

It is easy to understand that the sudden freedom was the occasion and the opportunity which gave the natural powers of the Puritans a chance to spread out into literature. But after the freshness of the change had passed, those natural powers must have still existed. The freaks and oddities may have owed all their vitality to the mere change; but can we believe that such substantial genius as that of Longfellow, Lowell, Holmes, Hawthorne, and Emerson was merely the result of an hysterical excitement, without other or deeper causes?

What may be the real fundamental causes of the growth of literature in a nation is of course hard to discover, and it is not unlikely that they will forever defy the power of human analysis. But we may fairly infer that, whatever the usual fundamental causes may be, they were the ones that produced the Massachusetts literature, because in its quality, power, and variety it was like the best literature of the greatest nations.

The attempt to explain its cessation by saying that in the last fifty years all the best minds of Massachusetts have emigrated to the Western States is of no avail, for this same emigration was going on at the time the literature was produced. Massachusetts was overflowing her boundaries in the fifty years after the Revolution as much as, if not more than, she has done since; and the enormous emigration out of England to her colonies has been contemporaneous with England's greatest literary activity. In fact, the population of Massachusetts increased more rapidly and gave her more overflow in her great literary period than it has since.

Nor does it afford an explanation to say that the men who would have continued Massachusetts' literature were all killed in the civil war. The men born between 1848 and 1861 were too young to go to the war. These men are now nearly all past forty years old ; and if a man has literary genius in him, he usually shows it before his fortieth year. The great literary men of Massachusetts made their reputations before they were forty.

Moreover, the men who went to the war were not all killed. Thousands of them returned stronger and abler in every way for the experience ; and it would indeed be extraordinary if the war had killed every one who had the literary instinct among a class who, as a rule, are not inclined to become soldiers.

The only explanation which seems broad and deep enough to fill the situation is that the great influx of foreign immigrants, Irish, Germans, and French, who since the year 1825 have poured into Massachusetts in an increasing stream until fifty per cent. of her population is foreign, has broken up the continuity and homogeneousness of her population and destroyed the nationality and unity of feeling which inspired her literature.

At the time her literary men were produced Massachusetts was a nation, and, though small, had all the distinctive features of nationality and a settled type of thought and feeling like England or France. This condition had been produced by a steady, uninterrupted development of two hundred years among a people of the same race and religion, who resented every outside interference and influence.

After the year 1640, when immigration to Massachusetts ceased, her development was entirely a native growth, and her native feeling was reinforced by the peculiarities of her religion and government. She not only rejected foreigners who were not of her people's race, but she rejected even Englishmen who were not of her way of thinking, and banished Roger Williams and Anne Hutchinson and persecuted the Quakers. Whatever may have been her faults in this direction, her people grew up united, pureblooded, and homogeneous, and when the year 1780 arrived they had been homogeneous for a hundred and fifty years, and formed the most intensely native and individualized commonwealth in America.

So far as can be discovered, it is this nationalized condition which produces literature of genius, rounded and complete in all its departments like that of Massachusetts. Such literature is not merely the expression of the man who writes it; it is the expression of the deep, united feeling of his people. The great schools of art and literature have all been national schools, the work of homogeneous peoples.

The great ideas we have inherited from the

past—indeed, all of value that we have inherited from it—are the result of nationality. The two nations of antiquity to which we owe most are the Jews and the Greeks. Our noblest inspirations in religion, morals, philosophy, literature, art, and government come from them, and they were of all peoples the most thoroughly homogeneous. If we pass down through history to colleĉt instances of genius, we find them only in communities intensely nationalized and homogeneous, like England or France.

The things that are worth preserving through the ages, the immortal things, cannot be produced by a man who is isolated from his fellows or unsupported by them, or lacks their sympathy; and the greatest things usually come from men who have a nation behind them. The supremely great man is the produĉt of the people among whom he was born and lived. A whole host of dramatists lead up to Shakespeare and surround him. They are all like him: all are on the same lines and of the same tone, but none so great. He and they spoke the thoughts and interpreted the feelings of the thousands of Englishmen among whom they lived; and he spoke best. Every investigation into the origin of the great ideas and movements of the past, whether they have been shown in the life of one man or in the lives of ten men, reveals a deep substratum of support among the people, going back in most instances for many generations.

One of the most important and strongest elements in the Massachusetts literature was the humor which pervaded a large part of it,—a humor which is more classical and more closely allied to wit than the modern humor of Mark Twain and others. It was the outgrowth into literature of the natural humor of the masses of the people which, as already shown, had been characteristic of them from the early colonial times. It had grown and developed until it had become a national and typical trait, sharpened and intensified without the slightest interference from foreign sources by two hundred years of use, and then it took the form of genius. Lowell seized upon it for the "Biglow Papers," in many respects the most original production of Massachusetts literature; it inspired Holmes, and in greater or less degree many of the others except Longfellow, whom it scarcely touched.

Why should it and the rest of the literary instinct have perished so suddenly, unless the swarms of Irish and other aliens broke its continuity and destroyed the united feeling of the people who had created and were continuing it? In a horseback journey through New England some years ago one soon learned to tell at a glance the house where an Irishman or other foreigner lived by the dirt and degradation which surrounded it, in striking contrast to the immaculate neatness of the natives; and the foreigners have poured mud into the pure stream of genius which was Massachusetts' greatest glory.

The literary men of Massachusetts were all born and passed through their impressionable age during a period of forty years in which the people of Massachusetts were more homogeneous than they were in any other forty years, either before or since. It is certainly rather significant that no man born since 1825 and brought up in the surroundings created by the immigrants has been able to reach anything approaching to the literary eminence which was reached by a dozen men born during the previous thirty years. The time has been ample. Men born between 1830 and 1840 would now be fifty or sixty years old.

If we look at English literature we find that twelve or thirteen distinguished characters have been born and raised to greatness since 1825: George Meredith (1828), Rossetti (1828), Ingelow (1830), McCarthy (1830), Farrar (1831), "Owen Meredith" (1831), Edwin Arnold (1832), William Morris (1834), Swinburne (1837), Green (1837), Lecky (1838), Morley (1838), Besant (1838), Black (1841),

Puritans and Philosophy

Buchanan (1841), Stevenson (1850), not to mention many others of minor and doubtful power.

In other words, English literature has moved on in its regular course under the influence of general causes. But the literature of Massachusetts has stopped. The old line of greatness is not continued. It is impossible to find for it any competent successor. Massachusetts has brought forth no man since that time who has written a poem equal to Morris's " Earthly Paradise," or Rossetti's " Blessed Damosel," or Edwin Arnold's " Light of Asia," or who has made such an impression on his time as Swinburne or even Jean Ingelow. Nor has Massachusetts brought forth an historian like Lecky, Green, or McCarthy, or a novelist like Stevenson or Besant.

On the other hand, the old order compared very favorably with their contemporaries in England. Longfellow, Lowell, Hawthorne, and Holmes are read and admired to-day in England as much as, if not more than, in America ; and Longfellow is credited with being more generally popular in England than Tennyson. But their successors, even in the United States at large, are weak and puny, and their faces in the pictures we have of them are a strange contrast to the vigorous lines in the features of the old order of

Massachusetts. They are simpering, superficial, and super-refined; devoted to mere dialect stories or strained descriptions of ephemeral or local phases. A deep, strong passion or a bold grasp at the eternal verities frightens them out of their wits.

The broad, deep sympathy of Longfellow, the keen wit of Holmes, the uncontrollable humor of Lowell, the tender, exquisite sentiment of Hawthorne, as well as the virile imagination of Stevenson, the wild fancy of Haggard, or Kipling's lust for nature, they seem to think not quite correct. They prefer needles and pins to broadswords.

In his recent book on emigration and immigration, Mr. R. M. Smith fixes the period of native increase in America from 1783 to 1820.* It was in one sense longer than that, and should be extended back for some years in most of the colonies, and in Massachusetts back to 1640. But there is no doubt that the period he has fixed was the period of the most nearly exclusively native growth and of the intensest native feeling, the time when the native feeling of previous years culminated, especially in Massachusetts. In fixing this period Mr. Smith was not thinking of the literature of the country, for he

---

* Smith's " Emigration and Immigration," p. 37.

says nothing about it; and it is important to observe that his period almost exactly covers the births of the men who made our only national and complete literature.

AT HARTFORD

CHAPTER III

THE LAND OF STEADY HABITS

CONNECTICUT, like Massachusetts, was made up of two colonies, and at first consisted only of a settlement of people in the neighborhood of Hartford. Afterwards there was another colony called New Haven established at the place of that name. The two were somewhat different in opinions, like the two colonies of Massachusetts, but were united in 1662 into one colony, to which the name Connecticut was given.

The colony at Hartford was founded by some Massachusetts Puritans who were very much opposed to the tyrannical ecclesiastical oligarchy which disfranchised the majority of the people, and if they had not gone away voluntarily they would probably have soon been banished. Hooker, their leader, was an able man, but not so pugnacious and intolerant as the Massachusetts ministers, and he believed in a Puritan democracy as the proper form of government. John Cotton, on the other hand, had said, "Democracy I do not conceive that God did ordain as a fit government either for church or commonwealth."

So Hooker, Haynes, Ludlow, and other refractory and democratic spirits led a number of those who were like-minded through the woods to the Connecticut River in the year 1636, driving their cattle before them. Soon after reaching the place that became Hartford, Hooker preached a sermon in which he maintained that the free consent of the people was the source of all authority, and this was certainly the form of government he and his followers established.

This migration was composed of three complete Massachusetts town organizations,—Dorchester, Watertown, and Newtown, which was afterwards called Cambridge. When transplanted within a few miles of each other on the banks of the Connecticut, they became Windsor, Hartford, and Wethersfield. The Puritans, as we have already observed, advanced into the wilderness not by isolated individual effort but by towns.

Not only three organized towns but three organized churches went with Hooker and his men into the woods. Hooker was a man of great stature and most powerful voice, which he used to its full compass in preaching. He was a popular orator of the pulpit, and whenever he visited Boston, crowds, which were no doubt largely composed of the disfranchised, went to hear him. We know little of his individuality; his life at Hartford was an unbroken record of tact, mild government, and strong influence.

Haynes, like so many of the Puritans, had been a man of fortune and position in England, where he was said to have had an estate worth a thousand pounds a year. He had also been governor of Massachusetts, and was the first governor of Connecticut. Little is known of him or of Ludlow, who was a lawyer, rather erratic and troublesome, and who finally went to Virginia.

The dominant party in Massachusetts expressed great regret at the departure of these people; they liked not, they said, to see the colony so much weakened, and they reminded the emigrants that the removal of a candlestick was a great judgment. But nothing could stop the movement. Efforts to accomplish it began to be made in 1634 and were completed in 1637, when about eight hundred Puritans had settled near Hartford.

The three towns were practically three independent States, and they joined together to create a general government over themselves. Each town elected two men whom they called magistrates, and the body of six thus formed was the General Court, which at first met in turn at the towns.

Each town decided for itself which of its citizens should have the right to vote. The privilege was given to all who had been admitted as inhabitants, and was never confined to members of the church. Like the General Court in Massachusetts, the magistrates performed the double function of a legislature and a court of law. Very shortly, however, this General Court met permanently at Hartford, and the character of the government was somewhat changed, each town electing three deputies, who met and elected the six magistrates.

The towns created the general government of the colony very much as the States of the Union created the general government of the United States; and curiously enough the system raised the question of town rights in very much the same way that the government made by the people of the thirteen original States raised the question of State rights.

In 1639 the colony drew up for itself a written constitution, the first written constitution that had ever been prepared on American soil, most strikingly liberal in its provisions and establishing the free suffrage and democracy which Hooker admired. There was no mention of the king or of allegiance to him, and the only oath of allegiance was one of allegiance to the colony.

But although the people were thorough believers in democratic government, and had no laws designed to create an ecclesiastical despotism like that of Massachusetts from which they had fled, yet in Connecticut church and state were in a certain sense one. They were one not so much by law as by tacit consent, and for the reason that the large majority of the voters were members of the church, and were at first very much in accord with each other in religious matters. The Connecticut ministers were always consulted in civil affairs, and the same men settled both civil and ecclesiastical questions in the same public meeting.

The dominant party had, however, little or none of that hard, intolerant, and prying spirit which made the history of Massachusetts. They were less intense, and though of determined and steadfast purpose, less learned and aggressive than the people of the colony from which they migrated; for whatever we may think of the cruelty and bigotry of Massachusetts, her system was a school of training which, when the bigoted part of it passed away, produced greater results and greater men than are to be found in Connecticut.

The Puritans who founded New Haven came direct from England. They touched at Boston, but resisted all persuasions to remain, and under their leaders, Davenport and Eaton, passed on to New Haven. So far as their sympathies and opinions were concerned, they might very well have stayed in Boston, for they were of precisely the same sort as the Boston Puritans, and they made of New Haven a little Massachusetts.

They first established a church, and then the church created the state. They relied on a passage of Scripture which speaks of wisdom having built her house and having hewn out her seven pillars, from which they inferred that church and state should rest on seven godly men.

Like the Massachusetts Puritans, one of their first enactments limited to church members the holding of office and the right to vote. The word of God, they declared, was to be the only guide of public officers and judges. They had no system of trial by jury; they could find, they said, no mention of it in the Old Testament.

Such was the town of New Haven, resting on seven Puritan pillars, who combined in themselves the legislature, the governor, and the court of law, and were fully persuaded that the rule of the many is not a good thing. The neighboring towns, Milford and Guilford, were in the same way composed of seven pillars, and followed closely New Haven as their model.

But in none of these governments was the King of England named. Like the people of Connecticut, the New Haven colonists quietly assumed all the attributes of independence. They also resembled Connecticut in having no title whatever to the land they occupied. They took the best they could find, and trusted to the future and good luck to secure all their rights.

New Haven began her existence in 1639. Five years afterwards Milford, Guilford, and Stamford formed with New Haven a confederacy of towns, and in a few years Branford and Southhold were added. This union, known thereafter as the colony of New Haven, had a constitution, a governor, deputy governor, and three magistrates, and each town sent two deputies. The disfranchised, who were a majority in New Haven and not quite so many in the other towns, were kindly allowed the right to inherit property and the right to engage in trade.

The dominant party in New Haven had the meddlesome inquisitorial spirit which characterized Massachusetts and was so conspicuously absent at Hartford. These were the two kinds of Puritans. The General Court at New Haven felt that they had an oversight of everybody's business, and could investigate their inmost thoughts, especially if those thoughts were supposed to be corrupt. Men and women were brought before the court to be punished for indelicate remarks made in private, for repeating an absurd request made in a prayer which had been overheard, and for improper kissing. The nearest approach to anything of this sort in Hartford was the punishment of Peter Bussaker for saying that he expected to meet some members of the church in hell, and hoped he should.

The General Court at New Haven of course undertook to suppress heresy by violence, and tried their hand at punishing the Quakers. But their attempts were weak and trifling compared with the tragic episodes of Massachusetts. The Quakers, who sought death and suffering in the cause of their faith as most men seek pleasure, hardly considered New Haven worthy of their attention, for the chances in Massachusetts were very much more abundant.

The peculiar proceedings of parental control over everybody which the magistrates of New Haven exercised are the source of all that has been said about the so-called Blue Laws with which Connecticut has been reproached for the last hundred years. If the reproach applied anywhere, it was to the New Haven colony alone. But it is unfair that even New Haven should bear the whole weight of the odium of blueness; for if by blue be meant that which is fanatical and absurd, the blueness of Massachusetts was far greater than the blueness of New Haven.

For the name Blue Laws, and for a great deal of the controversy about them, Connecticut has to thank a tory clergyman of the Church of England named Peters, who, having been driven from the country at the time of the Revolution, revenged himself by writing a history of Connecticut. Besides the supposed blue laws forbidding people to make mince-pies and kiss their children on Sunday, his book contains most amusing stories about bull-frogs invading a town and roaring so that the inhabitants fled to the woods, thinking that they were attacked by the French and Indians. He tells of a place where the Connecticut River runs through a passage only five yards wide, with rocks on either hand which intercept the clouds. The water, he says, in going through this passage is so consolidated that an iron crow-bar cannot be forced into it.

The blue laws of New Haven which were actually in existence were the usual ones of the extreme Puritans,—laws to prevent traders making more than a certain profit, laws to regulate wages, laws to compel every bachelor to live with some family, and laws against idleness and smoking. No one could begin the practice of smoking until he had obtained a license from the court, and even then could not smoke on the street. Massachusetts had similar blue laws, and such laws were enforced wherever extreme Puritanism had a strong foothold.

The two little colonies, the one at Hartford devoted to freedom, and the other at New Haven devoted to bigotry, prospered moderately for some twenty years, regulating their trade, providing for militia drill, the branding of horses, and the ringing of swine, until they were united by a charter from Charles II. in 1662. This charter was obtained by Connecticut, and greatly to the surprise of New Haven.

Young Winthrop, who was governor of Connecticut and son of the Winthrop who was so often governor of Massachusetts, went to England to procure a charter for the colony. Both Connecticut and New Haven had flourished for twenty years without charters, and in all that time, so far as official acts and records are concerned, they appear to have forgotten that there was such a person as the King of England, or such a country as Great Britain. Those were the days of Cromwell, the Commonwealth, and Puritan supremacy, and the colonies were let alone.

But in 1660 Charles II. returned to his own, and Connecticut deemed it wise to go and ask for what she knew would soon be forced upon her. Connecticut is nothing unless shrewd. She was determined to be beforehand and have an early influence in what was sure to be done, and she certainly secured for herself one of the most liberal charters ever given to an American colony.

The fawning address which accompanied the request for the charter is not creditable to colonial sincerity. If its statements can be believed, the people of Hartford had, during the civil wars, not only been royalists and loyal, but they had been depressed and broken-hearted, and had been hiding in the woods and mountains until the returning beams of his gracious majesty's sovereignty should cross the great deep and light them once more to happiness.

The Land of Steady Habits

By what means Winthrop secured such an unusually good charter is still somewhat of a mystery. The five hundred pounds furnished him by the colony over and above his salary is supposed to have had an influence at that careless and corrupt court, where both women and men made incomes by assisting suitors in obtaining favors from the king. It has been suggested that Lord Clarendon, the minister, was favorable to Connecticut because he was anxious to build up a strong colony which might quarrel with and weaken the unruly sectarians of Massachusetts Bay. There is also a pretty story told that Winthrop had a ring which had been given to his father by the father of Charles, and that this was very effective.

But we are inclined to lose confidence in these causes when we find that, fifteen months after the sealing of the Connecticut charter, Rhode Island got a charter which was still more liberal and free, and that it was obtained by John Clark, a Baptist minister, who made no pretensions to the diplomatic skill of Winthrop, and who had no money for courtiers and no ancestral ring.

It is useless to assign any reasons for the actions of Charles II., except his reckless and fickle temper. He was then flushed with victory and inclined to give anything a mistress or favorite asked. Within two years after granting this charter to Connecticut he gave half of the land covered by it to his brother, the Duke of York, and we have already seen how he lavished on favorites the land of Virginia.

The charter was so free and general in its terms that after the Revolution Connecticut lived under it as an American constitution until the year 1818. The governor was to be elected by the people, and not appointed by the king, the towns were to decide the qualifications of those who should vote, and the laws of the assembly were not to be submitted to the king for his approval.

When this charter was brought home and opened, behold, the boundaries given to Connecticut embraced New Haven. The second colony was swallowed up and lost; the little independent republic of New Haven had become a county of Connecticut. Before Winthrop set out for England he had been questioned by Davenport about this very matter, and had answered that he had no intention of absorbing New Haven, and that if the king should include her in the charter, she should be at liberty to join or not. Afterwards, when the charter was shown, he asked the General Court to respect and carry out his promise. But the charter, once given, was law, and as law it was entirely beyond the control of Winthrop or of the General Court.

The Land of Steady Habits

There is some evidence that Leete, the governor of New Haven, specially requested Winthrop to procure a union. Many of the leading men in New Haven were anxious for a union. Their spiritual despotism was dropping to pieces. The disfranchised majority were becoming unruly, and the persecution of the Quakers which occurred at this time made them worse. They became indignant at the cruelties inflicted, and thus the Quakers assisted in overthrowing ecclesiasticism in New Haven in very much the same way as in Massachusetts.

The disfranchised had everything to gain by a union and nothing to lose. Union meant an extended suffrage and larger liberty. When they heard of the provision for union in the charter they became unmanageable; refused to obey the laws of New Haven, and were continually asking the sheriffs and marshals whether their authority was from King Charles.

Two years and a half passed before New Haven, after many fastings and prayers and innumerable meetings of committees, finally accepted her fate. The long delay avoided any appearance of a tame submission and allowed the extremists time to reconcile themselves to the change, which was hastened when it was learned that Charles II. had in a careless moment given to the Duke of York a grant of land which included New Haven. Union with Hartford might not be desirable, but submission to the duke was worse. If New Haven remained outside of the union her land belonged to the duke; but if she joined with Hartford she had some chance of resisting his claims.

Connecticut had obtained her very liberal charter from Charles II. when he was fresh upon the throne and in the easy humor which soon afterwards gave to his brother part of the same land he had given to the colony; and when, on the death of Charles, that brother came to the throne as James II., he took Connecticut under his direct control, without regard to her charter, after the same plan he followed with the other northern colonies, except Pennsylvania, which he left in the hands of his friend William Penn.

Massachusetts' charter was cancelled by legal proceedings, the only way in which the validity of a charter could be destroyed. But a charter could be temporarily abrogated by the king taking possession of the province and ruling it according to his pleasure by virtue of that vague power called the royal prerogative. In such cases he set the charter aside for the time being, and when he restored the province, or ceased his direct rule over it, the charter was again in force. William III. took possession of both Maryland and Pennsylvania in this way. Pennsylvania was restored within two years; but Maryland was held for twenty-five years.

The Connecticut charter was never annulled by legal proceedings. Andros came and took possession of the colony in the name of the king, and seems to have demanded that the document itself should be surrendered to him. The people, it is said, spoke him very fair, and argued and pleaded with him for a long time. Then the charter was brought in and laid on the table. Suddenly the candles were put out, and when they were relit the charter was gone; for Captain Wadsworth had carried it off and hid it in an oak the site of which in Hartford is now marked by a stone.

This is the pretty story which we are taught in all our school-book histories; but it is not supported by good authority. There appear to have been several copies of the charter. One of these, which was in all probability the original instrument, Andros secured, and the duplicate Wadsworth got possession of and kept, but whether in an oak or in his own house is not known. In May, 1715, the General Court granted Wadsworth the sum of twenty shillings for certain services, " especially in securing the duplicate charter, in a very troublesome season, when our constitution was struck at, and in safely keeping and preserving the same ever since unto this day." *

No contemporary writers tell the story of the candles and the oak; and in after-years when the story was told we find the details of it varying so much that no faith can be placed in it. According to one account, Nathaniel Stanley took one copy and John Talcot the other when the lights were blown out; and Chalmers says it was an elm in which it was concealed. Still another account has it that the charter was surrendered to Andros and afterwards stolen from his room.†

In the dearth of romantic episodes in colonial history there has always been great temptation to uphold the myth of the charter oak. Historically it is of no importance; for so long as the charter was not annulled by legal proceedings, its validity could not be permanently destroyed by Andros. When his rule ceased the people still had one or two of the duplicates to read, and the old government under it was restored.

With the single exception of Andros, Connecticut never had a royal governor. She elected her own chief magistrate annually, usually re-electing the same one year after year, and was

---

* Palfrey's "New England," vol. iii. p. 543.
† Brodhead's "New York," vol. ii. p. 473.

in effect an independent colony from the beginning to the end of her history.

Her people were of the Massachusetts type, but in a milder form. Her laws were largely copied from those of the colony of Massachusetts Bay, and in some instances taken word for word. The public school system was the same and the township system the same, and there was also a general similarity in manners. It was sometimes reproachfully said of Connecticut that she was too much inclined to trot after the Bay Horse.

The Abbé Robin, after coming from Massachusetts, was much impressed with the mildness and moderation of the Connecticut people. He describes them as leading an easy life without any necessity for hard labor, and says that even the dogs and horses were unusually gentle.

In material prosperity there was considerable difference between Massachusetts and Connecticut. Massachusetts grew rich by ship-building and commerce; but Connecticut, though possessed of several fine harbors, had fewer ships. The soil, however, especially in the valley of the Connecticut River, was rather fertile, and considerable farm produce was raised and sent for sale to Boston. Horses and mules were bred and sold in the Southern colonies and in the West Indies. The trade in mules was quite large, and lasted down into the present century.

There is a good story told of John Randolph, of Virginia, who, seeing a drove of mules passing through Washington on their way to the South, said to Marcy, of Connecticut, "There go some of your constituents." "Yes," said Marcy, "going to Virginia to teach school."

Tobacco was raised in Connecticut in colonial times very much as it has been in recent years, and there was some slight business in lumber and staves; but in comparison with the population there was very little foreign trade.

The population of Connecticut increased slowly in comparison with the population of Massachusetts, chiefly because the colony could not support many people. They believed in large families as fully as the people of Massachusetts, and there were plenty of children born; but Connecticut could not supply them all with a livelihood, so they spread out into other parts of the continent. A large number of them moved to the Susquehanna Valley in Pennsylvania, where their descendants are to be found to this day, and the struggle for this valley is the most romantic episode in Connecticut's history. *

Eastern Long Island and Northern New Jer-

---

* See "The Making of Pennsylvania," p. 237.

sey were settled by them, and so were Western Massachusetts and Western Vermont. The middle and western parts of New York were developed chiefly by Connecticut pioneers; and finally, that part of Ohio known as the Western Reserve has acquired its characteristics of thrift, good government, and high intelligence from the Connecticut families who founded it.

There is no State in the Union which has been so well represented outside of itself. Whenever the members of any important body are arranged according to their nativity, it is very often found that the natives of Connecticut are more numerous than those of any other State. In the Constitutional Convention of New York, held in 1821, out of a total of one hundred and twenty-six members, thirty-two were natives of Connecticut. Only nine were natives of Massachusetts, which, according to the ratio of population, should have had seventy.

At one time one-fifth of the members of both houses of Congress had been born in Connecticut. Calhoun is reported to have said that he could remember the day when the natives of Connecticut, together with the graduates of Yale, lacked only five of being a majority of Congress.*

---

* Litchfield County alone is said to have produced thirteen United States senators, twenty-two representa-

The Land of Steady Habits

This migratory spirit has been very active during a large part of the nineteenth century, and has exerted itself in peopling what we call the Great West. It is largely the wanderer from Connecticut who, as a settler or a peddler of wooden clocks and hardware, or as an inventor and machinist, has made the peculiarities of the Yankee so well known throughout the world.

In the time of the Revolution, when the colonies were ranked according to the number of men they sent into the army in proportion to their population, Connecticut stood second. She went to war with the same steady thoroughness she showed in peace; and it is said that in one Connecticut brigade there were seven ministers as captains in command of men from their own congregations.

Yale University is as significant in Connecticut as Harvard is in Massachusetts. To the Puritan mind education of the highest kind was a necessity. The New Haven colony set apart land for a college in the ninth year after their arrival. Yale, however, was not actually founded till 1701, when it was established at Saybrook,

---

tives in Congress from New York, fifteen Supreme Court judges, nine presidents of colleges, and eleven governors and lieutenant-governors.

at the mouth of the Connecticut River. Some years afterwards it was moved to New Haven, and New Haven, it will be remembered, was, like Cambridge and Boston, the abode of the most intolerant and extreme kind of Puritanism.

It is perhaps significant that our two most famous institutions of learning grew up in the places where Puritanism was most bigoted and extreme. The mild, liberal democrats at Hartford seem not to have been so intensely devoted to learning. In fact, extreme Puritanism was so complex and subtle that it required the most exhaustive efforts of the mind to maintain it. Even in its worst complexity and subtleness it always openly professed to be founded on reason and knowledge, and if it could not be maintained by those means was willing to fall.

The doctrine of intolerance, for example, was always maintained by the Puritan preachers of Massachusetts with great ingenuity of language and show of knowledge. The more extreme the Puritan became the more need he had for intellectual training; and his system of belief was so constructed that every part of it called for much mental activity and the labors of the scholar.

But the general tone of Connecticut Puritanism outside of New Haven was comparatively mild, and softened the excesses of the New Haven citizens. Early in the history of the colony, about the year 1662, this mildness produced a controversy which resulted in what was called the Half-Way Covenant.

Democracy and ecclesiasticism under Hooker and his followers had gone along smoothly side by side and seldom interfered with one another; but the tax law, which assessed all, whether members of the church or not, for the benefit of the churches, soon gave trouble.

Those who were not church members, those who could not appear before the ministers and show a satisfactory conviction of sin and religious experience, were in the position of paying taxes for the support of a church in which they had neither voice nor vote. This was not a very terrible tyranny, and, compared with what the disfranchised majority in Massachusetts suffered, it was no tyranny at all; but still it was something to complain of, and after a most voluminous controversy it brought about the Half-Way Covenant.

The Half-Way Covenant was adopted by a synod of all the New England churches, accepted and admired by some who thought themselves progressive and were called Large Congregationalists, and denounced, rejected, and bewailed as part of the degeneracy of the age by those who wished to stand in the old paths.

The Land of Steady Habits

The synod had no power to force the system on the churches: it was merely an advisory body; but its decision was quite largely accepted and acted upon in Connecticut and, to some extent, in Massachusetts for many years.

It provided that the churches must accept as members all who had been baptized, if they were of years of discretion, not scandalous in life, and understood the fundamentals of religion. The children of persons so admitted must also be baptized whenever presented for it. Thus the severe examination into religious feeling and knowledge was abolished, and the simple formality of baptism became the only qualification for the right to an ecclesiastical vote.

This compromise quieted the democratic element in Connecticut until the year 1818. Up to that time the taxes for the support of the church continued to be levied, and were collected by the civil officers. For many years before the adoption of the new constitution in 1818 these taxes were paid by Episcopalians and members of other religious bodies whose belief would never permit them to become members of the Congregational churches.

The Half-Way Covenant was in effect a yielding of the church to the clamors of the masses who wished to get within it, and when within they are generally believed to have done the church no good. The severe examination into religious experience was one of the most energizing principles of Puritanism, and after it was lost in the Half-Way Covenant the churches are said to have been invaded by a decay of religious feeling which was not restored until after many years and many revivals.

But the comparative mildness of Connecticut Puritanism preserved it from change. There was no reaction, no renaissance, as in Massachusetts, because there was less from which to react; and Unitarianism, which has almost superseded the old faith of Massachusetts, has left Connecticut untouched. The Connecticut Congregationalism of to-day seems to be the nearest approach we now have to the Puritanism of colonial times.

The Connecticut Puritans who changed their religion usually became Episcopalians. After the Revolution, when the American branch of the English Church renewed itself, Connecticut became one of its most important strongholds, and was the first community in the country to secure a bishop.

The early settlers of Connecticut are said to have been of excellent English ancestry, the descendants of knights and gentlemen. Four-fifths of the landed proprietors of Hartford, Windsor, and Wethersfield belonged to families that had

had coats of arms granted to them in Great
Britain. They had come to a wilderness from
the stress of the times, as the Cavaliers went to
Virginia, willing to begin life anew, labor with
their hands, live in small cabins, and be laid to
rest in obscure graves above which were raised
no monuments emblazoned with heraldic emblems.

Certain it is that their names, like those of
the settlers of Massachusetts, are of the purest
Anglo-Saxon. The Ludlows, Winthrops, Wol-
cotts, Wyllyses, Trumbulls, Chittendens, Allyns,
Ingersolls, Pitkins, Lymans, Olmsteads, and
Treadwells are of no uncertain sound. We can
read through lists containing hundreds of these
names without finding a single one of alien
origin, which is a refreshment to all believers in
the importance of race after the modern lists of
Irish and Germans, mixed with Italians, Huns,
and Russians.

Their life and beginnings were very like the
early Massachusetts life, but on a smaller scale,
and not so immediately prosperous. The people
who began Hartford, Windsor, and Wethersfield
lived at first in wretched huts. Afterwards log
cabins were built, followed by frame houses, the
ministers usually having the largest and handsomest. Occasionally a large stone house was
built, like the Rev. Henry Whitfield's house at

The Land of Steady Habits

Guilford, of the year 1640, so massive that it was used as a fort. The houses of Governor Eaton and of Davenport in New Haven were also large; and Davenport's house is said to have had thirteen fireplaces in it.

The ordinary wooden house differed considerably from the modern one. It was constructed almost entirely of oak, even the clap-boards being made of oak, split from the tree and laboriously reduced with a shaving knife. The floors were also of oak, and the windows were leaden frames set with little diamond-shaped panes, swinging on hinges. Some pictures of these early houses represent them with the second story overhanging the first, and globular ornaments, no doubt also carved out of oak, hanging from the edges and eaves.

The outer doors were made of double oaken planks, fastened by wrought nails and spikes until they were like a solid mass, and were secured within by heavy wooden bars, a protection, probably, against an attack of Indians, who, though not so troublesome as in Massachusetts, were nevertheless a constant source of danger. The early laws of the colony compelled one member of every family to bring his arms to church.

The rooms were only about seven feet high. There were the same large fireplaces as in other

The Land of Steady Habits

parts of the country, where prodigious quantities of wood were burnt on the andirons. Even in summer these fires were lighted in the evening, and the family sat round them, telling stories, listening to the cries of the frogs and the whippoorwill, or startled by the gleam of a meteor seen through the diamond-shaped panes or open door, or the cry of a screech-owl when a cloud passed over the moon, both of which were believed to be of evil portent.

Swords were worn by the better class of people when in full dress, as in all the colonies, cocked hats, broad-brim hats, and as a luxury a sort of hat called a black beaverette. The coat was long, straight, coming below the knee, with a low collar showing the white neck-cloth fastened with a silver buckle behind. The small clothes, as they were called, now used only for playing games, were universal, and were tied with ribbons, at first above the knee and in later years below it. They were often made of buckskin, and bright red was a favorite color for the long stockings. The shoes were square-toed with enormous buckles, sometimes of silver. The lower classes wore knit yarn caps of bright colors with a heavy tassel.

As in Massachusetts, we find that high boots, usually very wide at the top, were considered an ornament, and worn to church. A handsome pair of them was supposed to last almost a life-time. The women of all classes were very fond of bright scarlet cloaks, which they wore on all occasions, and they must have been a striking contrast against the dark foliage of the pine forests. There was the same hoarding of great quantities of linen which we find in the other colonies. Everybody seems to have had abundance to wear, and we read of a Connecti-cut girl sent to boarding-school with twelve silk gowns, and a thirteenth afterwards ordered because she had not enough.

The men had wrestling, leaping, and running matches, shot at a mark, played ball, and bar-gaining for all sorts of trifles was a recognized amusement. Apparently there were more amusements than in Massachusetts. In winter, which was the time of leisure, there were sleigh-ing parties. Dancing and balls were common, and whenever a minister was ordained there was an ordination ball, which became a settled Con-necticut custom ; but it was always regarded as more or less of a scandal, and finally became so elaborate and hilarious that the more sedate people stopped it.

In the country districts the people went to church on foot and on horseback by roads or paths. " Many a time," says the Rev. Levi Nelson, of Norwich, " while passing over to the society, has my attention been arrested to notice paths now given up where they used to make their rugged way to the house of God almost as surely as the holy Sabbath returned. . . . To this day I love to think of their appearance in the house of God, of the seats they occupied, and of their significant motions to express their approbation of the truth."

Until 1750 there were no carriages. Everybody rode a horse or walked; and the same condition prevailed almost everywhere in New England, except near large towns like Boston. For over a century the New Englanders lived in the saddle like the Virginians, and yet there was no very great love of horses developed, nor a fine breed of them for saddle use. They were usually taught to pace, which was the gait regarded as easiest and best for a long distance. A good pacer could, it is said, without difficulty make fifty or sixty miles a day.

Even after 1750 there were very few carriages until the Revolution was over, and the first that appeared were two-wheeled, called chaises or gigs. They were not allowed to be used on Sunday, for the rumbling of their wheels was an irreverent disturbance of worship in the meeting-houses. When Governor Trumbull used to visit Norwich, at the time of the Revolution, in his chaise, the people crowded to the doors to see it pass, and there was no end of bowing and courtesying as the wonderful vehicle rolled by.

Flax was an important crop on most farms in all the Northern colonies; and, besides the planting of it, the rotting, breaking, dressing, spinning, weaving, and bleaching involved a great deal of labor. The women in all the colonies were industrious spinners, and those of Connecticut were in no way inferior to their sisters. A spinning-wheel was usually the most conspicuous part of a bride's outfit when she left her father's house. Girls who could annually add many skeins of linen yarn and sheets and towels to the supply they were amassing for the great event of their lives were sure of suitors.

Spinning nearly all day long was a common occupation of the women. Sometimes a brother would carry the small wheel over to a neighbor's, where his sister could spin and gossip with a friend. As they spun, the women often hummed old English ballads or Puritan psalms, and mingled with the whir of the wheel it made pleasant music, which, coming through the open windows in summer, caused many a traveller to pause and listen.

It has been said that spinning was very healthy exercise for women, and, unlike ordinary household drudgery, made them cheerful and added grace to their movements. In both Connecticut and New Hampshire there are traditions that the women among the masses of the people were much more vigorous and handsome in colonial times than after the Revolution, when domestic spinning and weaving had ceased.

A manuscript diary in the possession of the Connecticut Historical Society, written by a young girl, Abigail Foote, of Colchester, in the year 1775, confirms what we gather from other sources. She was the daughter of plain people apparently, but more intelligent and more inclined to books and education than people of her sort outside of New England.

She was extremely busy, knitting, spinning, weaving, cooking, teaching neighbors' children, helping her brother mend harness, riding horses, going to school, reading sermons and poetry, weeding in the garden, with a great deal of visiting among people of her own age. In fact, we often find evidence that the colonists were a very busy, active people with all their time employed, but taking delight in ordinary duties instead of being worried and discontented over them. There was no city life to set an absurd standard, and the work which Abigail Foote thought so honorable and pleasant as to deserve recording in a diary has been now so long performed by low-class foreigners that it is supposed to be necessarily degrading.

" Fix'd Gown for Prude Just to clear my teeth,—Mend Mother's Riding hood—Ague in my face—Ellen was spark'd last night—Mother spun short thread—Fix'd two Gowns for Welch's girls—Carded tow—spun linen—worked on Cheese Basket—Hatchel'd Flax with Hannah and we did 51lb a piece—Pleated and ironed—Read a sermon of Doaridges—Spooled a piece—milked the cows—spun linen and did 50 knots—made a broom of Guinea wheat straw—Spun thread to whiten—Went to Mr. Otis's and made them a swinging visit—Israel said I might ride his jade (horse)—Set a red Dye—Prude stay'd at home and learned Eve's Dream by heart—Had two scholars from Mrs Taylor's—I carded two pounds of whole wool and felt Nationly—Spun harness twine—Scoured the Pewter."

Wednesday was lecture day in Connecticut as Thursday was in Massachusetts. Thursday in Connecticut was usually training day for the militia and a sort of holiday. As the week wore on work relaxed, and Friday was often devoted to fishing, wolf-hunting, or easy occupations. On Saturday clothes were mended, and there was a general cleaning up for the solemn Sabbath, which began Saturday evening; and on Sunday the people seem to have been sometimes summoned to church by beat of drum, as in the old days at Plymouth.

Child, in his " Old New England Town," which was Fairfield, says that when young people were courting and compelled to sit in the same room with the girl's parents, they often spoke to one another through a long reed tube called a whispering rod. Methods of courtship were very peculiar, as we shall see.

In the opinion of the magistrates, young men were to be protected from the fascination of women. In New Haven, in 1660, Jacob Muiline went into a room where Sarah Tuttle was, seized her gloves, and then kissed her. The court asked Sarah if Jacob had "inveigled her affections," and, like the spirited girl she was, she said "No." So they fined Sarah rather than Jacob, and called her a "Bould Virgin." To which she replied "that she hoped God would enable her to carry it better for time to come."

It seems that at one time some of the women of Boston began to paint their faces, a fashion which is always coming and going. It was feared that it might spread to the country districts, especially in Connecticut, and one of the ministers who preached against it said that "at the resurrection of the just there will no such sight be met as the Angels carrying painted Ladies in their arms."

Children were expected to wear solemn faces and not laugh in the presence of a minister. They stood aside when any respectable person

The Land of Steady Habits

or stranger passed them in the street; the boys bowed and pulled off their caps and the girls courtesied. When playing together outside of the school-house they would sometimes arrange themselves in a row to do their manners, as it was called, to some elderly person who approached. These pretty customs were not uncommon in some of the other colonies.

Many of the farms had a shop where ox yokes and bows were made, also tool handles, and even some kinds of furniture. This Yankee facility in the use of tools was common all over New England, where farmers were usually traders and mechanics, and, if they lived near the water, boat-builders and sailors.

Connecticut vessels usually traded to the West Indies, and every farmer within reach of the water was apt to intrust the skipper with a small venture of poultry, a horse or two, or a small quantity of vegetables or grain. The vessels were usually small, varying from thirty to one hundred tons, and those of one hundred tons were often rigged with three masts and yards like a ship. The sloop-rigged vessels must have been larger than those of that description in modern times, for some of them carried thirty or forty horses.

The pursuit of whales began in Connecticut about the same time as in Nantucket in Massachusetts. At first whales could be captured in Long Island Sound, or just outside of it. They were pursued in large row-boats and brought ashore to be cut up. Many Indians were employed in this occupation, which, being full of excitement and very much like hunting, did not seem so degrading as most of the white man's work. They made excellent harpooners, and would even labor for days at the oars.

Soon the whalers began to use sloops, which went as far as the Grand Banks; then larger vessels, which cruised to the Azores and the West Indies; and after 1750 whaling was a great industry of New England. The ships visited Davis' Straits, Baffin's Bay, and the coast of Africa, and before the Revolution were to be found in almost every sea. Nantucket alone had one hundred and fifty whaling vessels, employing two thousand sailors; and the wonderful energy and skill shown in this calling were, in the opinion of Burke, proofs that the colonists could never be conquered.

The sharp humor, wit, and sarcasm which were so prevalent among all classes in Massachusetts were not, it seems, so common in Connecticut. A story, however, has come down to us, which is said to have been told at many colonial firesides, of a woman who, while crossing Windsor Plains from the Smoking Tree to

The Land of Steady Habits

Pickett's horse-shed, was overtaken by a terrible storm. Urging her horse to his utmost speed, she was able to keep ahead of it, while the torrents poured down just behind her; but her little dog, unable to keep up, was obliged to swim all the way.

Bride-stealing was a peculiar amusement in which the young people sometimes indulged. Those who were not invited to the wedding and felt affronted would watch their chance after the ceremony was performed, seize the bride and, placing her on a horse behind one of their number, gallop to a neighboring tavern where they had ordered supper. If they could reach the tavern without being overtaken by the wedding-party the night was spent there in feasting and dancing, and the bridegroom was in honor bound to foot the bills.

In one instance the wedding-party, expecting the trick, had dressed a man as a bride, and as he stood about in a conspicuous position he was seized and carried off. The wedding-party followed leisurely to the tavern, where they found the kidnappers just making the mortifying discovery that their bride wore boots; and this time the kidnappers paid the bill.

In a journey he made from Rhode Island to Hartford the Marquis de Chastellux stopped for a time in Voluntown, Connecticut, where an incident occurred which raises an interesting question of morals in colonial times, especially in New England. Chastellux stayed in Voluntown at a tavern, and was very much pleased with the family who kept it, describing them as charming, and the two daughters "as handsome as angels."

One of these daughters was confined to her room, and Chastellux tells us that he learned that she had been deceived by a young man, who after promising to marry her had deserted. Chagrin and the consequences that were to follow had thrown her into a state of languor. She never came down-stairs; but the greatest care was taken of her; somebody always kept her company; and her parents seem to have had no hesitation in telling her story to Chastellux and other travellers.

When the first edition of his travels appeared in France the marquis was very roundly abused for heartless indelicacy in describing this girl's misfortune and giving her name. But in the English edition the translator, who had travelled all over America, defended him in a note, in which he maintained that as the girl's parents had had no hesitation in telling her story, and as it was the custom of the country to regard such accidents not as irretrievable ruin, but as misfortunes which could be remedied, the marquis was merely giving an instance of American manners.

The translator further went on to explain that young women who were guilty of slips of this kind lost none of their rights in society; their mistake was lamented rather than condemned; and they could afterwards marry and take as good a position as ever, although their story was neither unknown nor attempted to be concealed. Morals, in America, he said, were in their infancy, in the sense that people had a very simple way of regarding these things which no right-minded person would attempt to ridicule; and he has some sharp words for French infidelities among married people, from which the Americans were quite free.

It turned out that the young woman's lover returned, and both Chastellux and the translator afterwards saw her perfectly happy with her child passing from her knees to those of its grandmother.

" The translator, who has been at Voluntown, and enjoyed the society and witnessed the happiness of this amiable family, is likewise acquainted with the whole of this story. He is so well satisfied with the justness of the liberal-minded author's reasoning on American manners in this particular, that he has not scrupled to give the name of this worthy family at length, not apprehending that their characters would suffer the smallest injury, where alone the imputation is of any consequence; nor does he fear opposing the virtue of this family and of these manners to European chastity, prudery, and refinement. The circumstances of this story were related to the translator . . . with the same sensibility and the same innocence with which they appear to have told them to the Marquis de Chastellux."

Some time afterwards, during another journey in Connecticut, the marquis found another instance of very much the same sort near Farmington, in which he was again impressed with the entire openness and innocence of all the people concerned, and their willingness to support and care for a young woman who had made such a mistake.

He and the translator comment at length on the circumstance, and the fairness and justice of not making the mother an outcast and a criminal for a lapse for which the father goes unpunished. The marquis suggests a possible explanation of the custom by saying that the acquisition of a citizen in a new country is so precious that a girl by bringing up her child seems to expiate the wickedness which brought it into existence. The translator adds that he hopes it will be very long before " the barbarous prejudices and punishments of polished Europe shall be introduced into this happy country ;" and he says that in his experience in America nothing was more

common than such slips among very young
people nor less frequent than a repetition of the
same weakness.

The remains of this condition of affairs have
been found in quite recent times in wild parts
of some of the Southern States, where no severe
social penalties are inflicted on a woman for her
first child born out of wedlock, although a second offence outlaws her. In these places travellers have talked with women who, without the
least hesitation or embarrassment, have described
their child as a first child or have distinguished
it by that name from others of their flock.

In New England and the other colonies the
young unmarried women had a great deal of
liberty allowed them, probably because the
villages and neighborhoods were at first composed of very few people all well known to
one another, and it seemed absurd, and was in
fact impossible, to bring up girls in the seclu-
sion which was imposed upon them in Europe.
This was no doubt the foundation of the liberty
still allowed to unmarried women in all ranks
of life in America, and which is now universally
regarded as proper and of most beneficial effect
in the development of their minds and characters.
The crudeness and simplicity—or innocence, as
the marquis and his translator called it—which
sometimes attended this custom in colonial times

with rather unfortunate results soon wore away after the Revolution, and more precautions were taken.

Among the Connecticut people there was also the practice of courtship by bundling, which has been already referred to as prevailing in Massachusetts, New York, and New Jersey. It has usually, however, like the blue laws, been treated under the heading of Connecticut, a commonwealth which seems destined to bear so much of the burden of everything peculiar or irregular which happened in New England.

Bundling, in all probability, originated in a habit which prevailed very widely in early times in America, especially on the frontier, where the cabins were often composed of only one room and a loft. In the lower room the whole family, father, mother, sons, and daughters, ate and slept, or sometimes they all slept in the loft above, which was seldom divided. In winter the extreme cold and in summer the heat made the lower room much to be preferred.

When a chance traveller stopped for a night's lodging he could not be refused and told to go sleep on the ground in the woods. He was taken in, and slept in the same room with the rest of the family, and often in the same bed. We have already given an instance in Virginia, related by the Rev. Dr. Burnaby, in which mother, father, daughter, and traveller all got into the same bed. Such incidents were common, are described in numerous books relating to the frontiers, and may still be met with in some of the wild regions on the borders of Kentucky and Tennessee.

The Abbé Robin, who was in Connecticut in 1781, says in his Travels,—

"The Americans of these parts are very hospitable; they have commonly but one bed in the house, and the chaste spouse, altho' she were alone, would divide it with her guest, without hesitation or fear. What history relates of the virtues of the young Lacedemonian women is far less extraordinary. There is such a confidence in the public virtue that, from Boston to Providence, I have often met young women travelling alone on horseback, or in small riding chairs, through the woods, even when the day was far upon the decline."

In homes of this sort, especially in wild places, when a young man came to court one of the daughters of the family, he was compelled to sit with her in the room that was common to all if it was winter. He had worked all day, as every man was compelled to do in those places. The evening was the only time for seeing the young woman of his fancy, and he had perhaps walked five miles or more to reach her house. It was natural to give him as good accommodation as was given to the stray traveller. The parents for the sake of keeping warm retired to bed early, or lay down on the floor of the cabin and covered themselves with blankets or skins, and the young woman and her friend covered themselves in the same way near by them to carry on their conversation. The custom gradually spread until it was universally accepted and believed to be entirely innocent.

One reason always given in justification was that it saved fuel and lights and prevented suffering from cold; and when other countries are investigated, we find similar customs growing out of the same necessity and supported by similar reasons. In many parts of Great Britain, and especially in Wales, courtship by bundling has prevailed down to quite recent times, and seems to have originated in the same habits which are said to have been the cause of it in America.

" At night a bed of rushes was laid down along one side of the room, covered with a coarse kind of cloth, made in the country, called *brychan*, and all the household lay down on this bed in common, without changing their dresses. The fire was kept burning through the night, and the sleepers maintained their warmth by lying closely." (Stiles, " Bundling in America," 23.)

The customs of rude people are often very shocking to the civilized, and sometimes the civilized have peculiar fashions. In France distinguished ladies used to lie in bed while their guests, both men and women, sat about the room and talked to them. In Holland bundling prevailed among some classes, and was there called queesting. It is said to have been sanctioned by the " most circumspect parents," and the origin of it traced to the economy of the people, who wished to save fuel and candles in the long winter evenings. Switzerland was also troubled with it.

In the early times in New England we are assured by numerous authorities that the practice was attended with very few unfortunate results ; not so many, the advocates of the custom maintained, as happened in the higher ranks of life, where the methods of courtship were different.

It was never countenanced by some of the people ; but it prevailed in spite of them, and is supposed to have become rather general about the year 1750. After that the French and Indian wars began, and the young men returning from the camp and army, where they had learned loose vices and recklessness, are supposed to have made sad changes in the simple ways of the colonists. Drunkenness and corruption are said to have greatly increased, and bundling was deprived of any innocence it possessed. The evil effects became so apparent that a decided movement was made against it. Jonathan Edwards denounced it from the pulpit, and one by

one the ministers who had allowed it to pass un-
noticed joined in its suppression.

Curious and startling results were sometimes
produced when a minister suddenly preached on
this delicate subject to a congregation a large
number of whom, men and women, were bun-
dlers or had been such in their youth. Written
confessions of sin were common at that time
when a person became a member of a church,
and when there was no long written confession
filed, short entries were often made in the
records. Some of these which related to bundling were in later and more self-conscious days
destroyed; but enough remain to furnish some
queer revelations. In one church one hundred
and twenty-four people were admitted to full
membership in a period of fourteen years, and
of these fourteen acknowledged having bundled.
In the same period two hundred became partial
or baptismal members, and of these sixty-six
pleaded guilty.

But bundling continued all through the century, and is supposed not to have entirely ceased
as an allowable practice until about 1790 or
1800, when changing circumstances, education,
and the continued attacks of the reformers accomplished its end. It had its defenders even among
elderly persons, and their arguments as collected
in Dr. Stiles's book are very amusing.

The Land of Steady Habits

As late as the year 1775 the custom seems to have been regarded with the most perfect innocence in some places. Miss Foote in her diary speaks of her sister Ellen bundling with a young man "till sun about 3 hours high," as if it was a matter of course, and a few weeks afterwards they were "cried" and married. In 1784 we find Mrs. John Adams referring to it in a letter, in a joking way, as still flourishing and well known.* The people of Cape Cod, it is said, held out longest against the efforts of the iconoclasts.

The final blow the custom received is believed to have been in 1785, when the reformers published some verses on the subject written in the homely way that was most likely to influence the lower classes. They were shrewd enough to have them published in an almanac, which was the surest and indeed the only method at that time of reaching great numbers of such people. This made them self-conscious about the matter; they began to think that they were looked down upon for it, which was a feeling they had never had before.

Counter-verses appeared in defence containing arguments, and all that were written on both

---

* Proceedings Massachusetts Historical Society, vol. vi. p. 508.

sides are curious, as showing a state of affairs and point of view which have entirely passed away.

" It shan't be so, they rage and storm,
And country girls in clusters swarm,
And fly and buzz, like angry bees,
And vow they'll bundle when they please.
Some mothers, too, will plead their cause,
And give their daughters great applause,
And tell them, 'tis no sin nor shame,
For we your mothers did the same."
* * * * * * *
" If I won't take my sparks to bed
A laughing-stock I shall be made."

" But where's the man that fire can
Into his bosom take,
Or go through coals on his foot soles,
And not a blister make ?"
* * * * * * * *
" But last of all, up speaks romp Moll
And pleads to be excused,
For how can she e'er married be
If bundling be refused ?"

With the exception of Jonathan Edwards, and possibly Benedict Arnold, Connecticut produced during the colonial period no very remarkable men. Aaron Burr, however, though born in New Jersey, was of Connecticut origin on both his father's and his mother's side. His mother was a daughter of Jonathan Edwards.

The Land of Steady Habits

General Putnam, who is usually assigned to Connecticut, was born in Massachusetts, and lived in Connecticut after his twentieth year. He was a popular officer and greatly trusted by Washington; but he never developed beyond the rough-and-ready type. There were few officers in the Continental army more competent to hold a position or lead an attack; but he was never given a large command, nor did he ever conduct a complicated campaign, or any of the parts of the art of war which require high intellect.

The most vigorous years of Putnam's life were passed in the French and Indian wars, and he was rather too old to become very eminent in the Revolution, which, like the civil war, demanded for its foremost military leaders men of less than fifty years. He was a rough, heavy man, with a broad, good-humored, florid face, rather unlike the typical New Englander, and overflowing with energy and exuberant life.

The famous story of the wolf's den is characteristic of his whole career. Having, in company with his neighbors, chased a she wolf into a cave, he was let down into it with a rope tied to his legs. He shot her, and when he had made sure she was dead, laid hold of her by the ears and gave the signal. He was hauled into daylight by the neighbors, dragging the prey after him and tearing his skin and clothes on the sides of the cavern.

He became a ranger in the French wars, learned to follow footsteps in the woods, to cut off outposts, and to creep into the enemy's camp at night for information. Desperate emergencies and daring expeditions were the situations in which he delighted. On one occasion, with only fifty men, he ambuscaded five hundred French and Indians, and killed and wounded nearly half of them. He captured a vessel on Lake Champlain by creeping up to her at night and wedging her rudder.

He was not troubled with aristocratic pretensions. Just before the battle of Lexington, though high in military rank and a man of prominence in the colony, he rode to Boston, driving before him a flock of one hundred and thirty sheep to relieve the distressed inhabitants. Important people in both Connecticut and Rhode Island seem to have had no scruples about work of this sort, and would haul wood and perform other manual labor without loss of dignity. No sooner had he arrived than he was entertained by the British officers, many of whom he had known intimately in the French wars, and with whom he was always a popular character. Afterwards, at the siege of Boston, he sent a present of some fine mutton through the lines to the wife of the British commander.

In his younger days he had been challenged to a duel by one of them, and having the choice of weapons, decided on a keg of powder with a slow match in it, both of them to sit together on the keg until it exploded. The Englishman soon left Putnam alone on the keg, and was ever after the butt of ridicule, for the keg contained nothing but onions.

Perhaps the most characteristic picture we have of him is just after the affair at Noddle's Island. He had waded with his men across the flats to attack the enemy's schooner, and, returning to his quarters at Cambridge, met General Ward and General Warren. He was exhilarated by his efforts and covered to the waist with marsh mud. "I wish," he said, "we could have something like this every day."

At Bunker Hill he commanded the fifteen hundred raw militia who took part in the engagement, and their heroic resistance against three or four thousand British regulars, of whom they killed and wounded between twelve and fifteen hundred, was doubtless largely due to his energy and leadership.

At the time of the battle of Bunker Hill, and for many years afterwards, no one appears to have had any doubt that "Old Put" was the commanding officer; but when a hundred years had passed and Massachusetts orators and writers began to look back for the purpose of glorifying that event, it seemed impossible that a Connecticut officer could have commanded Massachusetts men on Massachusetts soil and in a Massachusetts battle.

An attempt was accordingly made to give the credit to Colonel Prescott, who was a Massachusetts man and commanded that part of the line which was at the redoubt on Breed's Hill. He behaved well on that occasion, and held the redoubt until driven from it by superior force; but he exercised no authority over the rest of the line, which extended across Bunker Hill.

Putnam, on the other hand, not only had a large share in planning the battle, but went up and down the line encouraging and threatening, and on his old white horse rode to the rear, in the intervals of the firing, trying in vain to bring up reinforcements. When the retreat began, he put himself between the enemy and his own men to lead them back. He was a general and outranked Prescott, who was only a colonel.

Prescott had served in the French war, but had by no means the experience and reputation of Putnam, and he rose to no great distinction afterwards. There is no evidence that any of his contemporaries believed him to have been the commander at Bunker Hill, or that they awarded to him alone the honors of that day.

Benedict Arnold was a native of Connecticut, and before his treachery to the American cause was usually regarded as one of the most brilliant generals of the Continental army. His father was originally a cooper at Norwich, and afterwards, like many others in New England, engaged in commerce with the West Indies. He was successful, but generally believed to be dishonest, took to drink, and died in poverty and contempt. Young Benedict had greater ability and greater corruption. His moral nature was rotten to the core. From youth to age he was perfectly consistent, and he showed the same depravity in his youth at Norwich that he afterwards displayed as a man at West Point.

His physical courage was perfect. When a boy he liked to astonish his playmates by clinging to the arms of a mill-wheel and passing under the water with it. He was cruel and found pleasure in torturing birds. He became a navigator and a merchant, fought a duel, beat a sailor, seized a wild bull by the nose in the streets of New Haven, was reckless, turbulent, defiant of public opinion, and ended his mercantile career by a bankruptcy which left a stain on his integrity.

Jonathan Edwards deserves particular mention

because he was one of the very few men in the colonies who had much of a reputation in Europe. Very extravagant language has been used in his praise by the descendants of Puritans and Calvinists in both England and America, and he has been called the greatest of the sons of men.

As a metaphysician and an astute reasoner on the subtle problems of free-will and predestination his fame still endures, and is probably destined to last a long time. But his position in New England was in a great measure that of a reactionist. Gentle and benevolent, with all the liberal and tolerant ideas of Connecticut and none of the bigotry of Massachusetts, he attempted to retain a sort of enlightened extreme Puritanism based on pure reason and logic and freed from all superstition.

He was born in 1703, and his youth and early manhood were passed in Connecticut, but his mature years were spent at Stockbridge, Massachusetts; and in 1758 he was made president of Princeton College, New Jersey, where he died shortly afterwards from inoculation of the small-pox.

He was a combination of both Massachusetts and Connecticut feeling, and was one of the few who could be called a New England man and representative of its general religious thought;

and he was also broadly representative of Calvinism.

Long before he was twenty years old we find in him that intense earnestness which invariably marks the Puritan. Among the many resolutions he drew up, one was significant: "To live with all my might while I do live." His self-examination was very severe and, as often happened with Puritans, ran at times into morbidness. But his was too serene a nature to go very far in that direction. He was touched by the milder tone of Connecticut, and he was born when the excesses of the Cottons and Mathers were passing away.

He loved to walk in the woods and fields, and he took delight in nature, which for him was not peopled with terrors. His face in the portraits we have of him is gentle, serene, and almost beautiful, in striking contrast to the portraits of the older Puritan leaders.

His first controversy was in his parish at Northampton, which was in some respects a centre of opinion, and where the Half-Way Covenant prevailed in its greatest extreme. Not only were all baptized and respectable persons regarded as church members and given the right to vote in church affairs, but they were admitted to the communion, which was regarded as a means of conversion and not as a privilege of the elect. His predecessor in the parish, Dr. Stoddard, had been the leader of these extreme opinions, and they were often called by his name.

Edwards endured this situation for a time, and then in obedience to his instincts turned to resist it and stand back in the old ways. After the usual learned contest and trial he was compelled to retire, and moved to Stockbridge, Massachusetts, then a mission station for the conversion of the Indians, but now better known as a summer resort. Here he continued his metaphysical studies and his contest against the Half-Way Covenant, which he detested, and he would submit to no compromise.

He went more and more back to the ancient doctrines of Calvinism, predestination and election, which were becoming obsolete. At first he had been shocked by them. He could not believe them. He thought it horrible and absurd that God should at his mere pleasure choose a few to eternal bliss and send the rest to everlasting torment. But gradually, he knew not by what means, he was brought back to these doctrines, and, to use his own language, found them exceeding pleasant, bright, and sweet. He took endless delight, he tells us, in ascribing this absolute sovereignty to God.

St. Augustine, Calvin, and other upholders of

predestination and election had proved these doctrines from the Scriptures. But as time passed such proofs had ceased to affect men's minds; and Edwards, while not denying the Scripture arguments, set out to prove them by pure reasoning outside of authority and Scripture. He passed out of the strict domain of divinity, and joined the philosophers and metaphysicians.

Edwards's great fame rests principally on his essay on the freedom of the will. It is a short production, covering scarcely two hundred pages, but so closely and exhaustively reasoned that no one who has not mastered it can pretend to any thoroughness in metaphysics. Although it deals with a dry subject, no intelligent mind can fail to be interested. One is led on and on by the ingenious and powerful reasoning, and some are convinced in spite of themselves. Every effect, he says, must have a cause; and if the cause of our acting in a given way is a power of choice within ourselves, then that power of choice must have a cause, and that cause another cause, until we reach God, the original cause of all things, who has foreordained every action, thought, and choice of man from the foundation of the world.

All admit that God is omniscient and knows all things beforehand. If he knows all things beforehand, he either approves them all or he disapproves them all; he is either willing that they should be or he is not willing that they should be; but with a being of infinite power to be willing that they should be is to decree them. No one is absolutely happy unless everything is happening in accordance with his wishes. God is a being infinitely happy, therefore nothing is happening contrary to his wishes; therefore he has decreed all things that happen, the evil as well as the good.

In heaven, according to Edwards, the chief occupation of the blessed who inhabit that abode is in listening to the shrieks of misery from hell. In one of his sermons he describes parents approving in heaven of the condemnation of their children, and rejoicing, "with holy joy upon their countenances," in the torment of their little ones. He also describes a faithful pastor who has gone to heaven and spends his time in witnessing against the unregenerate of his flock as they appear for judgment; how he reviles and denounces them, and the delight he exhibits when they are condemned.

Edwards's effort has been very properly described as an attempt to stiffen Puritanism or Calvinism and to restore its bones and framework. It was also an attempt to restore the old belief by the aid of the process which was destroying it,—the subjective process of Mrs.

Hutchinson of relying on the inward consciousness of each individual, which was producing
Unitarianism in Massachusetts. The difference
between Mrs. Hutchinson and Edwards was, that
while Mrs. Hutchinson relied on a somewhat
vague and mystic inward feeling, Edwards relied
more exclusively on the intellect.

But this last heroic stand to stop the overwhelming tide was a failure, although Edwards
had many assistants, both in America and England, showing different phases of the contest.
They might as well have tried to stop a snow-
storm or check the rotation of the earth.

Edwards made of himself a famous metaphysician, but his metaphysics did not accomplish
what he intended or expected for his faith.
By carrying predestination and election to their
extreme logical limits he revealed their weak-
nesses and destroyed them. He showed that
the freedom of the will was a mere metaphysical
puzzle which could never be solved.

The Calvinistic sects of modern times usually
ignore it or accept it as a mystery, and their
belief in it is apt to be stated by saying that predestination is taught in the Scriptures, is reasonable, and should be believed; free-will is also
taught in the Scriptures, is undeniable, and should
be believed. It is impossible by human reason
to reconcile these two beliefs, for they are abso-

lutely contradictory of each other; but, doubtless, in the mind of God they are consistent.

In his efforts against the Half-Way Covenant Edwards was more successful; and, strange
to say, this man who was so much absorbed in
efforts of pure intellect was a revivalist. Several
years before Whitefield and the Wesleys started
the Great Awakening of 1740 Edwards had conducted revivals of his own, in which, according
to his extraordinary descriptions, even thoughtless
boys and girls were carried away by religion.
This, combined with his reaction against the
Half-Way Covenant, is supposed to have saved
the Connecticut churches from following those
of Massachusetts into Unitarianism.

VAN CLEUSE · PORTSMOUTH · R · I ·

CHAPTER IV

THE ISLE OF ERRORS

THE Isle of Errors and the Religious Sink of New England were the names given in colonial times to Rhode Island, because it was the refuge of Roger Williams, Mrs. Hutchinson and her Antinomian followers, Gortonites, Baptists, and various eccentrics and outcasts who were uncongenial to the orthodoxy of Massachusetts and Connecticut. It was a place for odds and ends and miscellaneous theology ; and Cotton Mather used to say that if any one lost his religion he would be sure to find it in Rhode Island.

Roger Williams and Gorton were the most prominent characters among these confused and discordant elements, and Williams was by far the more sane and sensible. After his banishment from Massachusetts in 1636 he helped to settle and build up Providence at the head of

The Isle of Errors

Narragansett Bay; and Mrs. Hutchinson and her followers performed the same service for Portsmouth and Newport at the mouth of the bay.

As finally constituted Rhode Island was made up of four different colonies,—Providence at the head of the bay, Portsmouth and Newport on the large island in the mouth called Rhode Island, and Warwick on the west shore, a few miles south of Providence. Rhode was a corruption of Roode or red, a name given to the island by the Dutch explorers from New York. Newport was founded largely by settlers from Portsmouth, and Warwick by dissatisfied persons from the other three towns.

The ruling spirit at Warwick was Gorton, a rough, pugnacious, honest-hearted mystic, who had arrived in Boston at the time of the Antinomian difficulties. He spent a short time at Plymouth, where his wife's servant got into trouble for smiling in church and was about to be driven from the town as a common vagabond. Gorton defended her, and this, combined with his heresies, caused his banishment. He was a strange creature who had caught up some of the ideas of the Reformation and had begun to work out religion for himself.

He had freed himself, like Roger Williams, from every kind of dogma, formalism, and church organization. Sermons, he said, were lies and tales, churches divided platforms, and baptism a vanity. When he first went to Rhode Island he refused to submit himself to the civil authority, because it was self-constituted and without recognition from England and had been altered from what it had been at first. These queer opinions and his unbearable insolence to the magistrates were too much even for the liberals of Portsmouth, and they banished him.

He went to Providence, and abused all the ministers and denied the necessity of any ordinances of church or state, until poor Roger Williams was almost distracted; for Williams was practical at the exact point where Gorton was unbalanced, and although he denied the validity of every form of religion, admitted that an organization of some sort, at least for the state, was absolutely essential.

Gorton's followers became so numerous and violent in their attacks on law and government that some of the people appealed to Massachusetts for advice, which gave the Puritans the sort of opportunity they were always glad to have. Without the least show of right they laid claim to all the land at Providence and also at Gorton's home, Warwick, in the hope of enticing him to Boston, where they could have a theological excitement with his queer opinions.

The Isle of Errors

Failing to entice him, they sent an armed force, which captured him with a number of his friends, destroyed a large part of their goods, and appropriated about eighty head of their cattle. When the prisoners reached the first town in Massachusetts the chaplain of the expedition offered prayer in the streets, and proclaimed that everything had been done in a " holy manner and in the name of the Lord." At Dorchester and Boston they were received with great rejoicing, a volley of musketry was fired over their heads, and the governor asked God to bless and prosper the soldiers who had brought them in. They were taken to church and preached at by Cotton ; and after the sermon Gorton rose up and answered him.

Several trials appear to have been held without securing a conviction, and meanwhile the ministers visited the prisoners and indulged themselves to the full in cross-questions. They were for putting all the prisoners to death ; but some of the General Court dissented, and according to Gorton the motion for death was lost by only two votes. They were, however, put to work in chains, and had been distributed to the towns for this purpose, when the indignation of the disfranchised majority became so great that they were set free and ordered to leave the colony within fourteen days, which was reduced to two hours when it was discovered that they were making friends among the people.

Williams's career was less eventful than it had been in Massachusetts. He was in strange uncertainty on all questions of religion, but held firmly to his belief in liberty of conscience. He lived in expectation of a new revelation which should give a new and pure commission to administer the sacraments and organize churches; and he talked about a " great slaughtering of the witnessess" and a general upheaval of society, which was to bring a new dispensation.

Until that time should come, he said, there was no authorized ministry or church, and all men should have liberty to maintain such ministry and worship as they pleased. At first he inclined to the sect of the Baptists, became convinced that his infant baptism had been invalid, and had himself re-baptized by immersion. But within three or four months he lost confidence in this second baptism and left the sect entirely.

He labored hard to persuade the people round him that liberty was not license; but most of his time seems to have been occupied in trying to convert the Indians; and among his published papers is a touching letter to his wife, written when he was among the savages, and sent to her with a bunch of wild flowers.

He probably understood the Indian character

as well as any man in New England, and prepared a grammar of their language which can
still be read with interest; but he describes the
difficulties of the language as almost insurmount-
able, and says that even Eliot, the famous Massachusetts missionary, who had translated the
whole Bible for the Indians, was often unable to
make them understand him.

There is a story told of Eliot, that when, in
translating the Old Testament, he came to the
passage in the fifth chapter of the book of Judges,
which says that the mother of Sisera looked out
at a window and cried through the lattice, he was
at a loss for an Indian word that meant lattice.
He went to some of the Indians and described
a lattice to them, and they gave him a word
which he put into his translation. Some time
afterwards, when he knew more of the language,
he discovered that the word they had given him
meant an eel-pot, which was made something
like a basket, and was the only sort of lattice
work the Indians knew of.

Williams had a great dislike for the Quakers,
who were very numerous in Rhode Island; and
he relaxed from his liberal principles so far as to
want to have them punished for using "thee"
and "thou" to superiors. When quite an old
man he rowed himself in a boat thirty miles down
Narragansett Bay to have a debate and contro-

versy with them at Newport, where, for two or three days, he labored to convince them of their errors, calling them, in the language of the time, "bundles of ignorance," and "a tongue set on fire from the hell of lies and fury." One of his best-known books was called "George Fox Digged out of his Burrows," which was intended to be a double joke, for Burrows was a prominent Quaker in the province.

Rhode Island was a strange New England colony, made up of Gortonites, Antinomians, Quakers, Baptists, and all sorts of nondescripts, who were wandering without a guide in the new-found liberty of the Reformation, and after centuries of restraint trying to think for themselves. Some declared that there should be no governors or officers or punishments, because all were equal in Christ, that it was murder and contrary to the Gospel to execute a criminal, and that no man was bound by a law that he could declare to be contrary to his conscience. There were tumults and riots as a consequence of these opinions and several trials for high treason.

Roger Williams rose to the emergency, and showed his good sense and strength of character by laying down the dividing line between liberty and law exactly as it is understood to-day, and in very much the same language in which it would be now expressed. All the liberty of conscience, he said, that he had ever contended for was that Protestants, Papists, Jews, and Turks should not be forced to any prayers but their own; beyond that they must obey the civil law.

He used the happy illustration of the ship, which was afterwards often repeated. The crew and passengers, he said, are not compelled to follow the captain's religion; they may say any prayers they please; but they must all obey the captain's orders in discipline and navigation. He had a fierce controversy with a certain William Harris, who wrote a book to prove that all kinds of taxation, laws, and magistrates ought to be abolished, and he had Harris indicted for treason.

We have the record of a curious debate in Providence, in which the wife of one Verin insisted on going to hear the sermons of Roger Williams and her husband insisted on restraining her. It was gravely argued on one side that liberty of conscience could never be allowed to extend to a breach of an ordinance of God, such as the subjection of wives to their husbands; that Verin was as conscientious in restraining his wife as she was conscientious in going; that they had all fled from Massachusetts rather than break a law of God to please men, and would they now break a law of God to please a woman? But Mrs. Verin triumphed in the end, and her husband was restrained from the liberty of voting for having attempted to restrain the liberty of his wife. All these difficulties experienced in practically administering the principle of liberty were very gratifying to the Puritans; for they had always declared that liberty of conscience would lead to lawlessness, immorality, and atheism.

The liberty and the strange variety of opinion in Rhode Island developed an extreme individualism and an extreme independence among the towns; and this is the key-note of the colony's history for two hundred years. Each town was a separate sovereignty, and nearly every one of them had at times entertained the notion of getting from the crown a charter for itself as a colony without regard to the others.

By the exertions of Williams a charter was obtained in 1643 for all the towns, but nearly three years passed away before they could be persuaded to unite under it. The charter was very short, and was the freest ever given. It simply said that the towns of Providence, Portsmouth, and Newport might unite together and make any form of government the majority should think best, and it gave them the corporate name of Providence Plantations.

When at last the towns decided to accept this charter the government they framed under it showed a most jealous regard for their independence. They created a president of the colony, with one assistant from each town, but these assistants had no legislative power. Any laws that were to be made were first proposed and passed by one of the towns and then sent about to the other towns for acceptance.

When a proposed law had run the gauntlet of all the towns it was handed to a committee composed of six men, one from each town, called the General Court; and if this committee decided that the law had been concurred in by a majority of the colony, it stood as law until the next General Assembly of all the people, who finally decided whether it should continue. There has seldom been a more elaborate system of self-defence against the supposed dangers of centralization. The towns retained all their rights of local government, and their union under the charter was simply a league.

So loose was the union of the towns under the charter that at one time Portsmouth and Newport attempted to detach themselves from the others and join the New England confederacy. Failing in this, Codington, one of their leading men, went to England and procured a commission incorporating them as a separate colony. For three years there were two governments, one at Providence and the other at Newport, holding separate assemblies for making laws, the cause of much strife and bitterness and great delight to the Puritans.

In 1663 a charter was obtained from the crown which made a close union of the towns, and was very much like the Connecticut charter which Winthrop had obtained the year before. It established religious liberty, allowed the people to elect their own governors and make their own laws as they pleased, and was so liberal in every way that it was not considered necessary to alter it in the Revolution, and the people lived under it until 1842.

After Charles II. came to the throne and Massachusetts lost her charter, Rhode Island was as lucky as Connecticut in retaining hers. There was no romantic episode of an oak; but when Andros came to Rhode Island for the charter it was quietly put out of sight. He never obtained it, and when William and Mary ascended the throne the charter was brought forth and the old government restored under it, as in Connecticut.

In the interval while the charter was in hiding Rhode Island showed a tendency to split up into fragments. The town of Providence sent an address to the king resigning its charter, asking to be annexed to the general government of New England, and disowning the address sent by the Rhode Island Assembly. Similar ad-

The Isle of Errors

dresses were sent by the Quakers and by various voluntary associations of citizens.

Indifference towards the rest of the world and a lack of cohesion among themselves were for a long time the prominent traits of the people, traits which might perhaps show themselves even now if an occasion should arise. Rhode Island was the last State to accept the National Constitution and join the Union. For many months after the other States had given in their consent and the general government had been organized and put in operation Rhode Island continued to retain her autonomy, and stood alone as an independent country in the midst of the American Union. When at last the little one condescended to join the company of the giants, the resolution accepting the Constitution was passed by a majority of only two votes.

As late as the year 1842 there was a formidable rebellion in Rhode Island. Many of the people had long been dissatisfied with the old charter granted by Charles II. and with the law which restricted the right of voting to freeholders. They formed voluntary associations in different places, and these associations called a convention to frame a constitution, and this without any authority from the government under the old charter and without the least regard for it. The new constitution was put to the vote of the people, and when its upholders believed that it had been adopted by a majority, they organized a government with regularly appointed officers. An individual named Dorr was elected governor, and the affair is now known as the Dorr Rebellion.

Rhode Island was once more under two conflicting governments. The charter government, however, had no idea of submitting to such a situation. They declared martial law, suppressed Dorr and his followers by force, and prepared a new constitution of their own, which, having been accepted by the people, has ever since remained the constitution of Rhode Island.

The extreme views on the subject of liberty prevented that unity and compactness of organization which gave Connecticut and Massachusetts their success as colonies. The discordant sects always tended to disintegrate the community; and they were so much opposed to ecclesiasticism and religious organization of any kind that their ministers were inferior. Their churches were not supported by taxation, and the people were too poor or too much afraid of encouraging ministerial tyranny to subscribe. The ministers were usually farmers, without salary or any means of support except their own labor. They had no leisure for study and little interest in it.

The Isle of Errors

As a consequence education was neglected; there was no system of schools like those of Massachusetts and Connecticut, and the public school system was not adopted until 1828. In fact, an attempt in Providence in 1768 to establish free schools showed that the lower classes of the people were decidedly opposed to them. Private schools were few and inferior; but the Baptists made some very creditable exertions, and in 1764 founded the college which is now Brown University.

It has often been observed that every settlement in Massachusetts and Connecticut grew up round a meeting-house and a graveyard. But it was very different in Rhode Island. Religious meetings were for a long time held in the fields or in private houses. The town of Providence was nearly a century old before it had a steepled church. There was not even a meeting-house until the year 1700, and the one then erected was shaped like a hay-cap, with a fireplace in the middle, the smoke escaping through a hole in the roof.

Individualism showed itself even in death. There were no common burying-places; families and sects had their own; and in later years there was often a difficulty experienced in laying out the streets of a town so as to avoid some Rhode Islander's last stand for independence.

The Isle of Errors

For the first fifty or sixty years Rhode Island struggled for bare existence, and at the end of that time her people numbered only ten thousand. They were scattered in small settlements clinging round the shores of Narragansett Bay, hemmed in on three sides by the powerful and jealous colonies of Massachusetts and Connecticut.

Their boundaries were always in dispute, and were not finally settled until the year 1883. Several times in the history of the colony she seemed on the point of being dismembered and divided among her neighbors. So strong were the fears and the ill feeling that for many years the people would build no highways to connect with the other colonies. Massachusetts and Connecticut had no love for the Isle of Errors, and would not admit her to the New England confederacy of 1643.

At one time the Plymouth colony claimed all the way to the bay on the eastern side, and also the island on which stood Portsmouth and Newport. Massachusetts claimed the rest of the eastern side and down the western side as far as Warwick, where lived the irrepressible Gorton. Connecticut claimed what was left of the western shore. If the Rhode Island people had admitted the claims of their enemies they would have had to live in the water.

The Isle of Errors

Rhode Island was not fairly started till 1700, and did not begin to flourish until after the Revolution. Her people produced nothing that was of any great value in the markets of the world. They had no great staple for export like the tobacco of Virginia or the fish of Massachusetts. Their harbors were as good as those of Massachusetts, but they had not the Puritan aptitude for commerce and ship-building.

In 1680, in answer to the questions of the Board of Trade, they said that they had no ships, only a few sloops; that their only exports were horses and provisions; that they had no fishing trade and no merchants; that the people lived chiefly by improving and cultivating the wilderness land. This statement must be taken with some allowance, for the colonists were always careful in their answers to the British government not to boast of their wealth and success, and they were apt to understate their population.

After the year 1700 a slight improvement began. Ships were owned in the colony, and Newport became a seat of commerce. In the year 1763 one hundred and eighty-four foreign-going vessels and three hundred and fifty-two coasters cleared from the custom-house of the little town, which is now chiefly known as a fashionable watering-place. Two-thirds of these vessels are said to have been owned in Newport, and together with the fishing-boats employed twenty-two hundred sailors. The profits of the slave-trade were also considerable, and many vessels were engaged in it.

The colony produced one remarkable man, General Greene, who was brought up a Quaker, and in the Revolution was usually regarded as the ablest soldier of the Continental army after Washington.

When the French army came to assist the patriot cause in the summer of 1780 they landed at Newport, and there the French officers received their first impressions of the strange New World of which they had heard so much. Some of the descriptions they have left are interesting.

Claude Blanchard, who was the commissary of supplies, preferred Providence to Newport. Providence was, he said, more lively and had more commerce. But he describes the wooden houses of Newport as very pretty. He visited a school where the children were all neatly clad, the room very clean, and the master an excellent man.

" I saw the writing of these children, it appeared to me to be handsome, among others that of a young girl nine or ten years old, very pretty and very modest, and such as I would like my own daughter to be when she is as old; she was called Abigail Earl as I perceived upon her copy-book, on which her name was written. I wrote it myself, adding to it ' very pretty.' "

He saw a great deal of the country between Providence and Boston. The men were tall and affable and wore good clothes; the women fair-skinned and good-looking. They lived easy lives, cultivating small farms which they owned, and in winter seemed to have nothing much to do but sit by the fire with their wives and eat a great many meals. They drank cider and Madeira mixed with water.

He found wall-papers, some of them quite handsome, in use instead of tapestry, and he was surprised to find carpets common, for they were then only just coming into use. They even used them, he says, on the stairs. There was a great deal of good furniture, especially among the better classes, and they were very choice in their cups, vases, and decanters. Everywhere, including Boston, he found what he describes as "immaculate cleanliness," and he comments on this quite often.

He had some difficulty with English; but found two persons who could converse with him in Latin,—one a Hessian dragoon, who had deserted from the British, and the other a native New Englander. Some of the manners of the people puzzled him.

The Isle of Errors

"I dined at the house of a young American lady where M. de Capellis lodged. . . . It is a great contrast to our manners to see a young lady (she was twenty at the most) lodging and entertaining a young man. I shall certainly have occasion to explain the causes of this singularity."

Chastellux on his arrival with the fleet was very busy with his military duties, and has nothing to say of Newport. He was anxious to get away as quickly as possible to explore and study all the colonies, and was soon on the road to Connecticut; but he stopped for a time in Providence, with which he was very much pleased, commenting on the neatness and good arrangement of the houses, and he breakfasted with Colonel Peck.

"This little establishment where comfort and simplicity reign gave an idea of that sweet and serene state of happiness which appears to have taken refuge in the New World, after compounding it with pleasure, to which it has left the Old."

The Abbé Robin, who visited Rhode Island the next year, says that before the arrival of the fleet and army the Americans had a great dislike for the French.

"They looked upon them as a people bowed down beneath the yoke of despotism, given up to superstition, slavery, and prejudice, mere idolaters in their public worship, and, in short, a kind of light nimble machines, deformed to the last degree, incapable of anything solid or consistent; entirely taken up with the dressing of their hair and paint-

ing their faces; without delicacy or fidelity, and paying no
respect even to the most sacred obligations."

This was, of course, the prejudice which all
Englishmen had at that time for their ancient
enemy across the channel. It was so strong
that on the arrival of the fleet at Newport the
people deserted the town. To overcome their
fears and dislike the French officers established
the strictest discipline and took advantage of
every occasion to show politeness and kind feeling. They were very successful in this, as the
Abbé tells us, and before long the most pleasant
relations were established.

Part of their endeavor to encourage friendli-
ness was abstaining from flirtations, and both the
Abbé and Chastellux comment on this in true
French fashion. When the fleet was afterwards
at Boston, Chastellux tells us that " though the
officers were admitted by the ladies of Boston to
the greatest familiarity, not a single indiscretion,
not even the most distant attempt at impertinence,
ever disturbed the confidence or innocent harmony of this pleasing intercourse."

The Abbé, however, after a sort of half complaint that the French nation had long been
upbraided " for paying no regard to the most
sacred of all connections when their gallantry
is concerned," admits that Newport had afforded several examples. One instance he re-

The Isle of Errors

lates of a French officer who won the affections of a young woman whose husband seems to have been equal to the occasion.

"He became more assiduous and complaisant to her than ever; with sorrow and despair in his soul, he showed a countenance serene and satisfied. He received at his house with attention and civility the very officer who was the author of his misfortune; but by the assistance of a friend so contrived matters as to hinder him from any private interviews with her whatever. These repeated disappointments appeared to the Frenchman to be mere effects of chance; he, however, grew sullen and peevish upon it, and consequently became less amiable in the eyes of the lady, and her husband more so than ever; and thus that virtue which had not lost all its claims to her seduced heart soon recalled it to its duty. Such a procedure as this in so delicate an affair discovers great knowledge of the human heart, and still more of dominion over itself."

At Middletown
R. I.

CHAPTER V

THE WHITE MOUNTAINS AND THE GREEN

NEW HAMPSHIRE, like Connecticut and Rhode Island, was an offshoot from Massachusetts, and out of New Hampshire arose Vermont. In the colonial period New Hampshire can hardly be said to have had a separate history; for a large part of the time she was under the direct government of Massachusetts and always under Massachusetts influence.

Stray adventurers had founded Portsmouth and Dover as early as 1623. In 1638 Exeter was settled by Wheelwright and a number of Antinomians who had been banished from Massachusetts during the difficulties with Mrs. Hutchinson. Hampden was founded in the same year by Puritans from England and Massachusetts.

The men who settled Portsmouth and Dover had been sent out by two enterprising individuals, Mason and Gorges, who had obtained enormous grants of land from the Plymouth Company. Gorges was a naval officer, a friend and companion of Sir Walter Raleigh. Mason was a merchant and at one time governor of Newfoundland. In 1629 these two men divided their property. Gorges took Maine and Mason took New Hampshire. Maine never became a separate colony, but remained under the jurisdiction of Massachusetts until 1819.

Mason had very grand ideas about New Hampshire, his vast estate of rocks and pine-trees. He looked forward to renting it out to tenants, like an English manor, he himself to grow rich on the proceeds, and, like William Penn and Lord Baltimore, become famous as the founder of an empire. But it was never anything but a dream. Men who had to contend with the savages, the long winters, and the barren soil of New Hampshire were not the sort who had rent to pay or who were willing to pay it to an absentee landlord. He sunk his fortune in the venture; his heirs sunk a large part of theirs; they finally lost their title, and their claims were a source of annoyance to the colony for nearly a hundred years.

Each of the four little towns, Portsmouth, Dover, Exeter, and Hampden, was of the usual New England type, an independent republic built up round a church. They quarrelled with each other continually, and their progress was slow. After twenty years of existence the population of the colony had not reached a thousand.

In 1641, tired of their separate unprotected state and unable to agree on any general plan of government, they were, by their own request, taken under the jurisdiction of Massachusetts. The law which allowed only church members to vote was relaxed in their favor, and they constituted a part of Massachusetts until, when Mason's heirs attempted to recover their rights, the court of King's Bench in England decided that neither the Masons nor Massachusetts should have them, and in 1680 they were put under the direct government of the king.

The growth of New Hampshire was very slow, and in 1730, after a hundred years' existence, there were only about twelve thousand people. But at the time of the Revolution there were supposed to be about eighty thousand. Laws, customs, and opinions were taken from Massachusetts, and fishing and trade with the Indians were the principal means of livelihood.

The most curious occupation in New Hampshire was masting. Officers of the crown went through the forests and marked G. R. on the tallest and best pines, and severe penalties were inflicted on any one who cut one of these trees which were thus reserved for masts for the royal navy. In winter they were cut down under the direction of a mast-master, and the labor of hauling them to the nearest stream which in spring would float them to the sea began.

From fifty to eighty yoke of oxen were hitched to a single tree to drag it over the snow, the end of the tree nearest the oxen being raised on a strong sled. A long time was always required to get the patient beasts started; but when once "raised," as it was called, they never stopped till they reached the water. Two tailmen walked by the hind yoke, and when the tongue of the sled, in passing over a hollow place, ran up so high as to lift up the hind yoke by their necks, the tailmen seized their tails and drew them outward, so that in coming down the tongue would not strike them.

So many of the people were Scotch-Irish that in the woods and country districts the Scotch dialect was constantly heard, and the people by their firesides told tales of the siege of Londonderry mingled with their recent adventures with the Indians. And such fireplaces! They were the largest of any in the colonies, eight feet long, and so very deep that the children had blocks on which they sat far within, and the child farthest in was the coldest and could see the stars up the chimney. In daytime, it is said, one could see to read inside of these fireplaces.

The White Mountains and the Green

There were no cranes in them, but a green stick called a lug-pole stretched across high above the flame, with iron trammels hanging down on which to suspend the pots.

Wooden plates and dishes were largely in use, and the women disliked earthen-ware because it dulled the knives. These women called their children bairns, were strong and hardy, worked in the grain-fields and broke up the ground for sowing.

The modern woman when in a hurry to kindle a fire takes a can of coal-oil, with the consequences of which we so often hear. But in New Hampshire she often took her husband's powder-horn. One whose name has become historic thought one day that she could quickly stop the stream of powder with her thumb, as she had often done before. But the flame followed up the stream into the horn, which flew from her hand up the chimney; and for years after people would say " as quick as Mother Hoit's powder-horn."

The elderly people went to church, as in Massachusetts, on horseback, and the young walked. In summer the young men walked barefooted, with their shoes in their hands, and the girls walked in coarse shoes, carrying a better pair to change before entering the meeting-house. At Concord it is said those coming from the westward stopped at a large pine-tree, where the shoes were put on, and the women left their heavy shoes under the tree until they returned, having no fear that any one would disturb them on the Sabbath.

In the "History of Barnstead" some curious court records are found. In 1649 Josiah Paistowe, for stealing four baskets of corn from the Indians, is ordered to be fined five pounds and hereafter to be called Josias and not Mr. as formerly. Captain Stone, for abusing Mr. Ludlow, who seems to have been a justice of the peace, and calling him Just-ass is fined one hundred pounds.

We find the men as carefully protected as in Connecticut from those allurements which we all know are hard to resist. Margery Ruggs, for enticing and alluring George Palmer, is ordered to be severely whipped, while George, who confessed that he had been unable to resist the enticement, was only set in the pillory.

The town histories have many accounts of fights with bears, which were very numerous and were often killed with axes. One man found a bear plunging his nose into a wasp's nest to rob it, and squealing and grunting as he was stung. Watching a chance when he was fully occupied, the hunter finished him with a blow of the axe.

The White Mountains and the Green

There were suspicions of witchcraft, and charmed crows which could be shot only with a silver button. One old dame who had all the usual signs and symptoms wore away to a mere skeleton before her death. But the shoulders of the strong men who carried her to the grave were bruised black and blue, crushed by the weight of sin.

Being the most exposed to the French and Indians of all of the New England colonies, the province could make no progress until repeated wars had reduced the power of the Indians and their white allies. Block-houses and garrisons were maintained all along the frontier, and scouting-parties were kept moving through the woods every day.

The Indians crept up to the settlements like wild animals and lay hid in the bushes, and even in the grain-fields and potato-patches. There was no safety unless these resorts were beaten up from week to week, for if the red men were allowed to collect in that way for any length of time they could rise up on a signal and massacre the whole community. A settler's family might go about their ordinary duties for several days and then suddenly discover by depressions in the grass or dusky forms disappearing among the trees that for all that time they had been watched by their enemies.

The White Mountains and the Green

The Indians used light charges of powder, waited till their victims were scattered, and then went up close and shot from behind a tree. Such surroundings turned every able-bodied man into a Leatherstocking. The rangers of New Hampshire, many of whom were Scotch-Irishmen, became famous, and their services were eagerly sought in the French wars. For following a trail and fighting from log to log they were unequalled in the colonies.

In the famous fight at Lovewell's Pond in 1725 the rangers saw an Indian standing on a point on the shore of a lake. They left their packs on the ground, crept to him, and soon had his scalp; but while they were gone after this decoy the Indians hid themselves near the packs, and when the rangers returned they received a volley which killed nine of them.

The fight continued from behind trees. John Chamberlain fought the chief Paugus, and when their guns became too foul to use they mutually agreed to go together to the stream to wash them. The others on both sides, understanding the arrangement, watched them without interference. When they returned to their places the Indian could load faster than Chamberlain, whose bullets could with difficulty be rammed down the barrel.

The White Mountains and the Green

"Now me kill you," said the chief, finding he was first to get his gun primed.

Chamberlain's gun was very open at the touch-hole. Giving it a smart blow on the stock, it primed itself, and his ball passed through Paugus.

The Indians grew weary of the contest and retired with the scalps they had secured. The remnant of the rangers escaped, but had to leave their wounded on the field, Lieutenant Robbins begging to keep his gun for a last shot before he died.

Hunting was a very profitable occupation when the Indians could be avoided. In an expedition to Baker's River in 1752 Stark and three companions collected within two months furs to the value of five hundred and sixty pounds sterling. But they never pocketed the profits of their success, for the Indians captured them and took them with their property to Canada, where the two who remained alive had to be ransomed.

Stark was a Scotch-Irishman, pugnacious, restless, and independent. He passed from the profession of hunter to that of guide, and from that to be a soldier and an officer in the French and Indian wars. He served under Lord Howe and other distinguished generals, and at the outbreak of the Revolution had had a military experience fully equal to that of Washington,

Putnam, or any other American in the Continental army.

When he heard the news of Lexington he started at once for Boston, and after the manner of a ranger called on all the people as he passed to follow him. He was at Bunker Hill and the siege of Boston. But his only distinguished service was the battle of Bennington, in which he cut off Burgoyne's foraging-party and so seriously checked his advance that Gates had ample opportunity to collect the army which defeated him at Saratoga.

General Sullivan, a conspicuous soldier of the Revolution, was born in Maine, but has usually been credited to New Hampshire, where he lived from his early youth; and Ethan Allen was the leading character of that part of New Hampshire which became Vermont.

The grant of land given by Charles II. to the Duke of York, which, as we have seen, gave so much trouble to Connecticut, included the whole of New England west of the Connecticut River. The colony of New York was thus brought eastward to that river, which runs north and south through the middle of New England.

The original charters of both Connecticut and Massachusetts gave them jurisdiction westward all the way to the Pacific Ocean, and they resisted the claims of New York, until finally as a compromise Connecticut had her western boundary settled where it now is, twenty miles east of the Hudson River; and using this as a precedent, Massachusetts succeeded in having her boundary settled in the same way. But the western boundary of New Hampshire was not brought into dispute until some years later, and its settlement was more difficult.

The New Hampshire lands which lay between the Connecticut River and Lake Champlain were, up to the outbreak of the French war in 1755, a complete wilderness, into which only the hunter and the Indian cared to venture. A few years previous to the outbreak of the war Governor Wentworth, of New Hampshire, had issued patents for lands in this section without regard to the grant to the duke or the claims of New York; and he announced that the western limit of his colony was, like that of Connecticut and Massachusetts, a line twenty miles east of the Hudson River.

The war, however, put an end to all attempts at settlement, for these New Hampshire Grants, as they were called, became the marauding ground of the French and their red allies. But no sooner was the war over and Canada given to the control of the English than settlers began to pour into the Grants, and within four years Governor Wentworth found that he had organized in them one hundred and thirty-eight townships.

The settlers took title to their farms from New Hampshire. The majority of them were from Connecticut, and the rest from Massachusetts and New Hampshire. They were hardy and ambitious, the flower of the colonial yeomanry, men whose love of independence and daring enterprise had been stimulated by their campaigns against the French. They cleared away the forests, planted, improved, and prospered; they believed that their labor and success gave them a perfect title to their land, superior to parchment or patent from either Wentworth or the governor of New York.

The New York colony, however, had obtained in 1764 a decree from the king in council confining the jurisdiction of New Hampshire to the eastern side of the Connecticut River. At first all parties appeared to be satisfied. The settlers themselves were indifferent. They thought that they were as likely to be prosperous under the government of New York as under that of New Hampshire. The decree seemed to them a purely political matter, without effect on the growth of crops or their individual rights of ownership; and the change of political authority should certainly have left all private rights of property unimpaired.

The White Mountains and the Green

But the government of New York, urged on by a clique of land speculators, announced that all titles in the grants west of the Connecticut River were invalidated, and must be repurchased from the new authority. The settlers, confident in the justice of their position, would not respond to this demand, refused to repurchase their lands, and when the three months had expired New York issued warrants to the land speculators.

These warrants included lands with orchards and houses which had been in the possession of the occupants for years, and had been redeemed from the wilderness and brought to a high state of cultivation. A more complete and deliberate piece of robbery can hardly be conceived.

The settlers sent an agent to England, who very quickly obtained an order from the king forbidding New York to issue any more patents. But nothing was said about the patents already granted, and under these the speculators began to take out writs of ejectment. The settlers were determined to exhaust all peaceable methods, and under the leadership of Ethan Allen they employed counsel to argue the ejectment suits at Albany. But almost every member of the New York government, including some of the judges, was interested in the land-jobbing, and the trial was a farce.

The White Mountains and the Green

Allen was advised to yield to the decision, and was reminded by the New York attorney-general that might often prevailed against right. To which in his grandiloquent way he replied, "The gods of the valleys are not the gods of the hills." He retired to his Green Mountains, and his followers allowed all the ejectment suits to go against them by default.

But it was no easy matter for New York to execute the judgments obtained against the people in the Grants and force them out of their homes. Allen organized a systematic resistance, and the New York officers succeeded in ejecting farmers in only one or two instances. Even in these cases the victims were immediately restored to their property by Allen's men. The New York sheriffs were often roughly handled, and a favorite mode of punishment was called " chastisement with the twigs of the wilderness," a phrase which sounds like Allen.

For ten years, from 1765 until the outbreak of the Revolution, this quarrel continued. The governor of New York issued proclamations declaring Allen and his lieutenants outlaws and offering a bounty for their capture. Allen replied by issuing a proclamation offering a bounty for the capture of the New York attorney-general. At one time New York passed a law by which if Allen and some others should not within a certain time surrender themselves they should be deemed convicted, and should suffer death as if indicted for a criminal offence, and the Supreme Court was authorized to award execution as if they had been tried, found guilty, and sentenced. But the Green Mountain boys held their farms, and when the Revolution brought a lull in the quarrel not a single land-jobber had been successful.

Allen took part in the Revolution, and made himself famous at the outset by taking Fort Ticonderoga. At the head of eighty-three men he marched into the fort in the dead of night, and when the astonished captain asked him by what authority he demanded a surrender he exclaimed, "In the name of the Great Jehovah and the Continental Congress."

This was Allen's only exploit in the war. He joined Montgomery on his expedition into Canada, and was taken prisoner in the attack on Montreal. He remained in confinement two years, and the narrative of his experiences reveals a condition of suffering among the American prisoners almost equal to Libby and Andersonville in the civil war.

When he was exchanged and returned to the New Hampshire Grants he found that his friends had taken advantage of the Revolution to declare themselves an independent State under the name of Vermont, had adopted a constitution, and elected the necessary officers of government. He immediately retired from the Revolution and devoted himself to securing the existence of his new-born commonwealth.

He kept up a secret correspondence with the British for the rest of the war, which led them to suppose that Vermont might come over to them at any moment. At the same time he occasionally disclosed this correspondence to Congress, and by showing how easily they might lose Vermont compelled them to respect her independence.

The backwoods diplomat continued his policy for many years after the Revolution was over. Vermont took no part in the formation of the national Constitution, but kept threatening to join Canada unless she were set free from her old enemy, New York, and Congress finally recognized her as a State in 1791.

Langdon House · Portsmouth · N·H.

WOODLANDS · PHILADELPHIA

CHAPTER VI

QUAKER PROSPERITY

PENNSYLVANIA, of which Delaware was a part, was before the arrival of Penn and the Quakers under the nominal control of the Dutch at New York. But they regarded the Delaware River merely as an avenue of trade, and made no attempt to settle the country round it. The few Dutchmen who were on the river confined themselves to the one or two forts which they had established, and were engaged almost exclusively in the fur trade and in the whale fishery at the mouth of the bay.

The Swedes entered the river in 1638, and being quite numerous may be said to have held possession for seventeen years, to the exclusion of the Dutch. In 1655 Stuyvesant conquered them in a battle, which Irving in his " Knickerbocker's History of New York" has described in the mock-heroic manner. But this conquest was of very little importance, for the Swedes, being the more numerous and also better colonists, cultivated and held the open meadow lands and marshes, and the Dutch control was nominal.

The Swedes were very contented and prosperous. Their way of living and their contests with the Dutch for the fur-trade have been described in "The Making of Pennsylvania," which also gives a full account of the Quakers, Germans, Welsh, and Scotch-Irish, with their peculiar customs and religious beliefs. In another volume, "Pennsylvania: Colony and Commonwealth," the general history of the province is given.

Pennsylvania was made up of so many nationalities and religions and there was so much contest in it that it is extremely difficult to summarize its history in a single chapter, which is usually amply sufficient for the other colonies. Not only were the elements of the population numerous and diverse, but a large part of the French and Indian wars was fought out within its borders. It was more severely and dangerously invaded in those wars than any of the other colonies; its position in the Revolution was peculiar and has been much misunderstood;

and this, added to the conflict of parties, has made its history very confused and elaborate. It will be possible here only to refer in a general way to some of its characteristics as contrasted with the other provinces, and to touch upon a few points not included in the two volumes which have been mentioned.

The central figure of Pennsylvania was William Penn, who in 1681 received a grant of the province from the crown, and the next year led to it the Quakers, who soon absorbed the Swedes. Like Lord Baltimore in Maryland, he was proprietor of all the land and the people were his tenants, paying him a small quit-rent for every acre they held of him. Like Lord Baltimore, he established religious liberty, but as a principle in which he believed, not as a policy to which he was driven; and religious liberty always prevailed in Pennsylvania without any of the overthrows or disturbances which it suffered in Maryland.

The two men and their people who owned the only successful proprietary colonies represented the extremes of religious thought at that time. The Quakers were the last important sect produced by the Reformation, and carried the doctrines and principles of that movement to their utmost verge. The Roman Church represented the belief in the innumerable dogmas, sacraments, and traditions of the Middle Ages, and the Quakers were as far removed as it was possible for Christians to be from that system.

The Roman Church had seven sacraments; the Quakers had none, not even baptism ; and of the numerous dogmas and doctrines they retained only the inspiration of the Scriptures and the divinity of Christ. The doctrine of the Trinity they explained in a simple way of their own, which was not accepted at that time even by the other Protestant churches.

The other Protestants who came to America —the Church of England people, the Puritans, Independents, Presbyterians, and others—usually had two sacraments, and clung more or less tenaciously to some of the old dogmas. The Puritans of Massachusetts, as we have seen, were very conservative and retained even the belief in the lawfulness of persecution for religious error, so that Pennsylvania under the rule of the Quakers was the most advanced of all the colonies.

Having cleared their minds of all the ancient dogmas, the Quakers naturally adopted religious liberty as a principle, just as we find the Antinomian followers of Mrs. Hutchinson and Roger Williams, who settled Rhode Island, adopting that principle. But the Quakers, being later in time, more numerous, better regulated and organized, and going to a more fertile country than Rhode Island, built up a more prosperous colony.

There were in Germany a number of sects, Mennonites, Tunkers, Schwenkfelders, and others, who held very much the same views as the Quakers. They were part of a great movement of thought, sometimes called Quietism, which towards the close of the Reformation had spread all over Europe, producing the Quakers in England, a whole host of sects like them in Germany, and even affecting to some extent the people of Italy and France. William Penn had travelled and preached among the Quaker sects in Germany, and he and his followers invited them to come to Pennsylvania.

They came in great numbers, and were followed soon after by German Lutherans and members of the German Reformed Church. Penn and the Quakers had not intended to bring the Lutherans and the Reformed. But the immigration movement once started could not be checked, and soon the German peasantry without regard to religion began to swarm into Pennsylvania. This migration continued for almost a hundred years, or from the foundation of the colony until the Revolution, and the result was that in colonial times one-third of the population of the province was German, or

Quaker Prosperity

Pennsylvania Dutch, as they were called, and this proportion is still maintained.

Pennsylvania and New York were thus the only colonies that had in them any considerable alien population. The people of the other provinces were all of English stock, with here and there a few foreigners, like the French Huguenots, but not enough to make any serious difference. Virginia and New England were exceptionally pure Anglo-Saxon, and remained so until some time after the Revolution.

In New York the alien element had been first in the field, controlled the government, and their influence was strongly felt after the English conquest. But in Pennsylvania the English Quakers held the government and were the controlling element until the Revolution. The Germans nearly all went out on the frontier and left Philadelphia in complete control of the Quakers.

Pennsylvania became a great colony, composed of a number of smaller colonies. The Quakers and the Church of England people had exclusive possession of Philadelphia and the neighboring counties, and lived and ruled in their own way. The Germans held Lancaster, Berks, Montgomery, and Lehigh Counties, retaining the language and customs of their native country and living to themselves. They developed a dialect of debased German and English, which is still spoken in the districts they first occupied, and to this day they retain a large part of their original German characteristics.

In the Cumberland Valley, near the Susquehanna and close to the Maryland line, the Scotch-Irish formed another almost separate colony. These settlers could not be called in any sense aliens. They were people of English stock, most of whom had lived in the Scotch Lowlands and migrated thence to Ireland, where they took up the confiscated lands of the native Irish rebels. They began coming to America in large numbers soon after the year 1700, when the long leases on which they held the Irish lands began to expire, and they spread themselves on the frontiers from Maine to Georgia; but most of them entered Pennsylvania and Virginia, where they were attracted by the fertile land.

Although they were not foreigners like the Germans, their life in Ireland, where they had been in continual conflict with the native Irish, had developed in them distinct characteristics. They were a hardy, excitable, aggressive people, and established customs and ways of their own on the Pennsylvania frontier without regard to the Quakers in Philadelphia or any of the other inhabitants of the province.

Quaker Prosperity

The Welsh Quakers, who came out in considerable numbers, had at first a colony of their own just west of Philadelphia on the Welsh Barony, as the tract of land was called which had been given them by Penn. They spoke Welsh to the exclusion of English, and attempted to have a peculiar form of government in which county and township affairs were managed through the Quaker meetings; but their separate existence and separate language did not last long, and before fifty years had passed they were completely absorbed.

The northern half of the province was claimed by Connecticut under her charter, which, like that of Massachusetts, gave her the land westward to the Pacific Ocean. This claim was stoutly resisted by William Penn's heirs; but they never could raise a sufficient force to resist the Connecticut people, who entered and settled the Wyoming Valley, forming another distinct community, which for many years maintained a petty civil war against the proprietary government at Philadelphia. The struggle for the Wyoming Valley is the most romantic episode in the history of the province, and its details, together with the curious customs of the Scotch-Irish, Germans, and Welsh, have been given in "The Making of Pennsylvania."

It will be seen at once from this brief review

that Pennsylvania was totally unlike her sister provinces. The two most important, Virginia and Massachusetts, were each composed of a homogeneous united people, of one religion, extremely conservative, driving out heretics and dissenters, and resenting all alien influences. Connecticut was very much like Massachusetts; and Maryland, New Jersey, Georgia, and the Carolinas, although they had some slight intermixture, were not so decidedly mixed in population as Pennsylvania.

New York had a large alien population of Dutch and some mixture of nationalities in New York City, and approached more nearly to the condition of Pennsylvania; while Rhode Island, though composed of various religions, was peopled almost exclusively by Englishmen. But neither in New York, Rhode Island, nor any of the other provinces were the people split up into distinct divisions, living by themselves in almost separate colonies, as in Pennsylvania.

Two conspicuous results followed from the conditions in Pennsylvania, one from the nature of the religion professed by most of the people and the other from their divided, disunited state. The religion of the Quakers and of a large part of the Germans, having rejected nearly all the ancient dogmas, allowed great liberty of thought. Penn and the Quakers enacted most liberal laws.

Quaker Prosperity

Hospitals and charitable institutions naturally followed, and soon scientific research appeared.

Franklin, finding the conservative atmosphere of Boston uncongenial, fled to Pennsylvania, where he soon became one of the leading men of science of the age, and discovered that lightning and the aurora borealis were forms of electricity. Medical science was rapidly developed. The first medical school, the first hospital, and the first dispensary ever known in America were established in Philadelphia, which in colonial times and long afterwards was the centre of study for botany, astronomy, natural history, and all the sciences that were pursued in that age.

The general opinion had usually fixed upon Virginia and the Carolinas as the most fertile portions of America and the land from which wealth could be most easily gained. In a certain sense this was true, but not in the way that was expected. It was supposed that those countries would produce a great variety of products, wheat, cattle, hemp, flax, as well as wine, silk, and drugs. But all these were failures in the Carolinas, and rice and indigo, from which nothing had been expected, became the important crops; and in Virginia tobacco absorbed all the efforts and devotion of the people.

Pennsylvania was the only province where there could be a really varied production under the conditions then prevailing. This, however, was not discovered until all the other colonies had been founded except Georgia. Although beginning less than a hundred years before the Revolution and half a century after Virginia, New England, New York, and Maryland had been established, Pennsylvania at the time of the Revolution stood third in population and importance, coming immediately after Virginia and Massachusetts.

Philadelphia increased still more rapidly. For more than a hundred years from the beginning of the colonial period Boston was the largest city in the colonies; but about 1750 Philadelphia was even with her in the race, and soon far surpassed her, remaining the metropolis of the country until excelled by New York in the first half of the nineteenth century.

This remarkable progress, which was primarily caused by the capacity of the province to engage in a varied agriculture combined with lumber, commerce, and manufacturing, was undoubtedly stimulated by the liberal laws, and still more by a circumstance which has not been often noticed.

The other colonies, especially the prominent ones, were held back during the early periods of their existence by the hostility of the Indians. The Virginians for more than fifty years lived under arms in palisadoed plantation houses. In Carolina the people for a long time dared not have a plantation far from the walls of Charleston, and during the seventeenth century the red man kept the New Englanders very closely confined to their trade and fishing on the coast.

But William Penn's famous treaty with the Indians, and the fidelity with which it was always observed, secured for Pennsylvania a long peace of seventy years, which was not broken until the French and Indian wars, which began in 1755.* Instead, therefore, of the massacres, contests, and continual watchfulness which fill the early history of Virginia and New England, the Pennsylvanians were from the beginning perfectly free to develop the interior resources of their province as they pleased. The Indians never caused them a moment's uneasiness; there were no forts or armies, and when the French and Indian invasions began in 1755 it was found that many of the farmers in the interior had no weapons and none of them knew anything of Indian warfare.

The rapid material prosperity which Pennsylvania enjoyed was deprived of its full fruition

---

* See " Pennsylvania : Colony and Commonwealth," chap. vii. p. 98.

by the divided condition of the people, the effects of which are still felt. The western part of the province, peopled largely by Scotch-Irish, felt itself to be a separate community; and at the time of the Whiskey Rebellion in 1791 there were serious thoughts of attempting to make it a separate State. Its people, with Pittsburg for their capital, still speak of themselves as Western Pennsylvanians. The Scotch-Irish always detested the Quakers and their government at Philadelphia, and this feeling survives in a hostility always shown by the country districts towards the city, which often surprises strangers who are unfamiliar with the history of the State. Instead of being regarded as the metropolis of which they can be proud, Philadelphia is looked upon as a rival to be disliked and injured.

The descendants of the Connecticut invaders in the Wyoming Valley in the northeastern part of the State have similar feelings, and also at one time entertained the idea of a separate State; and the Germans are still in many respects a separate community.

This lack of unity and homogeneousness deprived Pennsylvania of that high distinction and ascendency which were enjoyed by Virginia and Massachusetts. The province produced no political leaders of such vital force as the great Virginians and no literary men like those of Massachusetts.

John Dickinson was a Pennsylvanian in the sense that he was born and brought up in Delaware, which in colonial times was part of the province, and came to Philadelphia when a young man to practise law. He had a vast influence in shaping the early course of the Revolution. His " Letters of a Farmer" first aroused the people of the whole continent to an intelligent resistance against the stamp acts and tea acts; and they were the strongest statement of 'the legal relations between the colonies and the mother-country that was made.

From that time until the Declaration of Independence he draughted every important national document and was recognized as one of the most important leaders of the movement. But he refused to vote for the Declaration of Independence because he thought it premature. He wished to postpone it until our arms had met with some success which would induce an alliance with France.

This lost him his popularity and power. Pennsylvania turned against him with that unfortunate disunited habit she has always had of attacking her own important men. He was in effect banished; went to live in Delaware, became a common soldier in the Continental army, and did not appear again in national public life until he was sent by Delaware to the convention of 1787 which framed the Constitution.

Of the other prominent men, Robert Morris was born in England, Franklin in Boston, James Wilson in Scotland, and in later times Albert Gallatin in Switzerland. The prosperity of the State, and especially the advancement and liberality of Philadelphia, attracted able men from other places; but the mixed, confused population could not produce remarkable characters of its own, like the pure and united stocks of Virginia and Massachusetts.

For the same reason Pennsylvania, like New York, was slow in entering the Revolution; but once in, her people were earnest and persevering in the contest. But the extreme aggressiveness which conceived the idea of independence and forced it through originated in Massachusetts and Virginia, where the race was purest and most united.

William Penn, whose enthusiasm created the province of Pennsylvania and brought together in it the most incongruous elements of population that were to be found in any of the British colonies, was a very remarkable man. His character was almost as mixed and various as the population of his colony.

He was born in 1644, the son of Admiral

Quaker Prosperity

Penn, who conquered Jamaica before he was thirty, and passed a life of distinguished service on the seas. After Blake he was the greatest naval officer of the century in England. Between his twenty-third and thirty-first years he passed through the ranks of Rear-Admiral of Ireland, Vice-Admiral of Ireland, Admiral of the Straits, and Vice-Admiral of England. He had accumulated before the close of his life a valuable estate, represented for a time the town of Weymouth in Parliament, and held several of those offices of honor and profit which in that age were so liberally bestowed on the favorites of the crown.

He was determined to rise in his profession, no matter what political party was in power. He served with equal zeal under Cromwell and under Charles II. At the outbreak of the revolution he rightly judged that the popular party would have the best of it, and he joined them. But in 1655 Cromwell sent him in command of a fleet to capture Hispaniola and Jamaica. By that time he had made up his mind that Cromwell's cause was failing, and so soon as he got his fleet together he secretly offered it to Charles, then in exile on the Continent. Charles thanked him, said he had no place to keep a fleet, but that he would remember the offer.

Penn went on with his expedition for Cromwell, and conquered Jamaica; but from that time he took part in the plots for the restoration of Charles, and was largely instrumental in their final success. Neither Charles nor his brother James II. ever forgot these services, and their gratitude played an important part in the career of the admiral and also in the career of his son. Indeed, without this gratitude the son could hardly have secured such an enormous domain in America as Pennsylvania and Delaware, or held it against so much opposition.

If the admiral had any sincere political opinions at all, they were royalist, and arose from his extravagant respect for the aristocracy and his love of the excitements of a courtier's career. When ashore he spent a large part of his time at court, and his position there and in the navy gave him, as he thought, an unusual advantage for advancing his son. He educated him with that intent, and tried to press him on towards preferment.

We have a portrait of young Penn when he was about twenty-two, which has often been reproduced in engravings, and shows a face of most uncommon beauty and attractiveness. But there is about it a gentle, serious cast and a far-away look in the large eyes rather inconsistent with the father's schemes. What was the horror of that father when he discovered that while at Oxford his son had turned religious, and wanted to preach and groan in spirit, and despised the glorious art of war !

Young Penn had been at Christ Church College, where he had shown considerable taste and ability for athletic sports, but he had also attended the preaching of the Quakers and caught the infection. He had not then become a Quaker, but there was enough of it in him to alarm the admiral, and thenceforth the struggle between father and son reads like a comedy. The boy was whipped, and several times disowned and dismissed from the parental roof without a penny except what his mother gave him secretly, and as a last resort he was sent with some of the gay people of that age to travel in France, in the hope that he would pick up something besides fanaticism.

The scheme was partly successful, for, although Penn retained his religion, he added to it some of the qualities his father wished. Pepys describes him, on his return from France, as a " most modish person grown quite a fine gentleman," affecting French speech, gait, and clothes. He had become what we would now call a Franco-maniac.

He had succeeded in combining in himself the characters of religious enthusiast and courtier, and was perfectly sincere in both. He fought with a man in the streets of Paris, disarmed him, and then gave him his life. Soon after his return to England, when Pepys noted the remarkable change in his manners, he was again seized with the religious feeling and his father became alarmed. The remedy that had been successful once was tried again, and the young man was sent to Ireland, where the Lord-Lieutenant at that time kept a court of no little splendor and gayety. For the third time Penn's feelings underwent a change. His melancholy disappeared, he began to take an interest in military affairs, and made himself so useful in quelling a mutiny among the troops that the lord-lieutenant wanted to make him a captain, and Penn came very near accepting.

It was at this time that he had his portrait painted, and it is rather curious that the only picture taken from life that we have of the great Quaker is one in which he is clad in armor and wears the long hair of a cavalier.

But the old feeling soon got the better of him. He went to hear a Quaker preach, and this time the doctrine struck home and he never vacillated again. He formally joined the sect and was once more disowned by his father.

It would require a volume to tell the sufferings and struggles he endured in the early part of his religious career. The Church of England was determined to suppress Quakerism. Penn was often under arrest and often in prison, and he became almost as familiar with the interior of English jails as George Fox or Bunyan.

He was from that time a recognized leader and preacher and the author of numerous theological works. At the same time he passed a large part of his days at court, would dress handsomely on occasions, could be gay and witty, and took part in politics and other things somewhat inconsistent with what is supposed to be Quaker doctrine. So much was this side of his character developed that in spite of his great abilities his sect was at times a little inclined to dispense with his services.

All his life long he showed this double nature, and it was at the same time both his weakness and his strength. His father had been double in politics, belonging first to the roundheads and then to the royalists as suited his plans for advancement. The son belonged both to the world and to religion; not to one after the other, but to both at the same time, and seems to have been perfectly sincere in both.

This ability to combine the religious man with the man of the world—to be, in other words, that apparently impossible combination of qualities, a Quaker courtier—was the keynote of Penn's life and the cause of much advantage to his sect. By his presence, skill, and influence at court he was able to extend the principles of religious liberty and protect the Quakers as well as others who suffered from persecution. He released hundreds of his people from prison. He prevented thousands more from being imprisoned and suffering other indignities. He enlarged the liberty and strengthened the position of the Quakers in every way. Nor did he confine his exertions to his own sect, but spread the wing of his protection over other dissenters, and obtained pardons for political offenders of every sort.

He devoted himself to the whole cause of civil and religious liberty. He wrote pamphlets on it. He could scarcely write a letter without mentioning it. He even went so far as to maintain that it was an advantage to have a multitude of sects; that those nations were most prosperous that allowed the greatest liberty in religious opinions, and he gave Holland as a remarkable instance. Though probably in his heart believing that defensive warfare was excusable, he advocated the settling of all international difficulties by arbitration. He believed in peace congresses which would create an unarmed United States of Europe; and in this he was far in advance of his time.

These principles, it is true, were also part of

the doctrine of his sect; but he was the only man of his sect who could advocate them in the midst of their enemies at court. That he could advance such opinions, and at the same time retain not only his influence, but the respect, confidence, and even affection of royalists and bigots, is a striking proof of his courage and force of character.

He was continually writing books and pamphlets on the questions of his day. His published works fill two large volumes, and range through all the political and religious subjects of that time. Many of them were written in prison, and the three which have been longest remembered—"The Sandy Foundation Shaken," "Innocency with Her Open Face," and "No Cross, No Crown"—were written when he was only twenty-four years old.

"The Sandy Foundation" was an attack on the doctrine of the Trinity as formulated in the subtle metaphysics of the schoolmen. When he was imprisoned for it because he was understood to deny the divinity of Christ, he wrote "Innocency with Her Open Face," in which he explained the Quaker position of denying the metaphysical subtleties of the doctrine of the Trinity without denying the divinity of the Saviour.

"No Cross, No Crown," which was written

in prison about the same time, may be called his one stroke of genius. A deeply religious book, appealing to the religious sentiment of humanity without regard to creed, it seems to have expressed all that was best in the newly awakened feelings of the young cavalier. It has been translated into several languages, and new editions of it are still published.

As governor and proprietor of Pennsylvania he was very liberal and just, and the laws of the province expressed quite fully the advanced ideas which had brought into existence the Quakers. Penn wished to establish a community where government could exist without military force, justice be administered without oaths, and religion sustained without salaried ministers. An expression he used in one of his frames of government was so happy that it is still often quoted. He said that any government was free where the laws ruled and the people were parties to the laws.

He not only permitted religious liberty, but made it a penal offence to deride or annoy any one for a difference in religion. His punishments for crime were unusually mild. Death was inflicted only for murder and treason. This was remarkable when we consider that in England there were over two hundred offences for which death was the punishment, in the colony of New York the same number, and in Massachusetts and South Carolina over twenty. Every county, he said, must contain a prison, and every one of these prisons must be a workhouse and reformatory. He provided that punishments should be graded according to the enormity of the offence, which was a great advance; for it was the opinion of that time that what deserved to be punished at all deserved to be punished severely. There was a feeling that every crime, even the smallest, could be extirpated by thoroughness, and the most thorough methods that could be discovered were torture and death.

These ideas of prison discipline and graded punishments, now so wide-spread but then altogether new, were suggested and advocated by the Quakers at a time when Beccaria and Montesquieu, usually considered the great exponents of them, had not been born.

Penn also dispensed with the old laws by which the estates of murderers and suicides were taken from their families and given to the state, and he abolished primogeniture. But it is rather curious that it did not occur to him to abolish imprisonment for debt. Neither did he attempt to abolish slavery; he apparently thought it a permissible evil. But he made efforts to improve the condition of the negroes and attempted to have a bill passed in the provincial council to introduce marriage among them instead of the promiscuous intercourse which was supposed to be more profitable to their owners. He expressed excellent ideas on the subject of public education, but they were never carried out. Yet he accomplished so much that we should hunt the world over in vain to find another instance of one man putting into actual practice such a high ideal of a commonwealth.

He arranged Pennsylvania to suit himself, mapped it out into manors, counties, and cities, gave names, and directed the lines of future growth. No other colony was so completely the work of one man. He gave instructions that all highways should be straight lines from point to point, and Philadelphia was accordingly laid out on the checker-board plan with narrow streets all at right angles to each other. This unfortunate arrangement has caused great inconvenience in modern times and thwarted many attempts to improve the appearance of the city.

He received altogether a large amount of money from his colony; but during his lifetime there was no net profit to him. He mortgaged or sold all his estates in England and Ireland, and even mortgaged Pennsylvania itself in order to start the colony and carry it through its critical years of infancy. Inspired and enthusiastic with the vastness of his undertaking, he spared nothing, and reduced himself to such straits that he was at one time imprisoned for debt, and died in comparative poverty. But his heirs reaped a rich harvest and were more shrewd in money matters than their ancestor.

Not so reckless and exuberant as in Virginia, nor so repressed and restrained as in New England, the life of the Philadelphia people was full of enjoyment and substantial comfort. The houses were well built, usually of brick, with broad porches, projecting roofs, often with sundials set in the walls, and many of them were surrounded with gardens. The streets were planted with trees, following the original intention of Penn, who wished to have a " green country town" like those with which he was familiar in England. Posts a few feet apart marked the sidewalks, and there were pumps with lamps on them every thirty or forty yards.

Outside of the town a pretty, undulating country spread away to the north and west, covered with farms and innumerable country-seats. Every family of any means had a town-house and a country-house for summer. There was no part of the colonies where this country-seat life flourished as it did near Philadelphia.

Some of these country-houses are still standing,—the Woodlands, Mount Pleasant, Stenton,

Cliveden; but twenty-seven of them were destroyed by the British army when they occupied Philadelphia, and the rest have disappeared under the changes of modern times. They were usually built of stone or brick, in the best forms of the colonial architecture taken from the types of Sir Christopher Wren's school, which was flourishing at that time in England. They had ample grounds round them, often a hundred acres or more, which were cultivated as a farm. But close to the house the landscape gardening and the arrangement of the trees, shrubbery, and walks were in the best English style, and far excelled anything of the sort in other colonies.

These establishments had none of the varied life and rough plenty of the Virginia and Maryland plantation-houses or of the New York manors, and were generally occupied only in summer, like modern country-seats; but there was much entertaining in them, more elegant and formal than in the Southern houses, and some of them, like the Woodlands and Stenton, had fine libraries, works of art, and collections. Everything about them implied considerable wealth and leisure in their owners, and they were a step nearer modern life than the other colonial mansions.

There was less of a distinct aristocratic class than in the South, and less even than in New

MT. PLEASANT
Philadelphia
Built 1762

England. What was called the aristocracy was more like the upper classes of modern times, composed of the respectable, successful, or rich. To these the rest of the people paid a sort of deference, more from the habit which had become fixed in all European minds than from any power the upper classes possessed.

Philadelphia had many other characteristics which showed that the freedom of thought which prevailed in the province had advanced it into ways more like those to which the whole country is now accustomed. The first fire companies were started there, the first circulating library, the first company for insurance against fire, the first legal periodical, and the first bank. There were many good private libraries, and some important publishing houses, which issued editions of Blackstone's " Commentaries," Robertson's " Charles V.," and Ferguson's " Essays," larger enterprises of the kind than were undertaken in the other colonial cities. A general postal service was also attempted, which was extended by Franklin to cover all the colonies, and the Philadelphians often showed a touch of the modern impatience for early news.

Probably in no other place on the continent was the love of bright colors and extravagance in dress carried to such an extreme. Large numbers of the Quakers yielded to it, and even the very strict ones carried gold-headed canes, gold snuff-boxes, and wore great silver buttons on their drab coats and handsome buckles on their shoes. Nowhere were the woman so resplendent in silks, satins, velvets, and brocades, and they piled up their hair mountains high. It often required hours for the public dresser to arrange one of these head-dresses, built up with all manner of stiffening substances and worked into extraordinary shapes. When he was in great demand just before a ball, the ladies whom he first served were obliged to sit up all the previous night and move carefully all day, lest the towering mass should be disturbed.

The markets of Philadelphia were excellent from the beginning, as they still are. There was an immense supply of provisions of all kinds in great variety and of the best quality,—meats, poultry, vegetables, fruits, and the foreign delicacies which the active commerce of the city with all parts of the world supplied. Feasting and gormandizing to the verge of gluttony were the order of every day. There were private dinner-parties and entertainments without end, and all manner of clubs which were merely excuses for epicureanism.

The descriptions of the banquets and feasts, with twenty, thirty, and even a hundred different dishes, washed down by floods of Madeira, ale, and punch, are appalling, and at first incline one to the belief that the physical character of the people must have totally changed. But the same sort of thing was going on in England at that time, and in a less degree in other large American towns. The people led an out-door life, and were not in the nervous, depleted condition produced by the strain of modern life.

Gout was very common, and Dickinson, who drove his coach-and-four and made money rapidly, seems to have had severe attacks of it when comparatively a young man. John Adams, when he came to Philadelphia to the Continental Congress in 1774, fresh from Boston, stood aghast at this life into which he was suddenly thrown, and thought it must be sin. But he rose to the occasion, and, after describing in his diary some of the " mighty feasts" and "sinful feasts" which he attended, says that he drank Madeira "at a great rate" and found no " inconvenience."

Chastellux, our good friend who has given us so many glimpses of colonial life, complained that the breakfasts were very heavy. Loins of veal, legs of mutton, and other substantial dishes at an early hour in the morning were rather staggering to a Frenchman who was accustomed to a cup of coffee and a roll. One of these breakfasts, he says, lasted an hour and a half.

Quaker Prosperity

The drinking habits were also trying to him. They had, he said, the barbarous British practice of drinking each others' healths at a dinner party, calling out names from one end of the table to the other, so that it was difficult to eat or converse while you had to inquire the names or catch the eyes of five and twenty or thirty persons, being incessantly called to on the right and left, or pulled by the sleeve by charitable neighbors, who were so kind as to acquaint you with the politeness you were receiving.

Some would call out four or five names at once. "The bottle is then passed to you, and you must look your enemy in the face, for I can give no other name to the man who exercises such an empire over my will: you wait till he likewise has poured out his wine and taken his glass; you then drink mournfully with him, as a recruit imitates the corporal in his exercise."

At a ball at the French minister's, which he describes, he says it was the custom for a lady to dance with her partner the whole evening,—a severe rule, as he thought, which, however, occasionally admitted of exceptions. The handsomest women were given to the strangers. The Comte de Darnes had Mrs. Bingham for his partner, and the Vicomte de Noailles Miss Shippen; and, to the honor of France, they outdanced Mr. Pendleton, who was a chief-justice, and two members of Congress, one of whom, Mr. Duane, was supposed to be "more lively than all the other dancers."

There was a supper at midnight, and on passing into the room the French minister gave his hand to Mrs. Morris, a precedence which Chastellux says was usually accorded her as the richest woman of the town. The ball continued till two in the morning, but the marquis did not stay to the end. He had been examining the battle-fields round Philadelphia the day before, and had learnt, he says, "to make a timely retreat."

The French minister was certainly a valuable addition to society in Philadelphia, and on July 15, 1782, to celebrate the birthday of the dauphin of France, he gave a grand fête, of which we have an excellent description by Dr. Rush. A wooden dancing-room sixty feet long and forty feet deep was erected in the minister's grounds, open all round for the sake of coolness, the ceiling decorated with emblematic paintings, the garden cut into beautiful walks and divided by cedar and pine branches into artificial groves, seats placed everywhere, and thirty cooks obtained from the French army.

For ten days beforehand nothing was talked of but this ball. The shops were crowded; hair-dressers, tailors, milliners, and mantua-makers were to be seen, covered with sweat and out of breath, in every street. So great was the demand for the gentlemen of the comb that some ladies were obliged to have their hair dressed between four and six in the morning.

Half-past seven in the evening was the hour fixed for the entertainment, and as the time approached carriages thronged the streets, every window was filled with spectators, and nearly ten thousand of them gathered round the minister's house. Filled with French ideas of liberty and equality, and enthusiastic over the happy close of the American Revolution, the minister was not unmindful of this crowd. He had arranged the fence so that they could all look through it, and he would have distributed among them two pipes of Madeira and six hundred dollars in small change if some of the prominent people, fearing a riot, had not dissuaded him; so the money was given to the prisoners in the jail and the patients in the hospital.

As he entered the pavilion with his family, Dr. Rush found seven hundred people in the most brilliant and varied dresses, all ranks, parties, professions, and officers of government; the most learned mingled with those "who knew not whether Cicero pleaded in Greek or Latin, or whether Horace was a Roman or a Scotchman." Merchants and gentlemen, tradesmen

and lawyers, Whigs and those who formerly
had been Tories, governors, generals, congress-
men, judges, ministers of finance with their suites
and secretaries, made up the incongruous mixture, which nevertheless was in perfect harmony, because, as the doctor assures us, it was
truly republican, and pride and ill nature were
forgotten.

He saw Washington and Dickinson conversing
with each other, and Dickinson and Morris
frequently reclined against the same pillar.
The war was the great subject of reminiscence
and discussion, and men who had taken part in
every stage of it were there. Rutledge and
Walton from the South hobnobbed with Lincoln
and Duane from the North, and Tom Paine
wandered about analyzing his thoughts and enjoying the repast of his own ideas. Mifflin
and Reed accosted each other as if they had
always been friends. An Indian chief in his
savage dress and war-paint stood beside Count
Rochambeau in his splendid uniform, and talked
with him as if they had been the subjects of the
same government.

The heat was so intense on that July night
that few were willing to dance; but there were
fireworks, refreshments of cake, fruits, and
drinks continually served, and at midnight a
grand supper under three large tents. The

minister, the Chevalier de la Luzerne, passed about, addressing himself to every lady ; and so careful was he of every one's pleasure that he had provided a private room, where through a gauze curtain the strict Quaker ladies could see without indulging in the entertainment.

It seems to have been a principle with the chevalier that true republicanism included temperance and extreme decorum and good breeding. So far was this carried that Dr. Rush mentions it as marring the occasion, for the Philadelphians of that day were not accustomed to such a lack of "convivial noise." They complained that the people behaved more as if they were worshipping than eating. Everybody, it was said, felt pleasure, but it was of too tranquil a nature. Several people had prepared odes and songs, but there was no encouragement to produce them.

When the actual fighting of the Revolution began, and prices rose, giving opportunities for speculation of all sorts, the extravagance and recklessness in Philadelphia reached extraordinary heights. Afterwards, when the town became the seat of government, and Washington with his officials and the diplomats were living there, the luxury and display impressed Frenchmen like Rochefoucauld as very remarkable.

In colonial times the hour for fashionable

dinner-parties seems to have varied from noon until six o'clock, which is significant of the leisure and easy life the people must have enjoyed. The famous dinner given by Chief-Justice Chew, which Adams describes, was at four. Chastellux describes the fashionable hour as at five; and he says that calls and visits were paid in the morning. But there seem to have been also afternoon visits with much tea-drinking. In the evening the suppers began among the men; and they were heavy meals, almost banquets, at the taverns and clubs, with hard drinking and informal talk and discussion.

In previous years there had been another chance at funerals, which, as in New England, implied eating and drinking, with the distribution of scarfs and rings. It was the fashion for enormous numbers of people to attend funerals, —in some instances, it is said, several thousand, —and a long procession, mostly on horseback, followed the body to the grave. These extravagances were stopped in 1764 in all the Northern colonies by what would now be called a reform movement.

A wedding was another occasion which could not be allowed to pass unimproved, and even the Quakers indulged in great festivity. The banns were twice pronounced, and after each proclamation there was often a reception; and the wedding entertainment itself sometimes lasted two days, during which the parents of the bride kept open house.

In the midst of all this there was a great deal that was provincial and also simple in the best sense of the word. In summer, in Philadelphia, the young ladies appeared in full dress in the evenings and sat on the front door-steps, while the young men passed about, paying visits. A similar custom prevailed in Baltimore until long after the civil war. Although there were carpets in some of the houses, sanded floors were very common. Many of the people resisted the introduction of carpets, because they gathered dust and could not be easily and often cleaned. A bare floor scrubbed every day and sprinkled with fresh sand was best, they said, for all respectable people.

THE SHREVE HOMESTEAD · MT·PLEASANT · N·J·

CHAPTER VII

NOVA CÆSAREA

IN New Jersey, which the Indians called Scheyichbi, and the Dutch Achter Kol, we find faint and faded impressions of the colonies which were near by. Her people were a mixture of those who had created Pennsylvania, New York, and New England. But no one element of the population acquired exclusive control, as the Quakers did in Pennsylvania.

The province, mountainous in the north, and with a great deal of land which was evidently fertile, sloped off towards the east and south, with level sandy plains covered with a dense growth and interspersed with cedar swamps. Some of this southern land was valuable, especially for fruit and vegetables, but this use of it was not then fully available.

The province had the most obvious natural boundaries of any of the colonies. The Atlantic Ocean and the Hudson River on the east, and the Delaware River and Bay on the west and south, left only one artificial line to be drawn for the northern boundary from the upper part of the Delaware to the Hudson.

But New Jersey was not believed to contain any large quantity of fertile land, nor to be capable of furnishing gold, timber, fur, or any of the things that were eagerly sought by the worldly, and it so happened that no sect of religious enthusiasts chose it for a refuge.

The Dutch at New York took no interest in it, although it was within what they called New Netherland. They confined themselves to following up the valley of the Hudson towards the source of the fur supply, which was the chief object of their ambition. A few of them occupied Pavonia, on the present site of Jersey City; but they left few descendants there, and were not an important element of the population.

The Swedes who trespassed on the dominions of the Dutch on the Delaware usually preferred the Pennsylvania side of the river; but a few of them settled on the marshes and meadow lands of the Jersey side from Salem up almost opposite to Philadelphia, especially at Raccoon Creek, near the present village of Bridgeport, opposite to Chester.

Nothing more in the way of settlement was accomplished until Charles II., in order to have an excuse for seizing New York from the Dutch, in 1664 granted to his brother the Duke of York all the land between the Connecticut River and the Delaware. The duke kept the Hudson for himself, and gave to Lord Berkeley and Sir George Carteret the country between the Delaware and the ocean, "hereafter to be called," as the grant said, "by the name or names of Nova Cæsarea or New Jersey."

A few years afterwards, in 1676, Berkeley and Carteret divided the province between them by a line beginning at Little Egg Harbor, at the lower end of Barnegat Bay, and crossing diagonally to the northern waters of the Delaware a few miles below Milford. This made two colonies; East Jersey, on the New York side of the line, belonging to Carteret, and West Jersey, on the Pennsylvania side, belonging to Berkeley. But before this dividing line was finally decided upon, the two proprietors seem to have agreed that Carteret should have the part near New York and Berkeley the part on the Delaware.

Carteret was soon successful in getting people to settle in the neighborhood of Newark Bay. There were already Dutchmen there and a few Danes, and by these Danes the name Bergen, from a town of Norway, is said to have been given to the country; but why the Danes should have given a Norwegian name is not apparent.

These Danes, so called, may have been Norwegians. Denmark and Norway were united at that time, and Denmark being the more important, it may have been the custom to speak of all the people as Danes. The name still survives in one of the counties, the town of Bergen, and Bergen Point.

These Dutch and Danes were living in small villages, from which they went out to cultivate their fields, and the reason was the same which compelled the early New Englanders to this sort of life,—namely, fear of the Indians, who were very hostile in that neighborhood.

Puritans from Long Island established themselves at what is now Elizabeth just about the time of the grant to Berkeley and Carteret, and after the grant many more came in, some from Long Island and the rest from various parts of New England, establishing the New England town system. Scotch were added and also immigrants direct from England, until there were flourishing little villages,—Elizabeth, Newark, Middletown, and Shrewsbury.

Carteret appointed a relative, Philip Carteret, to be governor, who came out and lived at Elizabeth, sending agents into New England to encourage settlers to come to him. He remained at Elizabeth from 1665 until his death in 1682, governing by means of a council and a general

PYNE HOUSE
Princeton, N. J.

assembly elected by the people, and having considerable trouble with his people, who were dis united and unruly. Andros, who ruled New York, disputing his authority on one occasion, sent armed men to Elizabeth, who seized him and brought him a prisoner to Manhattan.

Lord Berkeley, who had West Jersey for his share, soon sold it to John Fenwick in trust for Edward Byllinge. Fenwick came out in 1675, and settled a few families at what is now Salem, on the Delaware. Byllinge, the real owner, was bankrupt, and turned over West Jersey to his creditors, appointing William Penn and some others to hold it in trust for them. This was Penn's first experience in American affairs, and a few years afterwards he received the grant of Pennsylvania. He and his co-trustees arranged with Carteret in 1676 the dividing line which has been mentioned.

They also sold a number of shares in West Jersey, and the purchasers prepared to establish settlements. Most of them were Quakers, and the story is told that as they lay at anchor in the Thames waiting to start, Charles II. came by in his barge, stopped alongside to look at them, and being told that they were Quakers, gave them his blessing. But whether he intended it as a courtly joke or whether they valued the blessing of such a man we are not told.

They reached the Delaware and proceeded up
it to Raccoon Creek, on the Jersey side, about a
dozen miles below the present site of Philadelphia, and landed among the Swedes, who took
care of them in their barns and out-houses, where
they were obliged to live for a time with snakes
under the floors. They purchased from the Indians the land from Old Man's Creek, a little
below Raccoon Creek, where they landed, up to
Timber Creek, near the present Gloucester;
from there to Rancocas Creek, and thence to
Assunpink, where Trenton now stands. Their
final settlement was made at a place they first
called New Beverley, then Bridlington; afterwards they gave it its present name, Burlington.

They found that fruit of all kinds would grow
in the greatest profusion. In Smith's History
some of the letters which these early colonists
wrote home are preserved, and they describe
the peaches and apples breaking down the limbs
with their weight, wild berries and nuts, with
great abundance of game. They had discovered
the cranberries which are still so plentiful in the
Jersey swamps, and were already making cran-
berry sauce for wild turkey and venison.

Other immigrants arrived, some going to the
colony at Salem which Fenwick had established,
and some to Burlington, and these two towns
composed the province of West Jersey.

Nova Cæsarea

For many years game and the wild fruits seem to have been the principal source of food, and in winter those who had no gun or had run out of ammunition were often in danger of starving. The family of John Hollingshead, on Rancocas Creek, being in great distress in the winter of 1682, their son, a lad of thirteen, killed two wild turkeys with a stick. Soon after the dogs chased a buck, which, attempting to cross on the ice of the creek, could not keep its footing with its smooth hoofs. When it fell on its side, young Hollingshead mounted its back, and kept his seat through its struggles until he killed it with his knife.

In 1687 the crops failed and the people were in great want. Some lived entirely on fish, and others, who were not near the water, on herbs. Fortunately, a vessel laden with grain arrived in the river from England. Finding a good market, vessels afterwards came with similar cargoes every year, and we hear no more of famine.

The proprietor of East Jersey, Sir George Carteret, died in 1679, and by his will left directions that his province should be sold, and William Penn and eleven others became the purchasers. They published an account of the country and succeeded in increasing the number of settlers, obtaining many from Scotland, who established themselves in the neighborhood of

Nova Cæsarea

Perth Amboy, named from the Scottish Earl of Perth and an Indian word which meant a point.

The new proprietors were Quakers, and they appointed Robert Barclay to be governor for life. He was the author of the famous book known as Barclay's "Apology," which has usually been regarded as the ablest of all the statements of Quaker doctrine. He remained in England and appointed deputies to go out and govern the colony. He seems to have ruled the colony in this way until his death, eight years afterwards.

East Jersey in the year 1682 contained about three thousand five hundred people. Most of them were collected about Newark Bay, with some scattered in the direction of the Shrewsbury River and Sandy Hook. Bergen, the oldest town, was inhabited principally by Dutch, who had come from New York many years before, and it was strongly fortified against the Indians.

The people lived on fish and oysters, and had small farms. The oysters they found growing wild on all the coast from Newark round to Cape May. Fish were also abundant, and in a letter of the time we read that "Barnegat or Burning Hole is said to be a very good place for fishing." But they could be taken anywhere with the greatest ease in all the East Jersey waters, and the people commonly fished

" with long sieves or long nets, and will catch with a sieve sometimes two barrels a day of good fish." There seems to have been none of the danger of famine in winter time which we read of in West Jersey.

The East Jersey people seem to have been a little free with their weapons about the year 1686, or else their peace-loving Quaker rulers were disposed to be strict with them. People, it is said, were put in great fear from quarrels and challenges, and a law was passed forbidding any one, under penalty of fine and imprisonment, to challenge, or wear pocket-pistols, skeins, stilladers, daggers, or dirks.

The numerous proprietors of both the Jerseys were a source of great confusion in the government of those provinces. Each promoted his own schemes and interests, and parties and cliques among them were constantly interfering with one another. It was difficult for them to agree on a governor; and when it was attempted to have both sets of proprietors agree on one governor for both provinces, the difficulties were increased. The remedy suggested was for the proprietors to surrender their governmental rights to the Crown, and make the two provinces into one under a royal governor. This was accomplished in 1702, just after Queen Anne had ascended the throne.

Nova Cæsarea

Lord Cornbury was immediately appointed the royal governor, with a council to assist him and an assembly elected by the people to make laws. This assembly was to meet alternately at Perth Amboy and at Burlington.

The proprietors had surrendered to the Crown only their right to govern, and still retained their ownership of the land, and the people always maintained that they also were entitled to the enjoyment of the rights and privileges they had had before the surrender. These two questions of the rights retained by the proprietors and the rights retained by the people became the subject of much contention, both proprietors and people struggling for the preservation of their privileges against the encroachments of the governor.

Cornbury, who was also governor of New York, was a violent, self-willed, injudicious man. He had the right to adjourn the assembly whenever he pleased, and he made free use of it. In the very beginning of his government he kept adjourning the assembly till one was elected which suited him and passed the laws he wanted.

But it was seldom he could have an assembly of this sort. Most of them were hostile, and protested against his rule, his long absences in New York, and his neglect of the affairs of the province. Convicted murderers, it is said, were allowed to go unpunished and wander about at large. He compelled the people from all parts of the province to go to Burlington to probate wills and transact all other business of the government. He granted monopolies, established arbitrary fees, and prohibited the proprietors' agents from selling land in West Jersey. He had also taken upon himself to pass upon the qualifications of members of the assembly, and had refused to allow three who had been duly elected to be sworn ; and finally he was charged with having been bribed by interested persons to dissolve the assembly.

At the same time that the assembly was protesting the proprietors appealed to the Lords of Trade in England against Cornbury's arbitrary administration, and Cornbury, through his council, appealed to the queen against the disloyal, factious, and turbulent people, as he called them. But he was soon recalled, to the great relief of every one, after a most unfortunate administration of six years.

Lord Lovelace, his successor, was popular, and seemed to be undoing all the evil of Cornbury ; but he died in about a year. The province, however, enjoyed quieter times, although there was always plenty of wrangling and disputes with governors, and in 1738 the people obtained a governor of their own instead of sharing with New York. In 1763 William Franklin, an illegitimate son of Benjamin Franklin, became governor, and held the office until the Revolution.

Jersey had no frontier near the French and hostile Indians. She was completely shut in by Pennsylvania and New York, and, like Rhode Island, she felt none of the sharp experience of those long wars which were such a discipline and training for the other provinces.

Her people who lived near New York partook largely of the Dutch ways. Their houses had the Dutch stoops or porches with seats, where the family and their visitors sat on summer evenings to smoke and gossip, while the cows with their tinkling bells wandered about the streets. Long Dutch spouts extended out from the eaves to discharge the rain-water into the street. In some villages there was a touch of New England life, and small towns can still be found in some parts of the State with neat white houses and broad shaded streets like their prototypes in Massachusetts and Connecticut. In West Jersey, along the Delaware, Quaker habits and methods were conspicuous.

The colony had no seats of commerce of her own. Her trade in wheat and provisions all went out by way of New York and Philadelphia. Her long line of sea-coast with dangerous inlets and bars offered no good harbors, and the places where there were good harbors on New York Bay or on the Delaware were close to the important marts of other colonies.

The people were engaged almost exclusively in farming. Each farmer's family raised almost everything they needed—their provisions, fruit, and tobacco—and wove their own clothes. The towns and villages were few and small.

The aristocratic class, which was always more or less vigorous in the other colonies, was of very little importance in New Jersey. There were some gentlemen farmers who were recognized as a sort of aristocracy, but class distinctions were not sharply marked.

There were not many indented servants, but there were a considerable number of slaves, and these slaves were very much dreaded. Several insurrections were attempted by them, and the laws against them were as severe as in the Southern colonies. For murder they were burned at the stake, in the presence of as many of their race as could be collected to witness the spectacle. One instance is recorded of a slave condemned to be hung, who first had his right hand cut off and burnt before his eyes.* In an old account-book of Essex County there

---

* Melick's "Old Farm," p. 225.

are several entries of the cost of wood for burning slaves, as, for example :

"June 4 1741 Daniel Harrison sent in his account of wood carted for burning two negroes. Allowed cur'y 0.11.0." (Hatfield's "History of Elizabeth," p. 364.)

The colonial custom in all the Northern colonies of entertaining expensively at funerals prevailed in New Jersey, and we find in the history of Elizabeth some details of the general movement which checked the excess and extravagance in 1764. Fifty heads of prominent families agreed among themselves to cut down the expense. Thomas Clark, a judge, who died in 1765, was buried in the new manner, and the newspapers reported, as a matter worthy of notice, that there was no drinking at his funeral.

The religious tone of the colony, except in West Jersey, which was largely Quaker, was controlled by the Scotch Presbyterians and New England Congregationalists, and they, of course, were strongly inclined to prohibit amusements.

The province was always disunited, and lacked the marked individuality which was so conspicuous in the others. The part near the Hudson was like New York, and the part near the Delaware like Pennsylvania. Princeton

College, which was established in 1746, was the result of a movement among the Presbyterians at large, in New York as well as in East Jersey, and was not in the full sense a Jersey institution growing out of the natural inclinations of the people, like Harvard in Massachusetts or William and Mary in Virginia.

New Jersey is still divided, but the line is not the same as the old one which the proprietors agreed upon. The divisions are now North and South Jersey, and the Pennsylvania Railroad from Trenton to Jersey City is supposed to mark the division quite accurately. North of the railroad is the hill country, and south of it the flat or tide-water district, as it is sometimes called; and the people of the two divisions are quite unlike, socially, economically, and intellectually. Close to the line the different types merge, and Trenton contains both.

Liberty Hall, Elizabethtown, N.J

END OF VOL. I.

MEN, WOMEN
& MANNERS
IN COLONIAL
TIMES

VOLUME II

BY SYDNEY GEO. FISHER

ROGER MORRIS HOUSE
High Bridge, N. Y.
Built 1764

MEN, WOMEN & MANNERS IN COLONIAL TIMES

BY

SYDNEY GEO. FISHER

ILLUSTRATED WITH PHOTOGRAVURES
AND WITH DECORATIONS BY
EDWARD STRATTON HOLLOWAY

VOL. II

PHILADELPHIA & LONDON
J. B. LIPPINCOTT COMPANY
1898

TABLE OF CONTENTS

VOL. II

LIST OF PHOTOGRAVURES

VOL. II

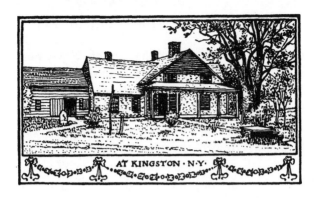

AT KINGSTON · N·Y·

CHAPTER VIII

MANHATTAN AND THE TAPPAN ZEE

IN the days of Columbus and Verrazzano the shores of New York Harbor were shadowed by goodly oak-trees and inhabited by swarms of red men, who dressed in garments made of the feathers of birds, with strings of copper round their necks. They rushed to the shore with delight to welcome the first white men, "raising loud shouts of admiration and showing us where we could most securely land with our boat."

They must have seemed comical enough, these red men in their feathers looking like half-picked chickens; and the Dutch who succeeded them were also funny fellows.

In the vast sweep of the coast of North and South America for ten thousand miles along the Atlantic there is no spot equal to this narrow entrance between high hills which now

9

opens into the bay and harbor of New York with its cities and teeming millions. Spaniards, Portuguese, Dutchmen, Frenchmen, and Englishmen were searching from Greenland to Cape Horn for gold and the passage to China. The Spaniards robbed the temples of Mexico and Peru, and spread themselves along the West Indies, the Amazon, and the Paraguay, laughing at the Frenchman struggling with the ice and snow of the St. Lawrence, and the Englishman in the swamps of Virginia. Each believed he had the best; but the nation that secured that narrow entrance where the red men dressed in feathers would have it all.

Fortunately for mankind and civilization, Columbus discovered only the West Indies and South America, and left the North American continent free from the curse of the Spaniard. If when he set out from Palos he had adhered strictly to his theory and steered due west, he would have reached some point on the coast of North Carolina or Virginia, Spanish migration and conquest would have followed him, and the history of the United States would be very different from what it is. But from Palos he sailed far to the southwest to the Canary Islands; thence he took a westward course, and if he had maintained it he would still have reached the North American continent at some point in

Florida or Georgia. But when near the New World he followed the flight of birds, and sailed again towards the southwest, which took him and Spanish civilization to the West Indies, Mexico, and South America.

He never saw the North American continent, and died without knowing of its existence. The birds had shaped a mighty destiny. In 1497, five years after Columbus's first voyage, John and Sebastian Cabot discovered North America for England, an event of vaster significance and benefit in the progress of mankind and more worthy to be celebrated than the accident which inflicted Spanish cruelty, rapacity, and failure on the continent of South America.

A hundred years after the Cabots had given North America to Great Britain, the Dutch, having freed themselves from the dominion of Spain, became enterprising explorers ; and Henry Hudson, an Englishman in their employ, entered both the Delaware and the Hudson River in the year 1609. By the merest good luck, England had only two years before, in 1607, taken advantage of the discovery of the Cabots to establish the Virginia colony at Jamestown, and had made a grant to the Virginia company of all the land from South Carolina to Halifax. This saved her title to the continent under the discovery of the Cabots, which might have lapsed from failure to make a settlement and take actual possession. The Dutch were just too late. But, relying on Hudson's expedition, they claimed a right to all the territory near the two great rivers into which he had sailed.

That the English title was superior to the Dutch is now no longer doubted, and the question has been authoritatively settled by the courts of New York. It seems strange that the ancient Dutch occupation and the voyages of the Cabots and Hudson should become practical questions of modern times in a litigation of the New York elevated railways.

But even the law must have its romance, and in 1889 some owners of property on the Bowery brought a suit for damages against the Elevated Railway Company for cutting off the light, air, and access to their buildings. The railway replied that the Bowery was an old Dutch street which had been laid out and property sold upon it when the Dutch nation had lawful jurisdiction in New York, and under the Dutch law there could be no damages for cutting off light, air, and access. But the court decided that the Dutch had never had lawful possession of New York; their occupation was a mere trespass and intrusion on the English title, which had originated in the discovery of the Cabots, and had been perfected by the grant and settlement of Virginia.*

In the year 1609, however, England had not fully awakened to her colonial opportunities, and allowed the Dutch to occupy the Hudson and the Delaware, and the French the St. Lawrence, without opposition. Against these two powerful nations, occupying important points on the continent, the British had only the miserable little colony in Virginia, dying of fever and ague.

The Dutch established themselves on the shores of the Hudson and the Delaware with a vigor which seemed to show that they would be the rulers of America. Brave little Holland had at that time only about two millions of people living at the mouth of the river Rhine, on a morass they had saved from the water by dikes, which they watched day and night. Their way was in the sea and their paths in the great waters. They built a thousand new ships every year, and the commerce of the world was at their feet.

At first their purpose at Manhattan and on the Delaware was merely to collect furs from the Indians, and they made no settlements.

---

* Mortimer *vs.* N. Y. Elevated R. R., 6 N. Y. Supplement, 898.

They had not the strong instinct of the English for establishing themselves in a new country. They were traders, and their idea of colonization was merely to assist the commerce of Holland, and not to build a new empire. They pushed their explorations rapidly, but only where they could follow the water, and they made few attempts to penetrate inland.

Adriaen Block's ship, the Tiger, was burnt at Manhattan; but in the winter of 1613 he built a small vessel, forty-four feet long, called the Onrust, or Restless, with which he sailed into Long Island Sound. The whirlpool in the East River he named Hellegat, from a branch of the river Scheldt, in Zealand, and passed on as far eastward as Martha's Vineyard, naming the Connecticut the Versch, or Fresh River, calling Narragansett Bay, Nassau, and leaving his own name to Block Island. Cornelius Mey explored the Delaware and gave his name to one of its capes.

The company of merchants who had been given by the States General of Holland the exclusive right of trading in New Netherlands, as their American possessions were called, had no political power like the English colonizing companies. They were merely armed traders, who occupied the country for the purpose of securing its furs and products. But every English company was given a distinct political government, and this difference is significant of the qualities of the two nations and their instinctive intentions.

The Dutch were very peculiar people. Thrifty, shrewd, enterprising in everything relating to commerce, ingenious in labor-saving devices, and with a very practical sort of intelligence, there was nevertheless a pleasing love of ease about them which was sometimes almost comic. They were liberal in their opinions, and less inclined than the other nations of Europe to tyranny or intolerance. They loved to contemplate their comfort and prosperity while they smoked their pipes, and they were willing that the rest of the world should enjoy the same pleasure. Although frank in speech, they paid most extravagant compliments and gave flattering titles to everybody, and they were very fond of firing salutes and sending important messages by a trumpeter. When they corresponded with the little colony of the Pilgrim Fathers at Plymouth, their letter began, " Noble, Worshipful, Wise, and Prudent Lords, our Very Dear Friends."

They fought heroically for their independence against the Spaniard, and won the gratitude of the civilized world by driving him out of Northern Europe. But, their independence once attained, they settled down to the substantial enjoyment of it and the commerce of the Indian seas, and have remained in that happy state ever since. They had no passion for conquest, and were not wandering over the earth with empires in their brains, like the Englishmen.

Their restful, contemplative qualities have been valuable material for humorous writers of other nations. The temptation to exaggerate them is almost irresistible, and immortalized Washington Irving in Mr. Knickerbocker's most veracious " History of New York."

When evening came upon the ocean a Dutch ship, we are told, always lay to, and the crew went to bed until morning. When a storm was approaching, the Dutch sailors climbed aloft to shorten sail, smoking their pipes, and in Holland distances were often measured by pipes instead of miles. Mr. Knickerbocker tells us how his ancestor, who was appointed to build a great cathedral, laid in as a preliminary a large stock of pipes and many pounds of the best Virginia tobacco, which he smoked peacefully for a year, contemplating the details of his mighty task before he began it.

When the privileges of the merchants who had been given the control of New Netherland expired, efforts were made to charter another and more powerful organization to take their place, and in 1621 the great West India Company was established. There was already an East India Company, which controlled the Dutch trade and colonization in the seas of Asia, and to the West India Company were given America and Africa. By these two great corporations the Dutch hoped to accomplish their designs on the commerce of the world.

The English, with sounder instinct and foresight, created companies for each one of their colonies, and in each one of these the colonists themselves had an interest, and in some instances almost the entire control. But the West India Company was a vast armed commercial monopoly, with an admiral and a fleet to rule everything Dutch on two continents, and destroy the power of Spain and Portugal on the sea. It could subdue, colonize, govern, make treaties with native states and princes, build forts, appoint and discharge governors and officers, administer justice, promote trade, and encourage settlers, and all for the benefit of itself and the trade it should bring to the ports of Holland. There was no provision for popular assemblies or legislatures, which were given to all the British colonies except Georgia, nor were the Dutch colonists to have the right to vote in any form.

As an assistance to Holland in fighting Spain

the West India Company was very successful. It captured and sunk the Spanish vessels and robbed them of the gold and silver they were bringing from South America; but in other respects it was a failure, and ended its career in bankruptcy and ruin.

From the time of the discovery of the Hudson and the Delaware, in 1609, until 1626, the Dutch had used those rivers merely as places to collect furs. But the West India Company now attempted to establish a permanent colony, and, seeing the evident advantage of Manhattan Island as the seat of commerce for the whole continent, they bought it for themselves. Farms were laid out on the land now covered by the streets of New York; the point of land where the East River flows into the Hudson was fortified, and still retains its name of the Battery; and the people built their little houses behind it, near Wall Street.

It was an ideal spot for such traders as the Dutch, for Long Island, or Sewanhackey, so near at hand, was the mint of the Indians, where the wampum, or sewan, was manufactured from shells and distributed to all the country. The Dutch, by their close neighborhood, could purchase it cheap and use it to buy furs from the northern tribes.

The ruler of the colony was called the director,

who was instructed to govern as a father, and not as an executioner of the people. He had his council to give him advice, a koopman, or secretary, and the schout, who was a combination of sheriff and prosecuting attorney. Only Dutch vessels were allowed to trade with the colony or in any of the dominions of the company, and in this respect the Spanish colonial system seems to have been imitated.

Among the first settlers were some Walloons, French Protestants who had lived between Belgium and France, where they spoke the old French language and had been savagely persecuted. They settled on a bay at the northwestern extremity of Long Island called Wahle Bocht, or bay of foreigners, and now corrupted into Wallabout. Here the first child of the settlement was born, Sarah Rapelje, a name still known in New York.

The settlement subsequently extended itself to the western extremity of Long Island, and was called Breukelen, after a Dutch village on the Vecht.

But New Netherland did not thrive; it barely supported itself; and the returns from it, contrasted with the spoil from Spanish fleets, disgusted the directors of the West India Company. Colonists did not flock to it as to the English colonies. The lower classes of Holland were too thrifty and contented to care to risk themselves in a wilderness. They had no means to buy extensive tracts of land from the West India Company, and they did not care to come out on chance or sell themselves as redemptioners, like the bustling and apparently reckless Englishmen.

The company accordingly attempted to people New Netherland with capitalists, rich men who, in exchange for a large tract of land and the title of patroon, would agree to establish a little settlement of fifty people. A patroon who should succeed in establishing a city or town was to be given power to rule it and appoint the officers and magistrates; and he was given almost absolute power over his tract of land, and none of his people could leave his service without his consent.

All New Netherland was to be taken up in this way by patroons except the island of Manhattan, which the company reserved for itself; and to Manhattan must be brought all cargoes, to pay the duty of five per cent. before they were sent to Europe. The trade in furs the company kept for itself, and any fish the patroons exported must pay a duty of three guilders a ton.

This system of feudalism was more aristocratic than that in Holland itself. The colonists of New Netherland were held down by a feudal as well as a mercantile monopoly. The mere statement of this condition of affairs shows at once the inefficiency of the Dutch as compared with the English colonial system, under which individual liberty, the right to vote, and representative government were freely allowed; and yet some of the descendants of the Dutch undertake to maintain that their ancestors introduced liberty and republican government in the United States.

There were many Dutch merchants who, having made fortunes in trade, were unable to join the landed aristocracy of Holland because the old nobility held nearly all the land outside of the towns, and were unwilling to part with any of it. The colonial patroon system appealed directly to this class, and a few of them, who also fulfilled the required condition of being members of the West India Company, took advantage of it. The intention, no doubt, was to turn large numbers of the rich Dutch middle classes into a colonial aristocracy, who would people, in time, the whole country. But the system defeated itself.

Kiliaen Van Rensselaer, a polisher of pearls and diamonds, secured for himself a large tract on the west side of the Hudson, near Albany. Michael Pauw obtained Staten Island and a tract called Hoboken Hacking, opposite Manhattan, where Jersey City now stands; and Pauw gave the name Pavonia to his great manor. Godyn and Blommaert had manors assigned them on the Delaware, near Cape May and Cape Henlopen.

Pavonia afforded Washington Irving much material for his history. When Argall, an English captain from Virginia, came to Manhattan to protest against the Dutch occupation of the country, the Pavonians, Irving says, smoked their pipes so violently that Argall, seeing nothing but what he supposed was a dense fog over Pavonia, never went near it.

These patroons were all directors in the company, had used their official position to obtain the best grants for themselves, and the indignation of the stockholders soon compelled them to disgorge. Van Rensselaer divided three-fifths of his manor with Moussart, Bissels, Laet, and others, and Godyn and Blommaert were also obliged to admit partners. But after all the dividing the result was that the land of New Netherland was in the possession of a few rich men, and immigrants were discouraged, for their condition would be a species of serfdom, with no prospect of advancement on what they already enjoyed in Holland.

A few settlers, however, were induced to come to the manors, and so far as the colony

was a mere trading station, it may be said to
have flourished. The furs sent to Holland,
which had been worth forty-six thousand guilders in 1626, were worth one hundred and forty-
three thousand in 1632. One ship is said to
have taken to Amsterdam a cargo of five thousand beaver skins. But agriculture languished;
for the Dutch, or Swannekens, as the Indians
called them, were such inveterate traders that
they regarded a farm merely as a place on which
to drive bargains.

In the course of time Van Rensselaer's patroonship became prosperous, and, in fact, it was
the only one which was at first successful. The
people are described as living amid the greatest
profusion of everything, cultivating grain on rich
land which was backed by forests full of turkeys
and deer. Nuts and blackberries were abundant,
and wild strawberries so plentiful that the jolly
Swannekens went out into the fields " to lie
down and eat them."

The more we examine the original records of
New Netherland which the patient research
of Mr. Brodhead has given us, the more the
comic side becomes apparent. It is rather interesting to read these original sources and then
turn to see how far they support Irving's statements in his Knickerbocker's " History of New
York." He has exaggerated them, of course, and

introduced at times imaginary incidents to help out the drollery; but in many cases the exaggeration is comparatively slight, and he could have amused his readers by an almost literal account of what happened or by reprinting the original records, some of which are more quaint and amusing than anything his genius could invent.

Van Rensselaer was always proud to call himself the "first and oldest patroon," and, finding all sorts of interlopers interfering in his exclusive trade in furs, he resolved to protect his monopoly by force. He built a little fort on Beeren Island, at the southern end of his patroonship, and appointed the good Nicholas Koom as "wachtmeister," to defend his staple right at Rensselaer's Stein, as he called the fort. Koom was to collect a toll of five guilders on all vessels except those of the West India Company passing the fort, and compel them to strike their colors in homage.

Soon afterwards Govert Loockermans, in his yacht the Good Hope, was passing down the river, when a shot from the fort aroused him.

"Strike thy colors!" shouted Koom from the shore.

"For whom shall I strike?" replied Schipper Loockermans.

"For the staple right of Rensselaer's Stein."

"I strike for nobody but the Prince of

Orange or those by whom I am employed," said the valiant schipper.

Koom then loaded with ball, and the first shot went through the sail and shrouds, a second passed overhead, and the third pierced the princely colors. But Loockermans kept on. Irving has given the incident almost as it stands in the old record, and then adds that the only effect of the shots was to make Loockermans draw more vehemently on his pipe, and for miles he could be tracked down the Hudson by his fierce whiffs of smoke.

The three principal Governors of New Netherland—Wouter Van Twiller, William Kieft, and Peter Stuyvesant—are called by Irving Walter the Doubter, William the Testy, and Peter the Headstrong, and the most accurate historian could not improve very much on that description. Van Twiller, Irving tells us, was an elderly man, descended from a long line of burgomasters who had dozed away their lives on the bench of magistracy in Rotterdam; but the actual origin of Van Twiller would have lent itself equally well to Irving's purposes.

He had been a clerk in the West India Company's office, had married a niece of Van Rensselaer, the pearl polisher, and had been employed by the patroon in shipping cattle to the colony.

He was a most ridiculously irresolute and ignorant man to be put in charge of an important province, over which he had complete power, without any assembly of the people to check him.

He had scarcely finished smoking his first pipe after arriving on Manhattan Island when an English vessel arrived, whose supercargo, or koopman, was one Jacob Eelkens, who had formerly been in the service of the West India Company. Eelkens insisted that the English owned the country, and he intended to trade for furs up the river. Van Twiller refused him permission to proceed, ran up the Orange flag at Fort Amsterdam, and fired three guns. This firing of guns for the sake of the noise was a species of intimidation the Dutch were very fond of, and, together with their habit of blowing trumpets for the same purpose, gave Irving large opportunities for satire.

Eelkens proceeded, however, in spite of all the fuss; and instead of trying to stop him with a shot aimed at his ship, Van Twiller summoned the people before his door, broached a cask of wine, filled a bumper, and called on all who loved the Prince of Orange to drink and assist him against the Englishman. Meanwhile Eelkens and his ship were out of sight up the river, and the broad-bottomed Swannekens, having finished their bumpers, returned to their homes laughing at their governor, but not much disturbed in their minds.

There was, however, in New Netherland one prominent person of whom Irving could not make fun. This was De Vries, a captain, ship-owner, patroon, explorer, and a man of energy and common sense. He was continually making voyages to the Delaware, or up the Hudson, or to and fro from Holland, laying out tracts of land for himself, stocking them with settlers, cows, and horses, and stopping at New Amsterdam to dine with Van Twiller and perform the surgical operation of inserting a little sense and courage into his head.

Dining and bumpers were an important part of governing at Manhattan. The day on which Eelkens escaped up the river, De Vries dined with Van Twiller and explained to him the situation. "If it had been my case," he said, "I should have helped him from the fort to some eight-pound iron beans; the English are of so haughty a nature that they think everything belongs to them." And finally, after reflection, it began to dawn on the Doubter that he could still send a ship in pursuit of Eelkens.

So a pinnace, a caravel, and a hoy sailed up the river to catch the koopman, and, finding him on shore near Fort Orange, with his tent pitched and driving a brisk trade, the Dutch soldiers seized all his goods, sounding their trumpet meanwhile "in disgrace of the English," as they said.

De Vries now wanted to send his own ship, the Squirrel, through Hell Gate to trade with the Puritans in New England. But Van Twiller had learnt how to be a governor, and ordered the ballast to be thrown out of the Squirrel. When De Vries protested, he was informed that "all princes and potentates" were accustomed to search vessels, and it was important to see if there was anything in the bottom of the ship subject to the company's tax.

Instead of firing in the air this time, Van Twiller trained the guns of Fort Amsterdam on the Squirrel, until De Vries, rushing to him in the fort where he stood, exclaimed, "The land is full of fools; if you want to shoot, why did you not shoot at the Englishman who violated your river against your will?" The Doubter was again in doubt, and De Vries and the Squirrel, with its ballast restored, passed out through Hell Gate, followed by a yacht which Van Twiller sent to watch them.

In order that the colony might be more confused and unsuccessful, the patroons began to quarrel with the company. They wanted, they said, to have their own monopoly of the fur trade. The company could have Manhattan Island to themselves if they liked, but each patroon should have a monopoly of trade on his own land; and they were continually begging and teasing for this privilege.

In 1640 smaller patroons were created, and each person who brought out five colonists was called a master and given two hundred acres of land. Commercial privileges were extended to all freemen, and trade was made free to all the world, which, however, merely meant that any one could trade if he carried his products in one of the company's ships.

At the same time the Reformed Church of the United Provinces was established as the religion of the province, an act which somewhat conflicts with the claim that the Dutch taught America the principle of separation of church and state. At the services of this church Indian wampum was put in the collection-plate, and wampum was the universal currency of New Netherland, as tobacco was in Virginia.

De Vries and Van Twiller dined and drank together without the slightest ill will. When De Vries arrived one day from the sea, with his ship badly leaking, he was cordially welcomed by the governor, and the ship hauled out for repairs in Smid's Vleye, or Smith's Valley, which was the name given to a marsh between East River and Pearl and Fulton Streets. Maagde Padtje, or Maiden's Lane, was in later days extended over this marsh, and a market-house built, called the Vleye Market, or market in the swamp, which was known by the English long after the Revolution as the Fly Market.

A few days after De Vries's ship was hauled out, he and Van Twiller went across the river to Pavonia, the patroonship of Michael Pauw, where Van Voorst had just arrived to take charge, bringing with him some " good Bordeaux wine." They took with them Dominie Bogardus, minister of the Dutch church, who had become an important man at Manhattan. Van Twiller, we are told, was always " glad to taste good wine." What were the tastes of De Vries and the dominie we are not informed, but they went with Van Twiller.

Van Voorst was delighted to see them, and the dominie and Van Twiller were soon quarrelling about a murder which had been recently committed in Pavonia; but that was soon settled, and everybody had such a good time that, when they were returning to Manhattan, Van Voorst fired a salute in their honor from a little swivel gun in front of his house. But a spark caught in the thatch of his roof, and his guests were compelled to see the whole establishment in which they had been so hospitably entertained burnt to the ground.

Soon after the constable at Manhattan gave a parting banquet to his friends, who were returning to Holland in the Seven Stars. Tables and benches were arranged under a tent in the fort at the Battery overlooking the bay which we all so often cross in going to New York, and while the people were feasting, the trumpeter, we are told, began to blow.

This was that same valiant trumpeter, Corlear, of whom Irving makes so much. But words passed, because the koopman of the ship and the koopman of the cargoes " scolded Corlaer the trumpeter." Whereupon " Corlaer the trumpeter" turned upon his scolders and gave them a drubbing, chasing them to their homes, where they got their swords and came back for vengeance. But they indulged themselves in nothing but " many foolish words," and the next morning, after having slept it off, " they feared the trumpeter more than they sought him."

So Van Twiller passed along in his administration, happy, festive, unconscious of his shortcomings, enriching himself at the company's expense, and getting for his own, among other tracts of land, the little island which is still called, in his honor, Governor's Island. Before he got it the Indians had named it Paggauck, and the Dutch called it Nooten "because excellent nut trees grew there."

It was in 1658 that the Doubter's administration came to an end, and by that time Fort Amsterdam was "open on every side except at the stone point," the church and houses were out of repair, it was difficult to discover where the magazine for merchandise had stood, the ships were rotting, only one of the three windmills was in operation, the five bouweries of the company were untenanted, and their cattle could not be found. But Van Twiller was the largest landholder in the province not a patroon. He owned nearly all the islands in both rivers, herds of cattle stocked his farms, and a few days after he was superseded he rented one of the untenanted company bouweries for two hundred and fifty guilders a year.

His successor, William Kieft the Testy, had been a bankrupt merchant, whose portrait, according to the laudable custom of the time, had been hung upon the gallows of his city in Holland. Afterwards he had been sent to ransom Christians in Turkey, and left some of them in bondage for the sake of leaving a larger balance of the ransom money in his own pocket. Less easy-going and uncertain than Van Twiller, and supposed to be more discreet and sober, the bustling and testy Kieft was nevertheless a most inquisitive and rapacious governor, and Irving is guilty of no exaggeration when he describes him as ruling by proclamations.

As a new broom which was attempting to sweep up the litter left by Van Twiller, he fired a proclamation at every abuse. The company officials must not carry on private trade in furs, there must be no secret traffic with the New Englanders, no guns or powder sold to the Indians, and all sailors must remain on their ships after nightfall. Proclamation after proclamation was poured out against theft, perjury, calumny, and "all other immoralities," against selling wine "except at a decent price," and the people were forbidden to leave Manhattan without passports. It was a riotous, disorderly community over which testy William had to rule, and murder, mutiny, and loose morality seem to have been rife among the people.

But it is a little unfair to laugh at Kieft for his proclamations. There were no legislature and no laws in New Netherland, and the orders or proclamations issued by the governor had to supply their place, as in the Spanish colonies.

De Vries was still coming and going, and dined with Kieft even more regularly than with his predecessor. In fact, the pair ruled the province between them. De Vries, we are compelled to state, had been instrumental in removing Van Twiller; for in one of his voyages to Holland he had not hesitated to tell of the sort of government which was carried on by his good friend of bumpers and dinners.

But it is not unlikely that Van Twiller bore him no ill will for this, and may have assented to it to give his friend a little importance with the authorities in Holland. He had got all that was to be had out of his office, and it was no more than fair that he should retire to his bouwery, rented from the company for two hundred and fifty guilders a year, and give others a chance.

Before Van Twiller's reign was cut short, De Vries had secured from him a fine tract of land on Staten Island, and in September, 1638, he sailed from the Texel with colonists to settle on it. They arrived off Sandy Hook in midwinter, and the Dutch captain seeing the shore covered with snow, and having only "old false charts" of the entrance, suggested that they return to the West Indies, where they could pass a pleasant winter and sail back to New Netherland in the spring.

The Dutch seem always to have had a fancy for lingering in the West Indies. In the voyage from Holland to Manhattan they often passed down by the Azores and Canary Islands and then across into the Caribbean Sea, anchoring at their leisure in pleasant places, whence they would sail north to Manhattan between the Bahamas and Bermuda. One ship is said to have made so many of these anchorages and stopped to fish so often that she was six months in making the voyage.

But some of the colonists on De Vries's ship, being within sight of their destination, thought it was hardly worth while to go back. They had heard that De Vries had once taken his own ship into Manhattan at night, so they asked him to be their pilot, and he steered safely up to Fort Amsterdam, where there was great rejoicing, because no ship was expected at that time of year, and Kieft welcomed him and helped to send his people to Staten Island.

Two years afterwards De Vries took it into his head to explore the Hudson, and on the shores of the Tappan Zee found a beautiful tract of land which suited him exactly. He soon had a colony on it, and named it Vriesendael. It was his favorite, and he spent many years there, not neglecting, however, frequent trips to see Kieft at Manhattan.

Among the first proclamations which Kieft issued was one aimed at the Swedes on the Delaware. The Dutch had been able to establish something like actual settlement and colonization on the Hudson, but on the Delaware they still remained traders, passing to and fro in their ships to collect the furs, and not making much of an attempt to occupy the country. Sweden was at this time looking about for worlds to conquer, and her people entered the Delaware in considerable numbers. They were better colonists than the Dutch, and settled themselves along the shores of the bay and river as far up as Philadelphia, while the Dutch scolded and stormed at them in vain.

Peter Minuit, a renegade Dutchman, was one of the leaders of the Swedes. " I make known to you, Peter Minuit," said Kieft, in one of his proclamations, " who call yourself commander in the service of Her Royal Majesty of Sweden, that the whole South River in New Nether-land has been many years in our possession, and has been secured by us with forts above and below and sealed with our blood ;" and he goes on with much bluster and flourish to hint of the terrible things that might happen to the Swedes if they persisted in their trespassing. But the Swedes stayed, and far outnumbered the Dutch, driving them out of the beaver trade, and the Dutch became mere interlopers in territory oc-cupied by the Swedes.

Manhattan and the Tappan Zee

In the same way the Dutch attempted to control the Connecticut River, where the Massachusetts people under the leadership of Hooker had settled. The coat of arms of Holland was nailed to a tree at the mouth of the Connecticut, as a token of possession. This was a method always adopted by the Dutch and some other nations when claiming new territory. It was a pompous flourish like the language of some of their proclamations.

The French often buried in the ground lead plates on which their supposed rights were engraved, in the hope, apparently, that when afterwards accidentally dug up they would be a proof of occupation. The English never resorted to any of these formal methods, and instead had a way of sitting down in new countries and staying there.

The Dutch hung up their arms on the present site of Philadelphia, where they were promptly torn down by the Swedes; and near Cape Henlopen, at the mouth of Delaware Bay, where they attempted to establish a little colony called Swaanendael, they set up a tin coat of arms of Holland, which an Indian took down to convert into tobacco pipes. Hossett, who was in charge of the place, made such complaints of this insult to their High Mightinesses the States General, that the Indians killed the chief who had made pipes of the tin heraldry, and his followers, to avenge his death, massacred every Dutchman at Swaanendael.

The arms at the mouth of the Connecticut were taken down by the English, who, as the Dutch complained, "engraved a ridiculous face in their place;" and the fort which the Dutch built near the present site of Hartford was treated with similar contempt. The Puritans occupied the country all round it, and even ploughed the land close up to the redoubt. "It was a sin," said the Puritan governor, "to leave uncultivated such valuable land, which would produce such excellent corn;" and when the Dutch resisted, the Puritans went up to the fort and pounded them on the head. Evert Duyckingk, we are told, while sowing grain, was struck "a hole in his head with a sticke, soe that the blood ran down very strongly."

The Swedes also amused themselves by pounding the Dutchman's head when he became too earnest in his protests. Kieft and others were always threatening "great calamities," and declaring that they would use "all the means God had given them to recover their rights." But Printz, the Swedish governor on the Delaware, had a short method of receiving Dutch envoys or messengers. One he threw out of his house, threatening to shoot him; and Hudde complained that "the subjects of the company, as well freemen as servants, when arriving at the place where he resides, are in a most unreasonable manner abused, so that they are often on returning home bloody and bruised."

But testy William soon had more serious difficulties on his hands. Determined to strip the province of everything, after the manner of his nation, he exacted tribute of corn, furs, and wampum from the Indians. He professed to be acting under instructions from Holland, but the Amsterdam chamber always denied that they had authorized such a measure; and it was a piece of foolishness from which the English colonists, recognizing the sturdy independence of the Indian character, had sense enough to abstain.

On a mere suspicion of some thefts, Kieft sent seventy soldiers and sailors, who attacked the Raritan Indians and destroyed their crops. In return, the Raritans wiped out De Vries's plantation at Staten Island, and soon after murdered a Dutchman at Deutel Bay, on the East River.

Kieft was now for war against the red man. But the serious-minded Dutch people of Manhattan told him that he was only seeking an excuse for "a wrong reckoning with the company;" and it was easy for him to talk of war "who could secure his own life in a good fort, out of which he had not slept a single night in all the years he had been here."

This is the first instance in New Netherland of anything like a popular movement or representative action on the part of the people. They had always quietly submitted to be ruled by the governor without laws or legislature, but now they seem to have found a voice which was so strong that Kieft dared not disregard it. He called a meeting of all heads of families near Manhattan, to be held at Fort Amsterdam, and there, on the 29th of August, 1641, the war question was submitted to the first meeting of the people that had ever been convened in New Netherland.

But the mass-meeting was unwilling to decide the question finally, and dispersed after referring it to twelve of their number, whom they called the Twelve Selectmen, known usually in New York history as The Twelve. Their decision was characteristic. The murder, they said, should be avenged, but nevertheless trade with the Indians must not be discontinued; and when the attack on them should be made, the governor "ought to lead the van."

De Vries, who was president of The Twelve, was, however, opposed to war, and The Twelve were in favor of delay. Kieft summoned and consulted them several times, but could get from them only advice for delay ; and soon becoming more representative of the people, they began to ask for reforms and improvements in the government.

This was going too far. They had been appointed only to give advice for war, or, in other words, to relieve Kieft of the responsibility if war was begun ; so he dissolved them, and forbade any meetings of the people without his express orders, because, he said, they tended to dangerous consequences and to the great injury of the country and authority. But he allowed the people to appoint four men to assist him in governing, whom he said he would consult when he felt the need of their advice. Free government was certainly not much encouraged at Manhattan.

Being unable to make The Twelve assume responsibility for a war, Kieft took the burden on himself, and sent an expedition of eighty men, commanded by a young ensign, Van Dyck, who crossed the Harlem River with the intention of surprising the Weckquaesgeeks at night. But the guide missed the way, and Van Dyck got into a petulant fit of Dutch temper and returned ingloriously.

The war-cloud rolled on ; there were terrible rumors of the preparations of the Indians, and another Dutchman was murdered while quietly thatching a house. The Mohawks, who lived north of Albany, were the great warrior tribe who ruled the inferior Weckquaesgeeks, Tappans, and Raritans living along the Hudson. In the winter of 1643 a party of nearly a hundred Mohawks, armed with muskets, came down to collect by force a tribute from their victims. Seventy of the river Indians were killed, and the rest began to flee towards Manhattan.

Four or five hundred of them took refuge at De Vries's colony of Vriesendael, and afterwards moved farther down and encamped on the oyster-banks at Pavonia, opposite Fort Amsterdam, where there were soon over a thousand savages congregated, and many of them crossed to Manhattan, seeking protection among the bouweries.

De Vries and others thought that this was an excellent opportunity to make a lasting peace with all these Indians, who were already grateful for the protection given them. But at one of those dinners which were such an important means of government in New Netherland it was suggested to Kieft that the innocent blood of the murdered Dutchmen was still unavenged, and that God had now delivered their enemies into his hands.

A petition was presented to him by some of the men who had been of The Twelve. Those who formerly had been for delay were now hot for war when they saw no necessity for a march into the Indian country, and that the enemy was panic-stricken and cowering at their feet. Kieft drank a significant toast, and swore that he would make the savages " wipe their chops."

De Vries and Dominie Bogardus protested in vain. In the dead of night Sergeant Rodolf and eighty men fell upon the unsuspecting Indians at Pavonia and murdered men, women, and children in cold blood. From midnight until morning they shot and slashed, threw children into the water and drove their mothers in after them, while the screams were heard across the bay at Fort Amsterdam.

" I sat up that night," says De Vries, " by the kitchen fire at the director's. About midnight, hearing loud shrieks, I ran up to the ramparts of the fort. Looking towards Pavonia, I saw nothing but shooting, and heard nothing but the shrieks of Indians murdered in their sleep."

Shortly afterwards, on the same side of the river with De Vries, another party of Indians were surprised and forty of them killed. The soldiers returned to Kieft in the morning with heads and prisoners, and he welcomed them by shaking their bloody hands. Even the women of Manhattan were aroused, and, in imitation of the savages, heaped indignities on the dripping heads. Not content with this slaughter, the

Dutchmen invaded the Long Island Indians, who had always been friendly, and robbed them of their corn.

The English settlers of America have not very much to boast of in the way of fair treatment of the Indians, but they never were guilty of anything so treacherous, cowardly, and cruel as these attacks of the Dutch. It was the brutality of weakness and fear, for the Dutch were utterly inefficient in real warfare against the Indians; and we are reminded of the execution of the aged Barneveldt, the great advocate of the States of Holland, which has always been a stain on the Dutch character.

But we need not concern ourselves very much about the Indians on this occasion. Within a few months they had completely squared accounts with the Dutch, and in fact had the balance on their side, just as De Vries and the wiser heads had prophesied. The poor river Indians, with the Dutch before them and the Mohawks behind them, made common cause with the Long Island Indians, and, hiding in the swamps and thickets, began those stealthy savage tactics against which the Dutchman was powerless.

The farmer and his cattle were shot down in the bouweries, grain, hay, and crops set on fire, and the women and children whose lives were spared carried into captivity. The outlying districts of New Netherland were almost depopulated, and the survivors fled to Fort Amsterdam, on Manhattan Island, where they crowded together, begging to be sent back to Holland. The province was on the eve of being emptied of its people; and to stop the calamity and prevent the people from returning to Holland, Kieft was compelled to take them all into the employment of the company.

Days of fasting and prayer were held, and when the Indians had had enough of plunder and slaughter they made a treaty of peace. But it could not last long. In a few months the war was on again, and the Indians swept the whole country, including New Jersey and the northern part of Manhattan Island, driving the frightened Swannekens into Fort Amsterdam.

There, in the little crumbling fort below the modern Wall Street, where the current of commercial prosperity sweeps by every day, was gathered all that was left of New Netherland. The women and children were hidden in the straw huts, and the men kept guard on the mounds of earth which formed the ramparts, while the Indian scouts came up close enough to shoot at the guards.

In his extremity, Kieft sent to the Puritans in New England for assistance, but received for answer that they were not satisfied " that the

Dutch war with the Indians was just." Provisions they were willing to send as an act of humanity, but they had not the slightest intention of protecting the Dutchman from his red enemy; and it is not unlikely that many a Puritan prayed to his terrible God not to deliver the Swannekens from the hand of the heathen, but to sweep them off the continent, so that the saints might inherit the earth.

Thrown on his own resources, Kieft organized such forces as he had, and as the Indians became weary of the success of their contest he undertook offensive measures against them. In this he received assistance from some of the Englishmen who for several years had been settling themselves within the limits of New Netherland. Many of them were Puritans from Massachusetts, who for various reasons had found the life at Boston uncongenial. But it is noticeable that they usually established themselves on the outskirts of the province, either on Long Island or close to the Connecticut line.

Among them was the famous Mrs. Anne Hutchinson, who had made a home for herself near New Rochelle, on what has since been known as Pelham's Neck, but which the Dutch called in her honor Annie's Hoeck. Here the Indians had murdered her and nearly her whole family. But there were two other prominent

Manhattan and the Tappan Zee

Puritan refugees who escaped, Daniel Patrick and John Underhill, both of whom had been soldiers of considerable experience.

Patrick had been employed to drill the militia in Massachusetts, but becoming "proud and vicious," as Winthrop tells us, he sought safety among the Dutch. Underhill had been at times very sanctimonious, and at other times much given to adultery, which he had confessed in all its details in true Puritan fashion with tears and wailing before one of the congregations. But the saints finally despaired of converting him, and he also removed to New Netherland.

Kieft sent a hundred and twenty men to assist Patrick against the Indians in the neighborhood of Stamford; but they wandered over the country all night without finding the enemy, and returning very weary to Stamford, full of that peculiar Dutch rage which seems to have afflicted the Swannekens whenever they had to walk very far for nothing, they upbraided Patrick for bringing them on a fool's errand. One of them was so abusive that Patrick resented his insults by rough language and spitting in his face, and as soon as Patrick's back was turned the Dutchman shot him in the head.

Underhill was more fortunate, and, when placed in command of fourteen Dutchmen, routed the Indians in one of their villages, and, assisted by a party commanded by La Montagne, they killed altogether one hundred and twenty of the enemy. Two of the prisoners were brought to Fort Amsterdam and tortured. One died under his sufferings, and the other was mercifully relieved by Kieft, who had him beheaded on the millstone in Beaver's Path, afterwards Beaver's Lane, near the Battery.

Kieft had now at last round some one who could protect his people. Underhill led another expedition, which fell upon the Indians in one of their fortified villages north of Stamford and killed upward of five hundred of them. This ended the worst part of the war, and New Netherland was delivered by the outcast Puritan adulterer.

The province was in a shocking state of ruin and confusion. The West India Company was now bankrupt, and The Eight, who had taken the place of The Twelve, demanded the recall of Kieft, whose misdeeds they set out at length in their petition. Everybody longed for a return of the old easy-going days of Wouter Van Twiller, the Doubter ; and even the Indians were said to go about crying, " Wouter, Wouter, Wouter !"

That good fellow De Vries had left the country in disgust. His advice had been neglected, his efforts to save the colony had been in vain, and his two estates at Staten Island and Vriesendael had been destroyed by the Indians.

He sailed away never to return; but, true to his old habits, he took plenty of time on his voyage to Holland. He coasted along the shore of New Jersey and entered the Delaware River, visiting the Swedes and telling them in his frank way that they had no business there trespassing on Dutch territory. But they liked him none the less, for he was always popular wherever he went; and we read that Printz, the Swedish governor, welcomed him most cordially and pledged him in " a great romer of Rhine wine."

From the Delaware he went to Virginia, and, as it was late in the autumn, he spent the winter there; and we can readily believe that he had a royal time with that cock-fighting, fox-hunting gentry, who were the people of all others who could appreciate his good qualities. At last he returned to Holland, where he amused himself by writing a most charming and simple narrative of all he had seen and done in New Netherland; and he died almost the only prominent man connected with the early days of that unfortunate colony who cannot be laughed at.

The colony had cost the company over five hundred and fifty thousand guilders after deducting the returns received from it; and after five years of Indian war there were comparatively few people in it. Besides traders, there were only about one hundred colonists at Manhattan. Outside of that island every settlement on the west side of the Hudson south of the Highlands had been destroyed, as well as those in the greater part of Westchester and Western Long Island.

Only the patroonship of Van Rensselaer and the few posts on the Delaware remained unharmed. The prosperous English colonies, with their rapidly increasing population, were pressing into New Netherland from all sides, and it was a question whether the remnant of the Dutch had not better be brought back to the fatherland.

But an effort was made to restore and renew. Kieft was dismissed, and Peter Stuyvesant, the headstrong, was made governor, or director-general, as he was called. He was to be compelled to rule, however, with the assistance of a supreme council, consisting of himself, a vice-director, and a fiscal.

In these reforms and changes it was recommended that the colonists should be settled in towns and villages, "as the English are in the habit of doing," which seems rather inconsistent with the claim advanced in recent years that the Dutch taught the town-government system to the New Englanders.

As a matter of fact, wherever the English

entered New Netherland they demanded a self-governing town for themselves. Kieft allowed the Puritans from Stamford, Connecticut, who founded the town of Heemstede, on Long Island, to elect their own magistrates, subject to his approval, and in general to manage their own affairs. In the same way, and insisting on the same privileges, the English founded Flushing, which the Dutch called Vlissingen, after a seaport of Zealand. But among the Dutch themselves in New York there was no town government or self-government of any kind which in the most remote degree resembled the New England town system.

Peter Stuyvesant was a pompous, vehement old soldier, fond of displaying his knowledge of Latin. He had been governor of the Dutch colony at Curacoa, and had lost a leg in an attack on the Portuguese island of St. Martin. The Indians called him wooden leg; and as he ornamented the artificial limb with bands of silver, he was often called silver leg, which, of course, gave Irving an opportunity for fun. He returned from Curaçoa to Holland for surgical aid, and on his recovery was sent out to rule New Netherland in place of Kieft. Among his instructions, he was told to allow the different colonies, as the settlements were called, to send delegates to his council. This was a weak, half-way substitute for representative government, intended to take the place of The Twelves, Eights, and Fours which prevailed under Kieft.

As soon as they heard that William the Testy was to be superseded, the people were wild with joy. Some of them, with true Dutch frankness, informed him that they intended to thrash him as soon as he lost the authority of his office, or, as they expressed it, as soon as he should " take off the coat with which he was bedecked by the Lords his masters." Dominie Bogardus also preached against him, declaring to his congregation that the great men of the country had been nothing but " vessels of wrath and fountains of woe" that plundered the people.

Against the dominie the only revenge Kieft took was to have drums beaten and a cannon fired during the Sunday service, and he encouraged people to indulge in all sorts of noisy amusements round the church. But against some of the others he was more severe, and they discovered to their sorrow that, though superseded, the last days of his power could be cruel.

He departed at last with a fortune of four hundred thousand guilders, which he had amassed during his administration; but the ship was wrecked on the coast of Wales, and Kieft and Dominie Bogardus with eighty others were drowned.

Manhattan and the Tappan Zee

At this time New Amsterdam, as the present
city of New York was then called, consisted of a
fort of earth ramparts, situated near the junction
of the East River with the Hudson, just above
the present site of the Battery, and surrounded
by high-peaked but rather low houses, thatched
with straw or reeds. The town was nearly all
below Wall Street, and above it throughout
Manhattan Island were the farms, or boweries,
as they were called.

From the walls of the fort towards the shore
and the present Battery was open space, and here
stood the lofty gallows and the whipping-post,
terrors to evil-doers. Near to the shore in both
the East and the Hudson River the queer-shaped
Dutch ships lay at anchor,—the hoys, pinks,
galleons, and yachts. The term yacht, which
has been adopted in English to describe a
pleasure-boat, seems to have meant in Dutch a
vessel of less than one hundred tons, the sort of
craft that was apt to be used for exploring expeditions or light trade.

The Dutch were very skilful gardeners, and
many of the great variety of vegetables which
are enjoyed in modern times were first produced
in Holland. In New Amsterdam they soon had
flourishing gardens round their houses, not only
of vegetables, but also of flowers, of which
they were equally fond. Van der Donck gives

a long list of flowers which he found blooming at New Amsterdam as early as 1653, most of which had been imported from Holland; and, besides these, they had domesticated many of the native wild flowers. Flocks of geese, ducks, and chickens were of course waddling all about, for the thrifty Dutch vrouws delighted in them.

These same vrouws and their goodmen slept on beds filled with feathers plucked from their own geese, and for covering they often used another feather-bed. They had great quantities of clothes, and appear to have found the climate very cold. The women wore innumerable petticoats, the men several pairs of trousers, one over the other; and in church in wintertime the men used muffs.

They had linen in what seems to have been unnecessary quantity, not only for wear, but for the table and bed. This was common in all the colonies, but the Dutch possessed unusually large supplies. Some families had five or six hundred dollars' worth; and we read of one man who had eighty muslin sheets, twenty-three linen ones, and thirty-two pillow cases. This is partially explained when we find that there were very few wash-days a year; and this custom of an enormous quantity of clothes and very few wash-days is said to prevail in modern times in some parts of Germany.

Manhattan and the Tappan Zee

But the Dutch were extremely clean and neat, especially about their houses. Cleanliness seems to have been a characteristic of the colonies, except among the German peasants in Pennsylvania, of whom there were many complaints. Several of the French travellers were much impressed with the cleanness of everything in New England, and the Moravians at Bethlehem in Pennsylvania were an exception among the Germans of that province. But even the German peasantry, who seem to have been very slovenly for some time after their arrival, became cleaner with the improvement of their condition in life.

A great change has taken place in this respect in the nineteenth century which is difficult to account for. Many people are still living who remember when farm-houses and all the homes of the lower classes had none of the tawdry dirtiness which now makes a visit to them anything but a pleasure. Some explain it by the modern labor-saving devices which seem to have destroyed the faculty for hard work, which is the only real dirt destroyer, and others trace it to the enormous immigration of low European peasantry.

Before the English conquest of New York the houses of New Amsterdam are described as built of bricks of various colors, laid in checkers, glazed, and very pretty. The front doors were divided into an upper and a lower half, which was a custom brought from Holland, and is now often imitated in reproductions of colonial architecture. Within the houses were neat and clean to admiration. The wood-work was scoured and rubbed until it shone like the decks of a man-of-war. The floors were rubbed and polished in the same way, and sprinkled with fresh sand every day, which when first put on was marked into patterns with the broom. Even the Dutch farm-houses had this virtue of cleanliness, for which the Dutch women were famous.

They loved to get their houses in perfect order every day, dress themselves well and neatly, with bags hanging from their girdles, filled with all the instruments of housewifery, and then spin busily at their wheels, or in summer sit on the stoop to receive visits from their neighbors, and gossip while the goodman smoked his pipe.

Sometimes they strolled in the evening to a grove of locust-trees on a bluff of the Hudson south of the present Trinity church-yard, or they wandered down the " Maiden's Path," now preserved in Maiden Lane. They were great gossips, it is said, and there must have been plenty to tell; for the Dutch were frank

to an extraordinary degree, and called everything by its common name.

The vrouws were very comfortable persons,
not vivacious, but with the most practical good
sense. Some of them engaged in trade or carried on small business occupations, in which
they were very skilful. They were probably as
good-natured and easy-going as the men; but
apparently it was not safe to presume too much
on their kindly disposition. We read in the
court records of Brooklyn that Mistress Jonica
Schampf and Widow Rachel Luguer assaulted
Peter Praa, the captain of the militia, when he
was at the head of his troops on training-day in
October, 1690. They beat him, pulled his
hair, and handled him so roughly with "Ivill
Inormities" that his life was despaired of.

It is said that the Dutch had few if any oaths
except "sacrament." When they wished to be
very offensive, they put their thumb to their
nose and wriggled their fingers, an insult for
which a Dutchman could be punished in court;
and Irving makes effective use of it in his
Knickerbocker History.

They were so extremely sensitive to impudent or insulting speeches that if they had had
many oaths the community would have been in
a continuous turmoil. People were brought before the court for saying of another, "If his

debts were paid he would have little left," or
that "he had not half a wife," or that he was
"a little cock, booted and spurred;" and Alice
Morse Earle, to whom we are indebted for the
description of many of these early Dutch customs, has collected numerous other instances in
her excellent volume, "Colonial Days in Old
New York."

Their love of gossip, combined with their
sensitiveness, kept the judges busy with suits for
slander. Dominie Bogardus and his wife Anneke sued a woman because she had said that
Anneke in crossing a muddy street lifted her
petticoats too high. Dominie Frelinghuysen
had painted on the back of his sleigh a rhyme
which Mrs. Earle has translated:

> "No one's tongue and no one's pen
> Makes me other than I am.
> Speak, evil speakers, speak without end,
> No one heeds a word you say."

The New York Dutch were certainly a very
curious people, and all the records and remains
of their life are full of quaintness. It is difficult
now to understand the mental condition of a man
who could call his yacht "The Pear-Tree."

The Dutch farmers lived in low, solidly built
houses, with small windows and very large
cellars, where they stored great supplies of

vegetables and hogsheads of salt beef, pork, and fish for the winter. Their fireplaces were, of course, large, as in the other colonies. You could drive a horse and cart through them, Kalm said, and they seem to have been built far out into the room.

The Dutch were in general not as heavy eaters as the English colonists, and drank less. The English called them milk-and-cheese men. They lived largely on the various products of milk, vegetables, bread, and very good little cakes. They were not, as a rule, great meat-eaters, like their neighbors.

Their drinking, though less by comparison than that of the English, seems, however, heavy enough in this less capacious age. After the English conquest of New York, the candidates in an election spent large sums for liquor. We read of sixty-two gallons of rum, several gallons of brandy, a pyd of wine, besides lime-juice, shrub, mugs, jugs, and bottles.

Before the English conquest, Dutch workmen on a building, as Mrs. Earle tells us, had to be sustained at every stage. In 1656 those who pulled down an old building in Albany received a tun of strong beer. When the first stones of the new wall were laid the masons were given a case of brandy, an anker of brandy, and thirty-two gallons of other liquor. When the beams were carried in by eight men, they had half a barrel of beer for every beam; and when the beams were laid, two barrels of strong beer, three cases of brandy, and seventy-two florins' worth of small beer.

Criminals were punished by the usual methods of that age,—the pillory, whipping, imprisonment, and hanging. When there was no prison, they appear to have been sometimes locked up in the tavern. Torture was used to force confessions of guilt. A number of instances of it are to be found in O'Callaghan's "Calendar of Dutch Manuscripts," and Dutch New York seems to have been the only one of the colonies in which this method of the Middle Ages was put in practice.

"Oct. 5, 1639. Hendrick Jansen, gunner's mate of the ship Herring from Bremen, charged with an assault on the deputy fiscal, was subjected to torture, but he persisted in the lie." (Trumbull: *Blue Laws, True and False*, 309.)

"Nov. 22, 1641. Jan Hobbesen, charged with theft (stealing a sheet from a tavern), persisting in denying the charge, is put to the torture, after which he confessed his guilt; is sentenced to be whipped with rods and banished." (*Ibid.*, 310.)

There seems to have been no hurry in getting Stuyvesant to New Netherland to take the place of Kieft. His departure was delayed for a long time; and when at last the little squadron of four vessels left the Texel, they spent six leisurely months in making the voyage. They captured a prize and lingered long in the West Indies.

But in May, 1647, they reached Manhattan; and although Stuyvesant's coming was "like a peacock's, with great state and pomp," and he was insolent and supercilious, keeping the principal people waiting bareheaded for hours before he would receive them, everybody was determined to be happy. The whole population appeared under arms, paraded about among the little thatched houses at the mouth of the East River, and fired their guns until they had burnt up nearly all the powder in New Amsterdam.

Stuyvesant promised that he would be a father to them, and paternal government was all that the people could hope for. In accordance with his instructions, he allowed a sort of compromise representative government. Four of the colonies—Manhattan, Amersfoort, Breuckelen, and Pavonia—held an election and chose eighteen persons, from whom Stuyvesant selected nine to advise and assist him in governing, but only when he chose to call upon them for advice. There were to be no future elections. The people were allowed their voice only in the first instance, and after that The Nine, like a close corporation, filled all vacancies in their body.

The people were not allowed to hold meetings of any kind, and The Nine had to go about from house to house to get their opinions.

The man who had arrived like a peacock soon became a hawk and a vulture. The people complained that he was everything. He had shops and breweries, and was a merchant and a trader in lawful as well as contraband goods. Duties and taxes were increased; the customs duties were so high that ships and traders were kept away, and Stuyvesant was eager to confiscate property of all kinds for the slightest infraction of his rules. Twenty-five vessels, it is said, would have visited Manhattan annually from the West Indies if their owners had not been afraid of confiscation.

A court of justice was organized and Van Durcklagen appointed judge; but Stuyvesant required that his own opinion should be asked in all important cases, and he reserved the right to preside over the court whenever he saw fit,— a most comical arrangement, which even Irving could not exaggerate.

The most extraordinary part of the whole system was that Stuyvesant, like the previous governors, seems to have had full authority to do what he pleased. Neither the company nor the States General of Holland appear to have been much interested or to have exercised much control, except to appoint a new governor after the excesses of the one in power had gone on for many years. If a governor could keep things tolerably quiet and prevent reports from reaching Holland, he could have his way. We read of the governor openly storming at the people and threatening to punish them if they should tell on him.

Stuyvesant was relentlessly cruel to some of the men who had abused Kieft at the close of his administration, or, in other words, had told on him. The headstrong Peter seemed to think it necessary to uphold all the rapacity of his predecessor. Kieft had upheld Van Twiller in the same way, and had ordered all persons to restore everything in their possession belonging to the company, unless they could " prove that they had bought it from the former director."

" If I were persuaded," said Stuyvesant on one occasion, " that you would divulge our sentence or bring it before their High Mightinesses, I would have you hanged at once on the highest tree in New Netherland. If any one during my administration shall appeal, I will make him a foot shorter, and send the pieces to Holland, and let him appeal in that way."

In some things headstrong Peter's reign was successful. He conquered the Swedes on the Delaware ; but it was a rather useless conquest. He also resisted with success the pretensions of

Van Rensselaer, who was trying hard to make his patroonship an independent colony, and had almost absorbed Fort Orange, which happened to be situated within his boundaries.

The laws or proclamations of New Netherland, Van Rensselaer claimed, ceased their operation at the entrance of his domain, and he refused to observe a general fast which Stuyvesant had ordered. This roused the ire of the valiant Peter, and he visited Rensselaerwick, where he was received with the full measure of Dutch pomp and salvoes of artillery. The long wrangling ended in his favor; Van Rensselaer was reduced to his proper dimensions, the independence of Fort Orange was secured, and it became the germ of the present town of Albany.

The Reformed Dutch religion was vigorously maintained, and a proclamation issued to suppress unlicensed preachers, and many of them were fined and imprisoned. The Lutherans and Baptists were forbidden to hold religious meetings, but the Lutherans finally obtained permission. When the Quakers appeared, they were treated with more severity than in any other colony except Massachusetts. Harsh rules were enforced against them, under which a number were banished, and those who harbored or assisted them punished with fines and imprisonment.

The people themselves were anxious for liberty, and constantly struggling for it, demanding the privileges they had enjoyed in Holland. They succeeded during Stuyvesant's administration in holding several Landtdags, or popular conventions, in which they set forth their grievances. But they gained very little, because the company and the mother country were indifferent, and the governor would grant no privileges that he was not compelled to grant.

The towns were, however, one by one given some little control over their own affairs. In 1652 the Manhattan people were allowed to have a schout, burgomasters, and schepens, but all these officers were appointed by Stuyvesant. Afterwards, when this burgher government was extended to Breuckelen, Amersfoort, and Midwout, they were allowed to nominate their officers for the governor's approval. But this was granted as a very great favor, and was intended to counterbalance the influence of the English villages.

The English were indeed pressing close upon New Netherland. Stuyvesant was in continual negotiations with the confederation of the New England colonies about his boundaries, and was beaten at every point. In 1654 the Connecticut people seized Fort Hope, which the Dutch had so long maintained at Hartford. The

Manhattan and the Tappan Zee

Yankee settlers of Long Island were in a continual state of disaffection, stirring up the Dutchmen to demand greater privileges and more liberal government.

The Dutch population of New Netherland was so small, and the New England population so large in comparison, that it was evidently a mere question of time when the Yankees by their vigorous overflow would absorb everything. "Many hounds," said Stuyvesant, "are death to the hare," and the Puritan hound was becoming very keen and hungry.

Under Cromwell, England was at war with Holland, and the English were becoming aroused to the importance of their American possessions. The intrusion of the Dutch in the best part of the continent was no longer regarded with indifference, and English diplomats and statesmen began to talk of the superior title of England to all the land from Labrador to Florida which the discovery of the Cabots had given. England was now becoming an important commercial nation, contending with Holland for the sovereignty of the seas. The New England Puritans, under direct encouragement from Great Britain, began to make deliberate encroachments on the territory of New Netherland, and Massachusetts granted lands on the Hudson opposite to Fort Orange.

Manhattan and the Tappan Zee

The relations between the two communities were strained, and the Puritans were evidently seeking an opportunity to begin an armed contest. They professed to have discovered a plot between the Dutch and the Indians to destroy the English in New England, who were to be massacred on Sunday when they were all in their churches. They openly charged Stuyvesant with this, and sent commissioners to Manhattan to collect evidence. They could find none, although they examined a great many Indians and other persons. But they still insisted on believing in the plot, which, with enlarged details, was the talk of Connecticut firesides for nearly a hundred years, and the ill feeling between Dutch and English increased.

A short peace had been patched up between England and Holland; but on the restoration of Charles II., in 1660, it was evident that no peace could be lasting between two nations who had become such bitter commercial rivals, and who were trying to cut each other out of trade in every part of the world. Stuyvesant and the company felt that the hounds were pressing them very close, and the weakness of their whole system is shown in their attempt to settle New Jersey with Englishmen. They seemed to think that English dissenters, being hostile to the Church of England, would be hostile to the whole British nation and government. They could not get their own people to leave the dikes and windmills of Holland, and in the hope of getting a large enough population to resist New England, they were proposing plans for gathering immigrants from all the countries of Europe.

But it was all in vain, for the British government had now decided to seize New Netherland. The argument which at this moment seemed most convincing was that as long as the Dutch remained at New Netherland they traded with the colonists of Virginia and of New England, and every shilling they gained in this trade was that much lost to England.

The English colonists were forbidden by the navigation acts to send their products to any country but England, and could buy their supplies only in England, and everything must be carried in English vessels. But, with New Netherland so near at hand, these rules were easily evaded. From Virginia alone it was estimated that the Dutch at New York received such quantities of tobacco that if sent to England in the regular way the duty on it would have amounted to ten thousand pounds a year. For a king who was so anxious to replenish his exchequer as Charles II., this consideration alone was decisive.

Manhattan and the Tappan Zee

But how was he to get possession of New Netherland? England and Holland were at peace, and Holland would not admit that England was entitled to all North America by the discovery of the Cabots. It was suggested that the crown should simply assume that the Dutchmen at Manhattan were British subjects on British territory, and begin to rule them. But this would lead to war as quickly as any other method; and it was finally determined that the best way would be to make a grant of New Netherland as English territory to some person, and then put him in possession by force.

Accordingly, in 1664, Charles II. gave to his brother, the Duke of York and Albany, afterwards James II., a grant of all the land between the Connecticut and Delaware Rivers. Four ships of war, under the command of Colonel Richard Nicolls, were at once sent to put the duke in possession, and Nicolls was to be the governor of the duke's province.

The object of the expedition was known at the Hague; but the West India Company refused to believe it. It was merely, they said, an expedition to reorganize the government of New England and establish Episcopacy there, and when that was done the Puritans would be more willing than ever to live under the Dutch. As for the States General, when called upon to defend New Netherland from the British, they replied that they would not be bothered with making a war for the West India Company. They had had trouble enough already with the East India Company, and they would rather pull them both by the ears.

But the valiant Peter prepared to defend his colony. Beer was forbidden to be brewed, artillery and ammunition collected from the Delaware and Rensselaerwick, and the people forced to work on the fortifications; and when the English squadron anchored just outside the Narrows and seized Staten Island, vigorous old Silver Leg refused to surrender.

The summons to surrender had declared that all the people should be allowed to enjoy their property; but Stuyvesant was determined that the people should not know of this, for they were not in the least heroic. No stronger comment could be made on the utter failure of the Dutch colony than that when the English enemy appeared, the only man who did not want to surrender was the governor, who, like his predecessors, was making a fortune out of New Netherland.

The people soon suspected that the terms of surrender were withheld from them for some reason, and demanded to see them. Stuyvesant stoutly resisted, and warned the burgomasters and council that if the people knew the terms

they would insist on capitulating. The English
seem to have been aware of this weak point, and
Winthrop, the governor of Connecticut, who
had accompanied the squadron, came to Man
hattan under a flag of truce, and assured Stuyvesant's council and burgomasters that if they
would surrender the Dutch could continue to
settle and trade in the province and pass to and
fro to Holland in their own ships.

Winthrop had also set forth these terms in
a letter which on his departure he handed to
Stuyvesant, and the burgomasters demanded that
this letter should be made public; but the governor, in a fit of passion, tore it in pieces before
them. When this became generally known, the
people refused to work on the palisades. The
one thing they cared for was to be given them,
—namely, trade; so what was there to fight
about? They crowded round the governor,
cursing the company and its management, and
crying, " The letter, the letter!"

The fragments of it were picked up, patched
together, and copied for the people to read; but
the governor, headstrong as ever against all opposition, kept up a show of resistance, although
he had burnt up a large part of his powder in
firing salutes to Winthrop and every messenger
who came from the squadron.

Nicolls, growing tired of the delay, landed

troops below Breukelen, and sent two frigates, which anchored between Fort Amsterdam and Governor's Island. Poor old headstrong Peter stood in one of the angles of the fort by a gun, watching their approach. An artilleryman with a lighted match stood by his side, and he would surely have had a shot at the enemy if two of the dominies had not come and led him away. Everybody remonstrated and pleaded with him, and at last he yielded, saying, " I would much rather be carried out dead ;" and soon after he met the commissioners at his bouwery to arrange the terms of surrender.

The Dutch troops were marched out of Fort Amsterdam with the honors of war, and immediately sailed for Holland. A corporal's guard of the English entered the fort, and in a few moments the British ensign was floating above the low walls, the windmill, the gallows and whipping-post at the river-side, and the queer little thatched houses huddling round the fort.

The fort was named Fort James, in honor of the conquering duke ; and when Nicolls went up the Hudson and secured Fort Orange, he called it Albany, after the duke's Scotch title, and New Amsterdam was called New York.

The Dutch had lost their best and greatest colony, and it must be confessed that they deserved to lose it. They had never really believed in it. They had allowed it to become the plundering-ground for a greedy, selfish corporation monopoly and its rapacious governors. They had not the force of character and energy to settle and rule it properly, and, unless they intended to make it a point of advantage for controlling the whole continent, there was no use in their keeping it.

After an existence of more than forty years, its population was less than ten thousand, who, although they held the present flourishing States of New York, New Jersey, Delaware, and Pennsylvania, the richest and best part of America, could barely maintain themselves, while the New England colonies, with an inferior and barren country, numbered nearly fifty thousand.

As for the Dutch peopling the whole continent and controlling it, that was, of course, impossible. There was only one nation competent for that task, and the sooner all others were cleared out of the way the better for civilization. The Dutch were traders, not colonizers, and they always succeeded best in tropical countries, where they still hold colonies or trading-stations. Even while they held New York they seemed to prefer the West Indies, and were inclined to linger there on their voyages to Manhattan.

Manhattan and the Tappan Zee

In Holland the seizure of New Netherland by the British was of course regarded as a deadly insult, and a long war began. Within ten years, in 1673, the Dutch succeeded in retaking New York, landing a force on the Hudson, just back of Trinity Church, near the present railroad ferries to Jersey City. They held the country for a few months, naming New York, New Orange; Albany, Willemstaadt; and New Jersey, Achter Kol. But at this time Holland had formed an alliance with Spain and Germany against England. Spain insisted that all conquests should be restored, and by the treaty of Westminster New York was given back to England in exchange for Surinam, which was given to the Dutch. The treaty was confirmed before it was known in Holland that New York had been retaken, and a trumpeter was sent to London to protest, but to no purpose.

Among the Dutch colonists in New York the English conquest was regarded almost with indifference. They rapidly took the oath of allegiance to Great Britain, and immediately began to talk about trade. They hoped for greater liberty than they had enjoyed under their own fatherland. They asked that New York should have the same commercial privileges as England or Boston, and, if these were granted, they declared themselves ready to "bloom and grow like the cedars on Lebanon."

Their expectations were in a great measure realized, for after twenty years of English rule the population of New York had almost doubled. But in civil government the duke was at first as great a tyrant as the West India Company had been. The Dutch laws and customs were allowed to stand, with the intention of gradually changing them, and the colony was to be ruled by the governor and his council, who were to make all laws.

There was to be a Court of Assizes, as it was called, consisting of the sheriffs and justices, meeting once a year to assist the governor and his council in law-making. These sheriffs and justices were appointed by the governor, and their yearly meeting was in no sense representative government, for the Duke of York despised anything of that kind. The Court of Assizes was enough privilege to allow the people; for the justices who composed it, he coolly remarked, would be the same persons whom in all probability the people themselves would choose, if they were allowed the privilege of electing them.

Stuyvesant had been among the first to take the oath of allegiance. He spent the rest of his life in the province, having first, like the thrifty Dutchman he was, secured from the British Privy Council a special license to trade. He lived on his little bouwery or farm, which was situated at the present Third Avenue and Thirteenth Street, where he died at the age of eighty years. He was buried under a little chapel of his own near his house, where a pear-tree brought from the fatherland and planted by his own hands was preserved by an iron railing until 1867.

New York under the duke was a proprietary colony with the most despotic power given to the proprietor. Maryland and Pennsylvania were also proprietary colonies, but their proprietors, Lord Baltimore and William Penn, could make laws only by consent of the freemen of the province or their delegates. The Duke of York, however, was under no compulsion to consult his people, and could make whatever laws suited him. He delegated this power to his governor, Nicolls, and Nicolls prepared a code of laws copied for the most part from the laws of the New England colonies, with additions and improvements.

The people were told to elect a convention of their delegates, which should meet at Hempstead and give the governor advice and information about this code; but as soon as the meeting began to make objections and suggest alterations, Nicolls promptly told them that they were there merely to approve what he had prepared for them, and he forthwith promulgated the code, which they submissively accepted.

This code established in the fullest manner religious liberty, which had not prevailed under the Dutch. The duke was a Roman Catholic, and in after-years, when he had been driven from the English throne, he told the Pope that it had been his intention gradually to establish by law the Roman faith in all the English colonies in America. When only a duke, and in possession of one colony, he dared not make his own religion exclusive, and, being unwilling to establish any other, he had no choice but to establish absolute freedom.

In 1665 he abolished the government of schout, burgomasters, and schepens which had controlled New York, and in its place established that government of mayor and aldermen of which we have heard so much in the modern politics of the city.

Finding that the Dutch, or Flemish, breed of horses was as slow as the schouts and schepens, he also, through Nicolls, established a race-course near Hempstead, on Long Island, where a great plain sixteen miles long and four wide was found to be covered with fine grass like the English downs, "with neither stick nor stone to hinder the horses' heels or endanger them in their races.'' There a silver plate was run for every year, to the great delight of all subsequent governors and the Long Island farmers, whose breed of massive horses in the course of years gradually improved in lightness and speed.

This open plain was regarded as a great curiosity in colonial times, when the whole country was covered with forests, in which travellers grew weary of the continual succession of trees. Visitors were taken to see it. The prairies of the West had not then been discovered, and Burnaby says in his " Travels" that it was the only natural open space on the continent.

The people in the rural parts of the province remained almost exclusively Dutch for a hundred years; but New York in the end became a mixture of Dutch, English, New Englanders, French, German, and a rabble from all parts of the world. Even under Dutch rule it was said that eighteen different languages were spoken round Fort Amsterdam.

In 1682, the people having become very clamorous for more liberal government, and refusing to pay duties and taxes, the duke found that if he wished to get any revenue from New York to pay the expenses of its government and garrison he must give the people a representative assembly; and that if he continued to refuse them this privilege he must either sell the province to the crown or have it a continual drain on his resources. Just at this time William Penn had received the grant of Pennsylvania, and had given his colonists a very liberal government and laws; and the duke, who was a close friend of Penn, was perhaps influenced by him.

In 1683 New York was given an assembly elected by the people, and the duke and his governor retained only the right to veto such acts of this assembly as did not please them. In return for this gift of liberty, the people were to raise funds to support the government and garrison.

Two years afterwards Charles II. died, the duke became king as James II., and as his title and power of duke were absorbed in royalty, New York ceased to be a dukedom and became a royal province. No longer feeling any necessity for keeping up the popular assembly, which he detested, James II. abolished it, and appointed Thomas Dongan to be governor of New York in 1686, with power to make laws as he pleased, without regard to the wishes of the people. The New England colonies were reduced by James to almost the same condition, and Edmund Andros was appointed to govern them.

Two years more passed away, and in 1688 James was driven from the throne by William of Orange. All authority being broken in the colonies by this revolution in England, the government at New York City was seized by an absurd, blustering German, Jacob Leisler, who, by extravagant talk about liberty and by accusing every one who opposed him of being a papist, secured a large following among the mixed population of the province, which was not yet under thorough control of Englishmen.

Some such seizure was justifiable under the circumstances, for all lawful authority had come to an end ; and in several of the other colonies competent men took possession of the colonial government, by a committee of safety or other means, to prevent anarchy, but always with the distinct understanding that they held it merely until the new king's pleasure could be known, and under these men the government was carried on in an orderly manner without injury to the province. It is another of those numerous instances which show the vast superiority of Englishmen in all political matters, and the instinctive manner in which in emergencies they adopt the sound and conservative course.

But when the German, Leisler, seized New York, having none of the Englishman's instinct, he threw everything into confusion. Full of insane suspicions of every one, elated, pompous, and ridiculous with the sudden possession of power, he soon had the whole province in a turmoil. Albany refused to submit to his wild rule, and for a time the colony was ruled by two governments: one at the head of the Hudson, under the Schuyler family, and the other at the mouth of the river, under Leisler, whose reckless conduct soon brought on a horrible Indian massacre at Schenectady.

His extravagance and incompetence might possibly have been forgiven on the ground that he was holding the government in trust for the new king, and knew no better than to make a fool of himself. But when Major Richard Ingoldsby arrived from England with two companies of British soldiers, he refused to let him into the fort. His excuse was that the new governor appointed by King William had not yet arrived, and that Ingoldsby had no authority to act in his absence. There was reason for not letting Ingoldsby assume the government, but none for abusing and storming at him; and if Leisler had had a little British common sense he could easily have smoothed over and compromised matters until the arrival of the new governor, who was expected every day.

But instead of a moderate course which would have pacified everybody, Leisler was so swollen with his own importance that he could not endure the thought of parting with his power. When he found that some of his personal enemies had been appointed to office by the king, he cried out in a passion, "What! those popish dogs, rogues—sacrament! if the king should send three thousand such, I would cut them all off!"

He collected militia in the fort to support him, and spread stories that Ingoldsby's troops were papists and disaffected persons from England who had forged their commissions. He received advice and requests from various quarters, urging him to peace; but as he seemed to be rapidly gathering his adherents into the fort and training the guns on the town, the members of the council and other respectable people collected the militia from the country and prepared to support Ingoldsby, who had quartered his troops in the city hall and was acting very quietly.

Leisler might still have escaped the worst consequences if he had not at this moment, in a fit of passion, fired a gun from the fort, with his own hands, on Ingoldsby's troops on parade. Volleys of musketry followed from both sides; several were killed and wounded; and Leisler was heating balls in the furnace to fire the town when hostilities ceased for the day. The next day a few more shots were fired from the fort; but Ingoldsby, acting very properly and prudently, refrained from attacking the fort, and stood on the defensive, expecting that Leisler would attack the town.

Fortunately, at this moment Sloughter, the new governor, arrived in the harbor, and after a day's parleying and foolish threatening, Leisler surrendered. He was tried for treason, together with some of his prominent accomplices, and convicted. Most of his followers escaped punishment, but Leisler himself and his principal assistant, Milborne, were hung.

It was afterwards thought that it was a mistake to hang him, because it gave him too much the character of a martyr and continued for many years the factions and disputes which he had started among the Dutch. But he had been so arbitrary and tyrannical, imprisoning and injuring people in every way, and almost driving the Mohawk Indians into an alliance with the French in Canada, that his death was clamorously demanded by the most important people, and even women petitioned the governor to execute sentence upon him.

It has been said that Sloughter, the governor, was unwilling to have him executed, and that those who were determined to be revenged on Leisler had to get the governor drunk before he could be persuaded to sign the death-warrant. In 1695 the British Parliament reversed the attainder of treason of all the rebels and annulled their convictions.

The prominent people and men of property had been Leisler's opponents and the lower classes his friends. The reaction against his excesses which naturally followed had put the upper classes in power, and they were determined to destroy him. In 1699, when the lower classes were more in control, under the favor of Governor Bellamont, who was inclined to side with them, the remains of both Leisler and Milborne were disinterred, exhibited in state, and reburied in the Dutch church.

The strong dislike and distrust of Roman Catholics which, as we shall see, was common in all the colonies was particularly pronounced in New York. The Dutch had had most bitter experience with the adherents of the Pope, and had more reason than the English to hate them. The Spanish Inquisition had slaughtered the people of the Netherlands by thousands. The liberty of Holland was finally gained by a long war with Catholic Spain, and was maintained for generations by a continual state of war with all the great Catholic powers of Europe, which believed that they could destroy the source of all Protestantism by crushing Holland. Nothing aroused so quickly the energy and vigilance of a Dutchman as to suggest the existence of a Catholic plot. Leisler, when he had seized the government at New York, kept himself in power by constant appeals to this sentiment.

In 1699 a severe law was passed ordering all popish priests and missionaries to leave the province by the first day of November, 1700. If any remained after that date they were to be treated as incendiaries, disturbers of the peace, and must suffer perpetual imprisonment. Those who should escape from prison were, when retaken, to be punished with death. This seems to have been the severest of all the colonial laws against Catholics.

Many of the negro slaves in New York City were Spanish Catholics captured by Dutch vessels from the galleons, and when, in 1741, nine buildings were set on fire within a month, there was at once a suspicion of a plot among these negroes to burn the town. England was then at war with Spain, and General Oglethorpe sent word from Georgia of a Spanish conspiracy to burn all the magazines and towns of the British in America. Priests were to be employed, who, pretending to be doctors or dancing-masters, should gain the confidence of families.

This, combined with the nine fires, created a panic on Manhattan Island not unlike the Salem witchcraft delusion; for to the Dutchman a papist seemed more dangerous than a witch that rode a broom.

Informers appeared just as fifty years before in Massachusetts, and soon one hundred and sixty negroes and twenty-one white men were in jail. Every sort of evidence was admitted, as at Salem, and the more ignorant and sensational the witnesses were the more they were believed. They related extraordinary tales of rites performed over black rings on the floor with bowls of punch held over their heads.

Thirteen were burned to death, eighteen hung, and seventy transported. Among those hung was a white man named Ury, who was believed to have attempted to officiate as a popish priest. As in the Salem witchcraft, the excitement was checked when the informers, running short of material, began to name important persons.

Leisler's outburst ended the formative political period of New York. King William gave the province the usual colonial government of governor and council and a general assembly elected by the people, which remained unchanged until the Revolution. The original Dutch population continued in the majority, with the English element increasing very slowly. There was no serious problem in the province, except the gradual absorption and control of the Dutch by the English; but the process was so gradual and so unconnected with exciting events that there is nothing to be said of it, except that there was comparatively little change until after the Revolution, when, the Dutch landholding system having been broken up, the New Englanders swarmed into the State.

The governors were, of course, Englishmen after the conquest, and appointed by the British crown; but the members of the assembly and many of the officials were Dutch.

At first the only change that could be noticed was that the population increased and there was more prosperity, which seems to have been caused by the more vigorous and steady government and the removal of the restrictions and burdens which had depressed the province under the imbecile rule of Holland and the West India Company.

But as the majority of the people were Dutch, there was for a long time little or no change in other respects. The men still wore the numerous pairs of trousers one over the other, and the women the innumerable petticoats of which Irving made such sport. They sat on the front stoop in the summer afternoons, and smoked their long pipes and drank their beer as contentedly under the British crown as under their High Mightinesses the States-General of Holland. New-Year's Day was as great a festival as ever, and holidays were still made as numerous as possible throughout the year.

They remained essentially traders, and were slow in developing agriculture and very slow in advancing into the wilderness. All through the colonial period the province consisted of the town of New York, on Manhattan Island, and straggling settlements and farms up the Hudson until the next important town, Albany, was reached. Beyond Albany, to the north and westward, the settlements branched out a little, but the development in this direction was comparatively slight. It was not until after the Revolution, when the overflowing New Englanders began to cross the Hudson and the province became thoroughly Anglicized, that the real development and prosperity of New York began and the name of the Empire State was earned.

The great mass of the Catskill Mountains, extending along the west side of the Hudson from New Jersey almost to Albany, was a serious obstacle to the advance of the colonists into the interior of the province, and confined them to the narrow valley of the Hudson. In colonial times, so far as settlement was concerned, the Hudson Valley was all there was of New York.

Manhattan and the Tappan Zee

The great region west of Albany, through the lakes Oneida, Cayuga, Seneca, and the Genesee Valley to Niagara Falls, was held by the Iroquois, as the French called them, or the Five Nations, as they were called by the English. The Mohawks lived nearest Albany, along the river which still bears their name, and they were in many respects the most vigorous, intelligent, and warlike of all the tribes. Next to them on the west came the Oneidas; and then, in order, the Onondagas, the Cayugas, and the Senecas, which last were the most numerous of the five tribes. In 1715 the Tuscaroras, a Southern tribe, defeated in war by the English settlers of South Carolina, moved up and joined the Iroquois, and were given land between the Oneidas and the Onondagas. From that time the Iroquois were known among the English as the Six Nations.

They numbered altogether about twelve thousand, and were the most civilized and powerful tribes on the continent. They were a confederacy with a regular system of representation and government, which, though not reduced to writing, was administered most effectively by their chiefs and leading men. Their national council was composed of fifty chiefs, of whom the Mohawks sent nine, the Oneidas nine, the Onondagas fourteen, the Cayugas ten, and the

Senecas eight. Their women were also allowed to hold meetings, and in important matters their advice was received with respect. They called themselves sometimes Aquanu Schioni, which meant the United People, and at other times by a name which meant the People of the Long House, possibly, as some have supposed, from the shape of their cabins, or from the long extent of their country from the Hudson to Niagara Falls.

When the first white men saw them they were already living in cabins built of wood, and they cultivated large fields of corn, beans, tobacco, and pumpkins, using stone implements to perform their work. They were more thrifty and provident than the other tribes, storing their crops against a time of want, and manufacturing rude pottery. They built strong forts palisaded with logs, which were proof against the white man's fire-arms of that time, and they made a sort of armor out of sticks and deerskins.

For many generations, and before the white men knew them, they had dominated all the tribes of the country westward to the Mississippi and southward to the Gulf of Mexico, and it has even been said that they had made hostile expeditions through Mexico and into the Isthmus of Panama. They collected tribute from the New England Indians and from the River

Indians, as they were called, along the Hudson. The Pennsylvania tribes were also their vassals, and they drove their western enemies, the Hurons and Ottawas, to the sources of the Mississippi.

Their superior intelligence and skill in the arts of their wild life gave them this dominion; and they had also by accident or natural shrewdness selected for their home the region which is the military strategic point for all the rest of the country. A glance at the map shows that from their Long House, across the lake region of New York, natural water highways led in every direction to the south and west.

On their left, as they looked south, was the Hudson; then came the Delaware and the Susquehanna with their sources along the southern edge of the house; at the southwest corner the head-waters of the Allegheny, leading into the Ohio, which leads into the Mississippi; and on the west Lake Erie with its long chain of inland seas. The rapid currents of all these streams could in a few days sweep their light war canoes into Long Island Sound, the Delaware Bay, the Chesapeake, or the valley of the Mississippi.

Military men from Washington to Grant have often called attention to the natural strength of this situation, and the Long House with the Hudson Valley is probably to-day the strategic position for the white man's dominion, as it was three hundred years ago for the Iroquois.

Receiving fire-arms, steel tools, and textile fabrics from Europeans, the Five Nations advanced considerably in civilization during the hundred and fifty years of the colonial period. They built houses of planks, instead of logs, planted larger crops, had fields of turnips and carrots, orchards of peach-, apple-, and pear-trees, and graveyards with wooden monuments. They held the balance of power between the French in Canada and the English colonies south of them, and were in a very important sense makers of American history.

They could have annihilated New Netherland at any moment and swept the Dutchmen into the ocean, but they were not much disposed to do so. Apparently an instinct of self-preservation restrained them; and they seemed to see their true policy in becoming a neutral nation, receiving knowledge and improved facilities from the white men north and south of them, prompt to resent aggressions and insults, but content to hold the Long House intact, without any desire for vengeance or conquest that might bring upon them swift destruction. As long as they held to this policy they flourished, and when they changed it at the time of the Revolution, their doom was sealed.

Manhattan and the Tappan Zee

The Dutch had been always well aware of the power of the Five Nations, and used the utmost care to keep on friendly terms with them. Fortunately, the Long House of these Indians was some distance from the Hudson Valley, and the Dutch, finding room enough for their purposes within that valley, did not press upon the lands of the Iroquois, and did not come in competition with them, as they did with the river tribes. Albany was at the eastern door of the Long House, and there the Dutchmen stood to receive the beaver skins from the Mohawk and the Seneca.

The great manor of the Van Rensselaers was also close to this eastern door, and on the conduct of that family in their dealings with the red man a great deal depended. Arendt Van Corlear was the Indian agent for the Van Rensselaers, and became so popular among the Five Nations that for more than a hundred years afterwards they called every governor of New York Corlear.

Close by, another family, the Schuylers, had their home and estate. They were not patroons, and had no special feudal privileges; but they owned great tracts of land with tenants, which gave them in effect the position of barons. They intermarried with the Van Rensselaers, and these two families had great influence in

New York long after the Revolution. The Van Rensselaers, it was said, furnished the money and the Schuylers the brains.

To the Schuylers, and especially to Peter Schuyler, the head of the family, has usually been given the credit of rendering most valuable service in securing the continued friendship of the Five Nations. The early Dutch traders had been very careful in their dealings with them; but the increase of irresponsible hunters and frontiersmen in the Mohawk Valley, who cheated the red men and furnished them with fire-water, and the reckless policy while Leisler held the government, were rapidly alienating them.

At this juncture, about the year 1692, Peter Schuyler began to interest himself in their affairs, and soon, by his ability and honesty in dealing with them, secured their respect. They called him Quider, which was their way of pronouncing Peter, and he was supported and assisted in his dealings with them by the families of his brothers and the Cuylers, who also had large estates in that region.

Peter Schuyler was mayor of Albany, colonel of the militia, judge of the criminal court, head of the commissioners of the colony for Indian affairs, and for many years conducted all negotiations, offset the intrigues of the French, and defeated an invading force of the French and Indians from Canada. He took five of the Iroquois chiefs to England in 1709, where they were duly impressed with the importance of an alliance with Queen Anne; and in return for his services, Anne wished to knight him.

But with his simple-hearted Dutch frankness he declined the honor. He already, he said, had more property than his brothers' families, and a title might arouse envy and estrangement among a large connection which had always enjoyed the most united happiness and whose unity was valuable to the province.

He died in 1724, and for some years the relations with the Six Nations were not so favorable as was desired, until that romantic character, William Johnson, appeared in 1738 to take the place of Quider.

Johnson belonged to a well-known and prominent family of the gentry of Ireland. He was intended for mercantile life, but his plans were changed by the refusal of his parents to allow him to marry a lady with whom he had fallen in love. His uncle, Admiral Sir Peter Warren, owned lands on the Mohawk River which he had from his wife, one of the De Lanceys of New York, and young Johnson was sent to manage these lands and encourage settlers to come to them.

Vigorous and genial in temperament and fond of hunting, he became fascinated at once with the wild life of the frontier. He settled near the Mohawk River, west of Schenectady, and soon surrounded himself with an establishment which resembled in some respects a Carolina or Virginia plantation. He colonized and laid out farms and villages, had stores and mills, traded with the Indians, and indulged himself to the full in the sports of the forest and a most liberal hospitality in his large mansion-house, which in appearance was not unlike the plantation-houses in Virginia.

He married a German girl of the country, by whom he had several children, and after her death he had several mistresses, the favorite and most famous of whom was an Indian girl of unusual beauty,—Molly Brant, sister of Joseph Brant, the Mohawk chief. She bore him eight children, and he lived with her until his death.

He had a most numerous household,—a secretary named Lafferty, who was also his lawyer; a physician, Dr. Daly; a bouw-master to take charge of his farm; a gardener, who kept lawns and flower-beds round his house, though in the midst of a wilderness; a dwarf, who played the violin; a school-master, who taught his numerous progeny, natural and legitimate, as well as those of his neighbors; and, besides these, he had fifteen or twenty slaves, house servants, a butler, dwarf waiters, a blacksmith, and a tailor.

He built lodges at various places for hunting and fishing, established churches and saw-mills, and introduced into the Mohawk Valley fruit culture, sheep, and thoroughbred horses. His fame spread through all the colonies, and he was petted and courted by every one, visited by governors and distinguished men, who never wearied of his conversation, and made a trustee of Queen's College, now Rutgers, at New Brunswick, New Jersey.

With the Six Nations he acquired a commanding influence from the beginning, learned their language, became familiar with all their customs and traditions, and the fierce Mohawks made him one of their chiefs. He had, it seems, a most fascinating manner and address, made up of mingled manliness and affability, which won the entire devotion of the strong as well as the weak. During his whole life he was the means of communication and friendship between all the English colonies and the Six Nations, and he saved the Six Nations from an alliance with the French. He was in constant employment, making treaties, settling land grants and small disputes with these Indians, and in an intercourse of this sort of over thirty years they never lost their confidence in his honesty and integrity.

He commanded the expedition which defeated Dieskau at Lake George, and for this victory he was made a baronet, and he certainly lived like one. His services were fully recognized by the British government, which lavished upon him land grants, salaries, and absolute power in dealing with all the northern Indians. After holding the Six Nations in check through the long French and Indian wars which followed Braddock's defeat, and preventing them from joining in the conspiracy of Pontiac, he died in 1774, just when the Six Nations were debating whether they should join the colonists or the mother country in the Revolution.

On this decision their fate depended. If they had remained neutral, as many of their chiefs counselled, or if they had joined the colonists, they would in all probability still be the Six Nations, inhabiting a country of their own in the heart of New York, and in almost as high a state of civilization as the white man. But they chose to take sides with the British, and after assisting in the campaign which ended in the defeat of Burgoyne at Saratoga, they began to massacre in the Cherry Valley, in New York, and finally made a descent into Pennyslvania, where they destroyed the settlement of Wyoming.

General Sullivan was sent to conquer them,

Van Cortlandt Manor
Croton, N. Y.
Built 1748

and, following up the Susquehanna Valley, he defeated them at the entrance of their Long House, and then invaded their pretty villages, cornfields, and orchards, which were all ruthlessly destroyed. Their alliance with the British was ended, and their spirit and existence as a confederacy broken. They relapsed into their separate tribal existence, and lost all of that interesting civilization which they had been building up so long. They became almost instantly mere ordinary degraded Indians, and their descendants are still to be seen in summer time selling colored baskets at the wateringplaces of Northern New York.

The New York of colonial times presents the curious picture of the vast territory from Niagara Falls to Albany an unbroken wilderness, save the occasional patches of cultivation of the Iroquois, who held the country with an iron hand, though under the shrewd influence of a most romantic and Bohemian white man. At Albany we have the great patroonship of the Van Rensselaers and the great estates of the Schuylers and Cuylers, with a large part of the population living as their tenants; and as we pass down the Hudson we meet with the manors of the Cortlandts and the Livingstons, and the great Philipse manor at Yonkers. At Manhattan Island the manors cease, and on Long Island, after emerging from the circle of Dutch at the eastern end of it, we find ourselves among the English Puritans, who had migrated from Connecticut and established the New England system of small towns.

Colonial New York was a strong aristocracy, with nearly all the available land, except on Long Island, in the hands of a few great families, who would not part with any of it, and insisted that every immigrant that came to the province should become their tenant. This was a serious check to the growth of the colony and the principal cause of its backwardness until the system was changed after the Revolution. Immigrants, especially English immigrants, and the Puritans of New England, who were seeking an outlet for their surplus population, refused to come to a province where they were compelled to be the tenants of Dutchmen, when in Pennsylvania or New Jersey they could take up all the land they pleased in their own right.

It was very different from the aristocracy of Virginia, where there were no tenants, and each aristocrat owned a plantation, which he cultivated with slaves. There were slaves in New York, rather numerous considering that it was a Northern colony; for the Dutch had been among the earliest slave-traders, and the West

India Company had brought many negroes to New Netherland. But they were used as house servants, seldom worked in the fields, and were most numerous in the town of New York, where they caused the serious disturbance which has been described. They intensified, however, as slaves always do, the aristocratic tone of the province.

The tendency of the patroonships and manors to check development and deter immigrants was increased by a sullen though quiet hostility of the Dutch against the English. They tried their best to keep them out; and not only the patroons and great men, but the small land-holders, clung to their property and refused to sell to Englishmen, who in colonial times had great difficulty in creeping into the province, except on Long Island and in the neighborhood of the town of New York. They could come in as traders and merchants, and they became numerous on Manhattan Island; but comparatively few of them could gain any real foothold in the rest of the country until after the Revolution.

Another serious injury to the progress of the colony was the corruption of its government. This corruption, having been started under the old Dutch governors, continued almost unabated after the English conquest. Dongan, an Irishman, appointed governor by the Duke of York, was as thrifty as Van Twiller. When the duke became king, this Dongan made use of the change, on the plea that it had vacated charters and patents, to demand that new charters should be taken and fees paid to him. New York and Albany each paid him three hundred pounds, and Rensselaerwyck two hundred pounds.

Governor Fletcher embezzled the revenue, allowed the fortifications and government houses to fall into decay, just as Van Twiller had done, and his officials made money by selling protection to pirates, and secured for themselves large grants of land. All this seems to have been done without protest from the people, who apparently regarded it as a matter of course.

As we read on through the colony's history in the eighteenth century, we find that the corruption continues. Land-grabbing and schemes to defraud the Indians of their land were numerous, and in some of these the Dutch clergy were interested. Dominie Dellius, the pastor at Albany, was charged with procuring fraudulent deeds from the Indians, and a Dutchman named Pinhorne obtained in a suspicious manner tracts four miles wide and fifty miles long by the banks of the Mohawk River.

Peter Schuyler was at first interested in this land purchase, but, unable to reconcile himself

to the fraud of the transaction, he retired from
it; and it is extremely doubtful if the lantern of
Diogenes could have found another man like him
among the prominent men of the province.

Lord Cornbury, who was governor for a
time, appropriated to his own use one thousand
pounds that had been raised for the defence of
the frontiers and fifteen hundred pounds that
had been raised for batteries at the Narrows.
He also received two thousand pounds as a
present from the assembly in such a scandalous
manner that Queen Anne prohibited any more
such gifts. He extorted money from ship-
masters, and was as wasteful and reckless with
the public property as Van Twiller.

He was fond of dressing himself in women's
clothes, and was frequently seen in the evening
in this costume, strolling about on the ramparts
of the fort with a fan in his hand; and a portrait of him, which is still preserved in England, shows him in this dress with the fan.
This strange whim was either a rakish joke—
for he had been heard to say that, as he was
the representative of Queen Anne, who, by
the way, was his cousin, he must dress as a
woman—or else he was crazy. Some said it
was in consequence of a vow.

The wife of this " peculiar and detestable
maggot," as he was called, was in every way his

equal. He had married her, it is said, for the beauty of her ear, and when the novelty of the ear wore off, he neglected her and would give her no money. She stole clothes and other things she wanted from all her acquaintances, by borrowing and never returning. She had a lordly way of going to visit people in their houses and ordering them to send to her home anything that caught her fancy, and she had eight or ten young women whom she compelled to come to her and do her sewing. As she was the governor's wife, few in those days of great respect for authority dared refuse. When the wheels of her carriage were heard in the streets, the people would say, " Here comes my lady ; hide this ; hide that ; take that away."

Governor Hunter devised a plan to import Germans at the expense of the British government, and ostensibly to benefit the colony by their labor in producing naval stores, but at the same time to enrich himself or Robert Livingston. There were at that time twenty or thirty thousand Germans in England who had been invited by Queen Anne to flee from cruel persecution in their native country. More had come than were expected or wanted, and, all being destitute, they had to be housed in tents in the fields near London until they could be got rid of.

They were shipped to Ireland, Louisiana, and various places, and Hunter obtained three or four thousand of them, together with a grant by Parliament of ten thousand pounds to assist his project. More than half of them died at sea from the dirt and disease of the ship. The rest were put to work on the Livingston manor; but, finding themselves in a condition of abject slavery, and discovering the fraud of the whole transaction, they deserted and scattered themselves through the country.

Many of them were given lands by the Indians, and after they had planted their crops and were flourishing, the governor informed them that they had no title to their land and must pay for it. Some submitted, and the rest were again scattered, many of them going into Pennsylvania; and ever after that the Germans, who at that period were coming to Pennsylvania in large numbers, carefully avoided New York.

The corruption of the whole system of management in New York is shown by the constant appearance of back claims against the government, invented on one excuse or another, and often thirty years old. They were paid, however, apparently without much indignation or protest, and in 1717 forty-eight thousand pounds in paper money had to be issued to meet one batch of them.

Manhattan and the Tappan Zee

But it is needless to multiply details and describe the governors who destroyed deeds and invalidated titles so that they could gain fees by reissues, or to tell of Clinton, who made a fortune of eighty thousand pounds out of his office, or of Clarke, who, beginning as clerk of the council, became governor, and returned to England worth one hundred thousand pounds.

New York is said to have had more colonial governors than any of the other provinces, and it is not surprising, because six or seven years seem to have been long enough for any one of them to amass a fortune, and it was but fair that others should be given a chance, or a "whack," as the Irish, who now rule New York, call it.

As the judges under the old Dutch rule had been mere creatures of the governor, and compelled to submit their important decisions to him for revision, so after the English conquest we find the bench shamefully controlled by political influence. The modern corruption in New York under the Irish, and the direct buying by the judges of their seats in the courts of law, which is the worst blot on our American civilization, seem to be a direct inheritance.

It is true that a great many of the frauds in colonial New York were the work of English governors; but they were committed because the Dutch, who composed the majority of the province, allowed them to be committed. They could have stopped it all by complaint, remonstrance, or aggressive attack; and it is noteworthy that the few people who protested against the corrupt condition of affairs were usually Englishmen, conspicuous among whom were William Smith, William Livingston, and J. Morin Scott, who founded a reform society called the " Sons of Liberty."

Rapacious and dishonest men often, in that age, sought employment under the British crown and obtained colonial appointments, and they robbed New York because her people allowed her to be robbed. Some of the men who were governors of New York were at other times governors of some of the other colonies, where they never dared even to attempt such outrages.

If such things had been attempted in Massachusetts or Pennsylvania, there would have been an uprising which would have given us some exciting pages of history; and when in Virginia Charles II. and his creatures started on similar courses of public plunder, there was instantly a bloody rebellion led by Nathaniel Bacon, which for a time destroyed the royal authority in the province.

The Dutch as a nation have had the general

reputation of being honorable in trade; but in political government and public transactions in New York they seem to have been rotten to the core, and they corrupted the English who came to them. The English governors imitated almost to the letter the methods of the old Dutch governors, because the opinion of the community had not changed, and they upheld the plundering by an Englishman as readily as they had that by a Dutch governor. We find Clarke, when he was in the midst of amassing his one hundred thousand pounds in seven years, writing home to the British government most gloomy descriptions of the prospects of the colony and the poverty-stricken emoluments of its governor, just as if he had been Van Twiller; and the people seem never to have been inclined to check him or, in headstrong Peter's words, "tell on him."

In the days of Washington and Jefferson, John Adams used to say that New York politics were always an inextricable mystery to him. If he had read the colonial history of the State he need not have wondered. The English race is by no means perfect or entirely free from corruption; but on the whole, if left to themselves, they are more honest, pure, and efficient in political matters than the Dutch, the Irish, or any of the alien nationalities which it has been our misfortune to have in such numbers among us.

The corruption in colonial New York produced a famous episode in the development of the law of libel, known as the Zenger case. John Peter Zenger was in 1734 one of the few men who seemed inclined to "tell on" the governors and their subservient courts. Old Peter the Headstrong would have threatened to make him a foot shorter and send the pieces to Holland; but there were no newspapers in Stuyvesant's time, and Zenger had the advantage of coming out suddenly with his statement in print. He asserted in the journal of which he was editor that some one had deserted New York and gone to Pennsylvania, giving his reason:

"We see men's deeds destroyed, judges arbitrarily displaced, new courts erected without consent of the legislature, by which, it seems to me, trials by juries are taken away when a governor pleases; men of known estates denied their votes contrary to the received practice of the best expositor of the law. Who is there in that province that can call anything his own, or enjoy any liberty longer than those in the administration will condescend to let them do it? for which reason I left it, as I believe more will."

Zenger was promptly arrested by the governor's order, and when the grand jury refused to indict him, he was prosecuted by the attorney-general on information. The lawyers of New

Manhattan and the Tappan Zee

York were at that time in as demoralized a condition as the judges, and consisted mostly of mere demagogues, pettifoggers, or worse. Two of the few good ones, Alexander and Smith, who were to defend Zenger, began their proceedings by attacking the validity of the commissions of two of the judges, De Lancey and Philipse, and for this impertinence were disbarred from practice, and John Chambers was assigned by the court as counsel for Zenger.

But when the day of the trial came, the services of Andrew Hamilton, a Quaker lawyer of Philadelphia, were secured. Hamilton was speaker of the Pennsylvania assembly, and a man of considerable learning and brilliant eloquence. The argument of the government was that, whether the libel was true or false, Zenger must be convicted because he had reviled those in authority, who were the king's representatives.

Against this Hamilton offered to prove the truth of Zenger's statements. He enlarged on the tyranny and cruelty of trying a man on information after a grand jury had refused to indict him. He described the condition of the province, and declared that free people were not bound by law to support a governor who went about to destroy it. They had a right to protest and tell their grievances. It was not the cause, he told the jury, of one poor printer, or of New York alone; it was the cause of every freeman that lived under the British government in America.

"It is the best cause, it is the cause of liberty; and I make no doubt but your upright conduct this day will not only entitle you to the love and esteem of your fellow-citizens, but every man who prefers freedom to slavery will bless and honor you as men who have baffled the attempt of tyranny, and by the impartial and uncorrupt verdict, have laid a noble foundation for securing to ourselves, our posterity, and our neighbors that to which nature and the laws of our country have given us a right—the liberty both of exposing and opposing arbitrary power, in these parts of the world at least, by speaking and writing the truth."

This was a most apt and strong statement of the modern doctrine of the law of libel; but at that time it was not recognized either in England or America. De Lancey, the chief-justice, charged the jury directly against it. But they accepted Hamilton's view, and acquitted Zenger amid cheers and shouts, which the chief-justice could not restrain by threats of arrest. The successful advocate was given a banquet and a gold box with the freedom of the city, and a salute was fired in his honor.

The patroons and other great landed proprietors spent much of their time in the town of New York, where many of them had winter houses. Even before the English conquest the thrifty habits of the Dutch traders had raised to wealth and refinement many of those families which now form what we have long known as the Knickerbocker aristocracy. Van Dam, Van Cortlandt, Van Curler, Philipse, Van Dyke, Van Ness, Ten Eyck, Van Schaack, Schermerhorn, Brinkerhoff, Van Brunt, Van Pelt, and Van Wart are some of the names which Irving found easy to ridicule, because they all sound absurd to English ears. It is a laughable chapter in which he describes how all these clans gathered to assist the mighty Stuyvesant in his war against the Swedes on the Delaware.

It was a curious aristocracy, unlike anything in Pennsylvania or New England; and though at first it seems to resemble the plantation nobility of the South, a close inspection shows a wide difference. There was none of the Virginian's intense love of sport, fox-hunting, racing, and cock-fighting. The Dutchman was a more reposeful aristocrat, and athletics were not within his tastes.

Though vastly more liberal-minded than the New England Puritan, he yet had a strange touch of the Puritan objection to amusements, except when indulged in by boys. A ride on a heavy Flemish horse, a peaceful pipe at the front door, where he watched the wrens and swallows, with billiards or a game of cards, was, he thought, quite enough. He cannot be charged with the excesses of gambling, rough pleasure, and the daring speculative life of the Virginian, nor with the Virginian's intellect and creative genius in politics.

But there was much that was worthy and fascinating among the Dutch patroons, and it would have been pleasant in those days to have passed from the mansion-houses of the Philipses, Van Dams, or Schuylers to Shirley or Westover on the James, and note the contrast.

The Dutch manor-houses were often large and beautifully decorated, with chimney-pieces of carved marble, arabesque ceilings, wainscoted walls, and panels of Dutch tiles. It seems to have been not uncommon for one of these establishments to have fifty white and black servants to assist at the entertainments and take care of the house and grounds.

There was usually a large formal garden, edged with box, which was the special care of the ladies of the family, and women of the better classes took a pride in working with their own hands in both vegetable- and flower-gardens. The New York Dutch, like their ancestors in Holland, were excessively fond of flowers, which they planted in beds, each kind by itself, in a mass of bright color.

"I think I yet see," says Mrs. Grant in her "Memoirs of an American Lady," "what I have so often beheld both in town and country, a respectable mistress of a family going out to her garden in an April morning, with her great calash, her little painted basket of seeds, and her rake over her shoulder, to her garden labors. . . . A woman in very easy circumstances, and abundantly gentle in form and manners, would sow and plant and rake incessantly."

The barns were of great size, like those of the Germans in Pennsylvania, and there were large herds of horses and cattle, and fine orchards. On the Philipse manor at Yonkers there were two rent days, one at Philipseburg and the other at Sleepy Hollow, where the tenants appeared to pay in money or in the produce of the land; and after the ceremony of paying was concluded, they were all indulged in a great feast for the rest of the day in the ancient feudal manner.

The Cortlandt, the Livingston, and the Van Rensselaer manors were each entitled to send a representative to the assembly; and in some if not all of them the lord had the privilege of holding court-leet and court-baron, with very liberal powers for administering justice and punishing offences, which in the early days of the colony extended to inflicting capital punishment.

Albany and Schenectady were situated near

each other, at the eastern end of the Long House of the Iroquois, and all through colonial times they were the principal frontier towns. They were very much alike, and both were entirely devoted to the fur trade; in fact, they were the centre of the American fur trade at that time. In the early days every house in Albany was a trading store, with furs in the second story. The people kept the trade to themselves as much as possible, and down to the time of the Revolution, and even after, no outsider could transact business in the little towns without paying five pounds for the privilege.

Dutch Albany consisted of a wide and long street, called Handelaer, parallel to the river, with the space between it and the river occupied by gardens. Another street, called Yonkheer, crossed it at right angles, leading up the hill to the fort. The houses were low, with high peaked roofs, on which were gilded weather-vanes in figures of horses, lions, geese, and sloops.

The gable ends of the houses, "notched like steps," were usually towards the street, and little lawns and gardens surrounded them. From the eaves of the roofs projected long water-spouts almost to the middle of the street, which on a rainy day were very apt to drench the passer-by, and the date when each house was built was usually let into the brick or stone in iron or black brick figures. The black bricks were used in contrast with the red to make flowers or patterns in the walls. The governor's house, it is said, had two black brick hearts on it.

The stoop or porch in front of each door was in summer, as in New York, the principal meeting-place, a sort of exchange or club for all the townsfolk. It was very churlish and rude to pass a stoop without saluting every one who was sitting on it, a custom which often made progress along the street very slow.

There they sat, smoking and watching the fluttering and swinging of the great weather-vanes; and as evening approached, tinkling bells announced that the cows were coming home. Each family had one of these patient beasts, so petted and tame that they all returned from the common pasture of their own accord in the evening, to be milked at the door under the trees. They stayed by the house all night, licking the salt and eating the vegetables that were given them; and after being milked again in the morning, walked tinkling away to their pasture.

The children ate their supper, composed principally of the milk of the cow that had just come in, sitting on the steps of the porch with their bowls in their laps, while their elders and the youths and maidens sat on the benches above, chatting and singing.

Almost every family of any means had negro slaves as house-servants, who were treated with great kindness, brought up in the same religion as that of the family, and often became as attached and devoted to their masters as sons or daughters. The first New Year's Day after a negro woman's child became three years old it was formally presented to one of the children of the family. The child to whom it was given immediately gave it a piece of money and a pair of shoes, and from that day the little negro was the child's servant. Every member of a respectable family was presumed to be supplied in this way with a slave or body-servant.

Most of the young men began life by entering the woods to trade for furs, and in these expeditions they were accompanied by their slaves, who often saved their masters' lives, or, when wounded or sick, carried them on their backs out of the wilderness.

The last resort in punishing a refractory slave was to sell him to the West Indies, and such was the dread of this punishment among the negroes that they would sometimes kill themselves when finally condemned to it. In the town of New York the condition of the negroes was not so ideal as in Albany. But the Albanians, we are assured, although friendly and familiar with their slaves, regarded with the greatest abhorrence any mingling of the blood of the two races. Mulattoes were almost unknown until after the Revolution, when the progress of the British army through the country could be traced by them.

In the spring of the year every boy and man became for a few weeks a pigeon and wild-fowl shooter. The wild pigeons, which are now almost extinct, existed in colonial times in countless millions. They are said to have fed in winter on the myrtle berries along the sea-coast of the Southern colonies, and on the first approach of spring they began to follow the shore, turning up the valleys of all the great rivers that led northward to the regions where they spent the summer.

When the vast flocks reached Albany, every occupation and amusement was dropped and the whole population turned out for the slaughter, which, with that of the geese and ducks, lasted for several weeks. It was not sport, for the game was too numerous and too easily killed. It was shot down by firing into the enormous flocks, and the dead were collected in the village in great heaps. In Cooper's novel of "The Chain-Bearer" there is an excellent description of this pigeon-slaughter in another part of New York, where a cannon was used to fire into the dense masses of birds as they swept by, and it is not improbable that in many cases this could have been done.

When the spring flight of birds had ceased, the sturgeon appeared in the river, and the people all took to their canoes, following the course of the fish far up the stream, spearing them by torchlight, and often remaining two nights upon the water until they had filled their boats.

When a young man had reached the age of about twenty, and thought of marrying, he procured for himself a canoe, forty or fifty dollars, and with his negro started up the river into the woods. He dressed almost like an Indian, and soon had more than the Indian's instinct in woodcraft. His small sum of money was invested in guns, powder, rum, blankets, beads, and other articles, to barter for the furs; and his object was to press far into the wilderness and buy the skins before they got into the hands of those Indians, usually Mohawks, who habitually brought them down to the regular dealers at Albany. These expeditions were usually made in the spring, after the winter trapping season of the Indians was finished.

Manhattan and the Tappan Zee

Paddling up the Hudson to the Mohawk, the first difficulty encountered was the high falls of Cohoes, ten miles above Albany. Here they unloaded their canoe and carried it and its cargo round the falls. After that they entered the wilderness, and penetrated to the Great Lakes or into Canada, passing many a carrying-place, where they dragged their property through dense thickets which made Cohoes seem mere child's play.

They could carry few provisions, and were obliged to depend largely on hunting and fishing; for on their outward journey the canoe would barely hold their articles of barter, and on the return it was filled with furs. The dangers of flood and field were numerous. An upset of their narrow little craft might send all their property to the bottom; and the possession of such a valuable cargo, especially the rum, was a temptation to rival Indians, or even white traders, to murder them.

They must keep clear of the Frenchman, who was an avowed enemy and always bitterly hated by the Dutch, who had won the liberty of their country against Catholic France and Spain. Their excursions directly into Canada were therefore comparatively few; so that, after exhausting the region directly north of Albany, now partly covered by the Adirondack Mountains, they made their way to the west, and even far to the southwest towards Pennsylvania and Ohio. They often launched their canoes on the Great Lakes, paddling along the shores for hundreds of miles, and sometimes took the dangerous chance of crossing one of those inland seas. They followed up streams and rivers, where every day they met with a great tree or a whole mass of trees fallen across and blocking their way, through which they had to cut with their axes or carry the canoe around them.

When the toilsome day was ended, they slept by their fire in the midst of the ague-breeding vapors of the primeval forest, devoured by mosquitoes and flies. The wolves sat round them in a circle, kept at a distance by the glare of the fire, but howling at it all night long. The plenteous animal life of the wilderness, which has now passed away, was in those times flourishing in its full vigor; and a night in the forest in spring or early summer, with the wolves howling, the mosquitoes and insects buzzing and stinging, and the bull-frogs answering one another from every swamp, was an experience which, according to a man's taste and previous training, would either interest or disgust him.

The Dutchman never quite equalled the Englishman or the French Canadian voyageur in woodcraft and love of wild life. He never penetrated so far or accomplished so much. The ocean and trade in the tropics formed the true field of his enterprise, and he was seldom highly successful in any other. But the young Dutchmen who ranged the New York woods did very well in their way, and when they had attained some distant spot far in the interior, where the furs could be had cheap at first hand, their patience and hereditary skill at bargaining procured a valuable cargo.

Then to get home with it was the question; and after incredible hardships and labors, carrying places innumerable, and nights with the mosquitoes and wolves, the deep-laden canoe was at last dragged round Cohoes Falls and floated down to the high-peaked houses and gilded weather-vanes at Albany. The boy who had started out with his negro a few months before had returned a man. Bronzed and sturdy from exposure, sedate and calm from danger, independent in bearing, and with a touch of the Indian's austerity and reticence, he sold his furs for what seemed to him a fortune, and was ready to marry.

The next year another expedition with slave and canoe was made, and the veteran woodsman was now very apt to feel an irresistible impulse towards those enterprises for which his nation had become famous. Going to New York with his profits, he bought flour and provisions, and procured for himself and his new property a passage to the Bermudas, where he sold out at a large advance, and, purchasing one of the small cedar schooners which were built in those islands, he traded for rum, sugar, or molasses to the West Indies.

Afterwards, perhaps, he brought his schooner home and sailed her up and down the Hudson for many a day; or, satisfied with the spoil of the forest and the ocean, he became a storekeeper in Albany, with a stoop and benches before his door, and the great spout pouring the rain from the roof into the middle of the street. Sometimes, determined on still deeper tranquillity and peace, he took unto himself a farm or bouwery in the country, where he lived as contentedly as if he had never known the excitement of adventure and changing scene.

Mrs. Grant describes the Dutch at Albany as often living to a great age, which was the natural result of their thrift, cleanliness, and contented dispositions. Ninety years were frequently attained, and she knew several who reached a hundred. Like the New Englanders, they all married very early in life; but children were not as numerous as in Massachusetts and Connecticut.

The children, however, seem to have had

freer scope, and were not held down so sternly as they were among the Puritans. They associated more familiarly with their parents, and had abundance of amusement. The Albany Dutch children were the inventors of that winter amusement of coasting down hill on the snow which has since become so universal in all the northern part of the country. Mrs. Grant describes it as unknown elsewhere, and cannot understand how any one could take pleasure in it. She tells us as a matter of wonder that Albanians who had been in England and ought to have learnt something better would, on their return to their native city, go out to the hill in winter and slide down with the rest.

The Albanians, young and old, were much devoted to this excitement which they had introduced into the world. They swarmed on the street that led down the hill from the fort, one line of children whirling by on their sleds, while another line was walking up ; the elder people meanwhile sitting wrapped in their furs on those stoops which they occupied with more comfort in the summer, and indulging in loud shouts of laughter when a sled was upset.

In that extraordinary list of American customs and institutions which Mr. Campbell assures us, in his " Puritan in Holland, England,

and America," was introduced by the Dutch,*
there is no mention of coasting, although there
is some evidence to prove its Dutch origin and
none whatever to prove the origin of those he
mentions. There is also very little doubt that
the New York Dutch gave us the custom of
celebrating New Year's Day, and possibly also
originated the word crank, to describe a person
of unbalanced mind. But to offset the beneficence of this and the delightful pleasure of
coasting, they were the first to introduce negro
slaves into the country, and they gave us that
deadly compound known as the doughnut, which
has wrought more destruction to American
stomachs than can be atoned for by all the
benefits that Holland has conferred.

In Albany the children divided themselves
into companies, containing as many boys as girls,
and the brightest boy and girl were the leaders
of their company. These associations managed
the amusements and arranged the excursions and
picnics among the hills and on the river, and
there was great rivalry among them. The
parents encouraged them, and every child was
permitted to entertain its company several times
a year. On these occasions the parents went
away from the house, which was turned over

---

* See " The Evolution of the Constitution," 315.

entirely to the children and their feast of chocolate, cakes, and cider.

Among people who married so easily and naturally, unchecked by artificial sentiments and conditions, bachelors, as in New England, were looked down upon almost as social outcasts. Each one lived in the house of some family, where he was given a room. Mrs. Grant describes them as passing in and out like ghosts, never speaking unless addressed, and seeming careless of the things of the world, like people who felt themselves above it.

They associated almost exclusively with one another, and were often very religious, or at least had the appearance of it ; and occasionally one would associate with the family with which he lived and take an interest in its affairs. There were no laws, as in New England, to regulate these unfortunates who were not in sympathy with the main object of the community, and the Dutch were tolerant of them, as they were of most people whom they believed to be in error.

Their position, as well as that of the bachelors in New England, reminds us very much of those animals, solitary or rogue elephants, as they are called, in the African jungle, or buffaloes on the plains, which are often found living a morose existence, separated from the herd in which the natural life of their species is to be found. They have been driven out, the naturalists tell us, by common consent, because they would not con-form to some habit or condition necessary to the preservation of the race. Similarly, in colonial times we often find the people living such a simple life that they instinctively fol-lowed some of the primitive laws which have peopled the earth.

But when a man married in Albany he was supposed to be deprived of two pleasures which he had before enjoyed,—coasting and pig- and turkey-stealing. The people raised great quan-tities of pigs and turkeys, and when young men spent an evening at the tavern, their feast was not complete unless the roast pig or roast turkey had been stolen from some of their neighbors, and as a consequence, pigs and turkeys were the only sorts of property that were ever locked up in that simple community. If the owner could catch the thief in the act and cudgel him it was considered a great joke, and the thief was in honor bound to accept his beating patiently.

On one occasion a young man, recently mar-ried, heard a disturbance among his turkeys. Rushing out, he found some of his old comrades robbing him, and from force of habit joined them in a similar raid on a neighbor, and shared the spoils with them at the tavern.

Another story which the jolly Albanians

laughed over for many years describes how some people who intended to dine slipped off to a tavern, where others were preparing dinner, and stole their pig, half roasted, from the spit. But the last party, not to be outdone, threw a pile of shavings in front of the tavern of their despoilers, set it in a blaze, shouting " Fire!" and, when everybody was out of the building, recovered their pig, now completely roasted, and returned to enjoy it undisturbed.

The home of the Schuylers was called the Flats, a level stretch of fertile land about two miles long, on the west bank of the Hudson, above Albany. Lofty elms adorned the bank of the river, which was there a mile wide, and in the middle was an island with a sand-bar stretching from it. On this bar, in summer, the bald-headed eagles, the ospreys, the herons, and the curlews arranged themselves in great numbers and in long rows, standing there all day to fish for perch. A great variety of ducks, white divers, and sawbills with scarlet heads swam about in the water with the young broods they had raised on the shore.

The house which overlooked this pleasing scene, backed by the interminable forest, was quite large, built of brick, and with a wide hallway running completely through it in the usual style of colonial times. It was full of very valuable furniture, like the Virginia mansions; but, being a Dutchman's house, the stoop or portico was of great importance. It had benches, lattice-work, and was covered with vines, in which the birds were encouraged to build their nests. Wrens, wood-sparrows, and hundreds of other birds were protected round the house.

Mrs. Grant, like all other observers of colonial times, describes the wonderful abundance of animal life, which has now so largely disappeared from America. She was an Englishwoman, and well accustomed to the immense numbers of animals and birds which even to this day fill the fields of old England; and yet America impressed her in this respect as quite extraordinary. "Life," she says, "swarms abundant on every side; the insect population is numerous beyond belief, and the birds that feed on them are in proportion to their abundance."

She spent much time at the Flats and describes how they lived on the portico:

"While breakfasting or drinking tea in the airy portico which was often the scene of these meals, birds were constantly gliding over the table with a butterfly, grasshopper, or cicada in their bills to feed their young, which were chirping above. These familiar inmates brushed by without ceremony, while the chimney-swallow, the martin, and other hirundines in countless numbers darted past in pursuit of this aerial population, while the fields resounded with the ceaseless chirping of many gay insects unknown to our more temperate summers. . . . This loud and not unpleasing insect chorus, with the swarms of gay butterflies in constant motion, enliven scenes to which the prevalence of woods, rising ' shade above shade' on every side, would otherwise give a still and solemn aspect.''

At the back of the house was joined a smaller and lower one in which the family lived in the cold winters, with the kitchen in a sunken story directly below the dining-room. At other seasons the meals were all cooked in out-buildings and brought into the main house, an arrangement which was common in the Pennsylvania and other colonial country houses. The house contained, of course, much silver plate, and some very fine paintings which Mrs. Grant describes as of more than usual excellence.

The most strange arrangement of all was the bare skulls of horses and cattle set on every fence-post,—unseemly ornaments. But let Mrs. Grant tell of their use :

" This was not mere ornament either, but a most hospitable arrangement for the accommodation of the small familiar birds before described. The jaws are fixed on the pole and the skull uppermost. The wren thus seeing a skull placed, never fails to enter by the orifice, which is too small to admit the hand of an infant, lines the pericranium with small twigs and horse-hair, and there lays her eggs in full security. It is very amusing to see the little creatures carelessly go out and in at this little aperture, though you should be standing immediately beside it. Not satisfied with providing these singular asylums for their feathered friends, the negroes never fail to make a small round hole in the crown of every old hat they can lay their hands on, and nail it to the end of the kitchen for the same purpose. You often see in such a one, at once, thirty or forty of these odd little domiciles, with the inhabitants busily going in and out.

" Besides all these salutary provisions for the domestic comfort of the birds, there was, in clearing the way for their first establishment, a tree always left in the middle of the back yard for their sole emolument, this tree being purposely pollarded at midsummer, when all the branches were full of sap. Wherever there had been a branch the decay of the inside produced a hole, and every hole was the habitation of a bird. These were of various kinds, some of which had a pleasing note; but on the whole their songsters are far inferior to ours. I rather dwell on these minutiæ, as they not only mark the peculiarities of the country, but convey very truly the image of a people not too refined for happiness, which in the process of elegant luxury is apt to die of disgust."

The wren, of which Mrs. Grant speaks so frequently, was in the colonial period and down to the time of the civil war very numerous about all country places in America. It is the most interesting and charming of all birds, and has delighted human hearts in every nation for a thousand years. Its sprightly neatness, appealing looks and gestures, fearlessness, and, at the same time, apparent love for man and his habitations, have led us to ascribe to it all manner of qualities and to invent romances for its life. Jenny Wren was one of the names the English had for it, and in France it is said to have more than a dozen pet names among the people. But with us it is now seldom seen, except in remote places and solitudes. Something—perhaps disgust at our artificial, strained life, or the detestable English sparrow—has driven it from nearly all our country homes.

In the home of the Schuylers, as described by Mrs. Grant, we notice that same ability to enjoy country pursuits and create pleasures and enlightened surroundings out of one's own resources which we found in Virginia. The Schuyler house was constantly full of visitors,— prominent officials of the colony, military men, travellers, and people connected with Indian negotiations. The family were all interested in the Indians, and even Mrs. Schuyler devoted considerable time to studying their habits and character.

Having no children of their own, they adopted many from time to time, whom they brought up with the greatest care and started in life, always giving them furniture and a slave. Adoption was very common at that time, for in those natural conditions children were not regarded as a burden. Few people had too many of them, and any who found their families too large could easily dispose of some to those who were not so well blessed. The Schuylers, Mrs. Grant says, always adopted the children of friends or relatives who had a superfluity. They brought up in this way fifteen, besides those who came to live with them only for a year or two to relieve temporarily an overcrowded home or to enjoy the educational advantages of the society at the Schuyler house.

Near the house a large field was left uncultivated as a sort of common, where visiting Indians or travellers passing to and fro to Canada could camp. Being on the great highway to Canada, there was seldom a time from spring to autumn when this common was unoccupied. The soldiers in passing always stopped there. Every summer there was an encampment of regular or provincial troops, and when the troops had gone northward, a colony of the women and children of their families remained. To all these campers, whether white or red, vegetables, fruit, and milk were freely given from the abundant supplies of the farm.

Sometimes in winter Mr. and Mrs. Schuyler, especially in their early life, went down to New York to enjoy the society, which Mrs. Grant describes as more varied and polished than in any other part of the continent. During the long French and Indian wars New York was the head-quarters of the British regulars, and the officers, having few duties in winter, devoted themselves to pleasure. They were sometimes profligate, we are told, but never ignorant or low-bred, and among the higher ranks of them Mrs. Grant found many finished gentlemen who had added experience, reading, and reflection to their natural talents.

Later in life the Schuylers were always at home on their country place, which in many ways resembled a Virginia plantation. Their servants seem to have been all negro slaves brought up in the family, to which they showed the greatest devotion. There were the old negro who made and mended the shoes for everybody, a carpenter, a horse-breaker, and a blacksmith who shod the horses and mended tools. Others had charge of the fishery, which was an important department, raised hemp and tobacco, or presided over the spinning and cider-making. Apparently they were more skilful and trustworthy than Southern slaves.

Mrs. Schuyler was a woman of strong character, intelligent, fond of reading, and well informed in colonial politics and Indian questions. She got more out of her country life on the edge of a wilderness than most people can now gain in the heart of a metropolis. She managed a very large household of slaves, visitors, and children; and, as we read the account of her duties and pleasures on a summer's day, we cannot but think of the modern women whose nerves break down with the management of three or four domestics, or who have no time for amusement unless they live in an apartment house in winter and a hotel in summer.

Mrs. Schuyler began the day with reading, and breakfasted early. A short time was then devoted to giving orders about her household, and she usually had some young woman, the daughter of a friend or relative, who acted as her executive officer. Her establishment had been so long well regulated and all her people so well disciplined that its operation was very smooth. She read again until eleven, and then joined her guests and Mr. Schuyler to discuss general topics,—the operations of the army, Indian treaties, and politics.

In these conversations she and her husband were able to give most valuable information and advice to officers and officials, who often made an excuse of a summer visit to receive this instruction. Young soldiers were told of the difficulties of campaigning in a wilderness so different from anything to which they had been accustomed, and were warned of the Indian methods of warfare which had been so fatal to Braddock and his expedition.

From her guests she went to give audience to new settlers who were taking up land and about to become tenants of the family, retainers and followers of all sorts, and people who were camping on the common and needed advice and assistance. Dinner was at two o'clock, when family, adopted children, friends, relations, visitors, and perhaps some travellers who were passing by that day sat down to a repast which was plain but very varied and abundant. There was none of the excessive feasting which we read of in other places in colonial times.

The defect, however, among the Schuylers seems to have been that they were a little too serious; and even Mrs. Grant admits that it would have been well to have had more gayety. In the afternoon visitors came out from Albany, usually young people to see the children. Walks and excursions followed, while Mrs. Schuyler sat on the portico reading or talking.

Such a life implies considerable expense, and in those days there were few interest-bearing investments by which people nowadays live. But agriculture, which has degenerated almost to the occupation of a peasantry, was then very profitable, and the resources of a great estate, even when it was largely composed of wild land, surprisingly abundant. In all the Middle and Southern colonies there were many moderate-sized farms from which the owners, besides having a home, all they wanted to eat, and a great deal of what they wanted to wear, received an income of two or three thousand dollars a year. Rochefoucauld describes the farm of Davies Randolph, on the James River in Virginia, which, though containing only three hundred and fifty acres of cultivated land, yielded its owner eighteen hundred dollars in the worst years, and in the best three thousand five hundred dollars.

The Schuyler estate seems to have furnished large supplies in the way of ordinary provisions, and, besides this, the game of the neighboring wilderness was an additional resource. The Indians, who were very friendly and grateful for the favors received, sent in large quantities of venison and smaller game. The slaves were constantly hunting, carried guns when they went to look for the cows or on any other errand that took them away from the house, and seldom returned empty-handed, and the river was full of fish.

The great supply of game in those times added not a little to the prosperity of the colonies, and game might even now become a valuable source of food and profit, as well as pleasure, by proper preserving; for there are millions of acres of land in the United States which are fit for nothing else.

In winter the slaves of Mr. Schuyler and of his two brothers, who had places near by, united in cutting and carrying timber to the saw-mills, where it was made into planks and staves, which were put on a vessel for the West Indies. Flour and salted provisions were added, and a member of the family went with the cargo. Any slaves who had proved themselves too refractory for endurance were also taken aboard; and the lading of this ship every spring was such a terror to all the negroes that it usually resulted in a temporary reform of even the worst.

Arrived at the islands, a return cargo of wine, rum, sugar, coffee, chocolate, and other products was taken on, and all that was not needed by the family or their friends sold at Albany. The return of the vessel and the distribution of the cargo was one of the great events of the year; and visitors, in return for hospitality, were constantly sending presents of wine, fruit, oysters, or whatever was choice to their homes.

In time the lumber industry of the river increased. The logs were made into great rafts, which floated down majestically with the current. The man in charge lived upon the raft in a little house with his family; and it was a pretty sight on a fine day to see the mother calmly spinning near the door, the children sporting about over the logs, and the father fishing.

In the neighborhood of the Schuyler estate and all through the colony Dutch remained the language of most of the people until the Revolution, and then was slowly replaced by English. There seem to have been some efforts made to encourage the acceptance of English, for in 1776 we read of children punished in school for speaking Dutch. In general it may be said that the Dutch characteristics held their own quite strongly until about the year 1800. As late as 1840 there were still a great many old people who spoke Dutch almost exclusively, and, as in the case of the Pennsylvania Germans, their language had become a debased dialect, full of English words, and not worth preserving.

The concentration of the land in a few hands helped to preserve the Dutch characteristics and held back in an inferior position the province that was capable of being the greatest of all. The Dutch population was very slow to enter the Revolution, and the toryism or indifference of New York was a cause of much anxiety to the patriots. But there were some individuals who were very earnest and forward, Alexander Hamilton, John Jay, Alexander McDougal, Isaac Sears, Philip Livingston, J. Morin Scott, and George Clinton, with whom was associated an eminent Dutchman, General Philip Schuyler. Although founded as early as the New England colonies and almost as early as Virginia, New York for some time after the Revolution held only the fifth place in population and importance.

In 1780 efforts were made to break up the land system, and laws were passed abolishing the feudal tenures. But the patroons and landlords avoided these acts by putting feudal tenures in their leases. In 1812 another attempt was made, but without success, and the irritation among the people increased. The New Englanders had now been overflowing into New York for some years. They began to come about the time of the Stamp Act difficulties, attracted by the fertile land, and the migration steadily increased. More vigorous, keen, and aggressive than the Dutch, filled with hatred of aristocracy and landlordism, and forever talking of liberty and independence, they were by no means welcome either to the old ruling class or to the masses of the people.

They were mostly rural Yankees, impudent, inquisitive, grasping, sharp, drawling in speech, and utterly without manners,—a class which has now fortunately passed away, but which once furnished the stock material for Charles Dickens and other English writers who ridiculed Americans. Occasionally, in remote parts of New England, you may find survivors of this class, and if one should fasten himself on you, as they are apt to do, you will never forget him.

Mrs. Grant describes their arrival and the terrible break they caused in the happiness of her own family, as well as in that of all the people whom she knew. "Conceited, litigious, selfish beyond measure, vulgar, insolent, and truly disagreeable," as she calls them, they squatted on the land as they pleased, over-reached in every bargain, and railed at aristocrats and "King George's Red Coats."

"Obadiah or Zephaniah, from Hampshire or Connecticut, came in without knocking, sat down without invitation, and lighted their pipe without ceremony; then talked of buying land; and finally began a discourse on politics which would have done honour to Praise God Barebones, or any of the members of his parliament." ("Memoirs of an American Lady," p. 286.)

Mrs. Knight, a bright woman, who kept a diary of a journey she made on horseback in 1704 from Boston to New York, shows the same dislike for the rural Yankee. At a house where she stopped for the night, the landlady, instead of telling her that she would be received or attending to her wants, drawled out,—

"Law for me, what in the world brings you here this time a night? I never see a woman on the Rode so Dreadful late in all my versall life. Who are you? Where are you going?"

Then, when Mrs. Knight's guide appeared, she turned to him with, "Lawful heart, John, is it you?" and kept up her questions until Mrs. Knight, unable to endure it any longer, stopped her.

At one point in her journey she met a girl who had been riding with her father thirty miles a day on a lean, hard-trotting horse, with only a bag for a saddle. "Lawful heart, father," she said, "this bare mare hurts me dingily. I'm dreadful sore, I vow."

But these horrible people were the making of New York, which would never have prospered under her heavy Dutch population; and, as Mrs. Grant laments, they soon converted the Dutch to their detestable habits. The long spouts which poured the water from the eaves on people in the streets of Albany disappeared, and picturesqueness and slow thrift gave place to energy and enterprise. Irving has described the astonishment with which Rip Van Winkle, when he awoke from his long sleep, saw the evidences of this change.

Manhattan and the Tappan Zee

In spite of its large foreign population, the Anglo-Saxon has always been the best as well as the final controlling influence in New York. The Dutchman had his day of power, but the descendants of the Vikings slowly, surely, and without effort or haste absorbed both him and his works until, in the constitution, laws, and framework of the State, there remains scarcely a trace of the Hollander. The Irishman still has his day of political corruption on Manhattan Island, and a most evil one it is; but he too will melt away before the race that has never had its equal in the world.

This influence of the New Englander was strikingly shown in the New York Constitutional Convention of 1821, already referred to in the chapter on Connecticut. Out of its one hundred and twenty-six members, thirty-two were natives of Connecticut and nine of Massachusetts.

The Yankees could not endure being tenants under the system which gave the landlord every advantage and made the tenant his slave. Their agitation increased every year against the leases and contracts, which were becoming more burdensome than ever under the ownership of a great corporation called the Holland Land Company.

After the Revolution the fertile tracts in the

interior of New York attracted speculators from all parts of the country, who hoped to enjoy the advantages of laws which were so favorable to the landlord, and the Hollanders joined in the rush, with the aid of this company. A map of the State, prepared in 1775, shows the central portion in the lake country, the old home of the Iroquois, laid out in large blocks, some numbered and others called Virgil, Homer, Dryden, Solon, Ovid, Scipio, and similar names, which are still retained by many of the towns in that region.

The journal of John Lincklaen, who was the agent of the Holland Company, gives us glimpses of these speculators: Cazenove, from whom Cazenovia was named, and others who were enthusiastically wandering through the woods with guides and surveyors, expecting great wealth from tenants and the maple-sugar industry.

Cooper's novel "The Chain-Bearer" gives another point of view of the life of some of the great landlords and their difficulties. Many of them, however, were successful, notably the Wadsworth family from Connecticut, who established themselves in the beautiful valley of the Genesee, where their descendants still live, and where there are still interesting country places, fox-hunting, and rural pleasures,—rather unusual now in America.

Manhattan and the Tappan Zee

In 1836, under the influence of the Yankees, the resistance to the land system became so pronounced that when a rumor was started that the Holland Company intended to enforce its liens against the people, a mob in Chautauqua County destroyed the land office with all its records. Three years afterwards, when the Van Rensselaers attempted to collect long arrears of rent and to enforce other rights which would give them a quarter title to the land, there was another outbreak, accompanied by bloodshed, and the assistance of the militia had to be obtained.

In these disturbances William H. Seward had his first opportunity for distinction, and displayed those qualities which afterwards gave him a statesman's career in the civil war. But the land question was settled very slowly, and as late as 1866 the militia had to be called out to stop a land riot in Albany County.

In consequence of the influx of the New Englanders and their progressiveness, New York grew very rapidly, and by the time the Erie Canal was completed, in 1825, was the most populous State in the Union. The canal added another chapter of atrocious political corruption to the long history of this sin in the Empire Commonwealth; but the effect of this water highway on material prosperity was enormous, and modern New York, as we know it to-day, is the result. Farm products on the line of the canal increased fifty per cent. after 1825, villages and factories sprang up by it, land rose in value, population increased by rapid strides, while the canal poured the products of the boundless West into New York harbor to increase her commerce and ships, and all this was followed by railroads, which performed the same task.

Apthorpe House · Harlem Heights

DOUGHOREGAN MANOR

CHAPTER IX

PURITAN AND CATHOLIC ON THE CHESAPEAKE

ABOUT twenty-five years after Virginia was established on the southern part of Chesapeake Bay, the family of Lord Baltimore took possession of the northern half of the bay for their colony, called Maryland. As the Baltimores were Roman Catholics, there has been much discussion of their motives in founding their colony; and the colony, as the only attempt to establish a Roman Catholic community in the British possessions, had a very peculiar history.

George Calvert, the first Lord Baltimore, occupied a rather curious position in England. It has been generally supposed that he was born, baptized, and brought up in the Church of England. He was a graduate of Trinity College, Oxford, and, after travelling on the continent of Europe, he became secretary to Sir

Robert Cecil, who had been one of the secretaries of state under Queen Elizabeth, and became Lord High Treasurer and Earl of Salisbury under James I. Cecil seems to have thought highly of young Calvert, and he was advanced in public employment until he became a favorite and trusted counsellor of James I., who made him his Secretary of State. He was also a member of the House of Commons, where he devoted himself to obtaining supplies for the king and to supporting his policy.

Calvert was soon interested in colonization schemes, and was a member of the Virginia Company. He also obtained in 1614 a grant of part of Newfoundland, and called his province Avalon, a name which it still retains.

Attracted by the valuable fisheries of the Banks, he seems to have expected to make a fortune out of this enterprise, or to establish a refuge for the English Roman Catholics. He spent twenty-five thousand pounds of his private fortune in building granaries, storehouses, and a handsome house for his own residence, without at all realizing the barren nature of the country.

About the same time that he received this grant of Avalon he publicly announced that he had become a Roman Catholic, and immediately resigned his office of Secretary of State. There has been much discussion and not a little violent controversy among the Protestants and Catholics of Maryland about this resignation. The view usually maintained by the Catholics is that Calvert had been recently convinced of the truth of Romanism, and conscientiously announced his conversion, at the same time resigning an office he could no longer consistently hold under a Protestant king, and was willing to sacrifice all his prospects of advancement for the sake of his new faith.

But the evidence, which has been well summarized by Mr. J. P. Kennedy in the pamphlets he wrote in the controversy, seems to show that Calvert had been a Roman Catholic for some years before he resigned, and that he was forced to resign by a movement in Parliament to drive from office all persons of Catholic proclivities.

The contest among the members of the Church of England, the Puritans, and the Roman Catholics was at that time raging with great violence in England, and it was a question which should capture and control the government. Under Queen Mary, the Catholics had been in power and had slaughtered the Protestants without mercy. Under Queen Elizabeth, the Protestants of the Church of England held the government and took their turn at persecuting; but the Catholics continued the struggle, and were assisted by the kings of France and Spain, under whom the Spanish Armada was sent, in the hope of making England papist at once and forever.

Although this great attempt of the Armada failed, plots of all sorts continued. The Pope claimed the power to depose monarchs, and, when deposed, their subjects were at liberty to assassinate them. He deposed Elizabeth, and an attempt was made on her life by an English Catholic. In the reign of James I., a few years before Calvert's resignation, some Catholics had organized the gunpowder plot to blow up Parliament. To defend the country against these attempts, and to retain possession of the government, the Protestant Parliament had enacted very severe measures against the Roman Catholics, with the intention of extirpating them from England. They were prohibited from performing the rites of their religion in public, and monthly fines and confiscation of their property were inflicted on them.

These laws were passed by the Puritans and the members of the Church of England. But King James, as head of the English Church, found the Puritan party growing too strong to suit his purposes, and he often favored the Catholics as an offset against the Puritans. He compromised their fines and forfeitures, and had several avowed or secret Catholics in high office as his advisers.

Calvert seems to have been one of these. He was of great assistance to the king, and favored the marriage of the Prince of Wales to the Spanish Infanta. He also, no doubt, was able to give much aid to the Catholics, save them from difficulties and loss of property, and help to secure more toleration for them from the government. But Buckingham and the Puritan party in Parliament were determined to enforce with greater strictness the laws against the people who were believed to be the enemies of England, and Calvert was compelled to resign his office.

There had been nothing dishonorable in his conduct of keeping his new religion to himself, although it was not so dramatic and striking as the sudden conversion and conscientious resignation for which some of his admirers contend. Hundreds of English Catholics at that time kept their religion a secret, and, if they had property to preserve or any worldly ambition or desire to gratify, secrecy was absolutely necessary. Calvert took the part of wise discretion and moderation, which enabled him to be of service to his own people, and he could have been of no service to them whatever if he had not been in power.

He had attained to such a position of eminence that the public announcement of his religion did him comparatively little harm. He suffered from none of the fines and confiscations which were inflicted on the obscure or unimportant. On the contrary, the king had such an appreciation of his ability that he retained him in the Privy Council, raised him to the Irish peerage the next year as Baron of Baltimore, and he sold his office of Secretary of State to his successor, after the manner of the time, for six thousand pounds.

He wished to go to his province of Avalon in Newfoundland, but the king detained him; for as an avowed Romanist he was almost of as much use to the king as he had been before the announcement of his religion.

Charles I., who succeeded King James in 1625, continued the same favor. Calvert was not required to take the oath acknowledging the supremacy of the Church of England, and he got leave to embark for his province of Avalon. He soon returned to England, and in 1628 went out again to Newfoundland, taking with him his family and a number of colonists. He probably intended that his province should be a source of profit to himself and at the same time a refuge for English Roman Catholics, just as William Penn intended that Pennsylvania should advance his own fortunes and at the same time shelter the Quakers.

He, however, soon saw the hopelessness of accomplishing anything among the fogs and icebergs, and, abandoning Avalon, he sailed to Virginia with the intention, apparently, of either settling there or of exploring the country to see what part of it he should ask a grant of from the king. His real intentions on this as on other occasions of his life are obscure. His own position, as well as that of the Catholics in England, had made discretion and silence habitual, and it was seldom safe for him to make his purposes conspicuous.

But he had scarcely landed in that royalist and Episcopal colony when the officials offered him the oath of allegiance, which also acknowledged the supremacy of the Church of England, and on his refusal to take it, he was quietly told that he must depart. He had attempted to enter the place of all others where his presence would be most resented, and there is evidence of some indignation among the Virginians, and a record that Thomas Tindall was to be pilloried for two hours " for giving my Lord Baltimore the lie and threatening to knock him down."

Leaving his wife and some of his children in Virginia, he returned to England and obtained a grant of land which included the southern part of Virginia and the northern part of North Carolina; but through the efforts of people interested in Virginia, this grant was revoked and he was given a tract north of the Potomac, which, however, was also a part of Virginia.

King Charles suggested that it be called Mariana in honor of the queen. But Lord Baltimore, with characteristic shrewdness, replied that it was also the name of a Spanish Jesuit who had written against monarchy, and the king thereupon proposed Terra Mariæ, which was adopted. The charter was written in Latin, and is the only one of the colonial charters the original of which is in that language. But before Lord Baltimore could receive it he died. His wife and several of his children, whom he had left in Virginia, had been lost at sea a few months before in returning to England.

His eldest son, Cecil Calvert, received the charter, which was confirmed June 20, 1632. It was almost precisely the same as the charter which had been granted for Avalon, and many of its provisions were followed in the charter granted fifty years afterwards to William Penn for Pennsylvania. It created a great feudal proprietorship, and introduced on the American continent the feudal system, which was gradually disappearing in England.

Lord Baltimore was to own all the land and

the colonists were to be his tenants, paying him a small quit-rent for every acre they held of him. He was to be the ruler and governor of the province, and also was given the right to make laws with the assent of the freemen or their deputies.

The most curious part of the charter was that it allowed Lord Baltimore to levy duties on goods imported to the colony. Such an extraordinary power to tax the products of the mother country was never again granted in any charter, and it was probably given in Baltimore's charter only because there had been little or no experience in managing colonies up to that time, and the government was disposed to encourage them in every possible way by privileges and favors, so as to extend the empire of Great Britain and check the expansion of the Dutch at New York.

Besides this favor of taxing imports, there was another clause in the charter by which the crown bound itself never to tax the people of the colony or their property. The usual situation of affairs was reversed, and, so far as taxation was concerned, Maryland was almost in the position which the mother country occupied towards the other colonies.

But it made very little difference in the final result, for the British government never allowed Maryland to take advantage of her right to tax imports. In subsequent charters such privileges were not given ; and in the Pennsylvania charter, which in many respects resembled that of Maryland, the privilege of taxing imports was omitted, and a clause inserted which, while it prohibited the king from taxing the colonists, gave Parliament full authority to do so.

Cecil Calvert immediately set to work to carry out his father's intention, and here we meet with another subject of much controversy in Maryland history. It has been said that the colony was founded on the principle of religious liberty, and was the first colony in America where that liberty was established.

But the religious liberty which prevailed in Maryland under the Roman Catholics was forced upon them by circumstances which they could not avoid. Neither the Church of England, the Puritans, nor the Catholics believed in religious liberty at that time. Each believed in a state church established by law, and each was intent on establishing its own faith by force, to the exclusion of every other.

The grandiloquent phrases in which the first settlement of the Maryland Catholics at St. Mary's on the Potomac is described as the home of religious liberty, and its only home in the wide world, can deceive only the ignorant. A few years before the Puritans had established a home for their religious liberty at Boston. Both the Puritan and the Catholic were seeking what was called at that time freedom to worship God. The phrase meant precisely the same in each case, and each hoped to be let alone, with no opinions near them which they did not accept.

The only difference between the Puritans at Boston and the Catholics at St. Mary's was that, the majority of the people in England being Protestant, the Puritan colonists were not regarded as dangerous, or as likely to be in league with the Pope and the kings of France and Spain in their designs against Great Britain; and they were accordingly let alone, and tacitly allowed to establish their religion and intolerance by law. But the Catholic colonists dared not establish their religion to the exclusion of others. It was a question in the minds of most Englishmen whether these people, who believed in the authority of a foreign power to depose English kings and foment rebellion against them, and who were continually plotting the overthrow of the British government, should be allowed to exist at all, and they would certainly never have been allowed to establish their peculiar system and theories as the exclusive system of a British colony.

In Virginia and Massachusetts, which were

then the only other colonies in existence, Catholics were in effect excluded; and during the whole of the colonial period, although there were a few Catholics scattered about in all the colonies, they were barely tolerated; and even when their presence and worship were allowed, it was generally considered unsafe to permit them to take any part in government. Under these circumstances the founding of a colony which should freely receive them was something of a feat, and it is probable that there were few, if any, people in England who could have accomplished it except the Baltimores, with their inherited influence at court and their habitual shrewdness and moderation.

Whether their opinions were in reality moderate, whether they accepted the extreme views of the power of the Pope over the English government, or whether they would have favored an attempt by the kings of France and Spain to inflict Catholicism on England by force, are interesting questions which have been discussed at times, but which cannot be answered, for the Baltimores expressed no opinions and made no arguments. They could not, like the Puritans of Massachusetts or William Penn and his Quakers in Pennsylvania, glory in their enterprise or explain it at large. If a colony to which Catholics could resort was to be established at all, it would have to be done quietly and unobtrusively, and in that case the least said the better.

Cecil Calvert prepared two vessels, the Ark and the Dove, and bore the whole expense of the expedition, which was forty thousand pounds. He collected emigrants, whose numbers have been variously stated at two hundred and three hundred; but it would seem from Cecil Calvert's own account that there were a few over three hundred.

Under the rising power of the Puritans the laws against the Catholics were now being more rigidly enforced than ever, and doubtless there were many who would have been glad to go but for the risk they ran of attracting more attention to themselves by seeming to establish a province of their own faith, which would at once be suspected of assisting the king of France to control the British throne. But a large number of the emigrants were Protestants, who may have been purposely obtained so as to avoid the charge of founding an exclusively Catholic community. Indeed, some writers have asserted that it is probable that the majority were Protestants; but the highest estimate that can be relied upon does not give the proportion of Protestants at much above a third.

Many of the emigrants were persons of means

or position, and they all seem to have been a steadier and less adventurous class than the early settlers of Virginia. Cecil described them as composed of two of his brothers, " with very near twenty other gentlemen of very good fashion, and three hundred laboring men well provided in all things."

Only by the high favor at court which Cecil had inherited from his father was he enabled to take these people out of the country. The Puritans seriously objected to the establishment of such a colony anywhere in the British possessions, every obstacle that could be devised was placed in its way, and Cecil found that he needed the full force of his influence at every step.

Charles I. and the officers of his government no doubt felt that as a few years before they had relieved the country of some very troublesome and dangerous people by letting the Puritans go to Massachusetts, so now they were lessening their difficulties for the future by getting rid of a few hundred Catholics.

Cecil almost slipped his people away without the oath of allegiance. In fact, he had got them all on board and they had gone to sea when Lord Coke, the Secretary of State, informed Admiral Pennington, who went in pursuit of the Ark and the Dove and brought them back. This was a serious matter, and the Jesuits and more than half the company immediately deserted the ships and went to the Isle of Wight.

When the "London Searcher" arrived, he found only one hundred and twenty-eight people to whom he could administer the oath. This oath had been rendered necessary by the Pope's bull freeing all English subjects from their allegiance to the crown, and by the position of hostility which the Catholics had assumed towards the government. It was an oath which was extremely difficult for a Catholic to take. He was obliged to swear that the king was lawfully a king, that the Pope had no power to depose him or to license his subjects to rebel against or assassinate him, that he would bear true allegiance to the king, that the Pope could not absolve him from this oath, and that the oath meant exactly what it said, and was taken without any mental or secret reservation whatsoever.

To allow Catholics to depart for the purpose of founding a colony in America without the sanction of this oath was considered utterly out of the question, and even the king had no power to help Cecil out of this predicament.

But Cecil's people seem to have been well able to take care of themselves. The one hundred and twenty-eight who took the oath were presumably the Protestants of the expedition, who had no objection to it, and perhaps some of them were Catholics who managed to settle such matters with their consciences in a way of their own. It is most likely, however, that these one hundred and twenty-eight were all Protestants, and show the exact number of that faith among the emigrants.

When the searcher asked the captain if there were any more, he was informed that "some few others were shipped who had forsaken the ship and given over the voyage." The one hundred and seventy people or thereabouts whom the captain described as "some few others" were all waiting at the Isle of Wight, and were picked up there when the Ark and the Dove were finally allowed to proceed; so that the principal part, if not all, of the Catholics of the expedition got away without taking the oath at all.

It was the 22d of November, 1632, when those who had dodged the oath were taken on board, and all started on the long voyage of those times down to the Azores and Canary Islands, across to the West Indies, and then up the coast to Chesapeake Bay. They spent the winter in the West Indies, and reached Point Comfort in Virginia on the 27th of February. They had some apprehension of serious interference from the Virginians; but the letters of safe-conduct given by the king protected them, and, proceeding up the Chesapeake, they established themselves on the north bank of the Potomac, at a place they named St. Mary's.

Cecil Calvert had remained in England, and sent out with the colonists his brother Leonard as their governor, who experienced none of the difficulties and hardships which had befallen the Virginia settlers at Jamestown. St. Mary's was a more wholesome spot, and the waters swarmed with wild fowl, fish, and oysters.

Some islands in the river near St. Mary's they called the Heron Isles, from the immense flocks of that species of bird which were found upon them. One of the earliest accounts of the colony describes the " eagles, bitterns, herons, swannes, geese, partridge, ducks, red bleu parti-colored birds and the like" which appeared everywhere in countless numbers. As for fish, they were in even greater abundance : bass, blue-fish, rock, shad, perch, and sturgeon mingled with the pompano and bonito of the South. Prodigious quantities could be taken with very little trouble. As late as 1763 the *Maryland Gazette* recorded that one haul of a seine at Kent Island brought in one hundred and seventy-three bushels, which were sold at two shillings sixpence a bushel.

They seem to have planted fruit-trees immediately, which flourished beyond all expectation. Within twenty-two years the orchards were a conspicuous feature about St. Mary's. Peach-, quince-, apple-, plum-, chestnut-, and walnut-trees, as well as grape-vines, grew luxuriantly, and are described by travellers in language so enthusiastic that we might doubt its truth if it were not confirmed from so many sources. In colonial times, in Maryland, Pennsylvania, and New York, there seems to have been some influence peculiarly favorable to the growth of fruit-trees, which were not so short-lived or so barren and diseased as they have since become.

Both Leonard Calvert and the Jesuits were very judicious in their dealings with the Indians. The colonists, though few in numbers, were for a long time left undisturbed. But as they increased and began to spread out the jealousy of the red man was aroused, in spite of all the efforts of the Jesuits. Murdering and fighting began, and growth and prosperity were checked for many years, as in Virginia and Carolina.

For the first ten years of its existence the colony prospered fully as well as could be expected, increasing slowly but steadily in population, until after twenty years the people are supposed to have numbered about eight thousand, gathered round the original settlement of

Puritan and Catholic on the Chesapeake

St. Mary's, in the extreme southern part of the province, and slowly and cautiously spreading out from it. They had small clearings, where, like the Virginians, they immediately began the cultivation of tobacco, which became the money of the province, and they kept close to the water, having few roads, and depending for their transportation on boats.

The policy of having Protestants in the colony was carefully continued by the Baltimores. In his first advertisement for settlers, Cecil Calvert had announced that he would accept people of all religious faiths, and he issued a proclamation forbidding " all unreasonable disputations on points of religion tending to the disturbance of the public peace and quiet and to the opening of faction in religion."

This order seems to have been enforced in at least one instance. Two Protestant servants were reading aloud, when a Catholic, William Lewis, entering the room, heard some such expressions as that " the Pope was antichrist and the Jesuits antichristian ministers," whereupon he exclaimed that it was a falsehood and came from the devil, as all lies did, and that all Protestant ministers were the ministers of the devil, and he forbade them reading the book. The servants, in a state of great irritation, are said to have prepared a petition to the governor of

Puritan and Catholic on the Chesapeake

Virginia, which was to be signed by all the Protestants in the colony; but before they could accomplish anything the matter was brought before the governor and his court, and Lewis was reprimanded and fined five hundred pounds of tobacco for his "offensive speeches" and "disputations."

Calvert dared not act otherwise than very liberally towards the Protestants. The slightest attempt to make Catholicism exclusive, or the slightest infringement of Protestant privileges, would have lost him his province. He could build up his province only by avoiding all offence to Protestants both in England and in his colony. The stock story which has just been given of the punishment of a Catholic for offensive speech to a Protestant shows the constant danger he was in; for the Protestants in that instance threatened at once to appeal to Virginia, and nothing would have pleased the Virginians more than to have received such an appeal, which they could have made use of with much effect.

Although the government of Virginia was obliged by the letters of the king to offer no opposition to Lord Baltimore, the Virginians were eager to resent the occupation by Catholics of a territory which had been carved out of their own province and on which some of their people had already settled.

Puritan and Catholic on the Chesapeake

One of the Virginians who had settled within the limits of Maryland before the date of Lord Baltimore's charter was William Clayborne, who had a trading station of some importance on Kent Island and another on Palmer's Island, near the mouth of the Susquehanna. He refused to submit himself to the jurisdiction of Lord Baltimore, and, assisted by Protestants in both Virginia and Maryland, carried on a petty warfare of annoyance until Leonard Calvert sent two armed sloops, which, meeting Clayborne's vessels in the Pocomoke River on the 23d of April, 1635, fought what has been called the first naval battle of America.

Clayborne was defeated, his island seized, his property confiscated, and Cecil Calvert's influence with the king prevented the Virginia government from taking sides with its unruly citizen. But the Virginians, especially the Puritans among them, sympathized with Clayborne, and before long they all had an opportunity for revenge.

Charles I. was now having serious difficulties with the Puritans. They were in open rebellion, and Cromwell was becoming their greatest leader. After the battle of Marston Moor, in 1644, the Puritans in England were in the ascendant and those in the colonies correspondingly elated. Many of the Virginia Puritans joined those already in Maryland, and, assisted by these, Clayborne attacked Kent Island, and, after taking it, went over to the west side of the bay and captured the settlement at St. Mary's.

Leonard Calvert fled to Virginia, and for two years Clayborne and the Puritans were masters of the province that had been founded for Catholics. The Jesuits were seized and sent in chains to England, many of the Catholics driven into banishment, and those who remained fined and stripped of their property. Thus, after a comparatively peaceful existence of ten years, Lord Baltimore's colony, so far as it was a Catholic community, was wiped out of existence.

In his retirement in Virginia, Leonard Calvert soon found that the royalists of the colony were willing to assist him. They had no interest in him as a Catholic, but they were trying to hold Virginia against Cromwell and the English Puritans, and they were willing that Calvert should defeat the Puritans in Maryland. Hill, who was acting as Puritan governor of Maryland, was unable to keep order, and within two years many of the people under him were very willing to have the Catholic proprietors restored.

Governor Berkeley, of Virginia, furnished Calvert with a small force, with which, in August, 1646, he repossessed himself of his former authority at St. Mary's without striking a blow. But Kent Island, Clayborne's stronghold, held out until subdued in the following spring, and soon after, in June, 1647, Leonard Calvert died.

Cecil Calvert had now to solve the difficult problem of retaining possession of his Catholic colony with Cromwell and the Puritans in power in England, and he went about the task in the only way that was possible. He appointed as governor, in 1648, William Stone, a Virginia Protestant, and bound him by a long oath, in which, among other things, he swore that he would not directly or indirectly molest for their religion any one professing to believe in Jesus Christ, " and in particular no Roman Catholic."

Having thus protected the Roman Catholics from the Protestant governor, he proceeded to protect the Protestants from the Roman Catholic legislature, and under his directions the assembly of the year 1649 passed the law which has become known as the Maryland Toleration Act. It provided, under penalty of fines, imprisonment, and whipping, that no one professing to believe in Jesus Christ should be molested in his religion; that no one should blaspheme God, deny the divinity of Christ or the doctrine of the Trinity, or speak reproachfully of the apostles or the Virgin Mary; and that no one in a reproachful way should call any one a heretic, schismatic, idolater, Puritan, Presbyterian, Independent, Popish priest, Jesuit, Jesuited papist, Lutheran, Calvinist, Anabaptist, Brownist, Antinomian, Barrowist, Roundhead, Separatist, or use any other name relating to religion in a disrespectful manner.

Clayborne and the Puritans were still at work as active enemies, and, being unable to attack and capture the colony, they spread rumors that the Protestants of Maryland were persecuted. To offset this, the " Protestant Declaration," as it was called, was obtained in 1650. It was a document signed by the governor, the Protestant members of the assembly, and many other leading Protestants of the province, declaring that under the Toleration Act they were enjoying full freedom in the exercise of their religion.

There were now many Puritans in Maryland who had been driven from Virginia by the severe measures of the Church of England royalists against them. They did not settle among the Catholics at St. Mary's, but went north of them and took possession of the country on the Severn River where Annapolis now stands; so that the colony was divided into a Catholic and a Puritan section. The Puritans, although living very much to themselves, were restive and uneasy at the thought that they were under a government in the control of Catholics, and they particularly objected to the oath of fidelity to Lord Baltimore, which they were compelled to take in words which described him as an absolute lord of royal jurisdiction. Cecil Calvert, with his usual moderation and tact, softened the oath to suit their scruples.

But in avoiding danger to his province from the Puritans, he found that he had unexpectedly offended another influence. Charles II. was then an exile in Holland, without so much as the shadow of power in the British dominions; but, offended at the leniency which his professed friend, Cecil Calvert, had shown to the Maryland Puritans, he deposed him from his proprietorship because he "did visibly adhere to the rebels in England," and appointed in his stead Sir William Davenant, who sailed for the province with a colony of Frenchmen.

If Davenant had reached the Chesapeake he might have involved Lord Baltimore in very serious difficulties with Cromwell, who would in all probability have made short work of the Catholic colony, which thus far had been allowed to exist by sufferance; but, fortunately, Davenant and his Frenchmen were captured in the English Channel by a Parliamentary cruiser.

By good luck Cecil Calvert had escaped this danger, which might have proved his ruin; but he was soon involved in another, in which there was but little chance for a happy accident in his favor.

Cromwell and the Parliament had settled their affairs in England, and in 1650 were ready to take up the subject of the colonies, and wherever it was necessary reduce them to submission. The New England people were all Puritans, and required no attention. The only other colonies on the continent at that time were Virginia and Maryland. Of these, Virginia had been as openly and palpably royalist as New England had been Puritan, and no one questioned that a fleet should be sent to subdue her. But about Maryland there was some doubt, and in the act of Parliament which was passed to authorize the sending of ships to the disaffected colonies in the West Indies and on the American continent, Maryland was not named.

Immediately, however, a clamor was raised that Maryland should be included. Many people had always been of the opinion that it was a mistake to allow the establishment of a Catholic colony, and they seconded the efforts of the Puritans who had been followers of Clayborne. So strong was the agitation that some of the Protestants in Maryland, fully believing that Lord Baltimore would lose his charter, refused to elect members to the assembly.

Puritan and Catholic on the Chesapeake

The question whether Maryland should be included in the expedition to reduce the Barbadoes and Virginia was debated at times for many months in the Council of State, and Cecil Calvert's arguments before that body show very clearly the careful policy by which he had preserved Maryland for twenty years.

The governor of his colony, he said, was already a Protestant in religion and a Roundhead in politics. He read the Declaration signed by the leading Protestants of the province asserting that their religious liberty was undisturbed; he exhibited and explained the Toleration Act which had been recently passed, and by the testimony of several merchants and traders he proved that Maryland had received and protected the Puritans who had been driven from Virginia.

He made, indeed, a very strong argument, and the only weak point was that after the execution of Charles I., while Governor Stone had been absent in Virginia, Thomas Greene, who was acting as governor, had foolishly issued a proclamation declaring Charles II. the rightful heir to the throne. But, to atone for this, Cecil showed that Governor Stone had immediately on his return disowned and recalled this proclamation.

The name of Maryland was finally omitted from the instructions, although twice inserted.

But, unfortunately, Lord Baltimore's enemies had procured the insertion of the general words, "to reduce all the plantations within the Chesapeake Bay to their due obedience," and one of the commissioners appointed to go with the two ships which composed the expedition was the troublesome William Clayborne.

On the voyage out one of the vessels was lost, but the other proceeded and, after reducing the Barbadoes to submission, reached Virginia, where the people, under the lead of Governor Berkeley, by a sufficient show of force and preparations for resistance obtained the very liberal terms which have already been described. Clayborne then, in March, 1652, went with the ship to St. Mary's, in Maryland, where, under the clause which empowered him to reduce all the colonies in Chesapeake Bay, he declared that no matter what the good conduct of the colony had been in the past, it must now expressly admit its submission to the authority of Parliament.

Governor Stone hesitated about yielding to this demand, which gave Clayborne the opportunity and excuse he wanted. He at once deposed Stone, declared all acts of the proprietor void, and appointed six commissioners to govern the province. He went back to Virginia, and after being appointed secretary of state in that colony, he returned to Maryland, where he appointed Stone governor, to rule with the six commissioners until the fate of the province should be finally settled by the Parliament in England.

The conflict was now transferred to England, where Lord Baltimore and the agent of the commissioners argued their respective positions before Parliament. The petition of the agent of the commissioners was dismissed; but Parliament being soon after dissolved by Cromwell, and the Dutch war coming on, the subject was dropped, and Lord Baltimore took advantage of the situation to re-establish his authority in Maryland, which he accomplished in 1654.

As soon as Clayborne and his fellow-commissioners heard of this, they determined on another invasion which would completely extirpate the Catholics of Maryland. Proceeding quietly at first, they demanded submission from Governor Stone, which he at first refused. But the Catholics besought him to yield, for the Protestants were rapidly joining themselves to Clayborne, and if the Catholics resisted by force, it would be remembered against them in the future. This was in the line of policy which they and Lord Baltimore had always followed. They must have a reputation of assisting and protecting Protestants; for the moment that they became known as fighting and resisting, they would have the whole English nation against them.

So Maryland passed again into the possession of Clayborne. An assembly was summoned for the following October, and no one who had borne arms against the Parliament or was a Roman Catholic could become a member or vote in the election. When the assembly chosen in this way met, an act was passed protecting Protestants of all opinions, but expressly refusing protection to Catholics, and forbidding any one to take the oath of fidelity to Lord Baltimore.

Cromwell was now well established as Lord Protector of England, and it became his interest, as it had been the interest of Charles I. and James I., who had preceded him, to preserve a balance among the various warring factions, and secure the support even of Catholics. Cecil Calvert had submitted to his authority, and his appeals to him were not in vain. Clayborne and the other commissioners received a letter from Cromwell, ordering them to refrain from disturbing Lord Baltimore in the possession of his province until his dispute with Virginia about boundaries could be settled in England. At the same time Calvert sent a messenger to Stone, upbraiding him for submitting so tamely, and ordering him immediately to restore the authority of the proprietor.

Stone could do nothing in the northern part of the province on the Severn, where the Puritans were in almost complete possession ; but he organized a force of about one hundred and thirty men among the Catholics of St. Mary's, and immediately captured a magazine of arms and the records of the colony, which were in the possession of some of the Puritans on the Patuxent. On the 20th of March, 1655, he set out northward against his enemy's stronghold at Providence. Part of his force marched by land, and the rest proceeded in boats along the shore.

The Puritans sent him some messages pro·fessing a willingness to submit under the condition of having the liberty of English subjects; but Stone paid no attention to them, and kept as prisoners the messengers, who had no doubt been sent merely to delay him or discover the disposition of his force.

He entered the harbor of Providence, now Annapolis, late in the evening, where he found that the Puritans had secured the assistance of a merchant vessel, the Golden Lyon, which opened fire on him. The captain of the Golden Lyon, Roger Heamans, was an ardent Puritan, and has left us an account of the battle. Stone turned aside to avoid the fire from the ship, landed in a creek, and went ashore for the night. The next morning he moved down openly upon the enemy, who appear to have been gathered at the water-side and on board the Golden Lyon.

When the Puritans saw him coming under the black and yellow flag of Lord Baltimore, they sent Captain Fuller with one hundred and seventy men to make a circuit and get behind him; but Stone seems to have turned and faced this force, and it was with them that the battle was fought.

Fuller set up the standard of the Commonwealth, and quietly waited till the Catholics fired upon it. Then, with the Puritan war-cry that had recently resounded over so many fields of England, "In the name of God, fall on!" they rushed to the charge. The Catholics shouted, "Hey for St. Mary's!" but the Cromwellian onset swept them from the field. The whole of Stone's force was killed or captured, except about five, who made their escape. "God," says one of the Puritan chroniclers, "did appear wonderful in the field and in the hearts of the people;" and Captain Heamans relates with true Puritan unction how they took among the spoil "their Pictures, Crucifixes and rows of Beads, with great store of Reliques and trash they trusted in."

Stone was wounded, and ten of his prominent

followers among the prisoners were immediately condemned to death, but only four were executed. A general confiscation of property followed, and the commissioners urged on the home government that not only should Lord Baltimore be deprived of his province, but the province should be restored as a part of Virginia, from which it had been unlawfully separated by the charter granted by Charles I.

Cromwell was uninfluenced by any of these requests. He regarded Lord Baltimore as a man who had submitted himself to the new order of things in England, who by his own efforts and largely at his own expense was adding a colony to the British empire, and he cared nothing for his Catholic opinions, which, in his case at least, were moderate and harmless. The Committee of Trade and Plantations took the whole question into consideration, and meanwhile the Puritans ruled Maryland for a year, and imprisoned the new governor whom Lord Baltimore appointed. The decision of the committee was wholly in favor of Lord Baltimore, and by their report of September 16, 1656, his authority was restored.

But he could obtain possession only of St. Mary's. The Puritans still held the Severn and the northern country. They had in their possession the records and great seal of the province, and they elected an assembly and carried on the government as if their authority was undisputed. This state of affairs continued for another year, when an agreement was signed by Lord Baltimore and Samuel Matthews, one of the leaders of the Puritans, which reads like a treaty between two independent nations, and, indeed, describes itself as a treaty.

After six years' contest with the Puritans, during which time Lord Baltimore had been alternately in and out of power in his province and never in full possession, he was now fully restored. By gifts of land and other favors he amply rewarded those who had stood by him, and provided for the support of the widows and children of those who had fallen in his cause.

There was another rebellion in 1660 when Charles II. was restored to the throne; but it was soon suppressed by Lord Baltimore's brother, Philip Calvert, who was sent out to be governor. The next fifteen years, until 1675, passed in prosperous tranquillity. Philip Calvert was succeeded in 1661 by his nephew, Charles Calvert, eldest son of Lord Baltimore. In those fifteen years the population is supposed to have increased from eight thousand to twenty thousand, most of it composed of Presbyterians, Independents, Baptists, Quakers, and a few members of the Church of England. The Catholics were only about a fourth of all the people, and some estimates make their numbers even smaller.

As a refuge for the Catholics, and as a Catholic colony, Maryland was not a success. It offered no advantages to people of that faith, and many of those who had settled in it were inclined to go away. In fact, when we consider all the contests and the confiscations of Catholic property, it is rather surprising that any of them were willing to remain.

Lord Baltimore had done his best; but, under the rising power of Cromwell and the Puritans, to have filled Maryland with Catholics would have been to invite destruction, and he was compelled to let his colony become merely a source of profit and distinction for himself. Instead of an asylum for the persecuted of his own faith, he was obliged to encourage Puritan refugees from the royalist colony of Virginia, and make his province an asylum for the people who were the enemies of his faith. He played the rather peculiar part of a Roman Catholic protector of Puritans.

We know little of his personality or opinions. He left no writings, and made no arguments or appeals that have come down to us. His colorlessness in this respect is in strange contrast to that other great proprietor of colonial times, William Penn, who founded Pennsylvania.

Puritan and Catholic on the Chesapeake

There were a number of these feudal proprietors who were given vast tracts of land in America, from which they all expected wealth and power. Besides those of Carolina, there were the proprietors of New Jersey, of New Hampshire, and of Maine. But, with the exception of William Penn and Cecil Calvert, they were all wretched failures.

Penn was an impulsive, enthusiastic man, devoted to philanthropy, liberty, and all the progressive movements of his day, who committed himself on every occasion, who told the world all that he thought and felt, who argued openly on all the great political and religious questions of his time, and whose letters, essays, and pamphlets have come down to us in several volumes. Of Calvert's opinions we scarcely know a single one with certainty; and while he was evidently a man of determined purpose, there is no evidence that he was an enthusiast on any subject.

In establishing a refuge for the people of his faith, Penn succeeded and Calvert failed. But Penn had little or no shrewdness in business affairs. His children grew very rich from Pennsylvania, but he himself lost money by the province, was cheated by the manager of his estates in England, and was at one time imprisoned for debt. He had no skill in judging character, and made most unfortunate mistakes in choosing his agents and governors. But Calvert was an incarnation of discretion, tact, and adroitness, with a natural instinct for governing which compelled the admiration and respect even of those who opposed him. The assembly of his province constantly voted him supplies and levied taxes for his benefit, which, in spite of all the turmoil and the money he had expended, enabled him to live through those trying years without bankruptcy.

There was a general resemblance in Maryland life to the life of Virginia, and yet with differences which show the gradual change in climate, soil, and topography of a more northern latitude. Maryland was close to the dividing line between South and North, and, while she was decidedly Southern, her civilization had a touch of the North.

The Marylanders occupied both sides of the upper half of the Chesapeake, in the same way that the Virginians occupied the lower half, taking advantage of the large rivers and estuaries that poured into the bay. Their first settlements clung to the shores of these rivers, and they penetrated backward into the interior very slowly. They travelled from place to place and exchanged their products usually in boats, and gradually developed for that purpose types of sailing vessels, small, fast, and convenient, which now survive in the buckeye and sailing canoe which are still seen in their waters.

The plantations were at first all on the river-shores, and each planter had his own wharf, where the ships from England came for his tobacco, and delivered to him the tools and manufactured goods he required, as in Virginia, without the aid of towns and local merchants. As plantations were established in the interior, the tobacco was brought down to the river-side in hogsheads, to which an axle was attached, so that they could be rolled and drawn by a horse. Narrow roads were cut through the forest for this purpose, which were called rolling roads, and many of them are still known by that name.

Each plantation was a little village and community in itself, like the Virginia plantations, but on a smaller scale than in Virginia; and in fact all the resemblances to Virginia were in miniature. Tobacco was not so excessively cultivated, and for some years before the Revolution large quantities of wheat were raised, especially on the eastern shore, which built up many flour-mills and allied industries in Baltimore.

The colony was cut in half by the wide bay, and the eastern and western shores were almost distinct communities, as they are to this day. To keep them united and to avoid controversy, great pains were taken to make the two sections equal in privileges, and give them the same representation in the legislature. The eastern shore was more given to wheat-growing than the western, and in many ways seems to have shown less resemblance to Virginia. Those large tracts of scrub oak and pine on the western shore which we now pass through on the railroad in going from Philadelphia to Baltimore are the old worn-out tobacco lands.

Traffic and communication being usually accomplished by boats, there were few roads. The country almost to the time of the Revolution was largely covered with forests, with plantations carved out of it along the winding shores of the bay and its rivers, and away from the water the plantations became fewer and more widely separated.

On these patches cut out among the trees the slaves broke up the land with great hoes, for the plough was seldom used except in new ground. The overseer rode about among them on horseback, with broad-brimmed hat, his whip under his arm, and his gun strapped to his back. He might want to defend himself or shoot game, or perhaps he might see in the woods a runaway negro or indented servant, whom every one was in duty bound to seize. In later times wood-rangers were employed to capture runaways.

They scoured incessantly the swamps and lurking-places, and any stranger wandering aimlessly about was apt to be bluntly asked, " From whom have you run away ?"

At the planter's house, after you had struggled through the circle of yelping hounds which crowded with you up the steps, you found the same rude plenty as in Virginia. Among the upper classes you found a well-furnished mansion, with gazettes, copies of the "Spectator" and British poets, with works on agriculture, and a family of no little pretension in dress and behavior. They led a jolly social life with all their neighbors, and had often been to the Annapolis balls in winter. But if, in the midst of your investigations, word was brought that a ship from England had come into the mouth of the creek, instantly you were deserted. Everybody rushed off to the shore to bargain for clothes, supplies, and knick-knacks, or hear the news ; and you were lucky if you could find an old crippled negro woman to give you a meal.

Attempts were made from time to time to improve the few roads, which were mostly mere trails in the woods ; and there was a curious road law passed in 1704, which provided that any road which led to Annapolis should be marked on both sides with two notches on the trees, and where it left another road, with the letters AA cut into a tree. Roads on the eastern shore that led to Port Williamstadt, now Oxford, were to be marked in the same way with two notches and the letter W. Roads which led to county court-houses were to have two notches and a third some distance above; roads leading to ferries were to have two notches all along, and where they turned aside from other roads, three notches at equal distances from each other; and where a road turned off to a church it was to be marked with " a slip cut down the face of the tree near the ground."

That devotion to out-door life and sports which was so conspicuous in Virginia we find repeated in Maryland. Game was so abundant that the accounts of it now read like fairy-tales, and in some respects it seems to have been more abundant than in Virginia. Not to mention the crabs and oysters which could be gathered on every shore, wild turkeys were often seen in flocks of a hundred, and deer were so numerous that some families lived on venison alone for nine months of the year. Alsop, who was a redemptioner, describes the family to which he was apprenticed as having hanging up on one occasion the carcasses of eighty deer.

From November to April the ducks, wild geese, and swans swarmed in the Chesapeake in such prodigious numbers that the writers of the time describe them as covering the water in compact masses like turf, filling the air like a cloud, and the vibration of their wings "like a great storm coming through the trees." Flocks a mile wide and six or seven miles long were sometimes seen feeding near the shores of the bay. They were shot from the shore without difficulty as they rose from the water or passed a point, and a man could often fill an ox-cart with them after four or five hours' shooting.

Every one was compelled to have arms, and for a long time ships were obliged to pay their port dues in gunpowder and lead. Most of the men had long, heavy duck-guns. An indented servant was supposed to practise shooting every Saturday afternoon, and when he was set free at the close of his term of servitude his master was obliged by law to give him certain clothes, shirts, shoes, two hoes, an axe, and "one gun of twenty shillings value, not above four feet in the barrel nor under three and a half feet."

Dogs which are said to have been a cross between the Newfoundland and the Irish wolf-hound were bred for retrieving the ducks; and they would swim far out into the bay in winter to fetch a cripple or attack a wounded swan. Attended by one of these dogs, the sons of the planters would stand up to their knees in water

on a cold day on the outer edge of a marsh, load-
ing and firing their long-barrelled guns at the can-
vas-backs ; and return to drink rum punch and
Madeira, smoke their clay pipes, and play cards
till midnight. If they went to visit a neighbor's
for a similar carouse and there were not beds
enough, they spread a blanket on a sofa or on
four chairs, near the fire, and snored with the
dogs and pickaninnies.

These young men often went to the frontier,
where they adopted the Indian dress, even to
the breech-clout, and, exchanging the long
shot-gun for an equally long rifle, hunted wild-
cats, deer, bears, and panthers. When once
they had tasted of this life, it was extremely
difficult for their parents to get them home again.
They clung to their Indian dress, would raise
the war-whoop to frighten peaceful villagers,
and sometimes insisted on going into church
with their breech-clouts, which did not assist the
devotion of the congregation.

A large part of the abundance of birds lasted
down to the middle of the present century,
and those who can remember the shores of the
Chesapeake at the time of and before the civil
war have most pleasing recollections of the interest created by this wonderful exuberance of
animal life. It was not merely the ducks, but
the quail, the rabbits, the foxes, the song-birds,

the blackbirds, and the wild doves in incredible numbers. On winter nights, on a Maryland farm, the sleeper would be awakened by a rumbling like distant thunder, when a vast mass of thousands of ducks rose from the waters of the bay or river. When summer came the small birds made it impossible to sleep after daylight, and the woodpeckers bored their holes into the eaves of the house.

In colonial times troops of horses ranged wild in the woods, as in Virginia, and were hunted with the same zest, and dogs were often bred to assist in the sport. Every Marylander and many of the women were fox-hunters; and Chief-Justice Taney, in his autobiography, describes himself as inordinately addicted in his youth to this sport.

A Maryland fox-hunt was often a long one; for many of the foxes went straight away, and not infrequently, on the eastern shore, crossed the peninsula from the Chesapeake to Delaware Bay. The horses used were not valued for their jumping power, but for endurance in a long ride through woods, swamps, and fields. If the hunters could not return home by night, they were welcomed at the nearest plantation, and a grand feast prepared, with drinking, dancing, and card-playing far into the night, and then to sleep on the floor before the fire if there were not beds enough.

Puritan and Catholic on the Chesapeake

The Marylander was a duck-shooter, a sailer of swift canoes, a most indefatigable rider to hounds, a hard drinker, and a heavy eater, and all these things he enjoyed in the greatest abundance. But, strange to say, it was not until after the year 1800 that he discovered the deliciousness of the terrapin.

The capacity for eating two or three ducks to a man, with enormous quantities of hominy and goblets of rum punch and Madeira, has passed away from the American race, along with the abundance and leisure which gave such a zest to their existence, in spite of agues and bilious fevers. The old planter, swollen with gout, bandaged his feet for the fox-hunt, shouting with the youngest, hauled the seine on the shore at the head of his negro gang, or rose early in the morning to go out and fish his weirs.

The women of his family followed very much the same pleasures, and lived in the saddle; rode to balls in the evening, with a scarlet riding-habit over their white satin ball-dress, most extraordinary figures, with handkerchiefs tied over the enormous mass of their puffed and pomaded hair, and their hoops spread out lengthwise on the horse.

To any one who wanders nowadays among Maryland farms and sees the almost total extinction of the birds and all kinds of animal life, it is a melancholy reflection to remember what once was. At houses where formerly as soon as you arrived a man went to the shore and with one haul of a small net took more fish than the family could eat in two days, you can now scarcely buy a fish of any kind.

The fields and the whole country are well cultivated, but songless, deserted, and stupid. No troop of baying hounds salutes you, shaking their long ears and pawing and entangling your feet, and the pet hawks and eagles and strange sights and sounds are gone. It was a mistake to allow all this life of pleasure to be ruthlessly extinguished, and the people are none the better for it.

The province was almost as townless as Virginia, but the natural conditions seemed to show somewhat more reason for the existence of towns, and the legislature at times made most frantic efforts to create them. At one time, in 1706, it attempted to bring forth forty-two of them in one litter, and many other efforts were made which were not quite so ambitious. The fate of nearly every one of them was swift and sure. They were staked out in the middle of fields or woods, and divided into lots of an acre each, with streets and alleys. The original owner of the land was given one lot, and the rest were distributed to whoever would take them in consideration of an annual quit-rent of a penny to the Lord Proprietor. Then when the failure of the attempt was evident, an act of the legislature was passed by which the tract of land was "untowned" and reverted to its former owner.

On the death of Cecil Calvert, in 1675, after his long rule of over forty years, his eldest son, Charles, became Lord Baltimore and proprietor of Maryland. Cecil had always governed the province from England, but Charles was sometimes in England and sometimes in the province. The peaceful conditions that had blessed the last fifteen years of Cecil's rule continued for a time; but Charles soon had difficulties and dangers of his own, the result of changed times in England. He was not so lucky in meeting them as his father had been, and lost the province.

The feeling of unrest and incipient revolt which had always characterized the Puritans of the northern half of the province was still strong, but there were no opportunities for an outbreak. Fendall, who had led the rebellion at the restoration of Charles II., was at large and engaged in one or two conspiracies for the overthrow of the proprietary power, but they were of trifling importance and easily suppressed.

Almost immediately after Charles Calvert took the government, the Church of England people appeared as a distinct party in the community and sent complaints to England. One of the clergy wrote to the Archbishop of Canterbury that the Catholic priests were provided for and the Quakers could take care of themselves, but that no measures had been taken for the advancement of the established church, which had only three clergymen; and as a consequence religion was despised, notorious vices committed, and the colony had become "a Sodom of uncleanness and a pest-house of iniquity."

Charles, who was then in England, resisted this attack, which he knew was intended to accomplish the establishment of the Church of England by law in Maryland, as it was already established by law in Virginia. He argued against it before the Privy Council, giving the old reasons which his father had so often given, that every form of Protestantism had full religious liberty in Maryland, that the majority of the people were Protestants, and that if any particular church or sect was not succeeding, it was its own fault.

He had not inherited, it seems, the full measure of his father's influence, for the Privy Council decided against him. They announced that there should be some maintenance for the clergy of the established church, that Lord Baltimore himself " should propose some means for the support of a competent number" of them, and that the laws against vice should be promptly executed. It was certainly a strange predicament for a Roman Catholic proprietor to be obliged to establish the Church of England in his own colony, and a difficulty into which Cecil Calvert had never fallen.

The question, however, was dropped for a time, and Charles returned to Maryland, where he took means to have laws passed for the suppression of vice and the better observance of Sunday. But the Puritans and Fendall were still at work, and the feeling against Roman Catholics was at this time aroused to new activity by the supposed " popish plot" which the infamous Titus Oates professed to have discovered in England.

Charles had to meet fresh complaints sent to England, which this time accused him of partiality to Catholics. He again repeated the old arguments, adding that the offices of government were divided equally between Protestants and Catholics, that the command of the militia was given almost exclusively to Protestants, and these assertions were supported in a document signed by prominent members of the Church of England. But the fear of trusting the adherents of the Pope with any governmental power had become very strong in England, and the ministry ordered that all public offices in Maryland should be given to Protestants. The colony was evidently becoming less Roman Catholic than ever.

William Penn had been given his vast province of Pennsylvania in 1682, and Charles Calvert was soon involved in a boundary dispute with him, which was continued by the two proprietors and their descendants for the next seventy years.* About the same time serious complaints were made against Calvert for allowing his officials to obstruct the collection of the royal revenue tax on tobacco. Two of the king's revenue officers were killed, and Calvert received a severe reprimand from the crown, was ordered to pay at once the two thousand five hundred pounds of duties which had not been collected, and was reminded that only the clemency of the king had saved his charter, which could have been forfeited for such misconduct.

His misfortunes steadily increased. James II. came to the throne in 1685, and, as he was a Roman Catholic, it might be expected that Calvert would now enjoy in the fullest manner the favor of the crown; but, instead of that,

---

* For a full account of this controversy, see "The Making of Pennsylvania," p. 318.

Puritan and Catholic on the Chesapeake

James had scarcely been king two years when he
began proceedings to annul the Maryland charter
and bring the province into more immediate de-
pendence on the crown. He had taken similar
action, as we have already seen, in some of the
other colonies.

Andros was made governor of all the New
England colonies, and soon after New York and
New Jersey were added to his jurisdiction.
Pennsylvania, however, escaped entirely, for
Penn was a close friend and favorite of James.
But the Calvert family seemed to have lost all
their favor and power at court, and to have in-
curred the hostility of the monarch who was of
their own faith. In truth, after the death of
Cecil the family steadily degenerated.

Charles inherited none of his father's courtier
skill. He spent a great part of the time in Maryland, enjoyed the life he led there, and expressed
a decided distaste for England. As a governor
in direct contact with his people he was very
successful, and, if we can accept as sincere the
votes of gratitude, thanks, and admiration for his
beneficent rule which the assembly passed, he
must have been very popular. But he failed to
appreciate the absolute necessity of a strong connection in England and at court; and the more
he lived in the province the more he acquired
its point of view, lost his position as an English

nobleman, and unfitted himself for acquiring influence with the king.

Before the proceedings to annul his charter could be consummated, William of Orange landed in England and drove James from the throne. Charles Calvert was now in England, whither he had gone to save his charter, and he had left a man named Joseph as temporary governor of Maryland. The contest between the Protestant William of Orange and the Catholic James II. renewed the fierce antagonism between the two religions which had been slumbering for years. The Maryland Puritans were alert and suspicious, and Calvert soon had some of his usual bad luck.

He had submitted himself to King William, and sent a messenger, ordering him to be proclaimed sovereign in Maryland. The messenger, unfortunately, died on the route, and the Puritans heard of all the other colonies proclaiming William, but had no instructions for a proclamation from Lord Baltimore. Virginia, always ready to seize such an opportunity, sent complaints to England, and some of the Puritans started a story that there was a Catholic plot to destroy the Protestants with the assistance of the Indians.

Messengers arrived reporting thousands of Indians assembled at certain points, and when none were found, they were reported farther on or in other places. John Coode, who had been concerned in previous rebellions, busied himself as a leader, and Kenelm Cheseldyn, Blakiston Beebe, and Colonel Jowles were active participants. An association was formed to protect the Protestant religion and the sovereignty of King William and Queen Mary. By the 16th of July, 1689, a small Puritan army, under the command of Coode, was collected on the Potomac, announcing that it was prepared to protect the Protestants from the papists and Northern Indians, who intended to descend on the province in August " when roasting ears were in season."

Coode and his followers soon seized the government at St. Mary's and published a Declaration of charges against Lord Baltimore and his methods. He had been building up his own power in the colony at the expense of the sovereignty of the crown, and to name or own the king's power was sufficient to incur the frowns of his lordship. He had affronted the king's officers of the customs, had forcibly detained one of them, and another one had been murdered by an Irish papist. He had oppressed the people, established popish idolatry instead of the churches and chapels of the ecclesiastical laws of England, given the most fertile lands to

Romish churches, and forfeited the lands of the Protestant ministry. He had vetoed the best acts passed by the assembly, disposed of Protestant orphans to be brought up in Romish superstition, separated a young woman from her husband and committed her to the custody of a papist, imposed excessive fees, seized Protestants in their houses by armed forces of papists and committed them to prison without warrant, allowed no redress for outrages and murders committed by Catholics, and used every means to divert the obedience of the people from the new Protestant king and queen.

His agents, the priests and Jesuits, the Declaration continued, had used solemn masses and prayers for the success of the popish forces in Ireland and the French designs against England, and on every side could be heard protestations against their majesties' right to the crown and vilification of their persons. For these reasons the people of Maryland had taken up arms to vindicate and assert the sovereignty of King William and to defend the Protestant religion.

Such was the Protestant indictment of the proprietary Catholic government of Maryland. Some of the charges seem exaggerated, but the obscurity and confusion of the colony's history make it extremely difficult to test the truth of any of them. Coode was soon in possession of the whole province, for the Catholics were powerless to offer any resistance, and in every quarter surrendered on demand. An address was then sent to the king, announcing that Maryland had been rescued from his majesty's enemies "without the expense of one drop of blood," and that it was held to await his further orders in regard to it.

Addresses to the king, asking him to take the colony under his direct protection and government, were soon prepared in all parts of the colony, signed by hundreds of names, and sent to England. The majority of the people were unquestionably in favor of the rebellion; but there was a respectable minority of Protestants who sent counter-addresses, accusing Coode and his followers of falsehood, tyranny, and misgovernment, denying all the charges against Lord Baltimore, and asking that his government and province be restored to him.

On this occasion Charles Carroll, founder of the family of that name, appears for the first time in Maryland history, and his letter to Calvert describes in strong language the confusion and misery in the province and the destruction of cattle and property under the rule of "such profligate wretches as Coode, Thurling, and Jowles, and such fools as they have poisoned by the most absurd lies that ever were invented."

Puritan and Catholic on the Chesapeake

In England, however, William III. took the side of the Maryland Protestant majority, approved their action, and accepted the province as they offered it to him. The leaders of the rebellion had held the government for six months before the king recognized them, and he instructed them to continue to hold it for him and keep the peace.

Meantime the Privy Council considered the charges against Lord Baltimore, and in August, 1690, a year after the rebellion had begun, ordered the attorney-general to proceed against the charter and collect proof of the proprietor's misconduct. At the same time the Puritan council in Maryland sent to the king a document in which they renewed the charges against Baltimore, declared themselves ready to prove them at any time, and added other " insolencys, misdemeanors, and outrages" which had been recently perpetrated by his agents. A certain tax on tobacco had, they said, been misappropriated by his lordship, who was now in arrears to the province at least thirty-six thousand pounds; but the exact amount could not be discovered, because his agents refused to show the account.

The proceedings against the charter were never completed, and there never was a final decision either for it or against it, which was unfortunate, because it has left the charges of Baltimore's misgovernment and oppression neither proved nor disproved. William III. finally grew tired of the slow procedure and took possession of the province without regard to Baltimore's rights, and the proceedings against the charter were abandoned. Sir Lionel Copley was sent out in August, 1691, to be the royal governor, after the leaders of the rebellion had been holding the province for two years.

Baltimore's ownership of all the land of the province and his quit-rents and revenues were, of course, left unimpaired, and in this respect he was in as good a position as ever. The political power or right to govern was all that was taken from him.

William III. had also in the same way deprived Penn of his right to govern Pennsylvania, without in this case even attempting to forfeit his charter. The chief reason for depriving Penn of his political power seems to have been that, the military force of the colony being weak and likely to continue so under Quaker rule, it might at any time be captured by the French or other enemies of England. Penn had also been a close friend of the dethroned James II., and might reasonably be suspected of favoring him. But Penn was a Protestant, and soon cleared himself of all suspicions; so that his government was restored to him within less than two years, while the Baltimores were kept from theirs for twenty-five years, when, as they had become Protestants, it was restored in 1715.

Under the new royal government almost the first act of importance was to establish by law the Church of England, and a yearly tax of forty pounds of tobacco on each taxable person was to be levied for its support. Maryland was now no more a Catholic colony than were the other colonies which contained a few Catholic citizens.

The Maryland Catholics were principally collected in St. Mary's County, on the Potomac, in the extreme southern part of the province, where the first landing and settlement had been made, and which always had been the seat of government. In 1694, however, it was decided to move the seat of government to the old Puritan stronghold which had been called successively Providence, Anne Arundel Town, and afterwards Annapolis, which was nearer the centre of the province, and in a more fertile and prosperous part of the country.

The people of St. Mary's, foreseeing the results, resisted this movement, but in vain. The presence of the seat of government had been their only hold on prosperity; and when it was removed, being unsupported by natural advantages, the interesting old town of so many contests and memories wasted away until it became as much of a desolation and ruin as Jamestown in Virginia.

St. Mary's had been the only town of the colony, and when the seat of government was moved to Annapolis, that, in its turn, became the only town; for Maryland was very much like Virginia in its civilization, with all the people living on plantations, which on the western shore were usually for tobacco and on the eastern for wheat.

The Protestants and their new government had progressive ideas and made every effort to improve Annapolis. They built a brick statehouse and a free school, also of brick, which was the first attempt at general public education that had been made in the colony. The free school in Annapolis, named King William School, was soon under way and flourishing; but the design of the people and the assembly was to establish a free school in every county, and from time to time acts were passed for this end, levying taxes on furs, beef, and some other exports. Assistance was obtained from England, the Archbishop of Canterbury was persuaded to encourage the undertaking, fines, forfeitures, and escheated estates helped to swell the fund, and after some years the schools were established under the control and encouragement of the Church of England.

The metropolis and centre of life in colonial times were always at Annapolis, which occupied very much the same position as Williamsburg in Virginia. The wealthy planters resorted to it for the dances and assemblies, and many of them lived there in substantial houses, where they indulged in the most extravagant hospitality. The governor's house and the homes of the Carrolls and the Pacas were the principal scenes of this festivity.

Situated on a peninsula overlooking the river and bay, with a view across to the eastern shore, the town was laid out with great care. A large circle was made on the highest point, which was occupied by the government buildings, and behind it was a smaller circle for the church. From these circles the streets radiated in every direction. A part of the water front was reserved for wharves and the rest devoted to residences with terraced grounds and gardens reaching to the river, a few of which still survive. The tradespeople were strictly confined to a certain district, and no offensive occupations could be carried on in the residence quarter. When the gentlemen were masquerading in their quarter, the common people were not even permitted to be in the streets of it.

Puritan and Catholic on the Chesapeake

It must have been a really beautiful little miniature city, reproducing English ways and customs. By the year 1750 its Puritan traits had all passed away, and one who knew it well said that there was not a town in England of the same size that could boast of so many fashionable and handsome women. The phantom pleasure was pursued with avidity; the races lasted four days, there were numerous dancing assemblies, the theatre was encouraged more than anywhere else in America, and there were sixteen clubs.

We are apt to think club life rather abnormally developed in our own time, but, in proportion to its numbers, no modern town could in this respect equal Annapolis. One was called the Hominy Club, and another the Drumstick. The Tuesday Club had among its members prominent men from the other colonies, and all these clubs were devoted to stimulating the social life.

From the short statements in their little newspaper, the *Gazette*, the typical amusements of a day of pleasure in Annapolis seem to have been to fire off guns, drink loyal healths, have a ball in the evening, with the whole town illuminated and punch distributed among the populace at the bonfire. They fired guns and salutes on every possible occasion. In the issue for July 15,

1746, we see the work of the clubs, some of which appear to have had houses of their own, as in modern times:

> "The gentlemen belonging to the '*Ancient South River Club*,' to express their loyalty to his majesty, on the success of the inimitable Duke of Cumberland's obtaining a complete victory over the pretender, and delivering us from persecution at home, and popery and invasion from abroad, have appointed a grand entertainment to be given at their club house on Thursday next."

There was also a jockey club which encouraged the horse-races, of which all classes in Maryland are still very fond. The subscription purses began at a hundred guineas and were afterwards greatly increased. The betting was high, and the Virginians, of course, came up in large numbers for these sports, which always closed with a ball. But Annapolis had not a monopoly of horse-races, for we find them held everywhere,—at Marlborough, Joppa, Chestertown, Elkridge, and Williamstadt, as Oxford was then called; in fact, wherever people congregated; and finally they began to have them at Quaker meetings.

The races were four-mile heats, and endurance rather than a sudden burst of speed for one mile was the test. The horses were usually six or eight years old instead of two or three, as in our times; and the system is supposed by some to have encouraged a sounder, healthier breed of animals than can be had under the modern forcing method.

Besides the ball, the races, not only at Annapolis but at other places, usually ended with a performance by Hallam Henry's Dramatic Company, which contained some good actors, and played in Maryland every season for more than twenty years. Annapolis has the honor of establishing the first theatre in the colonies. The first play-bill ever printed in America appeared in its newspaper, the *Gazette*, July 2, 1752. The plays announced were " The Busybody" and " The Lying Valet," " to begin precisely at seven o'clock ; no persons to be admitted behind the scenes." Afterwards the company played " Richard III.," " The Beggar's Opera," " Cato," " The Sham Doctor," " Miss in her Teens," and " George Barnwell."

But we are not yet through with the races ; for at the close of the week in which they were held there were also bull-baitings and cock-fights. Farmers, blacksmiths, carpenters, and gentlemen all bred cocks and fought them. The people were almost insane about this amusement, and Puritans who were inclined to look askance at the theatre never hesitated about a cock-fight.

" Did you ever make anything by cock-fighting ?" was asked of an elderly man, carrying an eight-pound cock under his arm.

" Make ! It has cost me thousands of dollars."

" What do you do it for, then ?"

" Why, it's the prettiest sight in the world."

The ladies of Annapolis were not without spirit, and we find an entry in the court records that Mrs. S. C., of Patapsco, was fined only one penny for whipping a man with a hickory switch, " it being imagined by the court that he well deserved it."

William Black, who in the year 1744 was secretary to some commissioners who came from Virginia to Philadelphia to assist in making an Indian treaty, gives us a lively picture of the life of the times. They embarked on the yacht Margaret, at Stratford, on the Potomac ; and after getting under way, he says, " we hailed with the trumpet the company who came to the water side to see us on board with ' Fare-you-well,' who returned the compliment, wishing us a good voyage and safe return ; for which, on the part of the company, I gave them thanks, with the discharge of our blunderbuss."

Stopping at Annapolis, they were entertained by the governor with punch, wines, strawberries, and ice-cream, followed by a series of dinners at all the principal houses, for their presence was a grand event for the townsmen. He describes one of several balls which were given them. The ladies made "a splendid appearance;" and "in a Room back from that where they Danced was several sorts of Wines, Punch and Sweet Meats, in this Room those that were not Engaged in any Dancing Match might either Employ themselves at Cards, Dice, Back-Gamon, or with a cheerful Glass."

Everywhere "the Glass was pushed briskly." When received by the governor, they discoursed for a while over glasses of punch; then dinner, and after that more discourse and the glass again.

In the "Sot Weed Factor," a rather clever satire on Maryland life, there is a description of a court day at a country village, which is, of course, an exaggeration, but assists in showing the conditions of the time. "Roaring planters" were drinking healths in circles, with their horses hitched to trees; and soon jury, lawyers, judge, and constables were engaged in a general fight, with the sheriff superintending and picking up stray wigs:

> "Where all things were in such confusion,
> I thought the world at its conclusion;
> A Herd of Planters on the ground,
> O'erwhelmed with Punch, dead drunk, we found,
> Others were fighting and contending,
> Some burnt their clothes to save the mending."

Puritan and Catholic on the Chesapeake

The factor found every room occupied in the inn, and had to sleep in a corn-crib. In the morning his hat, shoes, and horses were gone and his drunken servants stripped and left naked on the table. But a great planter, or Cockerouse, as the Indians always called such a man, politely invited him home "to take a Bottle at his Seat," which is described as an "antient Cedar House" buried among trees and vines.

In the harbor of Annapolis, in plain sight from most of the houses, lay vessels from all parts of the world; for the little town had its commercial day before the rise of Baltimore. The houses were in the most perfect forms of the colonial architecture. White Hall and the Chase, Scott, Ridout, Brice, Harwood, and Welch houses still remain as examples to reform our taste, and there are few other places in the country where such interesting and valuable treasures of this old art can be found.

The men and women, who, like the rest of the Maryland gentry, ordered champagne from Europe by the cask and Madeira by the pipe, also dressed expensively in the latest English fashions, and French travellers said that they had seldom seen such clothes outside of Paris. They had French barbers, negro slaves in livery, and drove light carriages,—an extremely rare indulgence in colonial times. The clubs got up

WHITEHALL
Annapolis, Md.
Built 1764

excursions, picnics, and fishing parties. Balls were given on all the great English anniversaries, and the birthday of the proprietor and saints' days were used as excuses. Saint Tamina had a society in his honor, for balls, masquerades, and May-pole dances.

They gambled, of course, after the universal custom of the times, flirted or pretended to flirt, like the modern Marylander, discussed the last vessel from England, the prospects of the tobacco crop, and the quarrels of the proprietors and the crown. Visitors were frequent from the Northern and Southern colonies. In spring the wealthy people departed for their manors or country places—De La Brooke, Kent Fort, Bohemia, or Bel Air—in great coaches of light yellow color with Venetian windows and projecting lamps.

One of the most interesting houses in Maryland, —Doughoregan Manor, in Howard County,— which is still standing, belonged to the Carrolls, who spent many a bright day in Annapolis. The buildings are long and rather low, but in beautiful proportion, and include a Roman Catholic chapel,—a relic of the times, which we shall soon describe, when the Catholics of Maryland were not allowed to have public places of worship. The whole length of the mansion is three hundred feet on the front, and only one room deep. At one end is the chapel, at the other wings, and in the centre the family residence, with a wide hall heavily panelled, a dining-room arched and recessed, and a library wainscoted high up in oak, in which Charles Carroll, one of the signers of the Declaration of Independence, passed his last days reading Cicero's " De Senectute."

We can understand how all this high life in Maryland was possible when we read that John Beale Bordley made nine hundred pounds on a single shipment of wheat to Barcelona. Farming was at that time, in both Maryland and Virginia, a paying business, and lawyers, doctors, and clergymen were all farmers. They were tempted to live beyond their means, and bankruptcy and disasters were frequent. When the shrinkage came after the Revolution, the grand life gradually went to pieces, as in Virginia.

The Bordleys were among the highest livers, and have left interesting memoirs. Stephen Bordley kept bachelor's hall in Annapolis, with a cellar full of wine, handsome plate, furniture, and linen, and a good library. He enjoyed a good income from his practice at the bar, and held important offices. The judges dined with him whenever they came to Annapolis,—everybody dined with him, and he died of the gout, like a hero.

His younger brother, John Beale Bordley, thought it necessary to call a halt in this life, so he went to live at Joppa, and became a fox-hunting planter, raising a large family and growing rich. But half of Wye Island was left to him, and there he set up a grand establishment, making his own flour, beer, and bricks, weaving cloth for his people, having his own carpenters, blacksmiths, and coopers, and even manufacturing his own salt. Visitors came to him, passing to and fro to the island, sometimes appearing in a ten-oared barge rowed by slaves, some of them staying all winter,—the Tilghmans, Hollidays, Lloyds, Pacas, Haywards, Blakes, Browns, and Hindmans. Baskets of fruit stood in the hallway, with tankards of sangaree and lemon punch, and everybody dressed for dinner in the ruffles and gorgeousness of the period.

After William III. came to the throne and the Church of England was established by law, Roman Catholicism was almost abolished in Maryland, and the few Catholics who remained were in a worse condition than ever. The Protestants were firmly settled in power, with the Church of England established on the ruins of the faith which the Calverts and their followers had fondly hoped would always control the colony. They were under the direct rule of a Protestant king who had spent a large part of his life in upholding the liberties of Holland against the combined Catholic armies of Europe. He had just fought his way to the English throne against the armies of a Catholic king, and he was continually discovering and suppressing Catholic plots to dethrone him.

The Catholics of Maryland were not the subjects of any European country watching its opportunity to invade England and turn it Catholic at the point of the sword; they were not the subjects of the king of France, who had supplied Charles II. and James II. with money and assistance to suppress Protestantism. It is not probable that in their depressed condition any of them were concerned in plots to dethrone William; and certainly none of them had been concerned in the Spanish Armada or the Gunpowder Plot.

But they were Catholics; they belonged to the faith and were a part of the people who believed that the British government and all the churches and cathedrals of England were the property of the Pope, and that it was justifiable to join the French in an invasion of England to dethrone any king who was a Protestant. The difference between Protestant and Catholic was at that time a political as much as a religious difference. The Protestants were the majority of the people of England, and the Catholics had been concerned in all the conspiracies and wars against the nation which for a hundred years and more had inflamed the Protestant mind. The Puritans and the English churchmen were too close to all these events to look upon them calmly or tolerantly. There were on both sides too many people alive who had taken part in them, and they could not believe that all danger was past.

They knew of the plots against King William, they knew that the dethroned Catholic James II. was in France, living under the protection of a Catholic people and king, with whom he eagerly watched for an opportunity to invade England and assist the English Catholics to seize the government, and they knew that on the continent of Europe, wherever Catholics were in power, Protestants were persecuted, tortured, and subjected to every indignity and misery that vengeance could devise. They had saved themselves from such things in England by force, and they believed that force would be necessary for many years to come.

The development of religious liberty had at that time reached a point where the different divisions of Protestants were willing to tolerate one another, although this toleration was not the free, absolutely willing, and open toleration of modern times. They were willing also to tolerate the Catholics in the sense of the former meaning of the word tolerate; that is to say, the Catholics were to be allowed to inhabit the country without deprivation of life or property; but they were not to be allowed any share in the government, or to have any influence in it which might be the entering wedge for attaining complete control; and they must keep their religion to themselves, not parade it in public or in any way attempt to proselyte and add to their numbers. If reduced to this condition, it was generally believed that in all English-speaking countries they would be comparatively harmless and unable to carry out the peculiar political doctrines which at that time were an essential part of their religion.

It was on this principle, which now, of course, seems strange and unnecessary, that the Catholics were dealt with in all the colonies, where they were very few in numbers, compelled to be very quiet and unobtrusive in their opinions, and usually conducted their religious services in private houses. Any priests among them were obliged to be as inconspicuous as possible, and both priests and laity were universally regarded as belonging to the most bitter and dangerous political enemies of England, who for humanity's sake were permitted to live in the community and enjoy the ordinary rights of person and property only on condition that they kept themselves in the background.

Where religious liberty was established by law in colonial times, it usually meant liberty only for Protestants, and Catholics were either expressly or impliedly excluded from its provisions. In the commission for New Hampshire of 1680 we find "that liberty of conscience shall be allowed to all Protestants." The Massachusetts charter of 1691, granted by William III., says, "there shall be liberty of conscience allowed in the worship of God to all Christians (except papists) inhabiting or which shall inhabit or be resident within our said province or territory;" and Oglethorpe's Georgia charter of 1732 says, "all such persons, except papists, shall have a free exercise of religion."

In the Rhode Island charter of 1663, in the constitutions framed by the proprietors of New Jersey, and in the constitutions framed by Penn for the government of Pennsylvania, religious liberty is given generally, without any exclusion of Catholics. In these instances there may possibly have been an intention to allow religious liberty in the modern sense of the term. Roger Williams and his followers, who founded Rhode Island, were adherents of obscure sects far in advance of their time, who seem to have been entirely sincere in their notions of liberty, although they were never put to the severe test of contending for political power with a rival sect, and there were few if any Roman Catholics in their colony. Pennsylvania and New Jersey were largely under the influence of the Quakers, in whose faith absolute freedom of religion was a cardinal principle.

But even in those colonies where there was no precise law on the subject, or where the law was broad enough to include Catholics, the force of general public opinion, and the strong conviction in all Protestant minds that the political integrity of England was inconsistent with Catholic power, was sufficient to make the treatment of Catholics the same as it was in colonies where the laws were expressly against them.

In Pennsylvania, where complete religious liberty was supposed to be allowed by law to every form of Christianity, and where the founder of the province and the people were more than usually liberal in their views, we find that the Catholics were obliged to keep very much to themselves. In 1708, Penn writes to his secretary of the colony, James Logan, "there is a complaint against your government that you suffer public mass in a scandalous manner ;" and again, " it has become a reproach to me here with the officers of the crown, that you have suffered the scandal of mass to be publicly celebrated."

It is to be observed that what Penn complains of is "public mass" and mass "publicly celebrated." He was willing that the Catholics should have it in their private houses, but the open celebration of it was an offence against the feeling of the time.

We read in Watson's "Annals" that in 1736 the people of Philadelphia opposed the building of a papal chapel because it was to be erected in too public a place; and another Catholic chapel, which is said to have been in existence about the same time a little north of Philadelphia, is described as being part of a private house, which enabled the worshippers to resort to it without inconvenience.

The priests commonly went about in disguise because they were at any time likely to suffer indignities from the masses of the people, whose instinctive dislike for them was very strong. A Jesuit who went from Maryland to Philadelphia in 1730 to see a Catholic lady of some importance found her disguised in the dress of a Quakeress, and made himself known to her only after cautious approaches.*

---

* De Courcy's "Catholic Church in the United States" (translated by Shea), pp. 209, 210.

Puritan and Catholic on the Chesapeake

Even as late as the Revolution and for some time afterwards, when the States were making new constitutions for themselves, we find the same general opinion prevailing. The constitutions of this period did not expressly except Catholics from the protection of religious liberty, but many of them expressly excluded Catholics from public office ; and the constitution of Vermont of 1777 provided that no Protestant should on account of his religion be deprived of any civil right, which would seem to imply that a Catholic could be so deprived.*

The Protestant government of Maryland under William III. proceeded to reduce the Catholics of the province to precisely the same condition which they occupied in the other colonies, and continued to occupy for the next century, until with the waning temporal power of the Pope and the change in some of the more violent of their opinions the fear of their political designs gradually wore away.

The benefit of religious liberty was allowed only to Protestants in Maryland, and the Catholic priests were strictly prohibited from proselyting, and from making any public or conspicuous display of their religion. In one instance, when there was an epidemic in the province, the as-

* " Evolution of the Constitution," p. 190.

sembly complained that the priests took advantage of it "to go up and down the country, to persons' houses when dying and frantic, and endeavor to seduce and make proselytes of them;" and, in the absence of a law on the subject, they asked the governor to restrain them by proclamation.

On another occasion the upper house of the legislature calls the attention of the governor to William Hunter, a priest, who had been very active in proselyting, and leaves it to the governor to decide whether he should be "wholly silenced, and not suffered to preach or say mass in any part of this province." In 1704 there was a complaint that mass was celebrated in the Popish chapel at St. Mary's when the County Court was holding its sessions there. For this too public exhibition of the Roman religion the chapel was ordered to be closed by the sheriff, and the priests were informed by the governor, "You might, methinks, be content to live quietly as you may, and let the exercise of your superstitious vanities be confined to yourselves, without proclaiming them at public times and in public places,"—a sentence which shows in brief the main principle which controlled the treatment of the Catholics in all the colonies.

In the year 1700, many conspiracies to dethrone William III. having been discovered, a severe statute was passed by Parliament, called "An act for the further preventing the growth of popery." By this law a reward was offered to any one who should secure the conviction of a priest for exercising any function of his office or for saying mass, and the punishment on conviction was perpetual imprisonment. Any Catholic who kept a school or educated or boarded young people was to receive like punishment. Those who refused to take the oath of allegiance and supremacy could not inherit land. No professed Catholic could purchase land; and to prevent Protestant children of Catholic parents from being compelled to embrace the Catholic religion for want of suitable support, the Keeper of the Great Seal could take charge of such children as were not given support by their parents, and make order for their proper maintenance. This legislation was reenacted in Maryland with some modifications, and those who refused to take the oath of allegiance and supremacy were not allowed to vote for delegates to the assembly.

It does not appear to have been always necessary to enforce all of this legislation. The ordinary policy which has already been described was sufficient to keep the few Catholics in Maryland within bounds, as in the other colonies, and the severe laws were held in reserve, to be let loose, as one of the governors said, to crush them if occasion should ever require it.

This plain statement of the actual condition of things in colonial times seems to be necessary because the facts have been distorted by Protestant writers on one side and by Catholic on the other. The severity of the repression not only in Maryland, but in England and all the colonies, has often been assailed as unnecessary and cruel bigotry, and no doubt it was often carried too far when public officials acted under the influence of excitement and yielded to popular clamor. Queen Elizabeth was as unjustified in slaughtering Catholics as Bloody Mary in slaughtering Protestants, and these excesses of Protestant rulers often injured their cause by producing reactions in favor of the Catholics. But we must not judge the situation exclusively by modern standards. We must put ourselves in the place of the men of that time, and understand their difficulties and the problems with which they were dealing.

If it had been merely a question of religion, the repression, even in the mildest form, would have been both bigoted and unnecessary. But there was a great deal besides religion at stake. The whole political fabric of England and the principles of liberty and free government of the Anglo-Saxon race were assailed. Catholic and Protestant did not then stand, as now, for a mere difference in religious doctrine. They stood for two different and absolutely inconsistent political theories which neither side would surrender.

The Roman Catholic Church of that time, although it contained, as always, many good and learned men, was unequivocally allied with despotism, and supported despotism in every country of Europe. It had not then accepted and it would not accept the new ideas of free government which were springing up everywhere, especially in England. Whenever it secured a king of England or gained influence over one, he became a despot, like the Catholic James II., who declared that he had power to annul or dispense with the laws whenever he pleased. If the Spanish Armada or any of the other Catholic designs against England had met with permanent success, there is no question that England would have become a despotism like France, which could have been broken only by the horrors of a French Revolution.

England escaped such a revolution only because in the previous two hundred years she had succeeded in fighting off the attempt of the Catholics to control her government and give despotism the sanction of religion. During those two hundred years the colonies in America were founded exclusively by Protestants, except in the single instance of Maryland, which became a completely Protestant government within sixty years. These Protestant colonists brought with them the principles of Anglo-Saxon freedom untainted by the influences from continental Europe which were attempting to smother them in England. The colonists represented the original Anglo-Saxon principles of liberty more thoroughly and completely than the mother country, and they and their descendants preserved them in that original purity which has created all that is valuable in the American Revolution and the Constitution.

But if in that two hundred years the British government had been controlled by Roman influence, the colonies would all have been turned into little despotisms, as James II. had started to turn them just before he was dethroned, our history would have been reversed, and our Revolution would have been another French Revolution.

We must remember also that under all the severely repressive laws the Catholics were always given ample opportunity to renounce their political doctrines as distinct from their religious doctrines. When they wanted to vote, or take part in government, or hold public office, they were offered an oath to the effect that they admitted the king then on the throne to be the lawful king of England, to whom they owed allegiance, and that they denied the authority of the Pope, or of any power outside of Great Britain, to dethrone him and absolve his subjects from their allegiance. But they would not take this oath, and openly put themselves in the position of rebels against the government under which they were living, and showed the sincerity of their opinions by joining in every conspiracy and attempt against the government. It is not at all surprising that they were taken at their word and treated as a dangerous class.

In modern times most Roman Catholics, or at least most English-speaking Roman Catholics, have practically abandoned their former doctrines of the authority of their Pope and church in political affairs, and as a consequence they are given the most complete political and religious liberty in all Protestant communities, a liberty which they might have had two or three centuries sooner if they had apprehended that religion and politics are not necessarily connected.

The only instances in which the freedom of Catholics has been disturbed in Protestant communities in modern times have been when a mistaken zeal on their part has aroused the people's suspicion that they still in secret nourished their ancient political doctrines and were watching an opportunity to carry them into effect. But every day that passes lessens the probability of such outbreaks for the future, and in the United States, when the Roman Church has acquired a native instead of a foreign priesthood, such difficulties will be impossible.

In 1708 the sheriffs of every county in Maryland made a careful enumeration of the Catholics, and returned two thousand nine hundred and seventy-four, of whom nearly half were to be found in St. Mary's County, where the original settlement had been made. As the total population was at that time about forty thousand, the Catholics were less than a tenth of the whole. They had not increased in proportion to the rest of the people, for thirty-five years previously Lord Baltimore had reported them as numbering one-fourth.

The Church of England people, however, who at first had been very insignificant in numbers, steadily increased, and their faith remained established by law until after the Revolution. They could not at first secure the absolute control they had in Virginia, for the Puritans were too numerous and had taken too important a part in the history of the colony; but the churchmen increased so rapidly that long before the Revolution they composed, it is said, two-thirds of the people.

The churches, as in Virginia, were usually built of brick. The pulpit was high above the congregation, with a great sounding-board like a candle extinguisher hung above from the ceiling. The pews were square boxes with partitions often seven or eight feet high, furnished according to the owner's taste, and owned like land, descending to heirs and transferred by will. When the floor was covered with pews, hanging pews were built against the walls on a level with the high pulpit.

The Maryland clergy are said to have been more vicious and corrupt than those of Virginia. They were appointed to their livings by Lord Baltimore, and, once appointed, it was almost impossible to remove them, no matter what their conduct. There were thirty-six parishes in the province, and the livings averaged two hundred pounds a year, which was a good income at that time, and few clergymen in the country could live so comfortably.

They were secure in their houses and glebes, with their incomes collected from taxes by the sheriff, and they set decency at defiance, it is said. They raced horses, hunted foxes, drank, gambled, joined in every amusement and gayety of the planters, and would extort marriage fees from the poor by breaking off in the middle of the service and refusing to go on until they were paid.

But in the midst of all this abuse we find that nearly all the good schools in the province were conducted by them,—the Garrison Forest School in Baltimore County, King William's School, Rev. Thomas Bordley's School in Cecil County, and the school at Chestertown. Parson Bacon, although for his accomplishments as a fiddler he was elected a member of the Annapolis Tuesday Club, was also a learned man, and compiled the valuable volume of the laws of Maryland. They were not quite so black as they have been painted, and a few notoriously bad ones affected the reputation of all. They lived under an evil system. There was no bishop or superintending head to control them, and the difficulty of punishing any of them by removal rendered the reckless ones open and defiant in their vices.

The detestable practice of sending convicted criminals to the colonies was indulged in by the British government to an unusual extent in the case of Maryland. In fact, the plain truth of the matter is that Maryland was made a penal colony, and was the only province into which convicts could be freely imported. To Virginia, as we have seen, comparatively few came; the people would not allow the practice to go on, and inflicted severe penalties on captains who brought them. But after the year 1750 Maryland was compelled to see English criminals turned loose among her people at the rate of four or five hundred a year; and it has been estimated that up to the Revolution she had received at least twenty thousand of these social pests, who were a severe injury to the general character of her people and interfered not a little with her advancement.

The Marylanders protested and resisted in vain. An act was passed prohibiting their importation, and when annulled by the crown was passed again and again, until finally the legislature fell back on that curious clause in the charter which allowed the colony to levy duties on goods imported from Great Britain; and as the convicts were sold like indented servants, a tax was imposed on them as imported merchandise. But the law was of course promptly suppressed by the home government, without regard to the charter, and the process of making Maryland a penal colony continued.

In this enormous importation of a low class, and in the presence of Spaniards, Italians, Dutch, Germans, and Bohemians who came to the province as adventurers, we find a reason for the failure of Maryland to attain a position of leadership and distinction like Virginia. The climate was said to be better than that of Virginia, tobacco-raising and plantation life very much the same, prosperity and wealth as quickly attained, and living was so easy that the Marylanders are described as larger and stronger than the Virginians. But no very remarkable men were produced, and the Maryland aristocracy was distinctly inferior in ability and accomplishments to the same class in Virginia.

The Spaniards, Italians, and other aliens were comparatively few. The majority of the people were English. But when to this alien element were added twenty thousand criminals, some of whom were actually employed as school-teachers, it is easy to see the degenerating influence which pervaded the masses of the people, on whom, in the end, the character of a community always depends.

Scharf, in his " History of Maryland," tells us that the manners and morals of the province were decidedly bad; and although this is perhaps too strong a statement, such a condition was naturally to be expected from the character of the population. Politics were corrupt and bribery common. Maryland and New York suffered more from this evil in colonial times than the other colonies, which were comparatively free from it. The Marylanders also showed a lack of intelligence in their political affairs, and injured themselves by imposing absurd duties on exports.

To complete the demoralization, treats were given by the government to the people on great occasions, like Washington's visit to Annapolis or a governor's visit to Baltimore. When the treaty of peace which closed the Revolution was signed, the State bought a hogshead of rum, forty-nine gallons of claret, thirty-two of Madeira, thirty-five of port, six of spirits, one hundred and seventy-six pounds of bacon, one hundred and twenty-six pounds of mutton, two hundred and seventy-two of veal, besides beef, lamb, fowls, loaf-sugar, bread, playing-cards, and candles, for a grand carouse of the mob. To celebrate the birth of the Dauphin of France, four hundred and eighteen pounds were spent in a similar way.

If the aristocracy had been composed of selected and unusual men, like the Virginia Cavaliers, they might have risen superior, for a time, to the masses. But very few people of this Virginia class came to Maryland. The Catholics, although in the first migration comprising not a few people of more than ordinary education, were not, as a class, of the high-strung Virginia order, and the Puritans were not of the keen, aggressive sort who settled New England.

The Maryland aristocracy indulged in the

sports and amusements and a great deal of the whole-souled out-door life of the Virginians, but they failed to combine with these the Virginians' love of knowledge, books, and discussion. They had no college like the Virginians, and no ambition for one, and this difference is at once suggestive.

The negroes were concerned in one slight rebellion, which was not like the usual slave rebellion, for they joined themselves to a disreputable party of white men, mostly of the insolvent class, whose object was to seize the government and force a general discharge of all debts and obligations.

The frequent rebellions in Maryland had naturally given the impression that the government could be seized to carry out any pet purpose of a clique or party; and this feeling was another injury to the province. There never seems to have been a time when there were not several restless, discontented spirits, who, having enjoyed the excitement and publicity of some of the Puritan rebellions, were on the watch for another opportunity. Coode was fond of boasting "that as he had pulled down one government, he would pull down another."

In 1711 Charles Calvert made a last attempt to regain the government of Maryland, but was distinctly told that it could not be restored to any one of his religious belief; and soon after, in 1714, he died, at the age of eighty-five, leaving his title and rights in the province to his son, Benedict Leonard Calvert.

While his father was still alive, Benedict had become a Protestant and joined the Church of England,—an act of policy rather than of conviction, as most of the historians have assumed; but there is no evidence by which we can thoroughly test the young man's sincerity. During his father's lifetime he suffered for his change of religion, lost an annual income of four hundred and fifty pounds which his father had given him, and was compelled to support his wife and six children on his marriage settlement of six hundred pounds a year.

Queen Anne, however, in consideration of the hard usage he had received from his father, gave him a pension of three hundred pounds a year, which was to continue only while his father lived; and she also, at Benedict's suggestion, appointed as governor of Maryland a certain Captain John Hart, who agreed to give Benedict five hundred pounds a year out of the perquisites of the office. George I., on ascending the throne a few months before the death of Charles Calvert, renewed the arrangement with Benedict which Queen Anne had made, and reappointed Captain Hart on the same condition.

Puritan and Catholic on the Chesapeake

As soon as his father was dead, Benedict expected that the government would be restored, and he undoubtedly would soon have received it; but he died only a little more than a year after his father. His eldest son, Charles, now the fifth Lord Baltimore, being under age, his guardian, Lord Guilford, petitioned for the restoration, and it was granted.

The last thread which had connected Maryland with Catholicism was now broken. It was a Protestant colony, with a Protestant church established by law, and under a Protestant proprietor. The earnest efforts of George Calvert and his son Cecil to build up a Catholic colony on the Chesapeake had not only failed, but had resulted in the establishment of an extreme Protestant colony, where Catholics were most severely repressed.

Almost immediately after the restoration of the colony to the Calvert family, one of those events occurred which showed the political opinions of the Catholics and the reason for the laws which repressed them. When the restoration was announced in Maryland, a number of them declared in favor of the pretender to the English throne, and used the guns of the government fort to fire a salute in his honor; the consequence of which was that the laws already in existence were more rigorously enforced and new ones passed increasing their disabilities.

Catholic writers have bitterly complained of these measures as a violation of the principles of religious liberty. But it is difficult to see that there was really any question of religion involved. If the Maryland Catholics chose openly to espouse the cause of a man who was watching his chance in a foreign country to invade England and overthrow the government, they were engaging, so far as lay in their power, in a rebellion against Great Britain. If their treatment was in any sense too severe, it was political, not religious, persecution. The Maryland assembly described them as people who had " openly, in treasonable manner, taken upon them to give the pretended Prince of Wales the title of King of Great Britain, and drunk his health as such."

The change from proprietary to royal government in 1691 had not interfered with the advancement of Maryland, but, on the contrary, the tranquillity of the Protestant rule seems to have increased both the productiveness and the population of the colony. The population more than doubled in those twenty-five years; and on the restoration, in 1715, young Charles Calvert received a province containing fifty thousand people, exporting every year thirty thousand hogsheads of tobacco, which required for its transportation one hundred ships and sixteen hundred sailors. Only two other colonies, Virginia and Massachusetts, surpassed Maryland in population at that time, and Virginia alone excelled her in the importance of her trade and the revenues derived from taxes on it by the British government.

This prosperity continued after the restoration of the Calverts, and the religious question having been decisively and finally settled, the political history of Maryland ceases to be of interest until the Revolution. Other colonies, however, were growing rapidly, and by the middle of the eighteenth century, Pennsylvania, New York, and Connecticut had caught up to Maryland and surpassed her.

The Calverts as Protestants proved themselves to be the same discreet, moderate rulers they had been as Catholics. The family seem, indeed, to have been well endowed with the faculty of governing, and, even when degenerated from the eminence of Cecil Calvert, were very successful in satisfying their people and in obtaining money returns from quit-rents, taxes, forfeitures, appointments to offices, and presentations to livings, which are said to have equalled twelve thousand pounds a year, and their loss sustained by the confiscation of all their property in the

Revolution was estimated at four hundred thousand pounds.

The steady decline of the family in character and ability is strikingly shown in their portraits, from Cecil's handsome, strong face down to the weak, inferior countenance of Frederick, the sixth Lord Baltimore, with whose death, in 1771, the family became extinct.

Frederick, whose conduct and character were what might have been expected from his portrait, left an illegitimate son, Henry Harford, who claimed Maryland, under his father's will, against Louisa Browning, who claimed under the will of her father, Charles Calvert, the fifth Lord Baltimore; and before the litigation between these two could be decided, the Revolution deprived both of them of the province.

The Catholic question soon settled itself in Maryland, and became a mere difference of opinion between individuals, instead of a contest for political ascendency. General public feeling and agreement controlled the subject. It was seldom necessary to enforce the laws, for the Catholics quietly accepted the conditions imposed upon them, and seem to have been treated with even more forbearance than in the other colonies. "Their priests," said Governor Sharpe in 1756, "have large tracts of land amongst us, and their children are frequently sent to St.

Omer's for education. These are, in my opinion, great indulgences, and such as are allowed in none of the colonies but Maryland and Pennsylvania."

At the time of the French and Indian wars, when the French threatened the complete destruction of the English colonies, all Catholics were strongly suspected, especially those in Maryland, of sympathy for France; and it is said that some of the Maryland Catholics openly rejoiced at Braddock's defeat.

The Protestant portion of the people was much aroused, and became still more uneasy when nine hundred of the French Acadians from Nova Scotia were landed in the colony. The assembly urged the governor to command the magistrates to execute the penal statutes with greater strictness. Nothing severe was done, however, and there is no evidence that any of the Catholics actually intended to assist the French, although some of the over-zealous may have expressed indiscreet opinions.

But many of the people were in favor of very radical measures, and those of Prince George County instructed their delegates to dispossess the Jesuits of their landed estates, exclude papists from places of trust and profit, and prevent them sending their children to foreign popish seminaries for education, where their minds were alienated from allegiance to the British government.

Living in an overwhelmingly Protestant community of Englishmen, the Maryland Catholics, being also Englishmen, gradually adopted a peculiar type of moderate Catholicism, free from the extreme claims of ultramontanism. There seems to have been but little about them that was inconsistent with the American republicanism which prevailed after the Revolution; and if they had remained the controlling influence, it is not likely that we should ever have had the public-school controversy or the Native American riots of 1844. But the enormous immigration of Irish ultramontanes after the year 1825 completely changed the character of the Roman Church in this country.

The original settlement in the extreme southern portion of the colony at St. Mary's had not been in the most productive part or the part most convenient for commerce, and the centre of population and trade kept moving northward, first to Annapolis, and finally to Baltimore. But Baltimore was of comparatively little importance until the Revolution.

Some of the attempts at artificial town making were more or less successful, until, after several experiments, the present site of Baltimore, on the Patapsco, was found. The first attempt was in 1683, when a town was ordered to be laid out on the Bush River, and as a result of this, a small village or settlement seems to have existed for some time on the left bank of the Bush, near the bridge of the Pennsylvania Railroad between Baltimore and Philadelphia, and this village was called Baltimore.

In 1706, when the forty-two towns were enacted into existence, three of them were in Baltimore County, one on the Patapsco, near the present site of Baltimore, one on the Bush, near Old Baltimore, as it was called, and the third on the Gunpowder, which is the next river south of the Bush. Of these only the one on the Gunpowder prospered, and was called Joppa. It had a court-house and prison, extensive wharves where vessels loaded for England and the West Indies, and the tobacco hogsheads were trundled down from the interior on the rolling roads.

Old Baltimore, on the Bush, was completely eclipsed by the vigorous rivalry of Joppa, which flourished down to the time of the Revolution, when it is said a war vessel was built there. But meantime the modern Baltimore, on the Patapsco, had been growing by force of circumstances and its obvious convenience. Without any suggestion from the legislature, vessels went there to trade, and the products of other rivers were brought to them.

Puritan and Catholic on the Chesapeake

In 1729 the assembly passed an act to establish a town on the north side of the Patapsco, and the commissioners appointed under this act laid out a town in what is now the centre of Baltimore, which in the end enlarged so as to embrace three settlements in its neighborhood.

Thirty years afterwards, in 1752, it contained twenty-five houses, and was becoming an important mart of trade. Germans came to it from Pennsylvania, and some of the unfortunate Acadians who had been torn from their homes in Nova Scotia settled there, the men becoming sailors and the women eking out a living by picking oakum. In most of the places where they sought refuge they left few if any descendants, but in Baltimore one still hears of the family names Berbine, Blanc, Dashield, Gould, and Guiteau.

At the time of Braddock's defeat there were great fears that the Indians would reach Baltimore; some of them came within eighty miles of it, and the women and children were put on vessels, ready to escape down the bay. In 1768 the county court-house and prison were moved from Joppa to Baltimore. Ten years afterwards Baltimore contained six thousand people, and Joppa, like St. Mary's, relapsed into desolation.

Many of the people who took part in creating Baltimore seem to have been fortunate in leaving descendants who are still prominent in the life of the town. In its early annals we find the familiar names Stewart, Carroll, Colgate, Tilghman, Howard, Ridgely, Van Bibber, Purviance, Fell, McKim, McHenry, Williams, Chase, Ellicott, and many others of families which continue to be well known.

By the time of the Revolution the intellectual energy of Maryland began to leave Annapolis and became centred in Baltimore, which in 1790 had over thirteen thousand inhabitants, at the close of the century had doubled, and in 1810 had almost doubled again.

Nearly all the prominent men that Maryland has produced have lived in Baltimore, drifting to it inevitably as they advanced in life. Chief-Justice Taney, although the most important of the principles he represented have been overthrown, was in many respects the most eminent of the Marylanders. He was born in Calvert County, of a Roman Catholic family, and went to live in Baltimore after his fifty-sixth year. His conspicuous ability as a lawyer had drawn him into politics as a young man. A Federalist in early life, he joined the wing of that party which supported the war of 1812, and after that gradually became a Democrat, and was United States Attorney-General under Jackson's administration.

Duane, who was Secretary of the Treasury,

refused to carry out Jackson's whim for removing the government deposits from the United States Bank. Taney was made Duane's successor, immediately removed the deposits, and precipitated the financial panic which followed. This was the beginning of Taney's vast unpopularity.

Some years afterwards he was made Chief-Justice of the United States, to succeed Chief-Justice Marshall, and immediately began to turn the decisions of the court away from the lines which had been laid down by Marshall and Story, and towards the doctrine of State rights. Some of his decisions, however, have been upheld, and have become settled principles of constitutional law; but his best-known decision, in the Dred Scott case, where he held that Congress had no power to prohibit slavery in the Territories, raised another storm of unpopularity, and contributed, perhaps more than any other one event, to bring on the civil war. But Taney's decision during the war, that the President could not suspend the privilege of the writ of habeas corpus without authority from Congress, is now upheld as sound.

In colonial times and during the Revolution the only Marylanders who were conspicuously prominent were Samuel Chase and Charles Carroll, both of whom signed the Declaration of Independence.

Puritan and Catholic on the Chesapeake

Chase was an extreme patriot in the Revolution, a violent opponent of the Stamp Act, and one of a party who seized the stamps and burnt the collector in effigy. He served in the Continental Congress for many years, and was an active and untiring member, although his name is not connected with any conspicuous opinions or act except his mission, in company with Carroll and Franklin, to persuade Canada to join in the Revolution. He was prominent in Maryland affairs after the Revolution, and became one of the justices of the Supreme Court of the United States.

Charles Carroll, like many other Maryland Roman Catholics, had been sent to France for his education, and most elaborately trained at those " popish seminaries," as they were called, St. Omer's, Rheims, and Louis le Grand, where, as the Protestants complained, Catholic children invariably imbibed a bitter hostility to England. Young Carroll afterwards went to England for a time, where he finished his elaborate education by studying the English common law, having already familiarized himself with the civil law on the Continent.

His ancestors, the O'Carrolls of Ireland, had been princes and lords of Ely and kings of Munster. His migrating ancestor came to Maryland after James II., in whose service he had been employed, was dethroned and the Protestants under William and Mary came into power. He soon became dissatisfied with the suppressed condition of the Catholics, and formed with some of them a project for migrating to the French possessions in the Mississippi Valley. He visited France for this purpose, and his plan would in all probability have been carried out if the French government had not thought the tract of land asked for too large to be granted to a subject.

In Maryland, Charles Carroll first became conspicuous for his opposition to the laws which taxed all the people of the province for the support of the established church. His opponent in this controversy was Daniel Dulany, a very prominent lawyer, well known in the other colonies, but a tory in the Revolution, and in consequence neglected by the historians.

Carroll was, like Chase, a man of much influence in provincial affairs and active in the Revolution; and, like Chase, he was an extreme patriot, favoring a public declaration of independence before most of the colonists were ready for such a radical measure.

William Wirt, William Pinkney, and Reverdy Johnson were all Marylanders, and during the half-century after the Revolution very eminent in public life as well as in law. Luther Martin was also a remarkable lawyer of similar distinction; but, though he lived in Maryland a large part of his life, he was born in New Jersey.

John Pendleton Kennedy, a Baltimorean, who was Secretary of the Navy, and took a leading part in promoting Commodore Perry's famous expedition to open the ports of Japan, enjoyed in his day considerable literary fame. His stories, "Swallow Barn," "Horseshoe Robinson," and "Rob of the Bowl," are not yet forgotten.

He was on intimate terms with Thackeray, and was with him in Paris when "The Virginians" was being published as a serial story. Thackeray complained that he was disinclined to supply the next instalment for the printer, and suggested in his jovial way that Kennedy write it. After familiarizing himself with the general trend of the novel and its author's style, Kennedy wrote what was required, and it now appears as part of the fourth chapter of the second volume, describing with greater accuracy than the great novelist was capable of the scenes of Western Maryland in the colonial period.

Edgar Allan Poe is often spoken of as a Marylander; but his early education and influences were all received in Virginia and England. He lived in Baltimore at times, and attained there his first real fame, when he was awarded the prize for his story, "The Manuscript found in a Bottle." But Francis Scott Key, the author of "The Star-Spangled Banner," was in the fullest sense a Marylander, and one of whom the State is justly proud, as it also is of the naval hero, Stephen Decatur.

Welch House · Annapolis

Gov. Tryon's House, N.C.

CHAPTER X

LANDGRAVES, PIRATES, AND CAZIQUES

CAROLINA was the great domain which in the year 1629 Charles I. gave to Sir Robert Heath, his attorney-general, and it was named after the king,—an attractive, soft name which, like Virginia, seems to suit the climate and surroundings. We have often made most lamentable failures in the names of our towns, especially the smaller ones. Indeed, we seem to be bereft of all taste and judgment in naming them. But in the names of our States, whether taken from kings or from Indians, we have always been most fortunate.

Carolina included the country from Virginia to Florida, but natural conditions and other circumstances soon split it up into three separate communities, which are now North Carolina, South Carolina, and Georgia. The way in which these divisions were created reveals the history and characteristics of each.

No settlement was made under the grant to Sir Robert Heath. It remained a mere piece of parchment among the records of the British government. But still it had a purpose to serve. It had given a name and described a territory. As years passed by Charles I. was beheaded, the people grew tired of Cromwell and his son, and the Restoration came in 1660, when Charles II. ascended the throne. He had many friends to reward for bringing him to his own again, and in 1663 to some of the most distinguished and devoted of these he gave Carolina, for which he found a name and boundaries in the old grant to Sir Robert Heath.

No other colony in America was ever in the possession of such distinguished and experienced men of affairs as was Carolina. Its proprietors were the Earl of Clarendon, who was the high chancellor of England; the Duke of Albemarle, who was captain-general of the army; Lord Ashley, afterwards Earl of Shaftesbury, chancellor of the exchequer; and there were also Lord Craven, Lord Berkeley, Sir George Carteret, and others,—all men of eminence who are fondly described in the charter as the " right trusty and well beloved" friends of the king.

If Charles II. had possessed our present

knowledge of America, he would hardly have selected Carolina as the richest gift to bestow upon his favorites. He would have given them Pennsylvania or New York. But he thought he was giving them the best land in America. Everybody else thought the same. The proprietors themselves no doubt selected Carolina, and suggested to the king that it should be part of the reward for their services; for it was in that way that such things were done at court.

The Southern colonies from Virginia to Florida always had a peculiar charm for the people of England. Every sailor and explorer that set foot upon their shores was carried away at once by the suggestion of riches, abundance, and easy life that appeared on every hand; the sunlight was so clear and yet so soft, the vegetation so luxuriant, the soil so black and rich. The coast was cut up into bays and sounds, winding in every direction among islands and shoals, and tempting the adventurer with strange scenes at every turn. The waters were full of every variety of fish, and a single random haul of a net supplied a fleet of vessels with food for a whole day. When they were tired of fish, they picked up on the shoals more oysters than they could use. Myriads of wild fowl, covering the water by acres, swam aside to let the boats pass through them, and the plover and snipe followed along the shoals and mud-flats in clouds.

When they stepped on shore the deer sprang aside among the trees, and the wild turkeys flew away, striking their wings against the branches. As they pressed inland, they found the level, low shores continue, interspersed with swamps and broad, deep rivers bearing slowly towards the sea the water discolored by the fertile soil. They struggled through dense thickets of the rankest growth, they waded up to their waists in the grass of open savannas, and they walked free and unimpeded along the dry ridges where the stately pine-trees grew.

The red men were there roasting turkeys before great fires and basting them with bear's fat, planting patches of corn and beans, setting fire to the woods and grass in a great circle to drive all the game on to an isthmus or into an angle of a river, where they slaughtered it at will for a feast. They lived easily or with labor that was sport. Their manners were, by turns, as soft and pleasant as the climate or as fiery and wanton as its sun. Almost every month and week tribe fought with tribe and band with band, creeping through the woods at night to surprise each other's hunting camps, and glorying in the scalp torn from the head of a child or an old squaw who had strayed too far from her wigwam.

Landgraves, Pirates, and Caziques

They received the white man with profuse hospitality, and their women willingly became his mistresses.

What a change it was from misty, cold Britain! The Englishmen were delighted with such a country, just as our own people of the North are still delighted, and pour into it to fill its hotels and resorts and lavish their money on its land for club sites or orange groves. It is a land which seems to have possessed a supreme attraction for men of great souls and daring enterprise, not always for their advantage; and was it with unconscious fidelity to its characteristics that they usually gave its places feminine names?

There was no more pathetic hour in the life of the gallant Ponce de Leon than when, as an old man, he landed on these shores with his followers and rushed from place to place, expecting every moment to find the fountain of perpetual youth. It seemed as if it must be there; and if you stand there to-day and dream for a while, you almost believe it. He never found it, nor did he see the trees which he was looking for with golden fruit plucked by beautiful maidens. He sailed away at last, disappointed, unsuccessful. But he called it Florida, the land of flowers, a name which could have been given only by a lover; and when he returned to try again, he was killed by the Indians.

Landgraves, Pirates, and Caziques

A grander and loftier spirit than Ponce de Leon, Sir Walter Raleigh, sent out his captains Amidas and Barlow, who landed on the outer beaches of the North Carolina sounds. They climbed about among the sand-dunes, breathed the bland air from the pines, and feasted their eyes on the soft, liquid light that they could almost feel. They never penetrated far inland; but they were infatuated, and described to Sir Walter a land where, as they said, the grape-vines were washed by the breakers of the sea; and he sent expedition after expedition to make the land his own until he had crippled his fortune.

He never succeeded. His small colony of about a hundred people, who settled on Roanoke Island, disappeared completely, and no trace of them could ever be found. Whether they perished of famine or were killed by the Indians is still a mystery. But he also gave the land a lover's name, and called it Virginia. Who would change it? Who could?

General Greene, of Rhode Island, who, after Washington, was the ablest soldier of the Revolution, was sent to drive the British from the South. He succeeded, and made for himself a deathless name. But the siren voice whispered to him through the pines, and the soft, warm wind caressed his cheek. When the war was over, his reputation, his wide opportunities in the North, seemed as nothing. He secured a tract of land on the Savannah River, to which he went with the enthusiasm of a boy, full of dreams of wealth and pleasure. But the siren took the hero to herself so completely that he perished within a year, and his grave has never been found.

But why multiply instances? for, beginning with the heroes of old, they come down through every decade of the centuries. In the days of Webster and Calhoun the capital and energy of the North were sent to help develop the rice and cotton plantations, and a large part of it remained in the fullest sense of the word a permanent investment. When the siren rebelled and fought us for her slaves, why did we not let the charmer go? It would have been cheaper. But no; we held her with the grip of death; and to keep her for our own we sacrificed in four years millions of lives and dollars, and we are still sending down our capital to develop those resources of which Raleigh and De Leon dreamed.

But we must return to the early settlement and the proprietors of Carolina whose eminence and practical skill were of little avail to them in their enterprise. Their tract of land was a complete wilderness from the English settlement of Virginia all the way to Florida, which was held by the Spaniards. They thought it would be safest to start at the northern end, close to Virginia; and, in fact, a number of Virginians had already passed over into this part of Carolina and established themselves on the Chowan River. These settlers were ordered to consider themselves separated from Virginia, a governor, William Drummond, was placed over them, they were allowed a representative assembly to make laws for their guidance, and soon after the governor was given a council of twelve to assist and advise him.

The Virginians who composed this colony were mostly of the reckless frontier class, with a strong love of independence, and they encouraged others of the same sort to come to them. They passed laws making their colony a safe refuge for insolvent debtors from England or Virginia. The eminent proprietors approved these laws, and in their turn made every effort to obtain immigrants and force on development. Both colonists and proprietors thought that all that was needed in that rich, warm soil was to bring in people and capital, and it would become a garden.

These same ideas still prevail, and always have prevailed, in the whole territory that was once called Carolina. As we read its history we find the most ardent encouragements to immigration; and when encouraging and coaxing failed to bring enough white men, the black man was brought in by the hundred thousand against his will. The insolvent debtor was encouraged until at last we find a whole colony established for his exclusive benefit. The obligation, legal as well as moral, of paying a debt was weakened until the individual became indifferent or indignant at the thought of it, and the States passed laws repudiating their bonds.

The constant cry was, "All we need here is people, more people." It has been repeated for two hundred and fifty years, and you hear it when you travel in the South to-day, for the delusion still prevails that the country is to be built up not by the energy and thrift of its own citizens, but by the assistance of the foreigner and the Northern capitalist.

Besides the colony on the Chowan, another one sprang up of itself at the mouth of the Cape Fear River, in the neighborhood of the present site of Wilmington. This place had been settled by New England people some time before the proprietors obtained their charter. The New Englanders had selected the spot after careful investigation and some experience of the country, and they bought the land from the Indians. But they soon abandoned their chosen spot, leaving fastened to a post a paper which expressed in strong language their opinion of the country. A company of explorers from the Barbadoes arrived, and, fascinated by the appearance of the place, read with contempt the paper on the post. Could they not see with their own eyes what the country was? and why should they heed the statement of some fools who had abandoned it?

These two settlements—one on the Chowan and the other on the Cape Fear—were at the extreme northern and southern limits of what afterwards became North Carolina. They were almost two hundred miles apart, great sounds and wide rivers and swamps lay between them, and the proprietors were obliged to manage them as two separate colonies, each with its own governor.

Their efforts to encourage immigration were partially successful, and, as they sent their agents soliciting colonists into almost every part of the British dominions, they collected in North Carolina a most motley and miscellaneous set of people. The controlling element was English, made up of adventurers and debtors from Great Britain and Virginia, with a large number of New Englanders who came to trade and often remained in the colony. Besides these, there were some French Huguenots, Germans, and Swiss who had been drummed up by the agents of the proprietors. But all the efforts to force development were of little avail; and at the time of the Revolution, when the settlements which made up North Carolina were a hundred years old, the whole population was only about two hundred thousand, of whom nearly half were negro slaves.

The province, as can be seen at once by a glance at the map, was shut in by sand-banks forming the outer boundaries of the great sounds. The inlets through these banks were dangerous to navigate, and there were no convenient places for a city or harbor, except at the Cape Fear colony, and even that offered comparatively few advantages. The land near the sounds and rivers was low and swampy, reeking with malaria, and not calculated to produce a population that would support a town. The people lived scattered far apart on farms and plantations, wherever they could find a suitable spot. Their isolation increased their love of independence, and the few occasions when they united for purposes of government usually ended in turbulence or riot. There were few laws and no lawyers. The laws were never printed, but only read aloud in the market-place, and the courts and the legislature met in private houses or taverns.

Virginia constantly complained that she was tormented by a nest of criminals and outlaws on her southern border. In one of the rebellions the insurgents captured the treasury and government of the colony, and when they were subdued, disorder and license still continued. In the course of forty years, from 1676 to 1717, the people had increased from fourteen hundred to only two thousand. Under the royal government, which succeeded the control of the proprietors, there was some improvement, and the people increased to one hundred and fifty thousand whites at the time of the Revolution. But as late as 1770 there was an insurrection which closed the courts of law and defied the government until it was suppressed by an army under Governor Tryon, who defeated the insurgents in a battle and hung the leaders.

The people lived an extremely isolated, independent life, each family sequestered on its small farm, surrounded by dense swamps, doing whatever seemed right in its own eyes, and living largely by hunting and a little agriculture, in which the women performed a large part of the labor. There were only three towns or villages,—Wilmington, Edenton, and New-Berne,—the largest of which scarcely contained six hundred people, and it was not until the next century that North Carolina began to have any importance as a State.

But her self-reliant, independent people, accustomed to insurrections, were very forward in the Revolution, which was a movement exactly suited to their taste. On May 31, 1775, more than a year before the Declaration of Independence was adopted at Philadelphia, the people of Mecklenburg County declared that all British authority had ceased, and chose officers whom they instructed to act independently of the crown and parliament. But they did not, as has been supposed, use the language of the Declaration at Philadelphia. It was most characteristic of them, and shows the disunited condition in which they had lived; for Mecklenburg County declared her independence, set up a government, and seemed ready to stand alone before the world without any regard for the rest of North Carolina.

In Georgia and North Carolina the slave population was not so excessive as in South Carolina. In Georgia the whites and blacks were about equal in number, and in North Carolina the white people considerably outnumbered the negroes, and there seems to have been, in consequence, less severe and cruel treatment of the slaves than in South Carolina.

Soon after the settlements on the Cape Fear and the Chowan, which became North Carolina, were established, the proprietors had an opportunity to begin another colony, which in time became South Carolina. The sand-banks and shoals with their dangerous entrances, which so effectually protected North Carolina from civilization, become less formidable farther down the coast, and about one hundred and twenty miles below the mouth of the Cape Fear there is a large, safe entrance into what is now the harbor of Charleston, and about sixty miles farther south is the harbor of Beaufort.

Beaufort had been visited one hundred years before, in 1562, when Jean Ribault attempted to establish there a settlement of French Huguenots. In 1667 William Sayle explored the coast, and two years later the proprietors of Carolina sent him out to colonize it. He began at Beaufort, which seems to have been the place best known to every one; but he soon moved his colony to Charleston harbor, the superior advantages of which were quickly discovered. His first colonists were adventurers and rough characters picked up in London and various parts of England, with a few New Englanders, and were more unpromising even than the people of North Carolina. Their numbers and their names are unknown.

The proprietors made great efforts to encourage other settlers, and as time went on the efforts were increased. Contracts, bounties, free lands, and every other inducement were offered, and anybody that would come was accepted. The result was, of course, a very miscellaneous population,—Cavaliers, Puritans, bankrupts, and every variety of the restless or unfortunate; people from the Barbadoes, a congregation of Puritans from Massachusetts, Dutch from New York, Scotch, Germans, Scotch-Irish, French from Acadia, and, after the revocation of the Edict of Nantes, a large number of Huguenots.

The reckless and desperate characters probably did not have large families, and in after-years gave little increase to the population. But the Huguenots were an important element. They remained in the country, and those famous names in South Carolina history, Legaré, Laurens, Marion, and Manigault, are from that stock. Besides these, who became well known, there was a large number of the most respectable families that were Huguenot: Boiseau, Chevalier, Dupré, Foissin, Gérard, Horry, Jeannerrette, Newville, Prioleau, Ravenel, Simons, Serre, and Trezevant are names that have been always more or less familiar to Carolinians. The Scotch-Irish were also important, and, as in all the other colonies, most of them went out on the frontier.

But although this recital of people gives an impression of a great increase and development, the immigrants were, in fact, comparatively few in numbers, and they failed to increase after their arrival. The flourish with which some of the historians have described the rush to South Carolina is soon dissipated by a careful investigation into the actual results. The numbers are seldom given or known, and, when given, are usually very small, and many of them refused to remain. The fifteen hundred French who came from Nova Scotia soon left the country.

At the time of the Revolution the whole population of South Carolina was only about one hundred and seventy-five thousand, hardly as much as North Carolina had, and of this number more than one hundred thousand were negro slaves. The blacks outnumbered the whites in colonial times usually two or three to one, and for a long time were imported at the rate of three thousand a year. This black compulsory immigration, of which no boast is made, was the principal source of the population and the controlling element in the history of the province.

The whites did not increase rapidly by births. Large families were not common among them, and there was none of that rapid native growth which was so remarkable in the Northern colonies, especially in New England. The climate, in spite of all its charms, was not favorable. The land near the coast, where the greater part of the people lived during the colonial period, was, like the coast land of North Carolina, low, malarious, and not as fertile as it seemed, except for the growth of rice and indigo, which were not introduced until after the lapse of many years.

In later times, as the people progressed more towards the western highlands, they encountered better conditions, and when, some years after the Revolution, the cotton-gin was invented, cotton-growing on the uplands gave a new impetus to prosperity. But the cultivation of rice, although covering large districts of the marsh lands, required a comparatively small population besides the negroes, and in colonial times rice and indigo, with some wheat and corn in the western districts, composed the principal productions of the Carolinians. The plantations were large, and the fertile land was all in the hands of a few people. There were no small holdings, and no manufacturing or diversified industries which would build up a large population and sound prosperity.

The proprietors, however, never doubted the success of their colonies, and their only fear seems to have been that they had not secured land enough. In 1665 they obtained another grant, extending their northern limits a few miles farther up into Virginia and their southern boundary far down into the Spanish possessions in Florida, and, like the first grant, giving them everything westward to the Pacific Ocean. Believing that they now had room enough to move in, they prepared in 1669 an elaborate constitution for the government of their enormous possessions. The document was prepared by the great philosopher, John Locke, whom they had interested in their plans, and who for some years served them as a sort of unofficial secretary. The Earl of Shaftesbury lent him some assistance, and the other proprietors made suggestions.

It was the most highly aristocratic form of government that has ever been attempted in America. The head of all was the palatine, who was always to be the eldest of the lord proprietors; next in dignity came the seven other proprietors, and after them the hereditary nobility, the landgraves, and the caziques. Besides these, there were to be admirals, chamberlains, chancellors, chief-justices, high stewards, and treasurers. Each county was to consist of eight seigniories, eight baronies, and four precincts, and each precinct was to contain six colonies; and there were also to be manors and lords of the manor, court-leets, leet-men and leet-women, a grand council, a parliament, a palatine's court, and courts for all the other dignitaries. And all this elaborate system was to be administered in a territory extending two thousand miles to the Pacific, including Alabama, Tennessee, Mississippi, Arkansas, Louisiana, Texas, New Mexico, Arizona, part of California, and a large part of Mexico.

Some years passed before any attempt was made to enforce this constitution, and meantime the colonists at Charleston established a government of their own, consisting of an assembly elected by the people, and a sort of upper house or governor's council. Afterwards Locke's constitution was partially enforced until the year 1693, when it was abrogated. There are still some people in South Carolina who are the descendants of the nobility which Locke created.

In 1693 the division between South and North Carolina was recognized, and ever after that they were regarded as separate colonies, but were for a long time under the same governor. They were radically different in their circumstances and development. The people of North Carolina were scattered over a vast extent of wild country of rivers and swamps, and saw very little of each other. Their towns or villages were few, small, and far apart. But South Carolina was essentially a colony of one town, and the life of the people centred in Charleston very much as the life of the colony of

Landgraves, Pirates, and Caziques

Massachusetts Bay centred in Boston. The South Carolinians advanced in the arts of life, and became a people of self-conscious civic pride, independence, and aggressiveness, which was curiously like what we find in Massachusetts.

Charleston would indeed be a better name for the colony than South Carolina. The governing classes lived there, the political riots and disturbances took place there, and the town ruled the rest of the province very much as Paris has ruled France. It was the most intensely centralized community in America in colonial times and for many years afterwards.

A large part of its history has been lost. The destructive fires and hurricanes which have so often visited Charleston have swept out of existence many documents and records, the British destroyed many more at the time of the Revolution, and the people were not careful to preserve what remained. Some years after the Revolution, through the efforts of Dr. Ramsay, much of the lost history of the province was recovered, but largely from the uncertain sources of tradition and recollection among the descendants of the early settlers.

What we have reveals a state of turmoil, contest, and struggle among the incongruous elements of the people so closely associated which throws considerable light on the characteristics of the State which have become prominent in modern times.

The majority of the colonists were English dissenters, mostly Presbyterians, and in some respects like the Puritans who settled Massachusetts. In fact, a Puritan congregation from Dorchester, Massachusetts, emigrated to South Carolina and established themselves, naming their settlement after the town they had left in New England. But the dissenters of South Carolina were by no means so severe and fanatical as the Massachusetts Puritans. The organization of their churches was less thorough, their doctrines less precise, and they were less disposed to reason keenly or intolerantly about religion. For many years there were no church services held outside of Charleston. The Carolinians, like the rest of the Southerners, have always taken their religion easily, and it rests upon them as lightly as they sit their horses; not because they are indifferent, but because they accept it simply without intolerance and without speculative inquiry.

The Presbyterians before long organized themselves throughout the colony; but the members of the Church of England secured possession of the government, and their church was the established religion down to the time of the Revolution. The proprietors favored the Cavaliers and Episcopalians, encouraged them in their control of the government, and at first this was bitterly resented by the dissenters.

The old contest which had raged in England in the time of Cromwell was fought out anew in the Carolina marshes. Mutual jealousy and contempt, ridicule of the austere morals of the Puritans, flaming indignation at the foppish vanity and luxuries of the Cavaliers, brought all attempts at orderly development to a stand. Of the few laws that were passed nothing is known. There were five governors within four years, each one compelled to give up in disgust. One of these, James Colleton, a landgrave under the Locke constitution, proclaimed martial law as a last resort. But the people rose against him, laughed at his attempt, and in 1690 passed a bill in the assembly abolishing his authority and giving him a set time in which to leave the colony.

After him a usurper, Seth Sothell, under an apparent authority from England, seized the government, and imprisoned traders from Bermuda as pirates until they ransomed themselves by paying what he called fees. He enriched himself by accepting bribes from criminals and taking violent possession of farms and plantations, until the people again arose and expelled him.

The arrival of the French Huguenots was another source of contention. Their numbers, as well as their industry and thrift, gave them considerable importance, but their presence was resented by the English. Their encouragement by the proprietors was regarded by the English colonists as a great imposition, and they would allow the refugees no rights. They gave them no representation in the assembly, and refused to pass a law allowing them to inherit land like natural-born subjects. At this time the assembly consisted of twenty members, all chosen in Charleston.

The opposition to the proprietors and all their plans was continuous. The colonists were supposed to be their tenants and to pay a small quit-rent for every acre they occupied. Very little of the rent was ever collected, but the proprietors for a long time believed that they would soon have enormous returns. For years they continued to send out supplies and spend money to force development, and in a short time had sunk in this way more than eighteen thousand pounds.

The colonists were not the sort of people who would readily pay quit-rents. Adventurous and reckless by nature, these traits were intensified by their contests with one another and the wild life they were compelled to lead.

The Indians were from the beginning extremely hostile and troublesome, and this was one of the circumstances which made the province a community of one town. In spite of their differences of opinion, the people were forced together for protection. While some were building homes, the rest stood on guard. They gathered oysters on the shoals with one hand while they carried their guns in the other. They planted crops at the risk of their lives, and when the harvest was ripe the Indians often relieved them of it in a single day. The soil was found unsuitable for grain, and they had not yet discovered that rice would grow in the swamp lands. The few patches of fertile land were covered with heavy timber, and the spots that were open were usually barren. In fact, the people were often on the verge of starvation in this land which had been thought by every explorer to be the paradise of plenty.

Piracy flourished along the shores of Carolina, and from there to the West Indies, as long as the proprietary rule lasted and for some years afterwards. Indeed, it extended northward into Delaware Bay, along the shores of New Jersey, and through the Long Island bays and coves to Rhode Island; but the principal source and home of it was in the Carolina sounds and the West Indies. The Vikings of the North Sea and the Baltic, the ancestors of the English race, had been pirates for centuries, and when opportunity offers their seafaring descendants take to the ancient occupation with supreme delight.

In her wars with France and Spain, England encouraged privateering, and privateering is conventional piracy. The step from one to the other is easy and natural. A captain and crew licensed to prey on the commerce of France or Spain, and having once tasted the sweets of plunder, often concluded that their profits would be larger if they made the commerce of the world the field of their operations.

There was a class of men known as Buccaneers, whose head-quarters were from time to time at St. Domingo, Tortuga, and what is now called British Honduras on the mainland. They existed in consequence of the efforts of Spain to monopolize for herself all the trade with her colonies in South America. With barbarous cruelty, and in a spirit of stupid short-sightedness, she drove away all ships of other countries and massacred the people who attempted to settle in any of her territories. In revenge, her commerce was considered fair game for all nations, and the men known as Interlopers, Brethren of the Coast, or Buccaneers, flourished on the plunder of it. They were mostly English, French, and Dutch Protestants, to whose love of adventure and wild life was added a vigorous hatred of the great Roman Catholic nation. They were not pirates in the full sense of the word, for they confined their depredations exclusively to Spain. They were well disciplined and organized, and many of them held religious services on their ships.

For nearly a hundred years they led a glorious life, hunting the wild cattle of St. Domingo, cutting mahogany in Honduras, and reducing the power of their great enemy as effectually as it could have been done by all the armies of Europe. To the protests of Spain, the other nations answered, " They are not licensed by us; attend to them yourself, for you are the cause of them."

They were the most daring and heroic of men. No disparity of numbers deterred them. In their small boats they would row up to a Spanish galleon, avoiding the direct fire of her guns, and pick off with their muskets the man at the helm and the sailors at the ropes. Securing themselves under her stern, where her guns could not be used, the crew of one boat would wedge her rudder, while the rest poured in a raking fire until they were ready to board and drive her people below the hatches.

Landgraves, Pirates, and Caziques

When at last their day passed and they were broken up and scattered by changing times and conditions, their success and the wealth they had acquired encouraged ordinary piracy. Sailors had become habituated to the idea of plundering on the seas. Many of them had been privateers-men or buccaneers, and they had all seen fortunes made in that way or in out-and-out piracy. Their success was wonderful, and a common seaman often had a thousand pounds to spend in drink and gambling. The British government was slow to punish them, for they were very numerous and skilful and their ships were very fleet. It was difficult to pursue them on the vast tracts of the Atlantic and Indian Oceans or to follow them into the intricate navigation of unexplored sounds and bays.

So for many a day they reaped their golden harvests, recruited from all classes of people and springing up in the most unexpected ways. Several women figured in their annals. Mary Read and Anne Bonny followed the fortunes of their pirate lovers to the last, and, when captured, respect for their sex saved them from execution. Any ship that sailed from port might be turned into a pirate by her crew before she had gone a thousand miles. One of the most successful of them was a large vessel belonging to the East India Company, the Mocha

Merchant, whose crew made her a pirate after they had left Calcutta. But it was not always the crew, for sometimes the captain would suddenly hoist the black flag and call on his men to join him.

There seldom has been such a field for writers of romance, and we have stories from De Foe's "Captain Singleton," in which a Pennsylvania Quaker is one of the characters, through the novels of Cooper and Marryat, down to Stevenson's matchless tale of "Treasure Island." But the subject has never been exhausted.

The pirates became so rich that they were a money power, and corrupted the administration of the laws which were enacted against them. They came to Charleston with perfect impunity, their ships lay peacefully at anchor in the harbor, and they bought their supplies and spent their money with a lavishness which made them popular with everybody. A few were brought to trial, but it was a farce. They employed the most respectable lawyers at enormous fees, and no jury could be found that would bring them in guilty. Some of them bought land and settled themselves in the province. Prominent people assisted them and became interested in the profits of their enterprises, until governors and secretaries of the colony were involved in this occupation, which will forever appeal to all that is romantic and daring in human nature. The condition of affairs is shown when we find that the proprietors of Carolina, in order to gratify the people and smooth over everything, granted an indemnity to all the pirates except those who had committed depredations on the dominions of the Great Mogul, an exception which every gentleman of the sea could easily show that he had avoided.

In varying degrees the pirates enjoyed privileges in the Northern colonies. The shores of New Jersey were wild, and full of sounds and inlets with shifting or dangerous bars, and Long Island had many secluded coves and harbors. Protections were openly sold in New York, and Governor Fletcher received handsome presents for himself and for his wife and daughters. When the business was finally suppressed in New York, the people complained that the province had lost a hundred thousand pounds a year. Rhode Island and Newport also enjoyed rich returns. In Philadelphia it was not so profitable, for the religious discipline of the Quakers kept them from it, and the distance up the river was nearly a hundred miles. But Blackbeard bought supplies in Philadelphia, and Evans owned property in the town.

The famous Captain Kidd was the son of a Scotch minister. He went to sea when very young, and became one of the most daring and successful merchant navigators of his time. He was a privateersman against the French, and not only captured valuable prizes, but won a high reputation for courage and skill. The year 1695 found him settled in New York, where he had married and retired on a competency. In that year Lord Bellamont came out to be governor of both New York and Massachusetts, and was specially instructed by the king to suppress piracy. But he met with very serious difficulties, for the men-of-war could not be used for the purpose, and the pirates were popular and scattered over the seas from America to India. No one cared to fit out a private vessel against them until Captain Kidd volunteered for the service.

A company was formed in England, consisting, besides Lord Bellamont, of Sir Edmund Harrison, the Earl of Romney, the Duke of Shrewsbury, Lord Orford, and the Lord Chancellor. These distinguished men subscribed six thousand pounds, with which they purchased a vessel of two hundred and eighty-seven tons, mounting thirty guns. Kidd was given command, and it is significant of the condition of the times that the greatest caution was taken in appointing him. Livingston, of New York, went security for his fidelity, and when the ship was equipped in England, great pains were taken to obtain respectable sailors of steady habits with families. Not enough of this class could be secured, however, and a large part of the crew was taken on at New York. In the voyage to New York, Kidd captured a French prize, and thence sailed to Madagascar, which was the principal resort of the pirates.

Kidd's authority from the crown was peculiar. He was commissioned as a privateersman against the French, and also against all pirates, for the purpose of bringing them to trial for their crimes. Another document, called a warrant, gave the members of the company all the property that should be taken from the pirates, and the company then entered into a recognizance to give one-tenth of the spoil to the king. It was in effect a piratical expedition to put down piracy, and the king was to share in the plunder.

That Kidd, when once in the Indian Seas, found plain, straightforward piracy more profitable than the arrangement with Lord Bellamont and his illustrious friends was natural. In the course of his ravages, which extended only over two or three years, a sailor, William Moore, when told by Kidd that he was a dog, replied that if he was it was Kidd who had made him one. Kidd instantly struck him dead on the deck with a bucket. Soon after he returned to

Long Island Sound in a small sloop, and sent word to Lord Bellamont, who was in Boston, that he was ready to prove his innocence.

Bellamont received him; but his answers to questions were so peculiar, and he distributed so many valuable presents to important persons, that he was arrested and sent to England. It has sometimes been said that there was not enough evidence to convict him of piracy, and that he was tried for the murder of William Moore; but according to the best accounts he seems to have been tried for and convicted of both offences. The booty which was taken from his immediate possession, or from places where he had deposited it in Long Island Sound, amounted to fourteen thousand pounds.

He was not in any sense a remarkable pirate, and perhaps would not have become so famous but for the suspicion that the members of the company who sent him out knew of his intention to turn pirate and hoped to share his profits. As they were nearly all distinguished noblemen, active in political life, a great scandal was stirred up, which absorbed the attention of Parliament and the English public for a long time. Learned arguments were made by lawyers questioning the right of the crown to issue such a commission coupled with an arrangement for reserving a tenth of the captured property and giving the rest to the company. The property taken, it was said, would have been stolen by the pirates from peaceful merchants, who were entitled to have it returned to them. By what right could it be given to the company? The apologists, of course, explained that all property for which a lawful owner could be found would have been restored, and that everything would have been conducted regularly and settled in courts of admiralty.

Edward Teach, or Blackbeard, as he was called, has always been a famous pirate in American annals; but his career, like that of Kidd, was a very short one of two years, from 1716 to 1718, and he was not remarkably successful in comparison with many others described in Johnson's " History of the Pirates" and other books. He was an Englishman from Bristol, and before he turned pirate had served in a subordinate position on privateersmen. His first appointment to command gave him the opportunity he wanted, and he made his headquarters on the coast of North Carolina, at Ocracoke Inlet, a place which is still very isolated and difficult of access.

From there he could communicate with Governor Charles Eden, of that province, with whom he is said to have shared his plunder. People still look for the treasure he is supposed to have buried; but Teach himself, when once asked where it was, replied, "Only me and the devil know, and the longest liver of the two will get it."

The picturesque element in his character accounts largely for his fame; for, besides his extraordinary brutality, he wore his long black beard twisted in curls round his ears, and in action he carried lighted slow matches in his hat. He was finally pursued into his retreat by Lieutenant Maynard of the royal navy, and killed in a fierce contest, in which the water round the sloops was covered with blood, but not until Blackbeard had destroyed more than thirty of the lieutenant's men. Maynard cut off his head and, mounting it on the bowsprit of his sloop, returned to the fleet, which was lying in the James River in Virginia.

In the end piracy wrought its own cure. As the chances on the Spanish main decreased, the pillaging of English commerce soon reached a point beyond all endurance. By the year 1700 the South Carolinians began to export rice, and, having vessels of their own, they suddenly saw piracy in a new light. A vessel had fitted out at Havana with a mongrel crew of English, French, Portuguese, and Indians, who, after capturing several Charleston ships, began to quarrel among themselves over the booty. The nine

Englishmen were turned adrift in a boat, and, making their way to the coast, walked overland to Charleston, where they said that they had been shipwrecked, a formal statement which a few years before would have been entirely satisfactory to every one. But they soon added to their knowledge of the hypocrisy of human nature. Several of them were recognized by Charleston captains who had lost ships; and they were all tried, condemned, and seven of them hung.

Charleston was no longer a rendezvous, and the pirates had only two strongholds, Providence Island in the West Indies and the Cape Fear River in North Carolina. Issuing from these shelters, they captured within four years more than thirty vessels on the American coast. The clamor against them was now so great that the British crown issued a proclamation offering pardon to all who should surrender within twelve months, and at the same time sent expeditions to suppress them. Captain Woodes Rogers, with several men-of-war, attacked Providence Island and took possession of it. Most of the pirates, when they saw that the day was against them, surrendered and accepted the pardon of the proclamation. But Steed Bonnett, who had been a man of education and wealth in the Barbadoes, and Richard Worley, still held possession of the Cape Fear River.

Landgraves, Pirates, and Caziques

South Carolina craved the honor of suppressing these remnants of her former friends, and Governor Johnson sent out William Rhett, who after a sharp action captured Steed Bonnett and his crew of forty men, of whom all but one were hung and buried on a shoal below high water, beneath what is now Battery Garden at Charleston. Johnson himself went after Worley, who fought a battle the fury of which it is probable that no romance could exaggerate. The pirates were killed or disabled, until Worley and another man were alone left standing, and they refused to surrender until they were desperately wounded. They were carried to Charleston, where their captors, with sanctimonious haste, tried and executed them before they could die of their wounds.

In 1695 John Archdale, a well-informed, judicious Quaker, who had become one of the proprietors, came out to be governor of all Carolina and to quiet the people. One might suppose that such a man would never be able to control the turbulent colonists; but he succeeded to perfection where all others had failed. The people at once gave him their confidence and support, which his sincerity and discretion enabled him to retain. He made no attempt at first to force the colonists to accept the Huguenots as citizens; but, on the contrary, he disfranchised all these French refugees and issued writs of election only for the two counties which contained the English.

Under his direction the assembly settled the land laws, made arrangements for payment of the quit-rents, appointed magistrates for hearing causes between the settlers and the Indians, built public roads, and cut passages through the marshes to shorten the distance in navigating the thoroughfares and sounds. He attempted to establish a friendly feeling between the colonists and the Indians, but if he had any success in this it was only temporary. The settlers were determined to cheat the Indians in trade at every opportunity, and even some of those high in office were interested in kidnapping the red men to be sold as slaves in the West Indies.

Archdale had no intention of remaining governor for any length of time. He had come out merely to quiet the colony, and he returned in 1696. In the same year that he returned the Huguenots were given equal rights with the other colonists and allowed to inherit land.

But although he had accomplished a great deal and had given the province its first appearance of prosperity, so that in the next fourteen years there were only four governors, he could not permanently alter the causes of discord. Regular and more orderly government continued to develop under the impetus he had given it, but the disputes and factions continued for a long time. In 1700 there was a contest between the upper and lower houses of the legislature. The lower house, under the leadership of Nicholas Trott, attempted to reduce the upper house to an inferior position, limiting it to a single day in which to pass the bills sent to it, and to a single hour in which to answer messages. In fact, the Carolinians undertook to shape their constitution without regard to the proprietors, and they largely succeeded.

In 1710 there was a small civil war. Gibbes and Broughton each claimed the office of governor. Gibbes appears to have been regularly elected to the office by the upper house, and took possession of the government. But Broughton and his friends, declaring that Gibbes had been elected by bribery, assembled at a plantation and marched to Charleston, which seems at that time to have been a walled town with a drawbridge, like the defence to an ancient castle. Gibbes, being in possession within the walls, refused to let down the drawbridge at the demand of Broughton, who thereupon rode around the walls with his party and tried to effect an entrance at what was called the bastion. Defeated in this, he returned to the drawbridge, and after a struggle succeeded in entering the town.

Both parties, being now inside, seemed unwilling to come to blows, and there was more manœuvring and tearing of ensigns than fighting. In the end Broughton's men, after proclaiming him governor, retired to a tavern, and it was agreed that Gibbes should remain governor until the proprietors settled the controversy.

The proprietors rejected the claims of both Gibbes and Broughton, and appointed as governor Charles Craven, a gallant and attractive young Englishman, who figures as the hero of Simms's novel, " Yemassee." He soon had to conduct the province through a terrible war with the Indians,—the Tuscaroras in North Carolina and the Yemassees nearer to Charleston. This war is made the subject of Simms's novel, which is written somewhat in the style of Cooper. The story is by no means unskilfully told, and is exceedingly valuable for its descriptions of the country, the schemes of the Spaniards in Florida to assist the Indians, and the strange tribes by which the colonists were surrounded.

The Indians, of whom there were more than twenty tribes in the near neighborhood, were indeed an important influence in the development of South Carolina. For many years their numbers were so great that a little unity and skilful leadership would have enabled them at almost any time to annihilate the colony, and on several occasions they came very near accomplishing it. The colonists saved themselves only by extreme vigilance, presents and bribes, and setting tribe against tribe.

Besides compelling South Carolina to become a province of one fortified town, the Indians soon wrought a change in its government. The contest with the Yemassees was so serious that in the midst of their difficulties the people sent to the proprietors for aid, but it was refused. The proprietors could not assist the province without involving their English estates in debt, and this they were unwilling to do; for they had already, they thought, lost too much money in Carolina. The agent of the colony thereupon applied to the king for relief, and it was suggested that the proprietorship be abolished and that the colony be turned into a royal government under the direct control of the crown.

This proposition soon received support from many quarters. The colonists favored it with enthusiasm, because they believed the king would be able to protect them from the Indians as well as from the Spaniards and pirates. The English merchants saw in it an increase of their trade to Carolina, because the people would be more prosperous and would probably be prevented by the king from issuing paper money, the depreciation of which was a great loss to all who dealt with them. Public men and statesmen saw in it a better prospect for the spread of the British empire; for they feared that if Carolina remained in the weak control of the proprietors, it would be taken by the Spaniards of Florida.

At the same time the proprietors succeeded in making themselves more unpopular than ever. Some lands taken from the Yemassees had been given by the assembly to some Scotch-Irish settlers who had been induced to come to the colony on the expectation of receiving the land. But the proprietors claimed the exclusive right of selling the land, and had it surveyed and laid out in baronies without regard to the Scotch-Irish, some of whom perished from starvation, and the rest sought refuge in the Northern colonies.

The proprietors also repealed a law which allowed elections to be held in the different parishes instead of compelling everybody to come to Charleston to vote. They had succeeded in winning to their side the popular leader, Nicholas Trott, and had made him chief-justice. He was accused by the people of a long list of thirty-one offences, which is a striking commentary on the way in which the colony was governed. He had contrived a fee for continuing cases from one term to another, he acted as counsel in cases pending before him, prepared documents the validity of which he afterwards passed upon as judge, he was sole incumbent of the Courts of Common Pleas, King's Bench, and Vice-Admiralty, and he was also a judge of the Court of Chancery ; so that no appeal could be taken to any one of these courts without his granting it against himself. But the proprietors, in answer to the protest of the people, not only continued him in office, but complimented him on his devotion to their interests.

One of the laws which was repealed by the proprietors was certainly a most extraordinary one. The high-spirited colonists had actually undertaken to levy a duty on all goods imported into the province from Great Britain. Half a century afterwards it became an important question whether Great Britain had a right to tax the colonies, but here was a colony taxing Great Britain. In Maryland, as we have seen, a clause of the charter expressly allowed such a tax to be levied, although the colonists never succeeded in acting under it. The Carolinians, however, levied the tax without the authority of any charter, and appear to have met with some slight success in executing their law, which was the only instance of a colonial tariff being enforced against the manufactures of the mother country. Even Massachusetts never went so far as this.

The enforcement of the law aroused great indignation among the English merchants, who were now more than ever in favor of a royal government which would put a stop to such high-handed measures. With the colonists the law was extremely popular, for they expected the proceeds of the tax would pay the expenses of government and help them carry on their wars with the Indians and Spaniards. Its repeal by the proprietors was considered such a grievance that they determined to deny the right of the proprietors to repeal any of their laws. In these proceedings, besides Trott and Rhett, we find the familiar South Carolina names of Bull, Barnwell, Butler, and Skrine.

The relations between England and Spain were at this time very much strained, and it was known that a Spanish expedition was preparing at Havana to attack South Carolina. The Carolinians had had several contests with the Spaniards of Florida, in which they had been usually successful; but when the governor called on them for a subscription to resist this attack, he was told that the duties on imports would be amply sufficient, because the people had determined to enforce this law, although it had been repealed by the proprietors, and in future " to pay no regard to these repeals."

The governor, Robert Johnson, thinking it would be best to have the militia ready, requested the field-officers to call a general meeting of their companies. Meantime the members of the assembly had prepared a plan for revolting from the allegiance of the proprietors, and, having reduced it to writing, it was presented at the meeting of the militia to be signed. They readily agreed to it, and soon after it was signed by nearly all the white people of the colony; and on the 28th of November, 1719, the announcement was formally made to the governor that the people had decided to dispense with the proprietary authority, and he was requested to accept the office of governor from them on behalf of the king. This he refused with much indignation, and the contest began.

The assembly, feeling confident of the support of the whole province, passed resolutions declaring that they were no longer an assembly, but a convention of the people to preserve the colony until his majesty's pleasure should be made known. They denied the authority of the proprietors to repeal laws, and denied also the authority of the governor and his council; but they provided that an address should be sent to the governor, asking him to continue the administration until the king's decision could be made known. Arthur Middleton, the head of a family afterwards famous in the history of the province, was president of the convention, and waited on Governor Johnson to persuade him to comply.

Middleton argued in a manner which seems strangely familiar, because it was in the same high-strung tone which is so well known to us in the history of nullification and secession in South Carolina. The governor had been approved by the king, so that he was already half a royal governor; and as for the remaining half, which rested on the proprietors, that had been abolished by Middleton and his friends. The convention representing the people had disowned the proprietors, and would not act with them on any account.

It was a serious predicament for Johnson. If he should attempt to dissolve the convention and dismiss the members to their homes, how was he to obtain money and militia for defence against Spain? On the other hand, if he allowed the convention to exist, was he not faithless to the trust the proprietors had imposed upon him? Messages and answers passed between him and the convention, each side trying to gain an advantage; but in the end Johnson took the only ground he could in honor take, and declared that he had been appointed by the proprietors, and by them alone could he be dismissed. He issued a proclamation dissolving the convention, but the document was torn from the hands of the marshal who attempted to serve it.

The convention then proceeded to complete the revolution by electing James Moore governor. There was a grand meeting of the militia in Charleston in the market square, with flags flying in the forts and on all the ships in the harbor. Johnson, arriving in the town and finding all these preparations for proclaiming the new government, had the courage, single-handed, to oppose them. He stormed and threatened punishments, reasoned and expostulated, and was about to seize with his own hands the commander, when the militia levelled their muskets at him. He had expected support from some of the people, but not a man joined him. The revolution seemed to be universal, and there was nothing that the governor could do against it.

He attempted to hold together the old government, but in vain. The convention proclaimed Moore governor, and set to work forming a new government, modelled on those in the other royal colonies, and consisting of a governor's council of twelve and an assembly elected by the people. Laws were rapidly passed, and among them, of course, the favorite tariff against goods imported from England. The fortifications were repaired, and the province strengthened in every way to resist the Spaniards. Taxes were levied on land and negroes, and a really vigorous and efficient government created, showing how natural and easy such work always is to the English race.

Meantime the Spanish expedition from Havana had sailed, and Johnson warned the revolutionists of what might happen if they attempted military operations without lawful authority. But the convention was confident, and the Spaniards never reached Charleston. They chose first of all to attack the island of Providence, where they were repulsed, and soon after a large part of the fleet was lost in a storm.

The convention was completely triumphant. Two British men-of-war came into the harbor, and Johnson immediately procured their assistance. With their men at quarters and portholes open, they lay before the town, and Johnson ordered the revolutionists to surrender or he would batter down the city over their heads. But the convention in possession of the forts and bastions of the little stronghold stood ready at their guns, and not a shot came from the men-of-war.

It was a most interesting revolution, so successful, and with such obvious influence on the greater revolution of the continent a little more than fifty years afterwards. One would suppose that the British government would have in some way punished or rebuked it; but while it was going on, Parliament was preparing to divest the proprietors of all their rights in the government as well as in the soil of Carolina. They were given seventeen thousand five hundred pounds in compensation, and the arrears of quit-rents due from the colonists were purchased for five thousand pounds more, making in all twenty-two thousand five hundred pounds, which probably very nearly compensated them for their outlay on the province, without giving them any of the profits which they expected to reap from their vast territory stretching all the way to the Pacific.

Some of the resemblances between this revolution and that of 1776 are worth noting. The two were conducted in very much the same way. Both of them began with complaints, remonstrances, and arguments, dignified and earnest for the most part, but interspersed, when occasion offered, with very decided and riotous action. Both were concerned with the question of taxation, although in a somewhat different way. The South Carolinians claimed the right not only to regulate their own internal taxes, but to tax at their pleasure the goods imported from the mother country. Both were an uprising of the people, represented by a body which in one instance was called a convention and in the other a Continental Congress, and in both instances, when the revolution was completed, these bodies became the government of the country.

In the South Carolina revolution Arthur Middleton was president of the convention. His son, Henry Middleton, was at one time president of the Continental Congress, and his grandson, Arthur Middleton, was one of the signers of the Declaration of Independence.

The British government, although it had no inclination to punish the revolutionists, would not accept Moore as the governor. General Francis Nicholson, a passionate, violent, but at the same time generous and firm man, very much like the typical South Carolinian, was appointed in 1721, and delighted everybody by his administration. He encouraged literature and religion, and under his administration the Church of England was more firmly established in the province.

The Huguenots in time showed a decided preference for the Episcopal service and doctrines, and the old Huguenot church now shown to visitors in Charleston is still in possession of the Episcopalians. The Huguenots joined the Church of England in South Carolina very much as the Lutheran Swedes joined it in Pennsylvania, where the old Swedish churches are now all Episcopal.

In fact, wherever the Huguenots appeared in America they were more easily absorbed among the English population than any other foreign element that has ever come to us. They rapidly joined the English religious bodies in preference to their own, and within two or three generations all their distinctive characteristics except their names had disappeared. The consequence of this and of their willingness to intermarry has been that no other foreign element except the English can trace its blood in so many distinguished and prominent people in the United States. They have been in this respect the reverse of the Germans, who, by attempting to keep up their nationality and segregating themselves from the rest of the people, have diminished their opportunity for usefulness to the nation.

But the most important benefit Nicholson conferred on the province was his treaty with the Cherokee Indians. He smoked their pipes and exchanged with them that eloquence about friendship as enduring as the sun and stars which is usually effective, or at least suitable, on such occasions. He regulated the standard of weights and measures by which trade with them was carried on, and appointed an agent to superintend their intercourse with the whites. In the same way he concluded a treaty with the Creeks.

Soon after, in the year 1730, Sir Alexander Cumming came out from England further to pacify the Southern Indians, with whom the French had begun to tamper as part of their plan of getting control of the Mississippi Valley behind the English settlements. They were already beginning to enter this valley on the north by way of Canada and the Great Lakes and on the south from the Gulf of Mexico. Cumming penetrated the Indian country three hundred miles west of Charleston, held many conferences, and returned in triumph with a crown decorated with scalps and eagle tails. Six chiefs accompanied him to England, were entertained and petted at court, and returned to their people with accounts of the wonders they had seen.

When the chiefs returned they were accompanied by Robert Johnson, who had been appointed governor to take the place of General Nicholson. Although as the last governor under the proprietors he had resisted the revolution to the utmost of his ability, he was much respected by the people, who knew that he had acted from a sense of duty and honor. They were not averse to having him over them again, and his administration, like that of nearly all the governors after the revolution of 1719, was quiet and satisfactory. After his death a monument with a very laudatory inscription was erected to his memory in St. Philip's Church.

The success of the negotiations with the Indians was a great relief to the Carolinians and was the beginning of their prosperity. Instead of living in terror of their lives, within easy distance of escape to a walled town, they could now spread out in all directions. The Spaniard in Florida was their only remaining enemy, and he was not so close and persistent as the Indian had been.

This peace which Nicholson and Cumming secured lasted for nearly thirty years, or until the breaking out of the French and Indian war after Braddock's defeat in 1755. During those years the South Carolinians pushed their settlements westward for a distance of over a hundred miles. The pioneers in this advance were the Indian traders and the cattlemen or graziers. The cattlemen occupied the districts where cane grew, the open grassy spaces in the forest, and also pastured their cattle in the woods. Places were established for bringing the cattle together, called cow-pens, a word which often occurs in the history of the province, and has given a name to one of the battle-fields of the Revolution.

The life of these men bore a slight resemblance to that of the cowboys of the Western plains in our own time. The traders, usually Scotch-Irishmen, advanced still farther, and were types of those curious characters who love isolation and a wild life. Some of them penetrated beyond the line of the Alleghany Mountains, hundreds of miles from the settlements, where they lived alone among the Indians with their squaw wives and the other pleasures of savage existence. One of them is said to have boasted that he had upwards of seventy children and grandchildren among the Indians.

This peace with the Indians followed some few years after the complete suppression of the pirates; and as the Indian peace gave the Carolinians the freedom of the West, so the suppression of the pirates gave them the freedom of the ocean. They were now at liberty to develop themselves and enjoy the chief advantages of their situation; for until the pirates were suppressed their discovery that rice would grow in the swamp lands was of very little use.

The cultivation of rice had been introduced by Thomas Smith, who was a landgrave under

the Locke constitution and a governor of the
colony. He had been in Madagascar, where he
had seen rice growing in low ground, and he
had long been convinced that it would grow in
Carolina. One day, about the year 1693, a
vessel from Madagascar, in distress, put into
Charleston harbor, and the captain, who was
an old acquaintance of Smith's, inquired for
him. In the course of their conversation they
talked about rice, and when Smith asked for
some, the cook of the vessel furnished him with
a small bag of it, which he planted in the back
of his garden. It grew, and the crop produced
was distributed among other people to make the
same experiment, which in every instance was
successful. Rice, negro slavery, and the extreme partiality which the British government
showed towards the colony were the foundations
of its fortunes.

The favor and encouragement which the
British government displayed were quite extraordinary. Massachusetts was also a royal
province, but the people were ground down and
oppressed by the crown until they became in
time the most inflammable revolutionists on the
continent. But every favor that could be shown
a colony was shown to South Carolina. The restrictions on colonial trade were waived for her
benefit, and she was allowed to send her rice

directly to any port south of Cape Finisterre, on the northwest coast of France. Parliament allowed her a bounty on hemp. The arrears of quit-rents which had been bought from the proprietors by the crown were all remitted, the king sent out as a present seventy pieces of cannon, and when Charleston was half destroyed by a fire, Parliament voted twenty thousand pounds to be distributed among the sufferers. The province was allowed, and even encouraged, to issue bills of credit, and men-of-war were stationed on the coast for the special protection of her trade.

It seems rather difficult at first to understand why there should have been so much partiality shown South Carolina. But the English aristocracy and governing classes had always been more interested in the Southern colonies than in the Northern ones. The Northern colonies were largely settled by Puritans, Quakers, and other dissenters, and were believed to have a cold climate, forbidding scenery, and to be suitable only for shopkeepers and petty occupations. The great plantations, country life, and genial climate of the South were more attractive; and as late as the time of our civil war, the English upper classes took sides with the Confederate States largely because their people were supposed to live like country gentlemen.

Landgraves, Pirates, and Caziques

The original proprietors of Carolina having been men of the highest distinction and influence in the Cavalier or high tory party, and having surrendered their province to the crown without a struggle, naturally left an inheritance of favor for Carolina, which was continued through generations of men of influence in the government, and it is probable that the Carolinians themselves were wise enough to cultivate this advantage to the utmost. They resorted to England, and passed to and fro more than the people of any other colony. The children of people of means were almost invariably sent to England for their education. English books were read, English clothes worn, and English habits and customs reproduced, especially in the country life of the planters. As the life of the colony was all centred in Charleston, which soon had many ships and a considerable commerce, the close connection with the mother country was easily maintained, and the route which ships from England followed at that time, by way of the coast of Europe and the Azores and Canary Islands, was much shorter to Charleston than to New York or Boston.

The English merchants, whose influence in British politics was strong, were always very fond of the Charleston people. London, Bristol, and Liverpool thought they saw great opportunities in South Carolina. They encouraged the slave-trade, and assisted the planters with credit and in other ways to purchase slaves, because the more slaves the larger the plantations and the greater the consumption of British goods.

So the five or six hundred wooden houses of which Charleston was composed began to give place to brick mansions and stores of a somewhat imposing appearance, and the walls, bastion, and drawbridge became of less importance. The plans which the proprietors had tried so often for coaxing immigrants into the province were renewed; but the reports of the large numbers who came must be scanned closely, and it is also necessary to investigate what happened to them after they arrived.

John Peter Pury, of Neufchâtel, Switzerland, visited Carolina, and, of course, was charmed. He entered into a contract with the government to bring in Swiss immigrants, but they sickened and died very fast, and those who survived spent their time in cursing Pury for the hardships of their lot. The Scotch-Irish immigrants went through similar experiences, and, in truth, all white people had to pass through a very severe ordeal before they were acclimatized. The negro, on the other hand, was acclimatized at once; and the sick and failing whites were all the more tempted to encourage the slave-trade, because to obtain credit with a merchant for a cheap negro to do their hard work was a matter of life and death to them.

And now began the process which supplied an enemy to take the place of the Indian and keep the South Carolinian keyed up to that high-spirited imperiousness which always comes to men who live with arms by their sides, in daily and nightly fear of their lives. Negro slavery in connection with the rice and indigo plantations became extremely profitable. Capital invested in planting and negroes would often, under favorable conditions, double itself in three or four years. A vigorous negro cost about forty pounds, or two hundred dollars, and after a year's labor usually paid for himself.

After the revolution of 1719 and the orderly settling of the royal government, slaves were imported in great numbers, until they outnumbered the whites almost three to one. They were not like the negroes we now see in the South, and still less like the Northern negroes, tamed by nearly two hundred years' contact with civilization and a large infusion of white blood. They were pure Congo savages, fresh from the African jungle, with their fetish worship, their wild dances, and their incomprehensible jargon which they called language. They were quick to learn certain things, and rapidly adopted the white man's dress and many of his ways. But they remained strange creatures for a long time, and it is not likely that there was much change until the second generation.

The lash of the overseer, the efforts of good people to Christianize him, contact with civilization, and a large infusion of white blood into his veins have been among the chief means which have changed the negro, and for a hundred years and more he has been mild enough; but in his untamed original condition in South Carolina he was a continual source of terror to the English colonists, whom he so far outnumbered, and who knew all the details of the terrible slave insurrections in the West Indies.

Of large stature; muscular; not only uninjured by the climate, but stimulated and strengthened by it; quickly becoming familiar with the effect and use of fire-arms, and with easy access to such weapons, as well as to the axes and tools used in his labor, it is little wonder that his masters were uneasy. He was by no means an inferior fighting man, and in this respect was more than a match for many of the Indians. Simms, in his novel, " Yemassee," describes the slaves pursuing some of the inferior tribes of Indians through the woods and smashing their heads with clubs. The imported negro was more of a fighting man and more dangerous than his descendants, and when the importation was prohibited it became safe to treat the slaves more mildly.

During the early days of the colony a regular watch and ward was kept round the walls of Charleston to guard against the red men; but now that that danger was past, a more intense and careful watch was necessary for protection against the blacks. The walls round the town were of no avail, for the negroes were everywhere,—in the houses of the town as servants, on the streets, and on the plantations. Every man, woman, and child must become a watchman and guard, and the whole community turned itself into an organized militia. Slaves could not leave the plantation to which they belonged without a ticket, and all white persons were authorized to disperse meetings of them. A slave found on the road could be stopped, examined, and, if necessary, whipped on the spot. If he resisted punishment, it was lawful to kill him. The white men all went armed to church, as in the early days of Massachusetts; and for any one to fail to give notice of the slightest symptom of disaffection in a slave, no matter to whom he belonged, was a heinous offence.

A justice of the peace and three freemen had the power to inquire into all crimes committed by slaves, and the judge could order death to be inflicted as a punishment in any mode he thought proper. Slaves were incapable of giving evidence, and were not allowed counsel for their defence. There was no marriage among them, and they lived in irregular association like animals, which, it was supposed, tended to increase their numbers, to the profit of their master. They were forbidden to learn to write, and could neither buy, sell, nor hire horses, nor travel in companies of more than seven. About the only mitigation in their condition was that they were allowed on Sunday to work for themselves.

That they were treated with extreme cruelty, the result largely of the terror their numbers inspired, is unquestioned, and it was unsafe for any one to intercede for them. Crèvecœur, in his "Letters from an American Farmer," tells of a clergyman who, having recently come to South Carolina, ventured to remonstrate with the people on their treatment of the slaves, and was promptly informed by his congregation, "Sir, we pay you a genteel salary to read us the prayers of the liturgy and to explain to us such parts of the Gospel as the rule of the Church directs, but we do not want you to teach us what to do with our blacks."

Crèvecœur also describes finding one day in

the woods a negro exposed alive in a cage to die of hunger and thirst. The cage was hung in a tree, and sitting on it was a flock of buzzards, which had already pecked out his eyes and were tearing the flesh from his arms, while the blood streamed down on the ground. This, as Crèvecœur was afterwards informed, was the punishment inflicted for the murder of an overseer, and its cruelty was defended as absolutely necessary to protect the community.

But Crèvecœur is probably wrong in describing him as in a cage. It is more likely that he was hung in chains, as it was called, which was a common way at that time of dealing with notorious criminals, although they were not usually hung in chains alive. It seems strange, from what we know of the habits of vultures, that they had begun to tear the negro before he was dead.

In many instances, of course, the slaves were well treated. Henry Laurens, Pringle, and other planters were well known as kind masters, and they were rewarded by a great increase in the number of their blacks; for when used with kindness and not overworked they bred much more rapidly; and this argument in favor of mild treatment was one of the few which it was safe to use.

The Spaniards at St. Augustine, knowing well the condition of things in South Carolina, made

every effort to incite an insurrection among the
slaves or to entice them away from the province. They offered them complete freedom
and protection if they would come to Florida;
and they had a regiment recruited in this way
from the Carolina slaves, whom they dressed
in full uniform of bright colors, which the darky
loves, and gave them equal rank and pay with
the Spanish soldiers. That they were not more
successful in these methods is proof of the sharp
watchfulness of the Carolinians, or, as the Carolinians would explain it, of the entire contentment of the negroes with their condition.

But in 1740 what every one had long expected
finally happened. A number of negroes at
Stono attacked a warehouse and, having killed
the men in charge, took possession of the guns
and ammunition which it contained, and immediately marched towards Florida, burning houses
and murdering every one they met until they had
killed about twenty people. They were continually joined by the slaves of the districts they
passed through, and had proceeded some distance when, in passing near a Presbyterian
church where the armed congregation was assembled, some one gave the alarm.

The men from the church pursued the slaves,
and, finding them in an open field feasting and
dancing and drunk with rum which they had

obtained from the plantations, at once attacked them. They were easily dispersed, many of them killed on the spot, and a terrible example made of the leaders who were captured.

South Carolina and, indeed, the whole South never forgot this and some other insurrections. The Carolinians redoubled their vigilance, and rangers were employed to patrol the frontiers. The dread of these servile insurrections became embedded in Southern feeling, and in the days of Clay and Webster and the Missouri Compromise many a speech in Congress was pointed with an allusion to it. At the time of the civil war nothing was so exasperating to the people of the Confederacy as the thought that the abolitionists of the North were attempting to bring upon them the horrors of a universal slave rebellion. But, as we all know, there were no rebellions in later times, and in the civil war the fidelity of the negroes to their former masters was remarkable, for the negro's blood had been diluted and his character changed.

The gift of freedom has, however, developed vices in him which were unknown in colonial times. He had not then the mad passion for raping white women and children, which causes so many lynchings in the South, nor did he show the inordinate criminal instincts which are now his characteristics.

Landgraves, Pirates, and Caziques

Besides rice and indigo, the people, as they were enabled to spread backward into the interior of the country, began to interest themselves in grazing, and to cultivate hemp, wheat, and corn, and cure hams, bacon, and beef. They followed the lines of the numerous great rivers, which gave them easy and cheap transportation for all their produce to Charleston, their common emporium and the centre of all their life.

Everything was made easy for them under the extraordinary favor which the British government lavished on its pet colony. Lands were given free of quit-rents for the first ten years, and taxes were a mere trifle. The mother country gave new settlers a bounty to purchase tools and start life on the land which they obtained for nothing. The settler then proceeded to procure some negroes on credit, and if after that, surrounded by an abundance of game and fish, he could not succeed, it was certainly his own fault.

The merchants both in England and in Charleston were very indulgent in the way of credit, and, as prosperity was increasing and values rising, found it for their advantage. They encouraged the people to buy both negroes and goods on long credit, and in this way they greatly stimulated the development of the country. They required settlements from their customers only once a year, and often extended them to two or three years; and on all the naval stores, indigo, hemp, and raw silk which the colony produced the mother country paid a bounty.

There were no manufacturing industries, and they were not desired; for, with bounties on most of their products, the people preferred to be producers of raw material. Slave labor was not suited to manufacturing, and white labor was high. The laws of the British Parliament forbidding manufacturing in the colonies and restricting their foreign trade, which were such a source of irritation in the Northern colonies, especially in New England, were regarded with entire indifference by the Carolinians.

From the point of view of Great Britain, South Carolina was the ideal colony, fulfilling in every respect the functions and duties of a colony, and entitled to all the assistance and favor that could be shown her. England intended that the colonies should all be mere producers of raw material, and buy all their manufactured goods from her, and at the same time trade with foreign nations in a way to help on the trade of the mother country. This was the foundation principle of her colonial policy, the principle that built up the colonies and finally lost them to her. If the colonies would accept the principle, she promised to help them to great prosperity, and in the case of South Carolina she certainly made good her word.

South Carolina was an instance which, so far as it goes, justifies the theory of those who maintain that a community may become prosperous, enlightened, and refined by the cultivation of the soil alone, without the varied industries of manufacturing. The seventy thousand white men, all planters and farmers, or merchants furnishing supplies to planters and farmers, were by the time of the Revolution a most united and happy people, with many of the characteristics of intelligence and intense patriotism which characterized the people of Massachusetts, much easier and more polished in their manners, and more familiar with the customs of Europe. There was probably no community in the world where such a very large proportion of the white people had means and leisure to enjoy themselves and cultivate the arts of life.

They were wholly engaged in agriculture, but they had all the advantages of city life, for everything centred in Charleston, which the rivers and roads made easy of access. The planters usually lived in the town, visiting their plantations, which were in charge of overseers, only when necessary, and some whose estates were close to Charleston dispensed with town houses.

Landgraves, Pirates, and Caziques

In summer every one congregated in the town to enjoy the sea-breeze, and for four or five months it became a very lively watering-place and was the resort of invalids from the West Indies.

There was a society for the promotion of literature, two libraries, and several temporary theatres at different times until 1793, when a permanent one was established. At the literary club, clergymen of several different denominations discussed religious topics in perfect harmony. Music was carefully cultivated long before much attention was given to it in the other colonies. Josiah Quincy, who visited Charleston in 1773, describes an amateur concert of the St. Cecilia Society at which two hundred and fifty ladies were present, and both men and women more richly dressed than in the North. And if there were any deficiencies in this civilization, the Carolinians themselves were not conscious of them.

The houses were usually of brick, with some pretension to architecture, and surrounded by large verandas. In winter, dancing assemblies were held every two weeks, and there were dinner parties, balls, and amateur concerts innumerable. Sports were fashionable,—fox-hunting, shooting, horse-racing, foot-ball, and also bear- and bull-baiting.

These pleasures were often interrupted by terrible epidemics of small-pox, yellow fever, and other diseases, which are obscurely described. Charleston was sometimes almost depopulated, and at times many of the people were so discouraged that they thought of deserting the province. But in spite of these attacks on their happiness, and the fires and hurricanes, they soon returned to their occupations and amusements.

There was a great deal of gambling and heavy drinking. The latter vice was common in all the colonies; but the climate of Carolina hastened its evil effects on the constitution. Few families had less than twenty slaves as house servants. Everybody had plenty of horses and many had fine carriages. Hospitality was boundless, and on many of the plantations the slaves had standing orders to bring in any respectable stranger they saw passing on the roads.

The plantation-house, surrounded by its stables, barns, and negro quarters, often looked like a small village. Bathed in the soft, indolent sunlight, in the midst of luxurious vegetation, the trees filled with mocking-birds, the horses and cattle wandering everywhere, and hundreds of blacks with their songs and irresistible humor breaking forth at every moment, it was a most attractive scene, in which many a traveller lingered long. Some of the plantations were laid out with handsome grounds, avenues of trees, and the landscape gardening of England.

Edward Middleton, who lived in the province in very early times, planted at his place, called The Oaks, a fine avenue of live-oak-trees, which still remains. Another place of the Middleton family is described as having in front of the house a spacious basin, probably something like a fountain, in the midst of a green lawn. Back of the house was a walk a thousand feet long, on each side of which was a grass-plot ornamented in a serpentine manner with flowers. On the left was a bowling-green, and at a little distance a large fish-pond with a mount in the middle of it as high as the top of the house, and on the mount a Roman temple.

Many of these handsome places were ruined by the British in the Revolution. They were rebuilt in greater magnificence, but were all destroyed in the civil war except Drayton Hall, which, being used as a hospital, was preserved, and is still shown to tourists and visitors from Charleston.

The typical South Carolinian, born and acclimatized in the province, was a man of rather large, well-developed frame, the result of good living, open-air life, and exercise in the saddle. The women were also of well-proportioned, rounded figures, less inclined to the slender, delicate type than in the Northern colonies; and it has been sometimes thought that the typical South Carolina female figure can be traced in their remote descendants in other States. They were lively and bright, took an important and active part in all sorts of affairs, and seem to have had a certain ascendency and superior position which were not attained by the women of the rest of the country.

We read of women managing plantations; and Mrs. Izard devoted herself to the introduction of silk culture, in the hope, as she proudly said, that it might be of benefit to Carolina. Many of the famous gardens in and near Charleston which were so much admired by travellers were the result of the skill and intelligence of women. Mrs. Lambol, Mrs. Logan, Mrs. Laurens, and Mrs. Hopton were among the remarkable gardeners, and Mrs. Logan wrote a book on gardening. About the year 1745 Miss Eliza Lucas, afterwards Mrs. Charles Cotesworth Pinckney, after several years of careful experiments, introduced the cultivation of indigo, from which for more than half a century, until it was superseded by cotton, the people of the province enjoyed very profitable returns.

A great many varied duties necessarily devolved on the women at a plantation. They took care of the sick; and as a plantation of any pretensions had usually two or three hundred slaves, this was by no means a trifling task. They superintended the spinning and weaving of cloth and the cutting and making of all the clothes for the plantation, and they usually had a great number of household servants to look after. They learned to command and enforce obedience among savages. They had to train slaves in habits of order, and teach them the small trades and occupations which were essential to the self-supporting character of their little community. They often taught their own children to read and write. Many of them were very zealous in giving religious and moral instruction to the negroes, teaching them to read the Bible, though not to write; and to this custom must be partially credited the taming and civilizing of the blacks, so that as years passed they became less dangerous. In the Revolution they did little or no harm to their masters, and in the civil war often saved valuable property and befriended their former masters when they were at the mercy of invading armies.

Besides these duties, which were especially assigned to the women, it was usually important for them to have a thorough understanding of the general management of the plantation; for the men were necessarily often absent, and it was not uncommon for a woman to be left

St. James's Church
Goose Creek, S. C.
Built 1711

alone for several months in charge of a huge plantation, with hundreds of slaves, and no white man to assist her but the overseer.

It seems to have been a more varied and broadening life than has been generally supposed, and it developed important qualities in both the women and the men. Each plantation was a little kingdom in itself, with its spinners, weavers, blacksmiths, carpenters, coopers, hospital service, religion, often its own vessel, and always its own laws and customs.

The animosities and factions which had been so rife under the proprietary government disappeared long before the time of the Revolution, and the white population were extremely homogeneous and united, imperious in temper, decided in opinion and judgment, and capable of prompt, unanimous action. They loved Great Britain and the British government, which encouraged and petted them, and we look in vain for any of those bitter complaints and quarrels which were so prominent in the other colonies. The history of South Carolina, although an important community, is in consequence very brief, as the history of prosperity and contentment always is.

Having such a strong and interested affection for the mother country, and always maintaining such close and constant intercourse with her, it might be supposed that the Carolinians would be slow to take part against the stamp acts and tea acts which brought on the Revolution, or that, at least, there would be many tories among them. But, on the contrary, South Carolina was the first colony outside of New England to send delegates to the Congress which met in New York to resist the stamp act. When afterwards the East India Company shipped tea to all the colonies, the cargoes sent to Charleston were stored and the merchants forbidden to sell them.

In Boston, as we all know, the tea was thrown overboard, and, as a punishment for this, the British Parliament passed an act closing the harbor of that town, which in effect destroyed its commerce. Acts of Parliament were also passed placing the government of the province almost completely in the hands of the king, and providing that persons indicted for murder could be sent to England for trial. When Massachusetts, finding her trade ruined and her people in want and suffering, called on the other colonies to stand by her, and by refusing to import English goods bring the Parliament to terms, South Carolina promptly complied. A meeting was called,— not a mere meeting of delegates, but a mass-meeting of all the people of the province, which assembled in Charleston, July 6, 1774, and voted unanimously to support the people of Massachusetts Bay.

The Carolinians on this occasion were not only prompt and unanimous, but their ideas on the subject were perfectly clear and definite; and, indeed, Carolina opinion, whether right or wrong, always had the merit of definiteness. They were not in the least injured by the acts of Parliament. They were still enjoying its favor as well as the favor of the crown, and had everything to lose by making themselves unpopular with the home government; but they declared in their resolutions that the recent acts, " though levelled immediately at the people of Boston, very manifestly and glaringly show, if the inhabitants of that town are intimidated into a mean submission to said acts, that the like are designed for all the colonies, when not even the shadow of liberty to his person, or of security to his property, will be left to any of his majesty's subjects residing on the American continent."

In the same resolutions they appointed Henry Middleton, John Rutledge, Christopher Gadsden, Thomas Lynch, and Edward Rutledge to be the delegates to the first Continental Congress to resist the attacks of Parliament. These delegates were an able and useful body of men. In general character and ability they were equal if not superior to Samuel Adams, John Adams, Robert Treat Paine, and Thomas Cushing, who represented Massachusetts, and they were nearly on a par with the Virginia delegation of Washington, Henry, Randolph, Harrison, and Pendleton. In their opinions they were in sympathy with both the Virginia and Massachusetts delegates, but were not so violent and not so determined to force the issue of independence as the Massachusetts men. The majority of the Congress and the friends of liberty in Philadelphia seem to have always placed most reliance on the representatives of South Carolina and of Virginia, whom they regarded as more statesmanlike and judicious than the Massachusetts delegates, who were headstrong, and played the part of agitators rather than of statesmen.

When the delegates returned from the Congress, in the last days of October, 1774, the Carolinians immediately set to work to create a government among themselves similar to the one by which they had accomplished their own revolution of 1719. They formed a provincial congress of delegates from every parish and district, which, like the convention of 1719, was to act independently of the assembly of their royal government, see that the non-importation resolutions were observed, and organize the militia.

Landgraves, Pirates, and Caziques

The facility with which the Carolinians could act together was strikingly shown in the Revolution. The non-importation agreements were so strictly enforced that not a single article of imported merchandise could be landed. Every man turned himself into a soldier; even the children were seen drilling with sticks in the streets; and the few who seemed out of sympathy with the general will were often roughly handled by the imperious majority.

They had no expectation, however, that there would be war. They confidently believed that their action and preparations would bring Great Britain to terms; and until they received certain information from England, they had no thoughts of actual bloodshed. The way in which they obtained this information was characteristic, and shows that high-handed alertness which all the conditions of their life had made habitual with them.

A packet from London, carrying the mail for the Southern colonies, arrived in Charleston on April 19, 1775. A secret committee had been appointed to watch for this vessel, and when she arrived, William Henry Drayton, John Newfville, and Thomas Corbitt demanded all the letters she carried. The postmaster refused; but the letters were taken from him, the private ones returned, and all despatches from the

British government opened and examined. There were letters to the governors of Virginia, the Carolinas, Georgia, and East Florida, showing conclusively that troops were to be sent to coerce all the colonies. At the same time a letter was found from the governor of Georgia to General Gage, the British commander at Boston, asking him to send troops to control the Georgia people. This letter was retained and another written to take its place, with an imitation of the governor's signature, telling Gage that there was no occasion for sending troops, as the Georgians were convinced of their errors and had come to terms. In the agitations which preceded the civil war of 1861 it will be remembered that the Carolinians took from the United States mails the pamphlets which had been sent by the abolition societies of New England for distribution in the South.

News of the battle of Lexington was received a few days afterwards, settling the question of war beyond a doubt, and a new incentive was now added in the fear of their slaves. They dreaded a great slave uprising, either instigated by the British government or tories, or of the slaves' own motion. Several of their public documents openly speak of this danger, and all their exertions were redoubled.

Twelve hundred stand of muskets, which were in the royal magazine, were instantly seized by a party of Charleston gentlemen and distributed among the militia. Soon after twelve others set out to take by surprise an English powder vessel which was lying near St. Augustine, and after overpowering the grenadiers on board and spiking the guns, they succeeded in removing from her fifteen thousand pounds of powder. They returned by the inland passage through the sounds, and delivered the powder in safety, while their pursuers were looking for them off the Charleston bar. A large part of this powder was sent to Massachusetts.

An association paper was prepared, describing the condition of the country, the danger of servile insurrection, and binding its subscribers to defend both the continent and the province. This paper was carried about to be signed by all the people of the province. Those who refused to sign were proclaimed as enemies, closely questioned as to their reasons, and forbidden to have intercourse with the associators. They were then required to take an oath of neutrality, and if they refused, were disarmed and some of them confined to their houses and plantations.

Such thoroughness was not to be found at that time even in Massachusetts. Only about forty persons in Charleston refused to sign the association paper, and they were for the most part officials or connected in some way with the royal government. In the interior of the country, where the people were less easily controlled, tories were more numerous, especially in the district between the Broad and Saluda Rivers. As they showed a decided disposition to enforce their opinions, the patriots promptly suppressed them by force of arms.

A British fleet of over forty vessels, which attacked Fort Moultrie and attempted to take Charleston, was driven off by the defences which the people had been so diligent to prepare, and soon after the Cherokee Indians, who had been roused to hostility by British emissaries, were subdued. If the Cherokees and tories had attacked on the west at the same time that the fleet was besieging Charleston, the province would have been taken. But the Carolinians were fortunate in being able to deal with each of these enemies separately, and conquer them both.

During the years 1777 and 1778, while the war was raging in the Northern colonies, South Carolina not only enjoyed complete immunity from invasion, but made money in commerce, and drove a thriving trade in supplying goods by wagons to North Carolina, Virginia, and Maryland. In 1779, however, her troubles began when the British invaded Georgia; and although the enemy was kept off during that year, Charleston was taken in 1780, and the British overran the whole State, dragooning the people into submission and creating tories by the same means that the Carolinians had used a few years before to create patriots.

An association paper of submission to the crown was passed about, and in Charleston alone more than two hundred people who had just before been in arms against the British signed it. Those who would not sign were treated as prisoners of war; some were crowded in loathsome prison ships and others confined to narrow limits on land. Severity after severity was enforced against them until hundreds submitted to escape starvation. Many of the people finally began to believe that they had been abandoned by the Northern colonies, and that South Carolina would in any event remain a royal province. Their pride was broken, and the pacification of at least one rebel province seemed complete.

The officers of the conquering army grew rich on the plunder of plantations and warehouses, and cargoes of indigo and negroes went out of the harbor for their advantage. About twenty-five thousand slaves are said to have been sold in the West Indies by the officers, and one of them, Colonel Moncrieff, sold eight hundred as his share of the spoils. They took what they pleased, helping themselves to the silver and plated ware with which the houses of the rich planters were furnished, and wantonly destroyed the beautiful gardens around Charleston. They enjoyed themselves with the concerts, assemblies, and amusements which the Carolinians had been so fond of, and brought to their entertainments the American officers who were their prisoners.

Many of the prominent people who had been released on parole were afterwards seized and imprisoned for nearly a year in St. Augustine. Henry Laurens, who had been appointed minister to Holland, was captured on his way to that country and imprisoned in the Tower of London for over a year; and, indeed, there were few eminent South Carolinians of that time whose histories do not contain an account of a long imprisonment.

The wealthy planters were in a deplorable state: their houses robbed, gardens and plantations devastated, buildings burned, and the negroes, without whom they were helpless, carried off. Many abandoned all their property and left the province, but others agreed to a submission which they intended to break at the first opportunity. The women, in many instances, showed greater resolution than the men, refused to attend the entertainments of the British officers, encouraged their husbands and fathers not to yield to save their property, and cheerfully followed them to the prison ships or into banishment, where they were usually dependent on charity for their support.

Among those who had fled to North Carolina was Colonel Sumter, and the exiles gradually gathered around him as their leader until he was able to carry on a sort of guerilla warfare against the British. Other similar bands were formed; and in the summer, when General Gates arrived from the North, he found himself with about three thousand men; but he was defeated at Camden, and Sumter, who was now assisted by the famous Marion, was left to continue the contest as best he could until the arrival of General Greene, who finally drove the British from the South.

But it was ten years and more before South Carolina recovered from that one year of ravage after Charleston was captured. The unity of feeling among her people had been broken. Impoverished debtors and angry creditors— those who had lost all by patriotism and those who had saved their property by temporizing —struggled and quarrelled together, filling the State with discord and confusion. But before the year 1800 they had settled down on the old lines. New negroes were purchased, houses rebuilt, and the second period of prosperity began, which was greatly accelerated by the introduction of cotton-planting and several improvements in the cultivation of rice.

In the year 1783 Gideon Dupont, a descendant of one of the Huguenot families, introduced the system of overflowing the rice-fields with water at certain seasons, which not only stimulated the growth of the plants but killed the weeds and saved all the labor of destroying them with hoes. Soon after this, machinery worked by the tides was invented for separating the grain from the husk, which had formerly been done by hand with most exhausting labor that broke down the strength of the negro men and often destroyed the fertility of the women. Other improvements followed which greatly lessened the cost of producing a crop and brought rice culture to a high state of efficiency.

Cotton-raising took the place of the culture of indigo, which soon after the Revolution was produced so cheaply in the East Indies that it was no longer profitable in Carolina. When the cotton-gin was invented by Miller and Whitney, of Connecticut, in 1793, an enormous impetus was given to cultivation. Cotton lands in South Carolina doubled in value, and the legislature, for fifty thousand dollars, bought from Whitney and Miller their patent and made it free to the Carolinians.

The cultivation of wheat and other products, which in her first period of prosperity had given variety to the industries of the province, was abandoned, and South Carolina became a State of two products, rice and cotton, dependent for their large profits on negro slavery. After the Revolution her people had the right to trade with all the world; but they soon returned to their old lines of trade almost exclusively with Great Britain, and the close relationship with what had been the mother country was renewed with the same characteristics of long credit which had prevailed in colonial days. This second period of prosperity was more vigorous than the first, and the English merchants reaped a richer harvest from South Carolina as a State than they had ever received from her as a colony.

In this second period of prosperity better houses were built in Charleston, the handsome gardens round the town and on some of the plantations were restored and enlarged, and the cultivation of flowers greatly increased. The imperiousness, generosity, and high spirit which had been the characteristics of the people in colonial times were intensified and carried to extremes. The hospitality of the planters was greater than ever, and very large sums seem to have been spent in charity in the town. Entertainments were numerous, long sittings at meals became common, there was not a little of fairly good education and general information, and much discussion of political questions and points of honor.

A novelist was produced in this period,— William Gilmore Simms,—born in 1806, who, though by no means great, won for himself a respectable position in American literature. Edgar Allan Poe considered him the best after Cooper, and he wrote somewhat in Cooper's vein. He had a most fertile brain, and his volumes are very numerous. His imagination was vivid, and he handled some of his most unpromising topics with a great deal of skill. But his most important merit is that he was a thorough son of the soil, describing conditions which he thoroughly understood and in which he believed, and this characteristic of his books is now all that preserves them from oblivion. In his later years he lived the life of a true Carolinian, in a good country house, in which he dispensed liberal hospitality.

This second period of Carolina's prosperity was remarkable for a great increase of duelling. Before the Revolution there had been a few duels fought with swords, notably one between

Landgraves, Pirates, and Caziques

Thomas Middleton and Colonel Grant, of the British regular army, about a question of rank at the time of the Cherokee war. After the Revolution pistols were invariably used, and the number of duels increased until, soon after 1800, there were four or five a year, and afterwards they became more numerous. Even boys sometimes fought, observing all the requirements of the code. At first the survivor was usually found guilty of manslaughter; but the punishment, burning in the hand, was always remitted. In later times the trial was merely an investigation into the manner in which the duel had been conducted, and if the procedure had been fair, the survivor was acquitted as a matter of course.

The rules and principles of the code were developed to excessive complexity and refinement. Men who had mastered all the intricacies and acquired that " exquisite sensibility," as it was called, in affairs of honor, were looked up to with great respect. Charles Cotesworth Pinckney was one of the most eminent in these matters, and Edward Rutledge also had a great reputation.

But all efforts by grand juries, petitions signed by thousands of respectable people, and the preaching of the clergy were unavailing to check the spread of the fashion, and an attempt was made to regulate it by law. A bill was draughted providing a legal tribunal to decide points of honor and to impose penalties affecting the character and civil privileges of the duellists, their seconds and abettors. The survivor was not to be punished by death, but was to be compelled to support the family of his antagonist, and this last provision probably prevented the bill becoming a law. Duelling continued until, when the men of high character who had enforced the fairness of the code were driven from influence and control after the civil war, it degenerated into the assassination and shooting at sight which we have known in the South in our own times, and which is now said to be slowly disappearing.

Among these high-strung but very charming and agreeable people, the planters were the aristocrats, and are said to have ignored and slighted the merchant class. But from other sources we hear of merchants attaining to positions of much eminence and importance, and becoming equal in every respect to the planters; and as many of them acquired considerable wealth, this was naturally to be expected. Henry Laurens, one of the most distinguished of the Revolutionary characters, was a merchant, Christopher Gadsden also, and Gabriel Manigault was both merchant and planter.

Landgraves, Pirates, and Caziques

The general tone was, however, set by the planters, and was not very consistent with mercantile pursuits. The sons of planters, unaccustomed to strict discipline, hot-headed, and full of what they had heard of honor, became extraordinary characters as clerks in a counting-house when they began to maintain what they considered their rights. Rather than break in such wild colts the merchants imported clerks from Europe, and the planter class was left to continue in those loose and desultory habits of business which ruined so many.

In fact, everything in South Carolina—the long credits which had always been allowed by the merchants, the assistance the province had received from England, and its good luck in so many ventures—encouraged debt contracting, and before the adoption of the National Constitution we find stay-laws and various contrivances for preventing the collection of debts.

The cultivation of rice and cotton was largely speculative, some years bringing large returns and others little or nothing. Prices were variable, and floods, frosts, hurricanes, and fires lent their assistance to make Carolina values very unstable. The people grew accustomed to sudden transitions from poverty to riches or from riches to poverty, and were extremely reckless. Sometimes the crash came in a man's lifetime;

but often, by the use of credits and other devices, he could keep up appearances throughout a long life. Men who for years had been supposed to be in the most prosperous circumstances were on their death often found to be totally insolvent and their large families left without a penny. In these circumstances the women rose superior to the situation, gathered together the remains of the estate, opened schools or lodging-houses, gave their children stricter training than they would have had under their father, and in the end restored the family to something like prosperity.

But nothing could shake the faith of the Carolinians in their methods. They believed most thoroughly in their system of speculative agriculture without manufactures. It was the only life worth living, and they had a supreme contempt for people who followed any other form of existence. That men who loved their country or respected themselves should want to build up manufacturing industries, which necessarily degraded the white man to the level of the slave, was to them inconceivable. Their furious resentment against the national protective tariff brought them to the verge of rebellion thirty years before the civil war, when with characteristic impetuousness they announced the doctrine that they had the right to nullify acts of Congress which were inconsistent with the system of civilization in their own State; and their hatred of the tariff was in the civil war almost as strong an incentive as their interest in slavery.

There seems never to have been an hour when they did not feel entirely competent to stand alone before the whole world, and their history seemed to justify them; for had they not maintained themselves unaided against the Indians, the proprietors, the Spaniards, the pirates, and their own slaves, who outnumbered them three to one? They saw their own interest and life with a sublime and ingenuous clearness which ignored every obstacle. They overthrew the proprietary system with unanimous and fearless self-confidence, and with cool courtesy invited the governor who was maintaining it to join them. For his manliness in refusing they respected him, and afterwards took pleasure in having as their royal governor the man who had resisted them courageously; for they were so overwhelmingly successful that they could afford to love their enemies.

In a similar spirit they undertook to nullify the acts of Congress, and graciously abandoned the attempt more from a conviction that the game at that time was not worth the candle than from any fear of consequences. But thirty years afterwards, when slavery was attacked and they believed their all was at stake, they moved with a unanimous promptness and high-spirited confidence, as though they intended to sweep the continent in one day, and, to use their own language, make slavery national and freedom sectional. Their State was the first to secede, and they fired the first shot of the rebellion. But they had reached their limitation at last, and their pride, their power, their wealth, and, unfortunately, also many of their highest and best qualities, were overwhelmed.

It was a pathetic fall and a serious loss; for whatever may be our opinion of the crime of slavery, the civilization which South Carolina built upon it had many merits, and her public men were not without important influence in the Revolution and in the Constitution. She had her day, and it was a pleasant one, and, as she will always believe, great. But in many respects it was the day of the successful spoilt child. Everything had been in her favor. When the proprietors could no longer afford to spend money in her aid, the crown and the English merchants began their system of coddling, and she was given a whole division of the human race to keep the mud from her hands and the sun from her head.

Robert Young Hayne was one of the prominent men produced in the nullification period of South Carolina's history. A typical Carolinian in thought and conduct, and of unusual eloquence, he was not in other respects of very marked ability; he is remembered principally for his speech in the Senate on nullification, to which Daniel Webster made his famous reply.

Calhoun, however, who belonged to the same period, was a most remarkable man, and undoubtedly the strongest intellect that was ever produced in South Carolina. He was somewhat unlike the others both in appearance and character, and impresses one as a variation of the type. He came from the frontier Scotch-Irish, and was not of the usual planter or merchant class. His deeply marked, rugged features, with heavy, prominent bones and cavernous eyes, are totally unlike any of the other faces that have come down to us in South Carolina portraits.

His father was a man of education, and Calhoun was trained in that Calvinistic mental discipline which has so often in this country given such good results. He is known now by the ordinary reader of American history only as the desperate champion of the lost cause of nullification; but we should remember that before he took up that cause he had a most useful career in national politics. He had been an enthusiastic supporter of the war of 1812, and had advocated internal improvements in roads and canals, the bank bill, and the protective tariff of 1816. As Secretary of War he organized and gave new life to that department, very much as Hamilton, years before, had organized the Treasury; and the War Department has existed on his system down almost to the present time.

Whether we agree with his opinions or not, it is impossible to deny the wonderful subtilty and analytical power of his arguments, and at times there is a touch of genius and charm in his language. Edward Everett said of him that as Clay was the great leader and Webster the great orator of that time, Calhoun was the great thinker. Clay and Webster also bore strong testimony to his mental power as well as to his incorruptible integrity, and John Stuart Mill thought he was the ablest of the American political philosophers.

The best service of South Carolina to the Union was her influence in forming the National Constitution which she afterwards tried so hard to destroy. When, in 1778, Congress sent out the Articles of Confederation for approval, South Carolina gave them more earnest and careful study than any other State. William Henry Drayton, the chief-justice, prepared a redraught of the articles, with suggestions which were afterwards embodied in the Constitution, and contributed materially to the formation of that document.

As a Carolinian and States' rights man, he, of course, was anxious to secure protection for States' rights, and especially the Southern interest; and he even provided that each State should keep up such military establishment as it pleased and have a naval seminary, all of which was, of course, very characteristic of the feelings of his people. But he also enlarged the federal power beyond anything contained in the articles prepared by the Continental Congress, and he strongly urged the necessity of it, suggesting that Congress should have power to define and punish treason and levy taxes independently of the States. These powers were not contained in the original articles, and they were afterwards found absolutely essential to any competent federal government. He also suggested regular executive departments of war, navy, and treasury.

He was a student of political theories and forms of government, a subject which was always popular among the Carolinians. Charles Pinckney, who in after-years was governor of South Carolina, a member of the United States Senate, and minister to Spain, had similar tastes, and when the Revolution was over he appears to

Landgraves, Pirates, and Caziques

have devoted considerable time to evolving a
more suitable form of government for the Union,
which resulted in the very advanced and suggestive plan which he laid before the Constitutional Convention at Philadelphia in 1787.

Drayton Hall · Ashley River · S. C.

CHAPTER XI

BANKRUPTS, SPANIARDS, AND MULBERRY-TREES

A FTER the proprietors of Carolina had surrendered all their rights in their province at the close of the revolution of 1719, the crown recognized North and South Carolina as two distinct commonwealths, and secured them in their territory; but the land now within the State of Georgia which lay between South Carolina and the Spanish possessions in Florida was taken by the crown, to be disposed of in future grants.

In 1717, however, two years before the revolution in South Carolina and the final surrender of the proprietors, Sir Robert Montgomery was seized with a desire to possess the territory which afterwards became Georgia, and plant a colony there. Like the other distin-

347

guished men who had taken a fancy to the South, he was carried away by enthusiasm, and in his prospectus advertising for settlers he described Georgia as the most delightful country in the universe. " Nature," he said, " has not blessed the world with any tract which can be preferable to it. Paradise with all her virgin beauties may be modestly supposed, at most, but equal to its native excellencies." The name he gave his province was the Margravate of Axilia, and he divided it into a complicated system of counties and districts, very much as Locke had done in his constitution for Carolina, but with more of a military intent, for these divisions were arranged so as to be a sort of self-acting defence against the Spaniards.

But the three years which the proprietors gave him to make the settlement or forfeit the land expired without his accomplishing anything, and nothing was attempted in Georgia until 1729, when it was brought to the attention of Oglethorpe, who was interested in the condition of the debtor prisons of England.

Oglethorpe had entered the army when very young, and enjoyed a most interesting experience of military life. He had been with Marlborough in the Low Countries, with Peterborough in Italy, and had served with Prince Eugene against the Turks. Returning home, he entered

Parliament, and at the time he became interested in Georgia was thirty-three years old, and had been a member of Parliament seven years.

One of his friends, named Caslett, who was imprisoned for debt, being unable to pay the customary fees to the warder, was forced to lodge in a building infected with the small-pox, where he died. This directed Oglethorpe's attention to the sufferings and horrors of these debtor prisons, and he had a committee of Parliament appointed to investigate them. On the information thus obtained, and in company with Lord Percival and other noblemen, he sent a memorial to the Privy Council asking for a grant of the land lying south of the Savannah River, where he agreed to establish a province for indigent people who had become a burden to the public.

In 1732 the crown gave a charter which was totally unlike any other charter of a colony in America. It did not create the usual government of governor, council, and assembly of the people; nor was it a proprietary charter giving the province to one or more persons for their own profit; but it created what would now be called a charitable trust corporation, making twenty-one noblemen and others " Trustees for establishing the colony of Georgia in America." These trustees were to govern the colony through a common council of fifteen persons, and make laws and ordinances to regulate the people who should go to the province. There was no representative assembly of the people, as in the other colonies, and there was no governor. The unfortunate and destitute, for whose benefit the enterprise was intended, were to be paternally managed by the trustees for twenty-one years, and at the end of that time the crown would establish such form of government as should seem best.

As a compensation for giving the people no political rights, the charter expressly provided that they should have all the other liberties of free-born British subjects. The controlling idea evidently was that, as the settlers would all be people who had failed to take care of themselves in England, they were to be treated as minors for twenty-one years, and after that given such government as their improvement should warrant.

The colony was named Georgia in honor of George II., who had granted the charter, as Carolina had been named after Charles I. Oglethorpe and his illustrious friends opened an office in Old Palace Yard, Westminster, and received many private subscriptions in addition to a grant of ten thousand pounds from Parliament. This money they used to defray the expenses of the government and in transporting the settlers and supplying them with necessaries and cattle until they were established on the land. They tried to get only the most worthy insolvents and unfortunates; but they also received people of means who went over at their own expense, giving each five hundred acres of land on condition that they carried over one servant for every fifty acres and did military service in time of war. The population, in consequence, consisted of an upper class of large landholders, a middle class of debtors, for whom the colony was founded, and a lower class of indentured servants.

Besides the philanthropic design, the colony was intended as a bulwark to protect South Carolina against the Spaniards. This being the purpose, the presence of a large slave population which could be incited to insurrection by Spanish emissaries must be avoided, and accordingly we find negro slavery absolutely prohibited.

But beneficence and military protection from the Spaniards were not the only objects to be accomplished. The wise and steady Oglethorpe and his friends were as much excited by the glorious prospects of their enterprise as Montgomery by the Margravate of Axilia. It was the old story over again. Some of the best and most illustrious men of England, who thought everything north of Virginia a frozen desert, had been exalted into wild enthusiasm by the magic touch of the South. Georgia was to be devoted to raising raw silk, wine, oil, dyes, drugs, and many other commodities which England was obliged to purchase at high prices from foreign countries. She was to be the ideal colony; have no manufactures, but furnish enormous supplies of raw material to the manufacturers of the mother country.

"Why, just think," said the enthusiastic trustees, "of the single item of raw silk. England now spends five hundred thousand pounds a year for manufactured silk from Italy, France, Holland, India, and China. But when Georgia supplies the raw silk, almost the whole of that five hundred thousand pounds will go to English silk weavers. Twenty thousand poor people will be employed in Georgia raising the raw silk, and at least forty thousand more in England weaving it. Nay, it is even probable that the Georgians will furnish the raw silk so cheaply that the silk-weavers in England will be able to undersell all the rest of the world, in which case England will have a monopoly of the silk trade, and the profits will be almost unlimited.

"Wine also can be raised in such quantities that we need no longer go to Madeira for it; and the flax, hemp, and potash of Georgia will reduce the balance of trade with Russia by one hundred and thirty thousand pounds. The indigo, cochineal, olives, and dyeing woods will have a similar effect on the balance of trade with the countries from which we now obtain those products; and this grand result will be accomplished simply by removing from England a body of indigent paupers and debtors who are now a burden to society, thus relieving the poor-rates and parishes and emptying the prisons."

All this was shown most clearly in that way statistics have of proving everything beyond the possibility of a doubt. It was to be the greatest province of the British empire. "Such an air and soil," says Oglethorpe, "can only be fitly described by a poetical pen, because there is but little danger of exceeding the truth. Take, therefore, part of Mr. Waller's description of an island in the neighborhood of Carolina, to give you an idea of this happy climate:

> " ' Ripe fruits and blossoms on the same trees live;
> At once they promise and at once they give;
> So sweet the air, so moderate the clime,
> None sickly lives or dies before his time.
> Heaven sure has kept this spot of earth uncurst,
> To show how all things were created first.' "

The soul of the enterprise was Oglethorpe, who in the benevolent purposes which animated him had probably been influenced by George Berkeley, afterwards the great Bishop Berkeley, whom he had known when he was with Lord Peterborough on his diplomatic embassy to Italy. Berkeley, a few years before Oglethorpe's Georgia enterprise, had planned his college for America, and his circular or prospectus for it is interesting to read, because it is another instance showing how the English upper classes were relying on the Southern colonies for the fulfilment of all their ideals.

After the most careful inquiry and consideration, Berkeley had decided to establish his college in the Bermudas, which he explains at length were at that time the centre of the British empire in that part of the world. They were in the track of all vessels to America, and they alone had a trade with all the other colonies. Their people were the most simple and moral and their climate the most genial in the world. That genial climate, which others believed would stimulate trade and commerce to unheard-of proportions, Berkeley relied upon to develop literature and the arts, and from his college were to go forth every year a highly trained clergy, who would convert the negro slaves and Indians to Christianity and forestall the efforts of the French and Spanish to establish the Roman Catholic religion in America.

Europe was worn out and decayed, but in the virgin air and soil of the New World life and beauty would spring forth anew, and on this prospect he wrote those verses which are as immortal as his discoveries in metaphysics:

> " There shall be sung another golden age,
> The rise of empire and of arts;
> The good and great inspiring epic rage,
> The wisest heads and noblest hearts.

> " Not such as Europe breeds in her decay;
> Such as she bred when fresh and young,
> When heavenly flame did animate her clay,
> By future poets shall be sung.

> " Westward the course of empire takes its way,
> The four first acts already past,
> A fifth shall close the drama with the day:
> Time's noblest offspring is the last."

General Codrington had attempted a similar college in the Barbadoes. Berkeley was more nearly successful, and raised five thousand pounds; but the grant from Parliament of twenty thousand pounds, on which he relied, was never made, and the money he had collected was turned over to Oglethorpe for Georgia.

In 1732, soon after obtaining the charter, Oglethorpe sailed for the province, carrying with him thirty-five families, who had been selected with the greatest care as the most worthy of the throng that applied. At the last moment the trustees examined each family separately in the cabin, to make sure that they were entirely willing to go, and only one man declined. The Duke of Newcastle sent letters to the governors of all the colonies, urging them to give every assistance in their power to the new enterprise, and the naval commanders on the coast had similar instructions. Encouragement and favor came from all sides,—a strange contrast to the conditions under which some of the Northern colonies were founded.

Noblemen, eminent people of all sorts, and the fashionable society of London were lost in admiration of Oglethorpe. Young, distinguished, cultivated, the delight of every drawing-room and literary gathering in the metropolis, already distinguished as a soldier, and with a great parliamentary career before him, he was going without reward, in a crowded emigrant ship, to conduct thirty-five families of broken debtors to the American wilderness.

In January, 1733, Oglethorpe and his company reached Charleston, where they were received with the greatest consideration and quartered at Beaufort, while Colonel William Bull went with Oglethorpe to select a site for their settlement in Georgia. In their sailing canoe they threaded the sounds and bays until they came to a low bluff covered with pines, where Savannah now stands. This spot was at once selected, a treaty made with the Indians who occupied it, and the emigrants brought down from Beaufort, supplied with cattle, rice, and everything they needed by the Carolinians, who were delighted with the prospect of this defence between their slaves and the Spaniards.

House-building began, and Oglethorpe worked with his own hands and took his turn standing guard at night. Assistance poured in from South Carolina. Prominent men came down, spending weeks at a time, to give advice, and bringing with them their slaves to work. Mr. Whitaker, we read, sent a hundred head of cattle, Mr. Joseph Bryan brought four sawyers, Mrs. Ann Drayton also four sawyers, Mrs. Hammerton gave a drum, the people of Edisto sent sixteen sheep, the assembly voted two thousand pounds, the people subscribed one thousand pounds, and Mr. Hume sent a silver bowl and spoon as a prize for the first child that should be born.

In the mild climate, and with the soft sea-air blowing through the pines, it was a sort of picnic foundation of a colony, and Oglethorpe must have thoroughly enjoyed it. He was in very much the same position as William Penn when he superintended the building of Philadelphia in the autumn of 1682. But Oglethorpe had the advantage of occasional trips to Charleston, where we find that he was entertained on one occasion by a public dinner, which he returned by giving a ball and supper to the ladies. Soon after he celebrated the founding of Savannah, naming the streets after the trustees and the benefactors in England, as well as the Draytons, Bryans, and Whitakers of Carolina, and concluding with a feast for all the people.

Oglethorpe also resembled Penn in his judicious treatment of the Indians. At the same time his military training led him to establish Fort Argyle, near the passes by which they had formerly invaded Carolina. He took similar precautions along the coast towards the south as a defence against the Spaniards, and fortified Savannah with palisades and cannon. Everything seemed to flourish under his wise management, he settled differences among the people, and met with the same success that Penn had enjoyed in this respect so long as he maintained a personal supervision of his colony.

New settlers continued to arrive. The trustees in England obtained from Parliament a grant of ten thousand pounds from the sale of lands in the island of St. Christopher, which was part of the money Berkeley had hoped to obtain for his college in the Bermudas. A botanist, aided by subscriptions from the Earl of Derby and the Duke of Richmond, was sent to scour the Madeiras, the West Indies, and South America for suitable plants for Georgia.

Olives, madder, and all kinds of strange plants soon arrived, and Oglethorpe laid out a tract of ten acres for experiments with them. Assisted by the Society for the Propagation of the Gospel, the trustees sent over some families of Salzburgers, who had roused the sympathies of all Protestants by the persecutions they had suffered in Germany, and they established a settlement in Georgia which they called Ebenezer.

After spending a year and a half with his people, Oglethorpe returned to England like a conqueror, bringing with him ten Indians, who were presented to the trustees and the king, entertained by the nobility, and carried about England as tourists to see the colleges, palaces, and churches. Oglethorpe himself was received by the king with every mark of respect, and at a grand entertainment he told the story of Georgia and its brilliant prospects. All England was stirred with enthusiasm. Four prizes were offered for the best poem on "The Christian Hero;" and the first prize was a gold medal, having on one side the head of Lady Hastings, one of the most liberal of the subscribers, and on the other the head of Oglethorpe, with the motto, "England may challenge the world." Pope expressed the feelings of the people and immortalized the hero in his verse:

Bankrupts, Spaniards, Mulberry-Trees

" Hail, Oglethorpe! with nobler triumphs crowned
  Than ever were in camps or sieges found,
  Thy great example shall thro' ages shine,
  A fav'rite theme with poet and divine.
  People unborn thy merits shall proclaim,
  And add new honors to thy deathless name."

Applications poured in upon the trustees from all parts of Europe, and Parliament voted twenty-six thousand pounds to fortify Georgia against the Spaniards and also against the French, who were beginning to encroach from the direction of Louisiana. The examination of the trustees into the character of applicants was so thorough that many were rejected ; and others were refused from lack of funds to assist them. In fact, the original plan of emptying the debtor prisons upon Georgia was largely abandoned, because it was found that those who proved themselves worthless in England were not much changed by the voyage to Georgia. The emigrants were now picked bankrupts and men from Scotland and the persecuted Germans on the Continent, and among these were a number of Moravians. Hardihood, religious zeal, and strict morals were the characteristics of a large part of "the great embarkation" which was prepared to return with Oglethorpe.

The care with which these people were provided by the trustees with everything necessary to start them on careers of prosperity was most extraordinary. Every man was to receive for one year certain allowances which are most minutely described, beginning with " 312 lbs. of beef or pork, 104 lbs. of rice," and running through a long list of articles down to " 12 quarts of lamp oil, 1 lb. of spun cotton and 12 lbs. of soap." Similar allowances were provided for every woman ; children over seven and under twelve received half an allowance, and those over two and under seven, one-third allowance. On the voyage out the people were to have every week four beef days, two pork days, and one fish day. Besides all this, there were allowances of blankets, bolsters, trousers, frocks, shoes, and long lists of the best tools and implements, enough to make one wish he could, even in these modern times, share the bounty of those trustees.

A man-of-war accompanied " the great embarkation" as a consort. Oglethorpe declined to live with the naval officers, and took quarters on one of the emigrant ships, which the historians describe as an heroic sacrifice ; but, in view of the beef, pork, and fish days, it could not have been a very great deprivation. On shore he delighted the Scotch Highlanders by dressing in their costume and sleeping on the ground wrapped in a plaid when he could have had a comfortable bed with fresh linen sheets in a tent.

He immediately exerted himself to fortify the colony against the Spaniards, and laid out elaborate works on those beautiful islands, St. Simon's and Jekyl, which are now the delight cf winter tourists and sportsmen. One small island in the neighborhood of these fortifications was called by the Spaniards San Pedro; but one of the Indians who had been in England took from his pocket a handsome gold watch that had been given him by the Duke of Cumberland, and requested that the island should be named after the duke.

And so the happy colonists continued scattering the names of their benefactors and of lord high chancellors, earls, and princes of the blood royal on every new scene that pleased their fancy. A thousand people had been sent out, fifty-seven thousand acres had been granted to settlers, five towns had been established, besides small villages and forts, and all done with the most enlightened judgment of the best and greatest men in England.

But what was the result of all this paternalism, and what, in the end, became of all the selected English, Scotch, Germans, Swiss, Italians, Salzburgers, Moravians, and Portuguese Jews who started with everything in their favor?

Their relations with South Carolina were soon very much strained. The trustees prohibited rum from entering the province, and wherever a cask of it was found it was staved by their officials. This cut off a great deal of trade which the Carolinians had hoped to gain, and they were still further restricted by a regulation which forbade all traffic with the Indians except under license from the trustees. From that time there was a strong undercurrent of ill will among the Carolinians against both Georgia and Oglethorpe.

The colony was soon involved in a most serious conflict with the Spaniards. In fact, the settlement of Georgia, instead of mitigating, increased the hostility of the Spaniards; for they claimed Georgia as part of their province of Florida, though while it lay unoccupied between them and the South Carolinians they had been comparatively quiet. But as the English wanted Georgia, they did well in occupying it, and Oglethorpe was the man for the occasion.

He soon realized that he was in a position of great danger; for the Spanish government was in a state of high irritation, and he learned of preparations at St. Augustine. He was so close to the Spaniards, and Georgia so weak and defenceless, that his little colony might soon be annihilated. He carried on negotiations with the governor at St. Augustine, and at the same time, with the art he had learned under Prince Eugene, so disposed his troops on several occasions as to give the impression of large numbers, the effect of which, however, was to increase the preparations of Spain. Oglethorpe at once set out for England, where, the situation being soon fully appreciated, he was made General of Georgia, and returned to the province in 1738 with a regiment.

Spanish spies and emissaries were now everywhere, even in the regiment which Oglethorpe had brought with him, and he narrowly escaped with his life. Two mutineers shot at him so close at hand that the powder of one musket burnt his face. The slaves in Carolina were being seduced, and the insurrection among them which has already been described soon took place. A similar danger was threatened from the Indian tribes; but Oglethorpe made a journey among them of nearly three hundred miles, and succeeded in securing their alliance. On October 22, 1739, war was formally declared between England and Spain, and Oglethorpe began it by burning Picolata on the St. John's River and capturing Fort St. Francis.

About the same time the plot of a German Jesuit, Christian Priber, was discovered. He had gone among the Indians in the interest of

France, with the intention of forming a confederacy of Indians, French, Germans, and runaway slaves which could be turned upon the English settlements. With that wonderful skill and unscrupulous subtlety which characterized his order in that age, and which finally led to its abolition for a time even in Roman Catholic countries, he gained a complete ascendency over the Cherokees, crowning the chief as king of the confederacy and giving flattering titles to his warriors. When captured and brought to Georgia, Oglethorpe found that although dressed in deerskins he was a man of ability, polished manners, and the master of Latin, French, Spanish, and English.

His conversation, papers, and a form of govment for his confederacy, which were found upon him, revealed that he intended to shelter criminals and tolerate every crime except murder and idleness. He had numerous agents and assistants and a secret treasurer in Charleston. Marriages were to be dissolved at will, women to be common property, and general licentiousness to be allowed in his government. This was to attract numbers, and, as he explained, was only a means to an end. " We never lose sight of a favorite point," he said, " nor are we bound by the strict rules of morality in the means, when the end we pursue is laudable. If we err, our general is to blame ; and we have a merciful God to pardon us." He died in prison before he could be executed, and in the mean time delighted all who visited him by his talents and accomplishments.

Oglethorpe next planned an elaborate attack on St. Augustine with the regiment he had brought from England, several companies of Highlanders and Indians, and a regiment from South Carolina, under Colonel Vander Deusen. He had altogether nine hundred troops and eleven hundred Indians, and was to be assisted by a fleet of men-of-war. He intended to take the place by assault; but the Spanish galleys prevented the fleet from assisting, and he was compelled to turn his attack into a siege. He bombarded the fort for twenty days, and had nearly starved out the garrison when they were relieved by supplies from Spanish vessels. It was the middle of July, the Indians were tired of the long siege, the white men were sickening in the hot sun, and the fleet, fearing the hurricane season, would remain no longer. The siege was reluctantly abandoned; but the Spaniards lost over four hundred killed and prisoners, while the English loss was only about fifty, and Georgia had a respite from the Spaniards for two years.

At the end of that time they attacked Oglethorpe in his fort at Frederica, on St. Simon's

Island, with an overwhelming force; but an ambuscade of Highlanders and Indians fell on their rear, and Oglethorpe, taking advantage of their confusion, routed them completely. Soon after, by a most ingenious letter sent to a Frenchman who had deserted to the Spaniards, he managed to give them an impression that he was about to receive large reinforcements, and they all fled back to St. Augustine. This ended the struggle, and Georgia and South Carolina were now secured for England.

Oglethorpe had been bitterly attacked for his failure at the siege of St. Augustine, especially by the Carolinians, who attempted to build up the reputation of their own soldier, Vander Deusen, on the ruin of Oglethorpe. But now Oglethorpe was receiving letters of congratulation from all the British colonies, and had become one of the great men of England.

He soon left Georgia, never to return. The struggle with Spain and the siege of St. Augustine had brought him enemies in Georgia as well as in South Carolina, and he was tried by court-martial in England for the failure of the siege, but triumphantly acquitted. He was of an impatient, hasty temper, rather fond of boasting, and with a very keen sense of personal dignity. These faults were continually involving him in difficulties, in spite of his great merit. He had been in the habit of drawing bills of exchange on the British government for the expenses of his campaigns, and, while most of these were paid, some were not; so that he not only served as governor and general without salary or reward, but was seriously injured in his private fortune by his self-sacrifice.

In 1745, when the Pretender invaded England, Oglethorpe was court-martialled for what was supposed to be a lack of energy in pursuing some of the rebels. He was acquitted, and in time became lieutenant-general of the British army, and afterwards general. He served in Parliament, was the delight of literary men, and the friend of Johnson, Goldsmith, Burke, and Hannah More. He lived to a great age, and could remember when, as a boy, he had shot snipe on what had become Conduit Street in London. He saw the colony he founded become an independent State. In the Revolution he refused to take a part in coercing the Americans; declared that he knew them, and that they could never be subdued; and when John Adams came to London as the ambassador from the United States, Oglethorpe was one of the first to call upon him.

" I have got a new admirer," writes Hannah More in one of her letters, " and we flirt together prodigiously. It is the famous General Oglethorpe, perhaps the most remark-

able man of his time. He is the foster brother of the
Pretender, and much above ninety years old. The finest
figure you ever saw. He frequently realizes all my ideas
of Nestor. His literature is great; his knowledge of the
world extensive; and his faculties as bright as ever. . . .
He is quite a preux chevalier—heroic, romantic, and full of
the old gallantry.''

As an encroachment on the Spanish possessions the planting of Georgia was a wise measure, but as a colony it was by no means a
success. The war had driven away some of
the original settlers and deterred immigrants.
Those that remained—an incongruous mixture of
several nations—are described as "ignorant of
their true interest and cursed with a spirit of
dissension." The trustees were unable to make
suitable laws for them, and the attempt to administer any laws at all was even a greater
failure. While Oglethorpe was present, all
authority centred in him, and his vigor and
power of command enforced obedience. But
he was often absent in England or fighting the
Spaniards, and the authority was in Causton, the
store-keeper who distributed the supplies which
the trustees sent out. By giving or withhold-
ing provisions he soon became an arrogant dic-
tator, and absorbed the power of all the other
officials. When he was finally dismissed, the
petty magistrates who were appointed made still

worse confusion, which the excellent trustees tried to obviate by sending out purple gowns edged with fur for bailiffs and a black tufted one for the recorder.

But nothing could stop the disorder, and we find the magistrates charged with blasphemy, drunkenness, false imprisonment, threatening juries, obstructing the course of the law, and general corruption. The trustees did their best in changing the form of government, but they were really powerless, and could do nothing with the people, who their own historians admit were utterly lacking in unity, morality, industry, and social integrity.

In " the great embarkation" Oglethorpe had brought out with him Charles Wesley and John Wesley, the founders of Methodism. Charles was Oglethorpe's private secretary and chaplain, and John was the missionary for the colony. These young men were then fresh from Oxford, learned in languages, literature, and science, and full of the most ardent enthusiasm. They were clergymen of the Church of England, and had not yet begun that course of thought and conduct which afterwards made them dissenters. The philanthropy and glorious possibilities of Georgia were well calculated to fire their imaginations. The English Church and thousands of the most important religious people in England were deeply interested in the new province.

There were at different times nine clergymen among the trustees. More than one hundred churches took up collections for the enterprise, and the Archbishop of Canterbury, bishops, and numerous collegiate and parochial clergy gave liberally. We read that one hundred and fifteen Bibles, one hundred and sixteen prayerbooks, seventy-two psalters, three hundred and twelve catechisms, fifty-six " Gibson's Family Devotions," and four hundred and thirty other religious books were put on board the first ship that carried out the emigrants, and within the next two years over two thousand six hundred Bibles and religious books were sent out. In fact, there were more books of devotion than there were people ; and if sincere effort alone could have made a province religious and moral, Georgia would have been the home of saints as well as the source of boundless wealth to England.

The Wesleys remained scarcely two years, and, in spite of their unusual ability, cannot be said to have accomplished anything. But although they made no definite impression on the province, the province made a deep impression on them, and it is probable that they learned there the most important lessons of their lives.

Bankrupts, Spaniards, Mulberry-Trees

They knew nothing of the world, and from childhood they had associated only with learned and academic people. They could hold services and preach in English, French, German, and Italian, and they were familiar with Hebrew, Arabic, and Spanish. Finding that their letters were often intercepted and opened in Georgia, they corresponded with each other in Greek, and when they feared eavesdropping, they conversed in Latin. They were totally devoid of taƈt and even common discretion; and, like young men fresh from college in our own time, they intended to reform the whole human race, and they rushed headlong at every evil the moment they saw it. Thrown suddenly into a wilderness, among people of gross immorality and offensive manners, they were taught sharply, but quickly and thoroughly, the one lesson they needed to make their intelleƈt, learning, and eloquence a living and praƈtical force.

One of their first experiences was with two coarse women of soiled virtue who they supposed had repented, and they persuaded Oglethorpe to accept them as respeƈtable. They then attempted to reform the other female colonists and reconcile their feuds. John was soon in love with a designing creature, Sophy Hopkins; but, being warned by his friends and the

Moravians, he broke off his engagement with her, and within eight days she married a man named Williamson. Soon after, John in his straightforward manner rebuked her for something reprehensible in her conduct, and later refused to administer the communion to her.

The whole colony, which was composed largely of the sort of people who are pettily malicious and vindictive, was now arrayed against the two brothers, and they were charged with a long list of offences which it is not necessary to repeat. Charles lost the favor of Oglethorpe, and it was suspected at one time that the people intended to get rid of him by violence. His former friends refused to speak to him, his servants would not work for him, he had to sleep on the ground, and when in a raging fever could scarcely get a bedstead to lie upon. John passed through a similar ordeal, was arrested on trumped-up charges, and finally had difficulty in getting away to England.

Other zealous clergymen had like experiences, and left in disgust. Others remained and accomplished something. Among these was George Whitefield, who took part with the Wesleys in the rise of Methodism. He succeeded in establishing an orphan asylum; but before long he drifted away to his real work of revivalism in all the colonies.

The prohibition of rum and negro slavery was another cause of trouble. The rum was smuggled into the province, there was a great deal of drunkenness, and the demoralization was increased by the evasion of the law and the fruitless efforts to enforce it. A few slaves were also smuggled, and the people were always clamoring for slavery, so that they might compete in prosperity with South Carolina. The raw silk, hemp, wine, olives, and drugs, which were to make Georgia the chief supply of England in these commodities, were not forthcoming, although the trustees tried in every way to compel the people to raise them. They would not cultivate them, and could not be made to see the advantage of it. They wanted to be rice and indigo planters like the Carolinians, with the assistance of slavery; and for fourteen years—from 1735 to 1749—they poured petitions and remonstrances on the trustees and the British Parliament.

Every other British colony, they said, was allowed slaves, and slavery was admitted to be the pillar and support of the British plantation trade in America. But the trustees were inflexible. They wished the colony to be a bulwark against the Spaniards and the Indians. Every slave that was introduced into it would be a weakness, and might be turned into a most dangerous enemy. They wished the colony to produce wine and silk, which could be cultivated only by the skilled and intelligent labor of white men. They wished the colony to be the refuge of worthy insolvents, and these had not the capital either to purchase or maintain slaves. They wished the colonists to labor with their own hands, assisted only by white indentured servants bound to labor for a term of years. The introduction of negroes would make all manual labor degrading, and encourage the very vice and idleness from which the colonists had been delivered by bringing them to America.

But nearly every one who lived in the province was convinced that without slavery it would continue to be a failure, and would not even have enough white people in it to resist the Spaniards. It had been founded fifteen years, and had hardly fifteen hundred people. There was scarcely a planter who could support his family with his own produce. The climate was so hot and unhealthy that from April to October no white man could work in the fields. The white indentured servants would not work, even if they could. They were refractory, filled with wild ideas of liberty, and near enough to Carolina to feel that manual labor was a degradation. Those who were willing to work were sick such a large part of the year that they cost more than they were worth. The consequence was that the people largely abandoned the cultivation of the land, and hung about the towns, drunken and dissolute, living from hand to mouth by any occupation they could find and the supplies from the trustees' storehouse. Many had already left the province, and soon all of them would go.

Among the most urgent in favor of slavery was Whitefield. Oglethorpe was not conspicuous in the controversy. He regarded slavery as an evil, and had said that it was "against the Gospel and the fundamental law of England; we refused as trustees to make a law permitting such a horrid crime." But he had a plantation and slaves of his own in South Carolina. The trustees were also interested in one way or another in the slave-trade. Whitefield had in Carolina a slave plantation, from the proceeds of which he supported his orphan asylum in Georgia; and one of his letters on the subject of slavery is one of the most curious and frank confessions of mixed motive that have ever been written:

"As for the lawfulness of keeping slaves I have no doubt. It is plain hot countries cannot be cultivated without negroes. What a flourishing country Georgia might have been had the use of them been permitted years ago! . . . Though it is true they are brought in a wrong way from their own country and it is a trade not to be approved of, yet as it will be carried on whether we will or not, I should think myself highly favored if I could purchase a good number of them in order to make their lives comfortable, and lay a foundation for breeding up their posterity in the nurture and admonition of the Lord. I had no hand in bringing them into Georgia, though my judgment was for it. . . . It rejoiced my soul to hear that one of my poor negroes in Carolina was made a brother in Christ." (*Tyerman's Life of John Wesley*, vol. ii. p. 132.)

Some of the Scotch Highlanders and the Salzburgers seemed able to work in spite of the climate, and were opposed to the introduction of slaves. A few others who were energetic hired slaves from South Carolina planters, on the understanding that if the law was enforced they would come over and claim their property. The majority of the people, however, continued their petitions, and in 1742 sent over Thomas Stephens to represent them before Parliament. An elaborate investigation by Parliament and the trustees followed, all sides and opinions were heard, and the whole question carefully considered. The restriction on rum was removed, but the request for slavery was denied, and Stephens was ordered to be reprimanded on his knees before the House of Commons for having brought a scandalous petition tending to asperse the characters of the trustees.

The people, however, were not appeased.

During the next few years their indignation was so great as to threaten rebellion or the abandonment of the province, and in 1749 the trustees and Parliament yielded and slavery was allowed.

The next year, 1750, in the hope of introducing some order among the people, the trustees allowed them to have a representative assembly, which, though it could not enact laws, might propose them for enactment by the trustees. But no one could be a member of this assembly unless he had planted a certain number of mulberry-trees to feed the silk-worms.

The people seemed to have been somewhat encouraged and improved by this sham of representative government; but the twenty-one years at the end of which the charter must be surrendered to the crown had almost expired, and the trustees, wearied and disgusted with their labors, surrendered it in 1752, some months before the full completion of the term.

The crown immediately established the ordinary colonial government of governor, governor's council, and assembly of the people, and the effect of this, combined with rum and negro slavery, was soon apparent. The people had what they wanted at last. Plantations were cultivated, vessels came to trade, and Georgia settled down to the development of her natural resources, which, like those of Carolina, were pitch, tar, lumber, rice, and deerskins.

The growth, however, was very slow, and Georgia was the smallest of all the colonies. When the trustees surrendered their charter in 1752 there were scarcely five thousand white people in the province. Ten years of royal rule increased the whites only by about a thousand; but as slaves had been allowed since 1749, the total population was about nine thousand. The next ten or fifteen years were more prosperous, and at the outbreak of the Revolution there were about twenty-five thousand whites and twenty thousand negroes. After the Revolution, in 1790, the whole population, white and black, was over eighty thousand.

But throughout the colonial period, and even in the next century, Georgia was a most disorderly commonwealth, filled with such anarchy and confusion that neither government nor justice could be administered. When an attempt was made to hold court, it was found necessary at times to conduct the judges from place to place by an armed guard.

The people near the frontier were generally considered the most lawless on the continent, idle, drunken, wandering about in bands to plunder both Indians and whites; and those in the interior and along the coast were not much better. In 1784, when there was to be a distribution of land-warrants, the people rushed into the office, seizing the warrants for themselves and carrying them off. The plantations and farms were usually small. Near the coast were some large ones, and some of the planters were men of respectability, leading a life somewhat similar to that of the great planters of Carolina. But the attempt to build up a decent community with English bankrupts and a mixed population was a distinct failure, and almost a century passed before the peculiarities of these people were reduced to a minimum, and Georgia could take a proper position among the States of the Union.

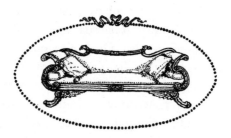

INDEX

Index

Index

Index

Index

Index

Index

Index

Index

Index

Index

Index

Index

The
Brown
House.
Providence , R. I.